Standing Your Ground

Standing Your Ground

Territorial Disputes and International Conflict

Paul K. Huth

Ann Arbor

THE UNIVERSITY OF MICHIGAN PRESS

First paperback edition 1998
Copyright © by the University of Michigan 1996
All rights reserved
Published in the United States of America by
The University of Michigan Press
Manufactured in the United States of America
∞ Printed on acid-free paper

2001   2000   1999   1998   5   4   3   2

A CIP catalog record for this book is available from the British Library.

Library of Congress Cataloging-in-Publication Data

Huth, Paul K., 1959–
     Standing your ground : territorial disputes and international
conflict / Paul K. Huth.
        p.   cm.
     Includes index.
     ISBN 0-472-10689-9 (hardcover : alk. paper)
       1. Territory, National—History. 2. Boundary disputes—History.
I. Title.
JX4085.H88 1996
320.1′2—dc20   95-48856
                                                          CIP

ISBN 0-472-08520-4 (pbk. : alk. paper)

To my loving parents and family:
I hope this book helps to answer the question
you so often ask of me—What is it that you do?

Contents

Tables

Figures

Acknowledgments

I owe a considerable debt to many individuals who have helped me in the completion of this book. A small army of undergraduate research assistants played an indispensable role in helping me collect data, and their efforts are greatly appreciated. In particular, I would like to thank the Undergraduate Research Opportunity Program at the University of Michigan for providing me with the chance to work with a number of bright and motivated undergraduate students. My greatest debt is to those who answered endless questions about research design, data analysis, and data interpretation; their expert advice and probing comments pushed me to rethink and improve the empirical analysis in many ways. The support of Chris Achen, Nancy Burns, Dani Reiter, Chris Gelpi, Pierre Landry, David Rousseau, Anne Sartori, Scott Bennett, and Alan Stam is deeply appreciated. The detailed and insightful comments of James Morrow, Paul Diehl, Robert Pahre, and Jennifer Shulman improved the manuscript throughout, and I would like to thank them for their efforts. I would also like to thank Bill Zimmerman, director of the Program for International Peace and Security Research at the University of Michigan, for his support and that of the program. The National Science Foundation provided financial support for my research, which is greatly appreciated as well. Finally, at the University of Michigan Press I would like to thank Malcom Litchfield for his support of this project at an early stage and Christina Triezenberg for her excellent work in preparing my manuscript for publication. In the end, I assume full responsibility for all the faults and defects that remain despite the best efforts of others to correct my errors.

CHAPTER 1

Why Study Territorial Disputes?

The opposing forces of change and continuity characterize international politics in the last decade of the twentieth century. The end of the cold war rivalry between the United States and the Soviet Union and the peaceful reunification of Germany have transformed fundamentally the national security issues confronting state leaders throughout the capitals of Europe as well as the United States. For centuries competition among major powers in Europe has resulted in international crises and the outbreak of wars.[1]

As we approach the twenty-first century, however, the threat of armed conflict among the major powers in Europe seems quite remote.[2] The cold war confrontation in central Europe has been replaced by an unprecedented level of security cooperation among former adversaries. Indeed, the "Partnership for Peace Program," which provides for limited forms of military cooperation between Eastern European countries and NATO (North Atlantic Treaty Organization), may be the first step in the eventual integration of these countries into NATO as

---

1. According to Evan Laurd, *War in International Society* (New Haven: Yale University Press, 1987), 421–43 a total of 177 wars were fought in Europe between 1500 and 1945 among both major and minor European powers. Jack Levy, *War and the Modern Great Power System, 1495–1975* (Lexington: University Press of Kentucky, 1983), 70–73 has identified 117 wars among the European major powers between 1500 and 1945. Also see Kalevi Holsti, *Peace and War* (Cambridge: Cambridge University Press, 1991), who has identified 98 wars among European powers since 1648.

2. Some analysts, however, argue that the end of the cold war will lead to a greater threat of crisis and war among the major powers in Europe. The primary argument is that increased instability in Eastern Europe will act as a catalyst to renewed competition between the major powers similar to the period prior to World War I. See, for example, John Mearsheimer, "Back to the Future," *International Security* 15, no. 1 (1990): 5–56. Opposing arguments are presented in Paul Huth, "The European Security Implications of the Dissolution of the Soviet Empire," in William Zimmerman, ed., *Beyond the Soviet Threat* (Ann Arbor: University of Michigan Press, 1992), 185–218; Stephen Van Evera, "Primed for Peace: Europe after the Cold War," *International Security* 15, no. 3 (1990/1991): 7–57; Jack Snyder, "Averting Anarchy in the New Europe," *International Security* 14, no. 4 (1990): 5–41; and Richard Ullman, *Securing Europe,* (Princeton: Princeton University Press, 1991).

full members. Through a combination of unilateral decisions and negotiated arms control agreements, NATO and former Warsaw Pact governments are significantly reducing, and in some cases eliminating,
conventional and nuclear weapons from their armed forces.[3] In addition, extensive confidence-building measures have been established to
monitor and regulate the location and movement of the remaining
military forces on the continent.[4] As a result of these ongoing changes
the capacity for many countries within Europe to engage in rapid offensive military operations has been measurably reduced, thereby weakening the pernicious effects of the security dilemma and greatly reducing
the threat of surprise attack.[5]

In a broader context, policymakers and scholars have argued that
international politics among advanced industrial countries have been
transformed in fundamental ways as a result of unprecedented levels of
economic interdependence and the prevalence of democratic political
institutions. The potential for stronger economic and political ties, linking Russia and Eastern Europe with the West as a result of their membership in international institutions such as the General Agreement on
Tariffs and Trade (GATT), the International Monetary Fund (IMF) and,

---

3. For example, across Europe member governments of NATO and the former
Warsaw Pact are reducing defense spending levels and the number of men under arms. The
Conventional Forces in Europe Treaty (signed in November 1990) requires Russia, in
particular, to make significant cuts in conventional armaments such as tanks, heavy artil-
lery, armored vehicles, tactical aircraft, and attack helicopters. Russian battlefield nuclear
weapons have been withdrawn from Eastern Europe, and NATO is in the process of
reformulating its doctrine of flexible response and first-use of nuclear weapons. NATO has
already issued statements indicating that the role of nuclear weapons will be downgraded
as a part of the alliance's deterrent posture, and there is growing support within NATO to
eliminate short-range and battlefield nuclear weapons. For a concise history of the fundamental changes in Soviet security policy under the leadership of Mikhail Gorbachev see
Coit Blacker, *Hostage to Revolution: Gorbachev and Soviet Security Policy, 1985–1991*
(New York: Council on Foreign Relations Press, 1993) and see Raymond Garthoff, *The
Great Transition: American-Soviet Relations and the End of the Cold War* (Washington,
D.C.: Brookings, 1994), chs. 5–13 and Jonathan Dean, *Ending Europe's Wars* (New York:
Twentieth Century Fund, 1994) for a history of U.S.-Soviet and European relations over
the past decade.

4. For example, the Stockholm Agreement signed in September 1986 requires all
NATO and former Warsaw Pact countries to provide advance notification of military
activities involving 13,000 troops or 300 tanks, to permit observation of planned military
activities involving more than 17,000 troops, and the right to conduct short-notice on-site
inspections. See Dean, *Ending Europe's Wars*, ch. 12.

5. The security dilemma refers to the difficulty states have in building up their
defenses without other states perceiving such measures as potentially posing an offensive
threat. For a discussion of the fundamental changes in European security issues see Ullman, *Securing Europe*, chs. 1–2.

the European Union, would further extend this process of transformation in the post–cold war era. According to these analysts, the emerging pattern of international politics among advanced industrial countries includes the following features.[6]

1. Territorial conflict and expansion are of secondary importance as causes of competition and rivalry between states.
2. The threat or use of military force is of limited utility to state leaders in achieving many of their foreign policy goals.
3. War is a remote possibility and therefore military security issues are no longer the dominant policy concerns of state leaders.

While the end of the cold war may lead to a new era of security cooperation between the major powers within and outside of Europe, armed conflict and adversarial relations are likely to continue to characterize international politics among many regional powers within and outside of Europe. For example, among the former republics of the Soviet Union and within Eastern Europe, territorial and ethnic conflicts, once suppressed by the threat of Soviet military intervention, have already escalated or threaten in the future to escalate into open disputes and armed conflict.[7]

Outside of Europe, the outbreak of the Gulf War aptly illustrates the

---

6. Analysts who have emphasized the implications of economic interdependence include Robert Keohane and Joseph Nye, *Power and Interdependence* (Boston: Little, Brown and Company, 1977) and more recently Richard Rosecrance, *The Rise of the Trading State* (New York: Basic Books, 1986). The theoretical implications of democratic systems for international politics are developed in Michael Doyle, "Liberalism and World Politics," *American Political Science Review* 80, no. 4 (1986): 1151–70. Also see Bruce Bueno de Mesquita and David Lalman, *War and Reason* (New Haven: Yale University Press, 1992), ch. 5 and Bruce Russett, *Grasping the Democratic Peace* (Princeton: Princeton University Press, 1993). Richard Ullman in *Securing Europe* has applied both of these bodies of literature to the analysis of European international politics in the post–cold war era.

7. A comprehensive survey of territorial issues within Eastern Europe and the former Soviet Union is presented in John Allock, Guy Arnold, Alan Day, D. S. Lewis, Lorimer Poultney, Roland Rance, and D. J. Sagar, *Border and Territorial Disputes*, rev. 3d ed. (London: Longman, 1992). In many cases territorial disputes have or may emerge as a result of disputes over the treatment and rights of ethnic minorities in neighboring countries. For a summary of potential conflicts that might emerge see J. F. Brown, *Nationalism, Democracy and Security in the Balkans* (Brookfield, VT: Dartmouth Publishing Company, 1992); F. Stephen Larrabee, "Long Memories and Short Fuses: Change and Instability in the Balkans," *International Security* 15, no. 3 (1990/1991): 58–91; Ted Hopf, "Managing Soviet Disintegration," *International Security* 17, no. 1 (1992): 44–75; Dean, *Ending Europe's Wars*, chs. 4–5; and Ted Robert Gurr, *Minorities at Risk* (Washington, D.C.: United States Institute of Peace Press, 1993), ch. 7.

persistence of armed conflict as an ever present feature of international politics in the 1990s. On August 2, 1990 Iraqi armed forces invaded Kuwait and quickly overran the country. In the months that followed, the United States sought to compel Iraq to withdraw from Kuwait by the use of economic sanctions and the threat of military force. Having failed to convince Saddam Hussein to withdraw, the United States led a coalition of states in a counteroffensive attack that successfully forced Iraq to relinquish its control over Kuwait.[8]

The conflicts within the former Soviet bloc and Yugoslavia as well as the Gulf War, highlight the following elements of continuity in international politics in the post–cold war era.

Territorial disputes remain an important source of conflict between states and can erupt into armed confrontation. In the case of the Gulf War, Iraq had territorial claims against Kuwait that can be traced back to the 1930s.[9] While the cold war rivalry between the United States and the Soviet Union was driven not by competing territorial claims, but by ideological conflict, long-standing disputes over territory have been a primary cause of rivalry between states since the end of World War II. Consider, for example, the Arab-Israeli conflict, the history of Indo-Pakistani conflict over Kashmir, or the Iran-Iraq conflict over the disputed Shatt-al-Arab Waterway.

Since the end of World War II there have been over 100 territorial disputes between states, and many of these disputes remain unresolved in the 1990s. Indeed, by the end of 1995 there were more than sixty ongoing territorial disputes between states in the international system.[10] Frequently these territorial disputes escalated into dangerous confrontations. For example, Michael Brecher and Jonathan Wilkenfeld have identified over 280 international crises between 1946 and 1988, and in close to 50 percent of the cases, territorial issues were a direct cause of the crises, or they played a primary role in the deterioration of relations between states and the onset of the crises.[11] Similarly, of the twenty-one

---

8. A comprehensive account of the Gulf War is presented in Lawrence Freedman and Efraim Karsh, *The Gulf Conflict 1990–1991* (Princeton: Princeton University Press, 1993).

9. See for example David Finnie, *Shifting Lines in the Sand* (Cambridge: Harvard University Press, 1992) and Hussein Hassouna, *The League of Arab States and Regional Disputes* (New York: Oceana Publications, Inc., 1975), ch. 6.

10. See appendix A for a listing and summary of disputes between 1950 and 1990. The figure for the number of current disputes is calculated from appendix A and Allock et al., *Border and Territorial Disputes*. In chapter 2 I define the concept of a territorial dispute in more detail.

11. See Michael Brecher, Jonathan Wilkenfeld, and Sheila Moser, *Crises in the Twentieth Century*, vol. I (New York: Pergamon Press, 1988), 143–346 and Michael

wars fought between states since the end of World War II, territorial disputes were a primary cause of the armed conflict in fourteen cases.[12]

Military force is still viewed by state leaders in many countries as a viable instrument for the pursuit of foreign policy objectives. While Europe since 1946 has experienced an unprecedented period of relative peace,[13] with no wars being fought between the major powers and few crises, armed conflict and international crises have been prevalent in regions outside of Europe. Of the twenty-one wars in the international system since 1946, all but two—the 1956 Soviet intervention in Hungary and the 1974 Cyprus War—were fought on territory outside of Europe.[14]

Similarly, of the more than 280 international crises identified by Brecher and Wilkenfeld, only about 10 percent were located in Europe while the remaining 90 percent were located in regions such as the Middle East, Africa, South America, and Central Asia.[15] While superpower rivalry during the cold war period often had an important impact on regional conflicts outside of Europe, many of these regional conflicts nevertheless had a dynamic of their own, independent of superpower intervention and involvement. The relative absence of political and military rivalry between the United States and Russia in the 1990s, therefore, will not prevent many of these conflicts from escalating in the future.

Because the threat of military force to overturn the status quo remains a distinct possibility in relations between many states, deterrence of armed conflict remains a central concern and problem for many state leaders.

My goal in writing this book is to examine one of the enduring features of international politics—the clash between states over disputed territory. In this book I examine the origins, evolution, and termination of conflict and rivalry between states over disputed territory between 1950

Brecher, *Crises in World Politics* (New York: Pergamon Press, 1993), ch. 2 for a summary description of the international crisis behavior (ICB) dataset. The complete ICB dataset covers the period between 1918 and 1988 and is available through the Inter-University Consortium for Political and Social Research at the University of Michigan.

12. The total number of wars was calculated from the list in Melvin Small and J. David Singer, *Resort to Arms* (Beverley Hills: Sage Publications, 1982), 92–95 with the addition of the British-Argentine war over the Falklands in 1982, the Israeli-Syrian War in Lebanon in 1982, and the Gulf War in 1990–1991.

13. John Lewis Gaddis has coined the phrase "the long peace" to describe the absence of conflict in Europe since 1945. See John Lewis Gaddis, "The Long Peace: Elements of Stability in the Postwar International System," *International Security* 10, no. 1 (1986): 99–142.

14. See Small and Singer, *Resort to Arms,* 92–95 and Laurd, *War in International Society,* 442–46.

15. See Brecher, *Crises in World Politics,* 70.

and 1990. I provide answers to questions such as why some bordering states become involved in territorial disputes, why some territorial disputes are characterized by high levels of diplomatic and military confrontation, and why some states seek a negotiated settlement of their territorial claims through compromise and conciliation.

There are two premises underlying my research on territorial disputes and international conflict. First, if we seek to develop a better understanding of international conflict since the end of World War II, we must focus scholarly research more directly on territorial disputes as a primary cause of crises and war. At present, the scholarly literature on the causes of war in the twentieth century is oriented toward the major powers, in general, and European international politics, in particular.[16] Two important consequences of this focus is that territorial disputes are not treated as a primary source of conflict between states, and international conflict behavior outside of Europe has not been studied extensively.[17] This book addresses both of these gaps in existing research.

The second premise of my research is that if we are to develop compelling answers to the questions of when and why territorial disputes lead to crises and war, then our analysis needs to integrate and draw on more general theories of international politics and the foreign policy behavior of states. Theoretical models provide the framework within which to generalize about state behavior in a logical and consistent fashion, and they also lead analysts to sharpen their focus and identify more clearly the potential effects of specific explanatory variables.

I believe it is appropriate to focus on territorial disputes as a distinct theoretical cause of international conflict because of the greater propensity of territorial disputes to escalate to the threat or use of military force, compared to other sources of conflict between states. Throughout

---

16. For example, the studies cited in the detailed review of existing scholarship on the causes of international conflict and war by Jack Levy, "The Causes of War," in Philip Tetlock et al., eds., *Behavior, Society, and Nuclear War*, vol. 1 (New York: Oxford University Press, 1989), 209–333 are heavily focused on the major powers, as are the works reviewed in Manus Midlarsky, ed., *Handbook of War Studies* (Boston: Unwin Hyman, 1989).

17. An important exception, however, is Brecher, *Crises in World Politics*. In addition, there is an emerging comparative literature on the security policies of Third World states which I have drawn on. See for example Stephen David, *Choosing Sides: Alignment and Realignment in the Third World* (Baltimore: Johns Hopkins University Press, 1991); Robert Jackson, *Quasi-States: Sovereignty, International Relations, and the Third World* (Cambridge: Cambridge University Press, 1990); Brian Job, ed., *The Insecurity Dilemma: National Security of Third World States* (Boulder: Lynne Rienner, 1992); Edward Rice, *Wars of the Third Kind* (Berkeley: University of California Press, 1988); Michael Barnett, *Confronting the Costs of War* (Princeton: Princeton University Press, 1992); and Mohammed Ayoob, "The Security Problematic of the Third World," *World Politics* 43, no. 2 (1991): 257–83.

history territorial disputes have been the principal source of conflict leading to war. For example, John Vasquez notes that in 85 percent of the major-power wars fought over the past 300 years territorial issues were a central feature of the conflicts. Vasquez further argues that territorial conflicts are unique in their propensity to escalate to armed conflict, and he concludes that war is quite unlikely unless there is a prior conflict between states over territory.[18]

In this book I integrate two different theoretical approaches to the study of international politics and the foreign policy behavior of states—realist and domestic politics models—to generate hypotheses about international conflict over disputed territory. My contention is that powerful explanations of international conflict behavior cannot be derived from theoretical models that fail to consider the simultaneous impact of both domestic and international-level variables. Prior scholarship has demonstrated quite convincingly that either approach (realist or domestic politics) by itself can provide only partial explanations of the causes of international conflict and the security policy decisions of state leaders. The critical theoretical task confronting scholars in the field of international politics is to develop generalizable propositions about state behavior based on the premise that foreign policy leaders are attentive to the incentives and constraints generated by both their domestic and international environments. If these widely utilized theoretical approaches to studying international politics can be integrated, such a theoretical framework should have considerable explanatory power regarding the behavior of states embroiled in territorial disputes. At the same time, I believe these theoretical models can be sharpened and refined through theoretical integration, and the hypotheses from this new model can then be carefully subjected to empirical tests.

Broadly stated, my objective in this book is to advance not only our understanding of the dynamics of interstate conflict over disputed territory, but also to try to contribute to international relations theory by developing a more integrated approach to theory building.

The Literature on Territory and International Conflict

If we turn to existing scholarship for answers to the questions of when and why states initiate, escalate, and terminate disputes over territory, we find only a limited body of work from which tentative answers, at

---

18. See John Vasquez, *The War Puzzle* (Cambridge: Cambridge University Press, 1993), ch. 4. Also see Stephen Kocs, "Territorial Disputes and Interstate War, 1945–1987," *Journal of Politics* 57, no. 1 (1995): 159–75.

best, can be identified. Scholars have argued that territorial disputes were a central cause of major-power armed conflict from the inception of the modern international system in the seventeenth century to the late nineteenth century.[19] In the twentieth century, territorial disputes have been prevalent outside of Europe, but in contemporary scholarship there is a lack of systematic and focused research on territorial disputes. For example, Robert Mandel stated that "our ability to explain why and when border disputes break out between adjacent states is severely limited," and, more recently, another scholar has noted that "comparatively little has been written that treats territory as a basic cause of conflict."[20]

I have already argued that one reason for this relative neglect of territorial disputes is the major-power bias in contemporary scholarship. There are, in addition, two other explanations for this gap in scholarly research. First, and somewhat paradoxically, because territorial disputes are often the underlying source of conflict in crises and wars they may be treated as a relatively constant feature of international politics. As a result, analysts may believe that the presence and characteristics of territorial disputes have limited value in explaining variation in conflict behavior among states. That is, there is always the potential for states to become embroiled in conflict over territory, and the really important question to answer is when and why state leaders choose to make territorial issues a point of contention. From this perspective we should then expect state leaders to initiate and resolve territorial disputes frequently as a tactical response to the changing needs of more pressing foreign and domestic issues. Two empirically based observations about territorial disputes, however, are puzzling from this perspective. Contrary to the position that territorial claims are often a cover for other sources of conflict, we find that in the post–World War II period less than one-third of all international borders have been disputed. Also, only a minority of post–World War II territorial dispute cases (approximately 40 percent) were settled by the challenger state withdrawing its claim or compromising—this, despite the skeptic's argument that the issues at stake in territorial disputes are often only of secondary importance to states. In short, territorial disputes are not that common between states, and, once initiated, state leaders are generally reluctant to give up their country's territorial claims. This suggests then that

19. See ibid.; Laurd, *War in International Society;* Holsti, *Peace and War;* and Rosecrance, *The Rise of the Trading State.*

20. See Robert Mandel, "Roots of the Modern Interstate Border Dispute," *Journal of Conflict Resolution* 24, no. 3 (1980): 427 and Alexander Murphy, "Historical Justification for Territorial Claims," *Annals of the American Geographers* 80, no. 4 (1990): 531.

questions about the origins and resolution of territorial disputes require more sophisticated theoretical and empirical analyses.

A second reason why territorial disputes are not very often the center of analysis in the current literature is that scholars in their theory-building efforts often take as given the preferences and goals of state leaders and examine the instrumental rationality of decisions to threaten or resort to the use of military force.[21] As a result, the issues at stake in a dispute or crisis are often not a central component of theoretical models.[22] Furthermore, even when the issues at stake are treated as an explanatory variable, the major-power bias in the literature leads analysts to conceptualize issues at stake in terms of reputations for resolve, the credibility of commitments to allies, or political and military leadership in the international system.[23]

When the issues at stake are analyzed in less abstract terms, scholars have observed that territorial disputes are prone to higher levels of conflict than are disputes centered around economic or ideological issues.[24] However, the weakness with these studies is that the analysts fail to account for variation in conflict behavior across the population of territorial dispute cases. Not all territorial disputes lead to armed conflict and bitter rivalry between states. In fact, in the post–World War II period over one-half of all territorial disputes *did not* involve the threat or use of military force. There is a good deal of variation then in the

---

21. See Frank Zagare, "Rationality and Deterrence," *World Politics* 42, no. 2 (1990): 230–60 for a useful summary of the literature in which this approach is adopted.

22. Gary Goertz and Paul Diehl, *Territorial Changes and International Conflict* (London: Routledge, 1992), ch. 1 and Paul Diehl, "What Are They Fighting For?" *Journal of Peace Research* 29 (1992): 333–44 argue along these same lines as does Holsti, *Peace and War*, ch. 1, and Vasquez, *The War Puzzle*, ch. 4.

23. In the rational deterrence theory literature emphasis is placed on reputations and commitments to allies. See for example Thomas Schelling, *Arms and Influence* (New Haven: Yale University Press, 1966); Robert Jervis, *The Illogic of American Nuclear Strategy* (Ithaca: Cornell University Press, 1984), ch. 5; and Paul Huth, *Extended Deterrence and the Prevention of War* (New Haven: Yale University Press, 1988), ch. 3. The literature on power transitions and the causes of major-power systemic or hegemonic wars emphasizes how the prevailing rules of the international system and the balance of power are at stake in major power confrontations. See for example Geoffrey Blainey, *The Causes of War*, 3d ed. (New York: The Free Press, 1988); Michael Howard, *The Causes of Wars*, 2d ed. (Cambridge: Harvard University Press, 1984); Robert Gilpin, *War and Change in World Politics* (New York: Cambridge University Press, 1981); and A. F. K. Organski and Jacek Kugler, *The War Ledger* (Chicago: University of Chicago Press, 1980), ch. 1.

24. See for example Charles Gochman and Russell Leng, "Realpolitik and the Road to War," *International Studies Quarterly* 27, no. 1 (1983): 97–120; Russell Leng, *Interstate Crisis Behavior, 1816–1980* (Cambridge: Cambridge University Press, 1993), chs. 3, 5; Holsti, *Peace and War*, ch. 12; and Vasquez, *The War Puzzle*, ch. 4.

patterns of conflict behavior across cases of territorial disputes. Much of the existing theoretical and empirical literature on territorial disputes, however, does not seek to explain the puzzle that while most wars and many crises involve conflicts over territory, many territorial disputes do not pose a high risk of war.[25] This suggests that patterns of escalation in territorial disputes are quite varied and complex, requiring careful theoretical and empirical analysis.

While much of the literature cited above does not treat territory as a central explanatory variable, there is a small body of work that does. This work can be divided into two broad categories. In the first category territorial issues are studied largely from the perspective of what impact geographic proximity between states has on the likelihood that they will become embroiled in conflictual relations, or that international conflict will spread (or diffuse) across national borders. Several studies have found that proximate states have a higher incidence of crises and wars than do more distant states. This literature argues that proximity facilitates conflict by providing states with greater opportunities to interact and disagree on issues as well as a greater capacity to threaten and resort to the use of armed force to resolve disputes.[26] Unfortunately, in these studies scholars typically have not analyzed the direct effects of border disputes as a cause of conflict. As a result, we cannot find in these studies answers to the larger questions of when and why some territorial disputes escalate to crises and armed conflict.

---

25. The resort to the large-scale use of military force in international disputes is very infrequent in general. For example Frank Sherman has identified over 500 international disputes over political-security issues (excluding territorial disputes) between 1946 and 1985, and during that period there were approximately thirty cases (less than 6 percent) in which states seeking to change the status quo resorted to the large-scale use of military force (more than 1,000 troops were committed to a military attack). During that same period there were 129 territorial disputes between states, and there were close to thirty cases (about 23 percent) involving escalation to the large-scale use of force by states seeking to overturn the territorial status quo. Thus, territorial disputes were roughly four times more likely to escalate to the large-scale use of force than other types of political-security issues. See Frank Sherman, "SHERFACS: A Cross-Paradigm, Hierarchical and Contextually Sensitive Conflict Management Data Set," *International Interactions* 20, nos. 1–2 (1994): 79–100; Herbert Tillema, *International Armed Conflict since 1945* (Boulder: Westview Press, 1991); and Brecher and Wilkenfeld, *Crises in the Twentieth Century.*

26. See for example Paul Diehl,"Contiguity and Military Escalation in Major Power Rivalries, 1816–1980," *Journal of Politics* 47, no. 4 (1985): 1203–11; David Garnham, "Dyadic International War 1816–1965," *Western Political Quarterly* 29, no. 2 (1976):231–42; David Garnham, "Power Parity and Lethal International Violence," *Journal of Conflict Resolution* 20, no. 3 (1976): 379–94; Peter Wallensteen, "Incompatibility, Confrontation, and War," *Journal of Peace Research* 18, no. 1 (1981): 57–90; Stuart Bremer, "Dangerous Dyads," *Journal of Conflict Resolution* 36, no. 2 (1992): 309–41; and Brecher, *Crises in World Politics,* ch. 3.

In research on the diffusion of conflict, the central question addressed by scholars is, When will bilateral disputes become multiparty crises or wars? In answering this question, geographic proximity is treated as one potential explanatory variable in a more general theoretical model of the diffusion of international conflict. Harvey Starr, in individual and collaborative work, has examined this question extensively.[27] While the results of his research indicate that proximity is significantly correlated with the diffusion of conflict, the theoretical and empirical analysis once again does not directly focus on territorial disputes as a cause of international conflict. Hence, given the different research agenda addressed in this body of work, it is not possible to learn a great deal about the dynamics of territorial disputes.[28]

In the second category of work, border and territorial disputes are the focus of analysis and are treated as a direct cause of crises and war between states. One body of work, while often rich in historical detail and description, does not attempt to develop clear and explicit generalizations about conflict behavior. Analysts either focus on a single case or examine multiple disputes within a particular region. In this literature, scholars often examine territorial disputes from a legal perspective and document

---

27. See Randolph Siverson and Harvey Starr, *The Diffusion of War* (Ann Arbor: University of Michigan Press, 1991); Randolph Siverson and Harvey Starr, "Opportunity, Willingness, and the Diffusion of War," *American Political Science Review* 84, no. 1 (1990): 47–68; Harvey Starr and Benjamin Most, "The Forms and Processes of War Diffusion," *Comparative Political Studies* 18, no. 2 (1985): 206–29; Harvey Starr and Benjamin Most, "Contagion and Border Effects on Contemporary African Conflicts," *Comparative Political Studies* 16, no. 1 (1983): 92–117; Benjamin Most and Harvey Starr, "Diffusion, Reinforcement, Geopolitics and the Spread of War," *American Political Science Review* 74, no. 4 (1980): 932–46; Harvey Starr and Benjamin Most, "A Return Journey: Richardson, 'Frontiers,' and Wars in the 1946–1965 Era," *Journal of Conflict Resolution* 22, no. 3 (1978): 441–62; Harvey Starr and Benjamin Most, "The Substance and Study of Borders in International Relations Research," *International Studies Quarterly* 20, no. 4 (1976): 581–620. Related work by scholars includes Stuart Bremer, "The Contagiousness of Coercion," *International Interactions* 9, no. 1 (1982): 29–55 and Fredrich Pearson, "Geographical Proximity and Foreign Military Intervention," *Journal of Conflict Resolution* 18, no. 3 (1974): 432–60.

28. Another body of work in the diffusion literature treats regional conflicts among minor powers as potential catalysts to conflict between major powers via intervention in support of opposing sides. In this context territorial disputes are often discussed but generally as a backdrop to the rivalry of the major powers in the region. The dynamics of the territorial dispute is less important than the fact that the dispute presents a dangerous opportunity for third-party intervention by the major powers. See for example Manus Midlarsky, ed., *Handbook of War Studies* (Boston: Unwin Hyman, 1989), ch. 3.; Alexander George, Philip Farley, and Alexander Dallin eds., *U.S.-Soviet Security Cooperation* (New York: Oxford University Press, 1988), chs. 17–23; Barry Blechman and Stephen Kaplan, *Force without War* (Washington, D.C.: Brookings, 1978); and Stephen Kaplan, *Diplomacy of Power* (Washington, D.C.: Brookings, 1981).

how well-grounded the positions of contending governments are in international law.[29] A legalistic perspective may provide some insights into the behavior of states involved in territorial disputes, but in many cases agreement cannot be reached between the opposing states to submit their dispute to arbitration or a ruling before the International Court of Justice (ICJ).[30] As a result, while the legitimacy of a state's territorial claim, based on international law, could be one piece of the puzzle in understanding the resolution of territorial disputes, there are too many cases in which legal considerations are not brought to bear for such an approach to provide a broad and general framework for analysis. Furthermore, whether governments will respect decisions based on international law may be a function of other conditions, such as the country's relative military power or the strategic and economic value of the territory in dispute. Thus, even when legal factors seem to play a central role in a territorial dispute, the independent effects of such factors must be considered in the context of the broader political and economic forces that may also be influencing the decisions of state leaders.

Related work focuses on the role of third-party mediation in the analysis of territorial disputes.[31] These studies once again often contain

29. For example see S. H. Amin, *International and Legal Problems of the Gulf* (London: Middle East and North African Studies Press Limited, 1981); Faridun Adamiyat, *Bahrain: A Legal and Diplomatic Study of the British-Iranian Controversy* (New York: Praeger, 1955); Kaiyan Homi Kaikobad, *The Shatt-al-Arab Boundary Question: A Legal Reappraisal* (Oxford: Oxford University Press, 1988); Ian Brownlie, *African Boundaries: A Legal and Diplomatic Encyclopedia* (London: C. Hurst & Company, 1979); Surya Sharma, *International Boundary Disputes and International Law* (Bombay: N.M. Tripathi Private Limited, 1976); Zaim Necatigil, *The Cyprus Question and the Turkish Position in International Law* (New York: Oxford University Press, 1989); Thomas Ehrlich, *Cyprus 1958–1967: International Crises and the Role of Law* (New York: Oxford University Press, 1974); and Roa Krishna, *The Sino-Indian Boundary Question and International Law* (New Delhi: Indian Society of International Law, 1963). Also see J. R. V. Prescott, *Political Frontiers and Boundaries* (London: Allen & Unwin, 1987) and Alan Day, ed., *Border and Territorial Disputes*, rev. ed. (London: Longman, 1987).

30. Of the 129 territorial disputes identified in appendix A, in only seven cases was the dispute brought to the ICJ for a ruling.

31. A sample of such works includes Hassouna, *The League of Arab States and Regional Disputes;* John Campbell, ed., *Successful Negotiations* (Princeton: Princeton University Press, 1976); M. A. Morris and V. Millan, eds., *Controlling Latin American Conflicts* (Boulder: Westview Press, 1983); Harold Saunders, *The Other Walls*, rev. ed. (Princeton: Princeton University Press, 1991); Kenneth Stein, *Making Peace among Arabs and Israelis* (Washington, D.C.: United States Peace Institute, 1991); Saadia Touval, *The Peace Brokers* (Princeton: Princeton University Press, 1982); Parker Hart, *Two NATO Allies at the Threshold of War* (Durham: Duke University Press, 1990); Douglas Kinney, *National Interest/National Honor: The Diplomacy of the Falklands Crisis* (New York: Praeger, 1990); and Christopher McMullen, *Mediation of the West*

excellent historical accounts of disputes as well as practical recommendations for policymakers on how to reach a negotiated settlement. The same shortcomings of legalistic analysis apply to this approach, however, and thus it is difficult to draw from these works broader theoretical or empirical generalizations. For example, often governments do not seek or cannot agree on a mediator, and, even when they do, solutions proposed by a mediator are not binding on governments.[32] Thus, while third-party mediation may help in some cases to prevent conflict escalation and promote resolution, the findings of this research are unlikely to provide a powerful explanation of conflict behavior across a broad range of territorial dispute cases.

A third body of work is more comparative in scope and directed toward generalization about the conditions under which territorial disputes escalate to crises and war.[33] This research is potentially the most promising, given its attention to the larger political and strategic context within which state decisions are reached. However, the empirical findings from these studies are mixed, making it difficult to draw general conclusions about conflict behavior over disputed territory. For example, Gary Goertz and Paul Diehl in their research on territorial transfers between states did not find a strong relationship between the balance of relative military capabilities and the use of armed force in achieving territorial changes from 1914 to 1980. Robert Mandel and Arie Kacowicz, however, in their studies of border disputes and peaceful territorial changes found that armed conflict was more likely between states of roughly equal

---

New Guinea Dispute, 1962 (Washington, D.C.: Institute for the Study of Diplomacy, 1981).

32. Of the 129 territorial disputes in the international system between 1950 and 1990, mediation was attempted by other states or international organizations in less than thirty cases.

33. Representative of comparative historical works are Saadia Touval, *The Boundary Politics of Independent Africa* (Cambridge: Harvard University Press, 1972); Naomi Chazon, ed., *Irredentism and International Politics* (Boulder: Lynne Reinner Publishers, 1991); Friedrich Kratochwil, Paul Rohrlich, and Harpreet Mahajan, *Peace and Disputed Sovereignty* (Lanham, MD: University Press of America, Inc., 1985); Rice, *Wars of the Third Kind;* Laurd, *War in International Society;* Evan Laurd, ed., *The International Regulation of Frontier Disputes* (London: Thames and Hudson, 1970); and Holsti, *Peace and War.* There are few quantitative studies of territorial disputes. The primary works are Goertz and Diehl, *Territorial Changes and International Conflict;* Mandel, "Roots of the Modern Interstate Border Dispute"; J. Brown Boyd, "African Boundary Conflict," *African Review Studies* 22, no. 3 (1979): 1–14, Arie Kacowicz, "The Problem of Peaceful Territorial Change," *International Studies Quarterly* 38, no. 2 (1994): 219–54; Arie Kacowicz, *Peaceful Territorial Change* (Columbia: University of South Carolina Press, 1994); and David Carment and Patrick James, "Internal Constraints and Interstate Ethnic Conflict," *Journal of Conflict Resolution* 39, no. 1 (1995): 82–109.

military capabilities. Similarly, Mandel argues that irredentist claims are more likely to lead to military conflict, whereas Goertz and Diehl's findings point toward the size of disputed territory and the pressures of population growth, and J. Brown Boyd concludes that ethnic irredentism is not a primary source of border conflicts in Africa.[34]

There are three general shortcomings to this third category of research on territorial disputes. First, the theoretical generalizations proposed and hypotheses tested are only loosely connected to, and derived from, more general theoretical models of international conflict. As a result, the logical foundation and therefore theoretical persuasiveness of the empirical findings are not firmly established. Second, even those works seeking to generalize about territorial disputes tend to focus on either domestic or international-level variables, but few studies carefully compare and then test hypotheses that incorporate both of these different levels of analysis. Third, the empirical findings are often based either on simple statistical tests or a limited set of cases.[35] More sophisticated multivariate analyses, conducted on a carefully selected set of cases and including controls for the effects of competing explanations, are required if we are to have greater confidence in the generalizability of results.

In sum, from the existing literature on territory and international conflict a list can be drawn up of hypotheses that identify a set of potential explanatory variables, and some tentative empirical generaliza-

34. Kacowicz, "The Problem of Peaceful Territorial Change"; Kacowicz, *Peaceful Territorial Change;* Mandel, "Roots of the Modern Interstate Border Dispute"; Goertz and Diehl, *Territorial Changes and International Conflict;* Boyd, "African Boundary Conflict." Irredentist claims are also emphasized by David Carment, "The International Dimension of Ethnic Conflict," *Journal of Peace Research* 30, no. 2 (1993): 137–50.

35. Goertz and Diehl, *Territorial Changes and International Conflict;* Kacowicz, "The Problem of Peaceful Territorial Change"; and Kacowicz, *Peaceful Territorial Change* are exceptions because they utilize more systematic methods of testing such as logit regressions and conduct their tests on a large number of cases. These studies, however, suffer from problems of case selection and research design which place limits on the conclusions that can be drawn from the statistical results. Goertz and Diehl restricted their cases to only those territorial disputes that were involved in a transfer of territory. As a result, their theoretical and empirical analysis fails to examine those territorial disputes that did not result in the transfer of territory. Kacowicz includes the population of peaceful territorial change cases in his analysis, but the sample of nonpeaceful territorial change cases that he also examines is not randomly selected from the population of such cases. As a result, it is difficult to know how representative this sample of cases is and therefore how much confidence can be placed in the statistical findings produced. Finally, Boyd in "African Boundary Conflict" limits his statistical tests of Africa border conflicts to only those states that experienced border conflicts between 1964 and 1967. The failure to include states not involved in border conflicts and to examine state behavior over a longer time period weakens the generalizability of his findings.

tions can be proposed. What is lacking is an integration of firmly grounded theoretical analysis with systematic empirical tests. In this book I improve upon existing work, then, in two basic ways.

1. More attention is given to developing a broad but rigorous theoretical framework for analyzing territorial disputes. By being more careful in the theory-building stage, I develop a stronger logical foundation for the derivation of a more complete set of hypotheses.
2. Hypotheses are tested utilizing multivariate statistical methods on a carefully selected set of cases. Greater rigor in the empirical testing stage will enable me to evaluate the relative explanatory power of competing propositions and to produce empirical findings from which we can generalize with greater confidence.

The Need for Theoretical Integration

In a realist framework, international conflict stems from the clashing national security interests of countries, and the military strength of states is the critical determinant of their relative influence and power. In this theoretical approach domestic political factors do not have a systematic or powerful effect on the security policy choices of state leaders.[36] A large body of theoretical and empirical work, however, has pointed out the weaknesses of a realist approach to explaining international conflict and the security policy choices of states. These works can be categorized as challenging realism from the perspective of the important role that international institutions[37] or domestic politics play in shaping the foreign policy behavior of states. In my judgment, the domestic politics approach has presented quite convincing evidence of the weaknesses of

---

36. Examples of scholars who analyze international politics from a realist perspective include Hans Morgenthau, *Politics among Nations*, 5th ed. rev. (New York: Alfred A. Knopf, 1978); Kenneth Waltz, *Theory of International Politics* (Reading, MA: Addison-Wesley Publishing Co., 1979); Joseph Grieco, "Anarchy and the Limits of Cooperation," *International Organization* 42, no. 3 (1988): 485–508; and John Mearsheimer, "The False Promise of International Institutions," *International Security* 19, no. 3 (1995): 5–49.

37. Examples of works that challenge realism from the perspective of the role and impact of international institutions include Keohane and Nye, *Power and Interdependence;* Robert Keohane, *After Hegemony* (Princeton: Princeton University Press, 1984); Robert Keohane, *International Institutions and State Power* (Boulder: Westview Press, 1989); Ken Oye, ed., *Cooperation under Anarchy* (Princeton: Princeton University Press, 1986); John Ruggie, ed., *Multilateralism Matters* (New York: Columbia University Press, 1993); David Baldwin, ed., *Neorealism and Neoliberalism* (New York: Columbia University Press, 1993).

realism. For example, from the perspective of domestic politics, critics have argued that realist models have important limitations when it comes to explaining alliance formation, deterrence outcomes, crisis bargaining behavior, military expansionism, the formation of grand strategy, and policies for defense spending and weapons procurement.[38] Nevertheless, critics of realism have not made a persuasive case that a purely domestic politics approach to theorizing is superior. Most scholars would agree, in fact, that the goal should be to develop a theoretical framework that incorporates in a coherent and generalizable way the impact of both domestic and international-level variables on the foreign policy decisions of state leaders. The objective then for scholars studying international security should be to move beyond critiques of realism and to begin to develop generalizable models of security policy decision making in which domestic politics play a central role. The challenge of pursuing this goal provides the intellectual premise for my theoretical analysis in this book. In sum, my goal is to rethink a realist approach by focusing specifically on the impact of domestic politics in the formation of the security policy of states.

When scholars attempt to theorize about international politics in the post–World War II era, it is essential to take into account that (1) many states have been beset by problems of internal economic and political development as well as external threats to their security and (2) the increasingly active role of the state in domestic economic and social affairs and public expectations that governments are responsible for social stability and economic prosperity. These features of the postwar period have potentially important implications for the foreign policy behavior of states, and I attempt to take into consideration these implications for the theoretical model that I develop and test.

One could argue that a domestic politics approach to studying security policy would imply that the foreign policy behavior of states is fundamentally inward oriented. That is, the initiatives and reactions of one state toward another are driven by the domestic political implications of international conflict and cooperation. It does not make logical

---

38. See for example James Morrow, "Arms versus Allies," *International Organization* 47, no. 2 (1993): 207–34; David, *Choosing Sides;* Barnett, *Confronting the Cost of War;* Bueno de Mesquita and Lalman, *War and Reason;* Jack Snyder, *Myths of Empire* (Ithaca: Cornell University Press, 1991); Russett, *Grasping the Democratic Peace;* Miroslav Nincic, *Democracy and Foreign Policy* (New York: Columbia University Press, 1992); Richard Rosecrance and Arthur Stein, eds., *The Domestic Bases of Grand Strategy* (Ithaca: Cornell University Press, 1993); Alan Lamborn, *The Price of Power* (Boston: Unwin Hyman, 1991); Thomas Risse-Kappen, "Ideas Do Not Float Freely," *International Organization* 48, no. 2 (1994): 185–214.

sense, however, to imply that we should expect state leaders to be inattentive to the international strategic environment within which their country is situated. Military defeats and diplomatic setbacks have often undermined the power and authority of political leaders within their own country, and it seems quite appropriate to expect that political leaders are aware of this.[39] As a result, scholars in their theoretical work must grapple directly with the recognition that security decisions, even if made by domestic political leaders, must surely reflect assessments of relative military power and the anticipated military and diplomatic reactions of allies and adversaries. In short, the domestic and international levels of analysis must be joined in a systematic way.

The integration of international and domestic-level variables in a single theoretical approach is not a simple task, however. In many respects, the underlying assumptions and logical derivation of hypotheses within realist and domestic politics models are just beginning to be carefully developed by scholars, and efforts at integrating the two approaches are even more tentative.[40] I will build upon the work of recent scholars who have applied greater rigor in the theoretical elaboration of each of these models and hopefully advance the theoretical debate by proposing a relatively simple but generalizable model drawing on elements of both.

Overview of Book

In chapter 2 I define the concept of a territorial dispute and describe the population of such disputes between 1950 and 1990. In chapter 3 I present the underlying assumptions and logic of a theoretical model that integrates realist and domestic politics arguments and the hypotheses

39. See for example Bruce Bueno de Mesquita, Randolph Siverson, and Gary Woller, "War and the Fate of Regimes," *American Political Science Review* 86, no. 4 (1992): 638–46.

40. Examples would include Waltz, *Theory of International Politics;* Barry Posen, *The Sources of Military Doctrine* (Ithaca: Cornell University Press, 1984); Stephen Walt, *The Origins of Alliances* (Ithaca: Cornell University Press, 1987); Emerson Niou, Peter Ordeshook, and Gregory Rose, *The Balance of Power* (New York: Cambridge University Press, 1989); Bueno de Mesquita and Lalman, *War and Reason;* David Lake, *Power, Protection, and Free Trade* (Ithaca: Cornell University Press, 1988); Robert Putnam, "Diplomacy and Domestic Politics," *International Organization* 42, no. 3 (1988): 427–60; Morrow, "Arms versus Allies"; Barnett, *Confronting the Costs of War;* Snyder, *Myths of Empire;* Lamborn, *The Price of Power;* Charles Glaser, "Realists as Optimists," *International Security* 19, no. 3 (1994): 50–90; Robert Powell, "Guns, Butter, and Anarchy," *American Political Science Review* 87, no. 1 (1993): 115–32; Joe Hagan, *Political Opposition and Foreign Policy in Comparative Perspective* (Boulder: Lynne Rienner, 1993).

that are derived from the model for empirical testing. In chapters 4 through 6 I empirically test by statistical methods the model and discuss individual cases to illustrate and critically evaluate the general findings. In chapter 4 I address the question, What is the probability that any two bordering states will become involved in a territorial dispute? In chapter 5 I turn my attention to only those bordering states that are involved in a territorial dispute, and I attempt to answer the question why some disputes are characterized by high versus low levels of diplomatic and military conflict. In chapter 6 I complete my empirical analysis by attempting to predict when a challenger state will seek a negotiated settlement of a territorial dispute. In the conclusion to the book, chapter 7, I discuss the overall explanatory power of the model tested, the broader theoretical implications of the findings, and policy prescriptions for the management of future territorial disputes.

CHAPTER 2

The Concept of a Territorial Dispute

In chapter 1 I argued that greater rigor was required in the theoretical and empirical analysis of territorial disputes. An essential first step is to develop a clear and valid definition of the concept of a territorial dispute between states. A well-grounded definition of the concept is critical in subsequent chapters to both theory building and empirical testing. In the first section of this chapter I present the definition of a territorial dispute, and in the second section I identify and describe the population of such disputes from 1950 to 1990.

Concept of a Territorial Dispute

Broadly defined, a territorial dispute involves either a disagreement between states over where their common homeland or colonial borders should be fixed, or, more fundamentally, the dispute entails one country contesting the right of another country even to exercise sovereignty over some or all of its homeland or colonial territory. More specifically, a territorial dispute exists between two states in any of the following situations.

At least one government does not accept the definition of where the boundary line of its border with another country is currently located, whereas the neighboring government takes the position that the existing boundary line is the legal border between the two countries based on a previously signed treaty or document. The scope of disagreement over the boundary line can range from a small section of territory to the entire length of the border. In all of these disputes the challenger does not question the existence of a border with the targeted country, but only the legitimacy of where the existing boundary line has been drawn. Of the 129 territorial disputes in the post–World War II period, twenty-five cases (or about 19 percent)[1] were characterized by such disagreements.

---

1. In a few cases the territorial claims of a challenger can be placed in more than one of the five categories to be discussed. As a result, the percentages cited will exceed 100 percent when totaled.

For example, since 1950 Ecuador has rejected the boundary line along its border with Peru, as fixed in the Rio Protocol of 1942, and has claimed a large section (some 125,000 square miles) of the Amazon basin of northern Peru.[2] In 1962 Venezuela officially renounced a prior agreement signed in 1899 with the British establishing the Venezuelan border with Guyana.[3] China has disputed its borders with both the Soviet Union and India by rejecting the legitimacy of border agreements concluded in the nineteenth century.[4]

There is no treaty or set of historical documents clearly establishing a boundary line, and, as a result, bordering countries present opposing definitions of where the boundary line should be drawn. In some cases, such disputes stem from the overly general and imprecise delimitation of a border in a previous agreement and, as a result, when the challenger and target actually attempt to demarcate the border, the terms of the border agreement are not detailed enough to resolve conflicting claims.[5] In other cases, however, there is no past agreement serving as the common reference point for establishing where the boundary is located. Instead, both challenger and target draw on their own set of historical evidence and documentation to claim that the border should be defined on terms favorable to themselves. Once again, in these types of disputes, the challengers do not question the existence of a border with the target but only the precise location of the boundary line.

2. See for example William Krieg, *Ecuadorean-Peruvian Rivalry in the Upper Amazon* (Bethesda, MD: William Krieg, 1987) and David Zook, *Zarumilla y Maranon: The Ecuador-Peru Dispute* (New York: Bookman Associates Inc., 1964).

3. See Jacqueline Braveboy-Wagner, *The Venezuela-Guyana Border Dispute* (Boulder: Westview Press, 1984).

4. See for example Alan Day, ed., *Border and Territorial Disputes* (London: Longman, 1982), 252–57, 259–69 and J. R. V. Prescott, *Political Frontiers and Boundaries* (Boston: Allen & Unwin, 1987), 222–27.

5. It is important to distinguish between problems of delimitation and demarcation of a border. Unfortunately, the two terms are often used interchangeably. Delimitation refers to the act of determining where the limits of a boundary line are to be drawn in a treaty or document, whereas demarcation refers to the act of marking on the ground the limits of a boundary line by means of pillars, beacons, and other physical means. Demarcation of a border typically presumes that two states have already reached agreement on delimitation of their common border. Agreement on delimitation, however, does not preclude disagreement or problems in demarcation because, for example, local conditions may make it impractical to mark the border in accordance with the guidelines of a written document. I view problems of demarcation as a second-order issue and therefore do not consider them to be cases of territorial disputes in and of themselves; my conception of a territorial dispute centers on the conflict between states in deciding whether and where a boundary line should be drawn. The distinction between delimitation and demarcation is clearly made in works examining territorial disputes from the perspective of international law. See Ian Brownlie, *African Boundaries* (London: C. Hurst & Company, 1979), 4.

Of the 129 territorial disputes in the post–World War II period, fifty cases (or about 39 percent) were characterized by such disagreements. For example, the governments of China and Nepal disputed their common border between 1949 and 1961 due to unclear and contradictory treaties previously concluded in the eighteenth and nineteenth centuries. The same type of problem characterized the dispute between Thailand and Cambodia over the Preah Vihear Temple and surrounding territory. Political leaders from each country claimed that the very same treaty (originally signed in 1907) established that the Temple was located within their own national territory.[6] In the Persian Gulf, the disputes involving Saudi Arabia and many of its neighbors have been based on the simple fact that historical documentation on the location of borders was quite limited and sketchy in detail.[7]

One country occupies the national territory of another and refuses to relinquish control over the territory despite demands by that country to withdraw. In the Middle East, examples would include the Israeli occupation of Syrian (the Golan Heights) and Egyptian (Sinai) territory following the Six Day War of June 1967. Another set of cases involves regional states pressing major powers to terminate the presence of a military base on their national territory. Examples would include Cuba's demand that the United States withdraw from its military base at Guantanamo Bay, or the demand by Egypt following World War II that the British military presence and base rights in the Suez Canal be terminated. In these cases the location of a border is not the issue in contention. Instead, the dispute centers on the attempt by the challenger to compel another state to withdraw from its national territory and thereby enable the challenger to reestablish full and effective control over its own national territory. Twenty-three (18 percent) of the 129 post–World War II disputes can be classified as involving such issues.

One government does not recognize the sovereignty of another country over some portion of territory within the borders of that country. The government may often be hesitant to openly and clearly issue its own irredentist claim to that portion of territory but, instead, may support separatist groups who claim that the disputed territory should form the basis of an independent and sovereign state. For example, since its independence in 1947, Pakistan has been involved in a dispute with

---

6. See Robert Butterworth, *Managing Interstate Conflict, 1945–74: Data with Synopses* (Pittsburgh: University Center for International Studies, University of Pittsburgh, 1976), 171–72, 263–64, 294–95.

7. See for example Husan Albaharna, *The Arabian Gulf States*, 2d rev. ed. (Beirut: Librairie Du Liban, 1975) and J. B. Kelly, *Arabia, the Gulf and the West* (London: Weidenfeld and Nicolson, 1980).

Afghanistan over sections of its eastern border populated by Pathan tribes. Afghan governments have openly called for the establishment of an independent state of Pakhtoonistan in the disputed territory while downplaying irredentist claims to the territory (though Afghan leaders have stated that they would welcome the incorporation of the disputed territory if the Pathan populations expressed a desire for such a union). At the same time, Pakistan has contested Indian control over Kashmir territory, claiming that the majority of the population within Kashmir would favor union with Pakistan if given the opportunity in a plebiscite.[8] Challenger irredentist claims or support for groups seeking to secede from the target, in fact, constitute only about 15 percent (nineteen cases) of the post–World War II population of territorial dispute cases.

One government does not recognize the independence and sovereignty of another country (or colonial territory) and seeks to annex some or all of the territory of that country. For example, Morocco refused to recognize the newly independent state of Mauritania in 1960 and claimed sovereignty over all of the country based on the historical argument that Mauritania had been a province of Morocco in precolonial times.[9] Following Israel's declaration of independence in 1948, Arab countries refused to recognize the state of Israel and advocated the establishment of a Palestinian state within the territory comprising Israel while also seeking to annex portions of Israeli territory.[10] Following the defeat of Germany in World War II for almost two decades the leaders of West Germany refused to recognize East Germany as an independent state, and even after recognition was granted in 1972, West Germany continued to support the objective of German reunification.[11] In this final category of cases, the directly opposed territorial interests of the challenger and target are very clear. In these cases the challenger typically seeks to annex all of the territory controlled or claimed by the target and therefore rejects any sovereign rights for the target. In the postwar period about 12 percent of all territorial disputes (15/129) involved such far-reaching claims by challengers.

The first two categories listed above represent conventional border

---

8. Day, *Border and Territorial Disputes,* 236–50, 283–94 and Prescott, *Political Frontiers,* 95–97, 228–30.

9. See Brownlie, *African Boundaries* 147–48 and Saadia Touval, *The Boundary Politics of Independent Africa* (Cambridge: Harvard University Press, 1972), 66–71, 125–31, 262–69.

10. See Mark Tessler, *A History of the Israeli-Palestinian Conflict* (Bloomington: Indiana University Press, 1994), ch. 5.

11. See William Griffith, *The Ostpolitik of the Federal Republic of Germany* (Cambridge: MIT Press, 1978).

disputes in the sense that two states have a disagreement about exactly where the boundary line between the two countries should be fixed. This is the classic problem of delimiting a border in which two governments seek to define the outer territorial limits of their recognized rights of state sovereignty. In sharp contrast, the fifth category represents a very deep conflict of interest because one government questions whether there even exists a legitimate border between it and another country. In this case the issue is much larger than just delimiting a border since the dispute is based on one country questioning the very existence of another country. The third and fourth categories are characterized by intermediate levels of conflict since they involve one state contesting the sovereign rights of another state over some portion of its national territory. In comparison, the first two categories involve no dispute whether territory along the border should be under the control of either country, nor is one country directly challenging the sovereign rights of another country by occupying some section of its territory.

To establish when a territorial dispute begins between two states, I rely on either written documents or public and official statements by state leaders in which the leaders of one government claim the territory of another state; question the existing location of the border and call for revisions in the border; or contest the right of a state to exercise sovereign rights over territory. In response, the targeted government rejects the challenger's position and maintains that the delimitation of the border or sovereign rights to territory are not open to question and negotiations. The dispute persists as long as leaders from the challenger state do not withdraw or renounce their territorial claim.

The end of a territorial dispute is marked by one or more of the following.

1. The occupation and assumption of control over disputed territory by the challenger is formally recognized by the target in a treaty, an international agreement, or in an official statement by the political leadership of the target.
2. The signing of a bilateral agreement with a target or an official statement by the challenger in which its territorial claims are either renounced or are satisfied with a compromise settlement.
3. The challenger agrees to abide by a ruling issued by the ICJ or an international arbitration panel.

My definition of a territorial dispute therefore relies on evidence of divergent positions being expressed by governments in bilateral diplomatic communications, or in international forums such as the United

Nations General Assembly or regional organizations like the Organization for African Unity (OAU) and the Arab League.

Before we consider the population of territorial disputes in the post– World War II period in table 1, I want to discuss explicitly what types of cases are excluded from my analysis.

I focus only on disputes between sovereign states (and their colonial territories), and therefore I do not include territorial disputes between a metropole and its colony, particularly struggles for independence by colonies against their metropole. For example, the attempt by France to reassert its colonial rule in Indochina in the early postwar period is excluded, as is Portugal's struggle to retain control over its African colonial possessions.[12] In addition, I do not include claims put forth by a political unit not generally recognized by the international community as a sovereign state or colony. Thus, I exclude the Polisario conflict with Morocco over the Western Sahara or Namibia's dispute with South Africa over Walvis Bay.[13]

My definition of a territorial dispute, with its emphasis on behavioral evidence of conflicting policy positions, excludes what might be described as "latent" disputes in which the leaders of governments might be expected to have (or are believed to harbor) territorial claims but fail to express them publicly or officially. As a result, there is no record of military or diplomatic actions taken by the challenger to contest the territorial rights of the target. For example, Finland was coerced into ceding Karelia and much of Petsamo to the Soviet Union during World War II but Finnish leaders did not call for the return of these territories during the cold war period. However, with the dissolution of the Soviet Union in 1991, this latent dispute has threatened to become an open source of conflict between Finland and Russia, since there is a growing public debate within Finland about whether to confront Russia with a demand for the return of Karelia and Petsamo.[14] Another example would be the postwar tacit agreement between Turkey and Syria over the territory of Alexandretta (or Hatay as Turkey refers to it). In 1939 France ceded to Turkey Alexandretta (then part of the French colony of

---

12. For a study of the conditions under which colonial powers will resort to military force in an attempt to forestall the decolonization process see Gary Goertz and Paul Diehl, "International Norms and Power Politics," in Paul Diehl and Frank Wayman, eds., *Reconstructing Realpolitik* (Ann Arbor: University of Michigan Press, 1994), 101–22.

13. See Day, *Border and Territorial Disputes,* 154–69.

14. See John Allcock, Guy Arnold, Alan Day, D. S. Lewis, Lorimer Poultney, Roland Rance, and D. J. Sagar, *Border and Territorial Disputes,* rev. 3d ed. (London: Longman, 1992), 69–74.

Syria). In the postwar period Syrian governments have not officially recognized Turkish sovereignty over the territory (which Turkey in turn has not insisted upon), but at the same time Syria has not officially called for the return of the territory either.[15]

In these two examples a previous exchange of territory serves as the basis for a potential dispute between bordering states. There are also potential cases of territorial disputes between states over border regions that are largely unpopulated and have not been delimited. In these cases differing definitions of where the border lies may exist but neighboring governments have decided not to press their claims against one another. For example, China and North Korea have opposing claims to a twenty-mile section of their common border but there is no available evidence indicating that the two governments have, in fact, confronted one another over the territory.[16] Similarly, Saudi Arabian borders with the former South Yemen have not been delimited, but Saudi claims to the territory of its neighbor had not until quite recently become a source of open confrontation.[17] While I do not include such "latent" conflicts in my population of territorial disputes, I do attempt to explain in chapter 4 why some bordering countries confront one another over territorial issues whereas others do not. As a result, I address important questions related to selection effects in theorizing about and empirically analyzing territorial disputes.[18]

As noted already, I do not include as examples of territorial disputes problems or failures of states to demarcate borders. A border that is not demarcated is not sufficient evidence to establish that there is an actual dispute over territory. For example, there are many cases of

---

15. See Daniel Pipes, *Greater Syria* (New York: Oxford University Press, 1990), 60, 98, 140–41.

16. The disputed territory is described in *International Boundary Study: China-Korea Boundary,* no. 17 (Washington, D.C.: The Geographer, Bureau of Intelligence and Research, Department of State, 1962).

17. See Day, *Border and Territorial Disputes,* 232. In 1992 the Saudi government warned Yemen to cease oil explorations along the border in disputed regions. See Clarke Dunbar, "The Unification of Yemen," *Middle East Journal* 45, no. 3 (1992): 472.

18. On the general problem of selection bias in social science research see Christopher Achen, *The Statistical Analysis of Quasi-Experiments* (Berkeley: University of California Press, 1986). Issues of selection bias in the study of conventional deterrence have been discussed by Christopher Achen and Duncan Snidal, "Rational Deterrence Theory and Comparative Case Studies," *World Politics* 41, no. 2 (1989): 143–69; Paul Huth and Bruce Russett, "Testing Deterrence Theory," *World Politics* 42, no. 4 (1990): 466–501; and James Fearon, "Signaling versus the Balance of Power and Interests," *Journal of Conflict Resolution* 38, no. 2 (1994): 236–69.

African states that have failed to demarcate borders for various reasons, but no dispute exists in principle over delimitation of the border.[19]

I do not include offshore disputes between states over maritime zones or continental shelves.[20] These are an important and frequent source of conflict between states, but I do not think that such disputes are similar enough to be included in my analysis of territorial disputes. First, many disputes over maritime zones do not involve any competing claims to national territory. Second, if territorial issues are involved but only extend to underseas territory, the political salience of the dispute is generally limited, in contrast with the importance and attention often given to land-based disputes. As a result, different patterns of behavior are expected in these two types of cases.

The Population of Territorial Disputes, 1950–90

In table 1 I provide a complete list of the territorial disputes in the international system between 1950 and 1990. This forty-year period was selected for the anlaysis because it ranges from the early stages of the emerging postwar international order to the collapse of that order with the end of the cold war and the breakup of the Soviet Union. For each territorial dispute case I list the countries involved, the duration of the dispute, and the total number of years in which militarized confrontations were initiated by the challenger over disputed territory.[21] A more detailed description of each dispute is presented in appendix A. In total there are 129 territorial disputes (and 116 disputed borders) with almost every region of the international system represented by a number of cases.

In figure 1 I summarize the different stages in the evolution of a territorial dispute. Two very different situations can characterize the

---

19. The reasons may range from lack of political interest by state leaders to practical problems and issues of cost in surveying isolated and rough terrain along a border. See Brownlie, *African Boundaries* for a description of borders that are neither demarcated nor in dispute.

20. See Henry Degenhardt, *Maritime Affairs: A World Handbook* (London: Longman, 1985) and J. R. V. Prescott, *The Maritime Political Boundaries of the World* (London: Methuen, 1985).

21. A militarized confrontation or dispute is initiated when one state conveys either a possible threat to use force by means of verbal statements and/or military actions, or actually resorts to the use of force. The targeted state may respond with a counterthreat/ military retaliation or limit itself to diplomatic protests and other noncoercive countermeasures. See Charles Gochman and Zeev Maoz, "Militarized Interstate Disputes, 1816–1976," *Journal of Conflict Resolution* 28, no. 4 (1984): 585–616 for a similar definition of a militarized interstate dispute.

TABLE 1. Territorial Disputes, 1950–90

Countries	Years	Number of Militarized Confrontations
The Caribbean, Central, and South America		
Argentina vs. Chile	1950–90	10
Argentina vs. UK	1950–90	2
Argentina vs. Uruguay	1950–73	2
Bolivia vs. Chile	1950–90	0
Cuba vs. US	1959–90	1
Ecuador vs. Peru	1950–90	5
Guatemala vs. UK	1950–90	3
Honduras vs. El Salvador	1950–90	1
Honduras vs. US	1950–72	0
Mexico vs. US	1950–63	0
Netherlands/Suriname vs. France	1950–90	0
Netherlands/Suriname vs. UK/Guyana	1950–90	2
Nicaragua vs. Colombia	1980–90	0
Nicaragua vs. Honduras	1957–60	1
Nicaragua vs. US	1950–71	0
Panama vs. US	1950–77	0
Uruguay vs. Brazil	1950–90	0
Venezuela vs. UK/Guyana	1951–90	5
Europe		
USSR/East Germany vs. US/West Germany/France/UK	1950–71	2
France vs. UK	1950–53	0
Greece vs. Albania	1950–71	0
Greece vs. UK/Turkey	1951–90	3
Ireland vs. UK	1950–90	0
Netherlands vs. Belgium	1950–59	0
Netherlands vs. West Germany	1955–60	0
Spain vs. UK	1950–90	1
West Germany vs. Czechoslovakia	1955–73	0
West Germany vs. East Germany	1955–72	0
West Germany vs. France	1955–57	0
West Germany vs. Poland	1955–70	0
Yugoslavia vs. Italy	1950–75	1
Middle East		
Egypt vs. Israel	1950–89	7
Egypt vs. UK	1950–54	1
Iran vs. UK/Bahrain	1950–70 1979–90	0
Iran vs. UK/United Arab Emirates	1950–90	2
Iran vs. Iraq	1950–90	9

TABLE 1—*Continued*

Countries	Years	Number of Militarized Confrontations
Middle East-continued		
Iran vs. Saudi Arabia	1950–68	0
Iraq vs. Kuwait	1950–90	5
Jordan vs. Israel	1950–90	1
Jordan vs. Saudi Arabia	1950–65	0
North Yemen vs. UK/South Yemen	1950–90	3
Oman vs. United Arab Emirates	1977–81	0
Qatar vs. Bahrain	1967–90	1
Saudi Arabia vs. Iraq	1950–81	0
Saudi Arabia vs. Kuwait	1961–90	0
Saudi Arabia vs. UK/Qatar	1950–65	0
Saudi Arabia vs. UK/United Arab Emirates	1950–74	1
Syria vs. Israel	1950–90	14
Africa		
Benin vs. Niger	1960–65	1
Comoros vs. France	1975–90	0
Egypt vs. UK/Sudan	1950–90	1
Ethiopia vs. Sudan	1950–72	1
Ethiopia vs. UK/Kenya	1950–70	0
Ethiopia vs. France/Djibouti	1950–77	0
Ghana vs. France/Ivory Coast	1959–66	0
Lesotho vs. South Africa	1966–90	0
Liberia vs. France/Ivory Coast	1950–60	0
Liberia vs. France/Guinea	1950–58	0
Libya vs. France/Chad	1954–90	1
Madagascar vs. France	1960–90	0
Mali vs. Mauritania	1960–63	0
Mali vs. Burkino Faso	1960–87	2
Mauritania vs. Spain	1960–75	0
Mauritius vs. France	1976–90	0
Mauritius vs. UK	1980–90	0
Morocco vs. France/Algeria	1956–72	2
Morocco vs. Mauritania	1957–70	0
Morocco vs. Spain	1956–90	1
Seychelles vs. France	1976–90	0
Somalia vs. Ethiopia	1950–90	6
Somalia vs. France/Djibouti	1960–77	0
Italy/Somalia vs. UK/Kenya	1960–81	2
Togo vs. Ghana	1960–90	0
Tunisia vs. France	1956–62	1
Tunisia vs. France/Algeria	1956–70	0
Uganda vs. Tanzania	1972–79	3
Zaire vs. Congo	1970–90	0

TABLE 1—*Continued*

Countries	Year	Number of Militarized Confrontations
Africa-continued		
Zaire vs. Zambia	1980–90	2
Zambia vs. Malawi	1981–86	0
Central Asia		
Afghanistan vs. Pakistan	1950–90	4
China vs. Afghanistan	1950–63	0
China vs. Bhutan	1979–90	0
China vs. Burma	1950–60	1
China vs. India	1950–90	7
China vs. Nepal	1950–61	1
China vs. Pakistan	1950–63	0
China vs. Soviet Union	1950–90	3
India vs. France	1950–54	0
India vs. Portugal	1950–74	2
India vs. Bangladesh	1973–90	0
Pakistan vs. India	1950–90	12
USSR vs. Iran	1950–54	0
USSR vs. Turkey	1950–53	0
East and South East Asia		
China vs. Japan	1951–90	0
China vs. Taiwan	1950–90	3
China vs. South Vietnam/Vietnam	1951–90	8
Indonesia vs. Netherlands	1950–62	4
Indonesia vs. UK/Malaysia	1961–66	1
Japan vs. USSR	1951–90	0
Malaysia vs. China	1979–90	0
North Korea vs. South Korea	1950–90	1
North Vietnam vs. South Vietnam	1954–75	1
Philippines vs. China	1956–90	1
Philippines vs. Malaysia	1961–90	1
Portugal vs. Indonesia	1975–90	0
South Korea vs. Japan	1951–90	2
South Vietnam/Vietnam vs. Cambodia	1956–83	6
Taiwan vs. Japan	1951–90	0
Thailand vs. France/Cambodia	1950–82	8
Thailand vs. Laos	1984–90	2
Vanuata vs. France	1982–90	0

Note: See appendix A for a description of the territorial issues in dispute, the outcome of the dispute, the dates when states initiated militarized confrontations, and sources consulted.

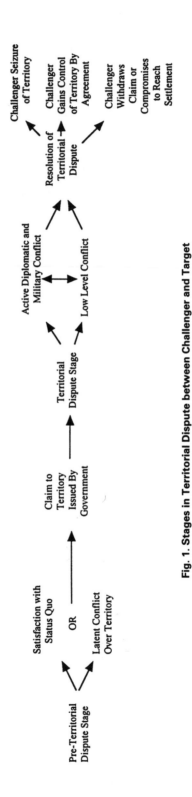

Fig. 1. Stages in Territorial Dispute between Challenger and Target

preterritorial dispute phase. In the first case, both states are satisfied with the territorial status quo and therefore a dispute is unlikely to emerge. In the second case, however, there is a latent claim or conflict over territory and the likelihood is greater of a dispute eventually emerging. Once a claim is issued by the challenger and rejected by the target, the period of open dispute has commenced. During this phase the challenger's pursuit of its claim can alternate between periods of active diplomatic and/or military confrontation and low level protest and conflict. In the final stage—the resolution of the territorial dispute—a number of outcomes are possible. For example, the target may capitulate to the use of force by the challenger, the challenger may withdraw its claim to territory, or the two states may settle by means of mutual compromise.

If we now turn to the population of dispute cases, we see the full range of situations presented in figure 1. For example, the disputes vary in length of time with a number of disputes spanning the entire 1950 to 1990 period, but some cases are as short as two or three years. In total, twenty-three disputes (18 percent) were less than ten years, forty-seven disputes (36 percent) lasted thirty years or more, and the largest number of cases (fifty-nine or 46 percent) were between ten and thirty years. In the large majority of disputes one state is designated the challenger, but there are a small number of cases in which both states seek to overturn the territorial status quo. For example, if we look at the 116 disputed borders we find that there is a single challenger in 104 cases (or 90 percent) and in only twelve cases (10 percent) did both states simultaneously claim the territory of the other. The largest number of disputed borders were located in Africa with thirty-two cases, while the fewest number of disputed borders (thirteen) were located in Europe.

Many states were embroiled in multiple disputes over the 1950 to 1990 period. The two most disputatious countries were China and Saudi Arabia. China was the challenger in nine different disputes while Saudi Arabia was the challenger in six disputes. There were numerous cases in which the same country was involved in two or three different disputes as a challenger. Conversely, some countries were the targets of claims by multiple challengers. For example, Great Britain was the target in twenty disputes and France in fourteen cases. In general, colonial powers were targets in multiple cases as were very large states with multiple borders, such as China, India, and the Soviet Union.

The frequency of militarized confrontations was highest in the Middle East with over forty cases, including five wars and over 1,000,000 battle fatalities. In contrast, despite a greater number of territorial disputes than in the Middle East, there were less than twenty-five militarized confrontations and only one war (3,000 fatalities) in Africa, and there were only seven militarized confrontations in Europe and two wars totaling over 11,000 fatalities.[22]

There is also substantial variance in the outcomes of these territorial disputes. At the end of 1990 there were fifty-four borders still in dispute with the highest ratio of unresolved disputes relative to total disputed borders located in Central and South America (67 percent) and the Far East and Southeast Asia (78 percent). In contrast, fifty-seven borders once in dispute were settled with the highest ratio of resolved disputes relative to total disputed borders (77 percent) located in Europe. Of the fifty-seven borders where disputes were resolved, forty-three were settled by means of compromise or capitulation by the challenger, while in the remaining fourteen cases the challenger gained control over disputed territory by either unilateral concessions by the target in the absence of coercive pressure by the challenger (eight cases), or by the challenger's effective threat or use of military and/or political pressure against the target (six cases).

These 129 territorial disputes, with their global coverage and substantial variance in duration, number of militarized confrontations, and outcomes constitute the primary database for testing theoretical propositions by means of statistical analyses. In chapters 4 through 6 this population of cases will be analyzed in order to address a series of hypotheses about the conflict behavior of states involved in territorial disputes.

---

22. Fatality figures were taken from Melvin Small and J. David Singer, *Resort to Arms: International and Civil Wars 1816–1980* (Beverly Hills: Sage Publications, 1982), ch. 4 and the updated Correlates of War Project dataset on "International Wars, 1816–1990" at the University of Michigan and Lawrence Freedman and Efraim Karsh, "How Kuwait Was Won," *International Security* 16, no. 2 (1991): 37.

CHAPTER 3

A Modified Realist Model

In this chapter I present a modified realist model that incorporates the central role that domestic politics can play in shaping the foreign policy behavior of states. In the first section of the chapter I break down the analysis of territorial disputes into separate stages and discuss the assumptions of a rational choice approach to theory building. In the second section of the chapter I describe the basic assumptions and logic of the modified realist model and derive a series of hypotheses that will be tested in chapters 4 through 6. In the final section of the chapter I compare and contrast the hypotheses derived from the modified realist model with those that would be derived from a more conventional realist approach.

Introduction

Conceptually, I divide the analysis of territorial disputes into three stages, and at each stage the theoretical focus is on explaining the behavior of the challenger in a dispute. As a result, in my analysis I do not test propositions about how the target state responds to the actions of the challenger. The anticipated reactions of the target, however, are clearly of primary concern to the challenger, and therefore the logic of strategic thinking is incorporated into many of the hypotheses concerning the decisions of the challenger. The reason for my theoretical focus on the challenger is that *it is the actions and decisions of the challenger that are the fundamental causes of conflict and accommodation over disputed territory.* It is the challenger that issues a claim to territory, decides whether to pursue its claim aggressively or to seek a settlement, while the target responds to these actions. Thus, a theoretical analysis of the emergence, escalation, and peaceful resolution of territorial disputes that focuses on the behavior of the state that consistently assumes the initiative at each of these stages (i.e., the challenger) should provide substantial insight into the dynamics of territorial disputes. The three stages I analyze in a territorial dispute are as follows.

1. At stage one policymakers must decide whether to confront their neighbor with competing claims to territory, or to accept the territorial status quo. In the period between 1950 and 1990 approximately 33 percent of the borders were at some point the source of a territorial dispute between states. In chapter 4 I will test hypotheses derived from the model to explain why some bordering states become embroiled in territorial disputes whereas other neighbors avoid such conflicts.

2. In the second stage of analysis I examine all of those states that became embroiled in a territorial dispute. The question I address is, What level of diplomatic and military pressure will the challenger apply against the target in support of territorial claims? In approximately 50 percent of the 129 territorial dispute cases the challenger initiated one or more militarized confrontations in which military units are deployed and placed on alert, indicating a threat to use force. The actual resort to the large-scale use of force (an attack involving 1,000 or more troops) by the challenger, however, is quite infrequent. In less than 20 percent of the militarized confrontations initiated does the challenger escalate to the level of armed conflict involving substantial numbers of military forces. In chapter 5 I test the model to determine why some territorial disputes are characterized by high versus low levels of diplomatic and military conflict.

3. In the third stage of my analysis I try to explain when the challenger will seek a peaceful resolution of the territorial dispute with the target. In less than half of the cases does the challenger, in fact, seek such a resolution of the dispute. The theoretical question I address in chapter 6 is, Under what conditions will the challenger seek a resolution of the territorial dispute by means of compromise or conciliation and, conversely, when will the challenger persist in diplomatic and/or military confrontation with its neighbor?

To answer each of the basic theoretical questions posed above and to provide a framework for understanding what policy choices will be selected by the challenger state, I develop a new realist model that acknowledges that domestic politics within states cannot safely be ignored when trying to explain the security policy choices of state leaders. As noted in chapter 1, realist and domestic politics models are typically presented as largely competing theoretical approaches to the study of international relations. At the same time, the logic and assumptions underlying each of these models are often not clearly articulated or fully developed, and, as a result, it is actually quite difficult to determine how divergent the two models really are, or to assess the relative explanatory power of each model. My objective therefore is to describe in some detail the basic assumptions and logic of the modified realist model in order to show how domestic politics can be incorporated into a realist framework in a logically sound and generalizable way.

In my view, if powerful explanations of the foreign policy behavior of states are to be developed, three basic questions must be addressed by any theoretical model.

1. What are the most salient policy goals of decision makers?
2. What motivates decision makers to pursue their goals?
3. What features of the domestic and international environment of decision makers are most important in shaping their policy choices?

The basic assumptions of the modified realist model were therefore formulated in order to provide answers to each of these critical questions. I drew upon and synthesized the work of other scholars in order to identify what I believe are the essential features of this new model. The assumptions of the model are explicitly presented in order to: (1) clarify the theoretical foundations of the model, (2) facilitate an assessment of the logical consistency of hypotheses derived from the model, and (3) identify more clearly the theoretical differences of this new model with a conventional realist approach. While my hypotheses are not derived from the assumptions of the model in a formal or mathematical setup my objective is to try and make as clear as possible the logical steps involved in moving from assumptions to testable propositions. In presenting the assumptions of the model I believe it is important to establish whenever possible their logical and/or empirical plausibility. As a result, I will cite appropriate findings from previous scholarship that lend support to the validity of the stated assumptions.

Before I turn to a discussion of the model it is necessary to discuss briefly the use of a rational choice framework for conceptualizing how decisions are reached by foreign policy leaders. The rational choice framework I employ for the modified realist model begins with the assumption that decisions regarding national security policy are made by a single unitary actor. The unitary actor assumption enables me to derive testable hypotheses by conceptualizing the decisions of a challenger state as being made by a single key individual who must make the final choice between attempting to change the territorial status quo or accepting it as it stands.[1] Empirically, I believe this assumption is justifiable when applied to modeling decisions on foreign policy with potentially important national security implications. In such situations there is a good deal of variance in the size of the groups providing advice and consulting closely with a central decision maker, but it is not typical to find that the final choice is actually being made by some collectivity of decision makers. The more prevalent pattern is one in which a single leader (e.g., President, Prime Minister, First Secretary, or General) makes the final choice after consultation with an inner group of advisers.[2] From the unitary actor assumption, however, one cannot infer what are the policy preferences of the decision maker,[3] or what conditions affect his/her assessment of the expected utility of policy alternatives. Furthermore, the unitary actor assumption does not imply that the central decision maker is isolated from the influence of other groups and political actors within and outside the government. Indeed, the central decision maker will typically receive advice from many sources, consult with other policymakers, and consider the reactions of many other political actors before reaching a final decision.

The second assumption is that the unitary actor chooses the policy option with the greatest expected utility. This assumption is necessary because a rational calculation of policy choices requires that a decision maker assess the relative costs and benefits of alternatives and select the option that maximizes expected gains or minimizes expected losses. This

1. See Bruce Bueno de Mesquita, *The War Trap* (New Haven: Yale University Press, 1981), ch. 2 and Bruce Bueno de Mesquita and David Lalman, *War and Reason* (New Haven: Yale University Press, 1992), ch. 1 for a discussion of how the unitary actor assumption deals with the problem of Arrow's Paradox.

2. This conclusion is based on case studies of crisis decision making and war initiation such as Glenn Snyder and Paul Diesing, *Conflict among Nations* (Princeton: Princeton University Press, 1977), ch. 5; Evan Laurd, *War in International Society* (New Haven: Yale University Press, 1987), ch. 5; Jonathan Wilkenfeld and Michael Brecher, *Crises in the Twentieth Century*, vol.II (New York: Pergamon Press, 1988), 57–60; Michael Brecher, *Crises in World Politics* (New York: Pergamon Press, 1993); Alan Dowty, *Middle East Crisis* (Berkeley: University of California Press, 1984); Michael Brecher, *Decisions in Crisis* (Berkeley: University of California Press, 1980); Avi Shlaim, *The United States and the Berlin Blockade, 1948–1949* (Berkeley: University of California Press, 1983); Karen Dawisha, *The Kremlin and the Prague Spring* (Berkeley: University of California Press, 1984); Robert Jervis, Richard Ned Lebow, and Janice Gross Stein, *Psychology and Deterrence* (Baltimore: Johns Hopkins University Press, 1985), chs. 3–5. Supporting evidence drawn from experimental tests can be found in Patrick Haney, Roberta Herzberg, and Rick Wilson, "Advice and Consent: Unitary Actors, Advisory Models, and Experimental Tests," *Journal of Conflict Resolution* 36, no. 4 (1992): 603–33.

3. In addition, my use of a rational choice approach does not imply a normative judgment about whether the goals of state leaders are "sensible" or "reasonable."

assumption does not imply that the decision maker has complete information about all the costs and benefits of alternatives,[4] or considers an exhaustive list of options. In fact, as already described in the beginning of this chapter, the policy options of the challenger at each stage of a territorial dispute are simplified to a choice between a limited number of basic alternatives. I do assume, however, that in processing information, decision makers do not engage in systematically biased appraisal of options as a result of cognitive limitations or motivated misperceptions. Finally, my use of a rational choice framework does not necessarily imply that leaders follow a systematic and structured process of reaching decisions that can be readily documented. The only requirement is that the final choice by leaders between policy alternatives meet the basic assumptions described above.[5]

Within this rational choice framework, an explanation for the

4. As a result, uncertainty about expected costs and benefits can lead to misperception and miscalculations by decision makers. One of the central developments in game-theoretic work over the past decade has been the incorporation of incomplete information into models with the result that these models better approximate the decision making context of state leaders. Examples of such work pertaining to the study of international relations include Bueno de Mesquita and Lalman, *War and Reason;* James Fearon, "Signaling versus the Balance of Power," *Journal of Conflict Resolution* 38, no. 2 (1994): 236–69; James Morrow, "Capabilities, Uncertainty, and Resolve," *American Journal of Political Science* 33, no. 4 (1989): 941–72; Barry Nalebuff, "Rational Deterrence Theory in an Imperfect World," *World Politics* 43, no. 3 (1991): 313–35; Robert Powell, *Nuclear Deterrence Theory* (New York: Cambridge University Press, 1990); R. Harrison Wagner, "Uncertainty, Rational Learning, and Bargaining in the Cuban Missile Crisis," in Peter Ordeshook, ed., *Models in Strategic Choice in Politics* (Ann Arbor: University of Michigan Press, 1989), 177–205; and Ben Mor, *Decision and Interaction in Crisis* (New York: Praeger, 1993).

5. The descriptive accuracy of the rational choice model is the subject of a large empirical literature that cannot be cited fully here. Some of the key works, however, include Janice Gross Stein and Raymond Tanter, *Rational Decision Making: Israel's Security Choices, 1967* (Columbus: Ohio State University Press, 1980); Robert Jervis, Richard Ned Lebow, and Janice Gross Stein, *Psychology and Deterrence* (Baltimore: Johns Hopkins University Press, 1985), chs. 3–4; Snyder and Diesing, *Conflict among Nations,* ch. 5; Dowty, *Middle East Crisis;* Brecher, *Decisions in Crisis;* Brecher, *Crises in World Politics;* Shlaim, *The United States and the Berlin Blockade, 1948–1949;* Dawisha, *The Kremlin and the Prague Spring;* Steven Hoffmann, *India and the China Crisis* (Berkeley: University of California Press, 1990); Richard Ned Lebow, *Between War and Peace* (Baltimore: Johns Hopkins University Press, 1981), chs. 5–6; Jervis, *Perception and Misperception in International Politics;* Gregory Herek, Irving Janis, and Paul Huth, "Decision Making during International Crises: Is Quality of Process Related to Outcome?" *Journal of Conflict Resolution* 31, no. 2 (1987): 203–26. Also see Irving Janis and Leon Mann, *Decision Making* (New York: Free Press, 1977) and George Quattrone and Amos Tversky, "Contrasting Rational and Psychological Analyses of Political Choice," *American Political Science Review* 82, no. 3 (1988): 719–36.

conflict behavior of a challenger state centers on answers to each of the following questions.

1. What is the probability of altering the territorial status quo by means of diplomatic and military pressure for the challenger?
2. How much utility would the challenger attach to altering the territorial status quo?
3. How much utility would the challenger attach to accepting the existing territorial status quo?

The hypotheses derived from the model will therefore be directed at answering each of these questions. The calculation of costs and benefits for a challenger will vary depending on what stage in the analysis of a territorial dispute we are examining.

At the first stage, for example, when the challenger decides whether to initiate a territorial dispute and then to maintain that claim over time, the potential costs of simply disputing territory—military, economic, or political—should not be that substantial. In fact, several hypotheses derived from the model argue that there are costs to the challenger in *not pursuing a territorial claim* under certain conditions. Furthermore, conventional realist type variables such as the relative military strength of states should have modest explanatory power, since there are limited military risks involved in simply staking a claim to territory. The target will not undertake direct military action unless the challenger initiates a militarized confrontation over disputed territory. Thus, the costs of a military conflict at this stage are not of central concern to the challenger. Nevertheless, the challenger does face some risk once it advances a territorial claim that the target or other states will respond by reducing cooperative economic, political, or military ties that it has with the challenger.

At the next stage, when the challenger must decide in pursuit of its territorial claim what level of diplomatic and military pressure to apply against the target, then potential costs should become much more important to the challenger. For example, the risks of a military conflict are now much more salient, and therefore we would expect that the balance of military forces would have much greater explanatory power at this second stage of analysis. Similarly, the other potential costs of confronting the target (i.e., loss of diplomatic and military support by the target) should be greater at this stage, since the target is more likely to retaliate if the challenger applies substantial diplomatic and military pressure. The benefits of disputing territory continue to provide incentives to the challenger to apply coercive pressure, but at this stage the potential costs of disputing territory should be more salient to the challenger.

In the third stage, when the challenger must decide whether to seek a resolution of the dispute through compromise, both costs and benefits should play a prominent role in the challenger's calculations. For example, I will argue below that domestic political factors generally provide only weak incentives for a challenger to settle a dispute. In contrast, changes in the international strategic environment of states can generate strong pressures for states to seek a settlement reflecting new diplomatic and military realities.

The general implication of this summary of the challenger's cost-benefit calculus is that the factors considered by the challenger at each stage can vary and even the same factors considered at several stages can be expected to have stronger or weaker effects at different stages. We now turn to the modified realist model to discuss in more detail the cost-benefit calculus of the challenger state.

The Modified Realist Model Summary

In this section I present the theoretical model to be tested in the remainder of the book. This model integrates assumptions from both traditional realism as well as theoretical works that challenge realism from the perspective of domestic politics. This modified realist model portrays state leaders as foreign policy decision makers who seek to maximize their chances of staying in power; seek to promote the military security of their country; are very careful to pursue foreign policies that strengthen their domestic political position; and are therefore judicious in limiting the threat or use of military power to international disputes where politically salient issues are at stake and the costs of military conflict are not substantial.

The integrated model developed in this chapter incorporates a number of assumptions from conventional realist approaches, but the critical differences lie in the role that domestic politics plays in the formation and conduct of foreign policy. More specifically, the model argues that the domestic context of states decisively shapes the foreign policy decisions of state leaders. To explain the national security policies of states, this model posits that one must examine the domestic political institutions within which foreign policy leaders operate as well as the broader domestic political environment within which leaders make decisions on foreign policy.

In the scholarly literature on the causes of war, the conventional realist framework has been applied largely to the analysis of the behavior of the major powers in the international system. For example, structural realist arguments developed by Kenneth Waltz,[6] concerning the relative stability of bipolar and multipolar international systems, focus only on the major powers. The territorial disputes to be analyzed in chapters 4 through 6, however, include not only major power cases but a large number of regional conflicts involving non-European developing countries. Thus, of the 116 borders that have been the subject of a postwar territorial dispute, eighty-four (or 72 percent) involve a Third World or non-Western developing country as a challenger.

The question to ask then is, Should a realist model be utilized to analyze the conflict behavior of nonmajor powers? The answer, I believe, is that there is no compelling argument to be made for limiting a realist model to only the major powers. Many of the assumptions and implications of Waltz's theoretical approach should be applicable to the decisions of all states on questions of national security.[7] Waltz and other realists such as Hans Morgenthau and John Mearsheimer[8] focus on the major powers because they are militarily the most powerful states, and therefore their foreign policy decisions may have very important implications for the likelihood of war in the international system.[9] This does not mean, however, that the national security policies and conflict behavior of nonmajor powers cannot be analyzed within the same general realist framework. Indeed, if realism is to serve as a general theoretical model for the study of international politics it is necessary that it be applied to the behavior of major and minor powers alike.

The final point to make is that state behavior in territorial disputes lies squarely within the domain of issue areas to which realist theory is properly applied. The territorial integrity of states is perhaps the fore-

---

6. Waltz, *Theory of International Politics*.

7. For example, Stephen Walt, *The Origins of Alliances* (Ithaca: Cornell University Press, 1987) utilizes a realist approach in studying the alliance behavior of Middle East states in the postwar period.

8. Hans Morgenthau, *Politics among Nations*, 5th ed. rev. (New York: Alfred A. Knopf, 1978), John Mearsheimer, "Back to the Future: Instability in Europe after the Cold War," *International Security* 15, no. 1 (1990): 5–56, and John Mearsheimer, "The False Promise of International Institutions," *International Security* 19, no. 3 (1994/95): 5–49.

9. The results of quantitative empirical studies generally do not lend strong support to the argument of "structural realists" that the polarity of the international system has a powerful effect on the likelihood of Great Power war. See Paul Huth, Christopher Gelpi, and D. Scott Bennett, "The Escalation of Great Power Militarized Disputes," *American Political Science Review* 87, no. 3 (1993): 609–23 and Paul Huth, D. Scott Bennett, and Christopher Gelpi, "System Uncertainty, Risk Propensity, and International Conflict among the Great Powers," *Journal of Conflict Resolution* 36, no. 3 (1992): 478–517.

most concern of leaders in a conventional realist model and, as argued in chapter 1, territorial disputes have been a primary cause of international crises and wars in the post–World War II period. The threat of force and armed conflict, the central concern of realists, is therefore a danger confronted by states in many territorial disputes.

I present the model by laying out each of its basic assumptions and related corollaries and then derive a series of testable hypotheses. As I describe the model I will discuss where the assumptions and logic of the new model contrast with a traditional realist approach. The assumptions of the modified realist model are as follows.

Assumption 1. Due to the anarchical nature of the international system, state leaders cannot depend upon a recognized supranational authority to settle disputes with other countries.[10] As a result, state leaders are ultimately responsible for protecting their country from possible military attack and other international security threats.

Assumption 2. A central concern of state leaders is to retain their position of domestic political power and to expand their base of political support when opportunities arise.

Assumption 3. The ability of state leaders to remain in office is strongly related to generating support among various domestic political constituencies.[11]

---

10. Waltz, *Theory of International Politics,* 104 uses the term "self-help system" to describe how individual state security must be pursued in the international system.

11. One of the most important features of the modern state (be it democratic or authoritarian) is the far greater scope of national government involvement in the economy and society and the general public's expectation that national political leaders are held responsible for the state of the economy and a wide range of social problems related to such basic issues as education, crime, and health. There is a voluminous literature (too large to cite here) on the rise of the modern state and the historical trend toward greater state penetration of society. There is also a large body of empirical work in American and comparative politics providing support for the assumption that a leader's tenure in office is strongly related to the government's record of success on domestic policy issues. For example, in the literature on American voting behavior one of the central findings is that the outcome of presidential elections are strongly influenced by the state of the economy and that a strong record of local constituency service contributes to congressional reelection. See for example Donald Kinder, Gordan Adams, Paul Gronke, "Economics and Politics in the 1984 Presidential Elections," *American Journal of Political Science* 33, no. 2 (1989): 491–515; Gregory Marcus, "The Impact of Personal and National Economic Conditions on the Presidential Vote," *American Journal of Political Science* 32, no. 1 (1988): 137–54; Gerald Kramer, "Short-Term Fluctuations in U.S. Voting Behavior," *American Political Science Review* 65, no. 1 (1971): 131–43; and Morris Fiorina and Bruce Cain, *The Personal Vote* (Cambridge: Harvard University Press, 1987). Comparative studies of the domestic political economy of elections in advanced industrial societies include Douglas

These first three assumptions establish that state leaders must juggle two critical political roles: (1) they are held accountable for preserving the national security of their country, and (2) they are politicians who seek to remain in power and thus are concerned with current or potential political opposition from counterelites. If political leaders attempt to meet the demands of both of these roles then two important implications follow. First, military security issues are not given the highest priority by state leaders. The material and financial resource demands of national security policy do not have a privileged position in comparison to domestic policy needs.[12] Second, decisions on foreign policy, *including security policy,* are examined in terms of what the consequences are for the domestic political position of state leaders, and security policy may be used to advance the domestic political interests of state leaders. Taken together these corollaries imply that: (*a*) political leaders will define the foreign policy agenda of their country in terms broader than just military security issues, and (*b*) the domestic political needs of leaders will lead them to consider trade-offs and possible conflicts of interest with strictly military security concerns.

In contrast to these two corollaries, in the conventional realist model military security is the first and foremost concern of the state leaders. The realist approach would argue that states pursue a multiplic-

---

Hibbs, *The Political Economy of Industrial Democracies* (Cambridge: Harvard University Press, 1987); John Freeman, *Democracy and Markets: The Politics of Mixed Economies* (Ithaca: Cornell University Press, 1989); and Michael Lewis-Beck, "Comparative Economic Voting: Britain, France, Germany, and Italy," *American Journal of Political Science* 30, no. 2 (1986): 315–46. In nondemocratic systems as well, political elites often act on the belief that their authority, legitimacy, and tenure in office are linked to stable domestic economic conditions. Scholars have applied this argument even to the case of the former Soviet and Eastern European communist systems as well as China. See James Millar, "The Little Deal: Brezhnev's Contribution to Acquisitive Socialism," *Slavic Review* 44, no. 4 (1985): 694–706; Peter Hauslohner, "Gorbachev's Social Contract," in Ed Hewett and Victor Winston, eds., *Milestones in Glasnost and Perestroyka* (Washington, D.C.: Brookings, 1991), 31–64; George Breslauer, *Khrushchev and Brezhnev as Leaders* (Boston: Allen & Unwin, 1982); Gordon Bennett, "Economy, Polity, and Reform in China," *Comparative Politics* 18, no. 1 (1985): 85–100; Franz Michael, Carl Linden, Jan Prybyla, and Jurgen Domes, *China and the Crisis of Marxism-Leninism* (Boulder: Westview Press, 1990); Andrew Nathan, *China's Crisis* (New York: Columbia University Press, 1990); Vivienne Shue, "China: Transition Postponed?" *Problems of Communism* 41, nos. 1–2 (1992): 157–68; and Tang Tsou, *The Cultural Revolution and Post-Mao Reforms* (Chicago: University of Chicago Press, 1986).

12. Some empirical evidence for this corollary can be found in public opinion data on national security policy among Western European countries, which show that the public is generally unwilling to sacrifice domestic economic and social welfare programs to meet the financial needs of national defense. See Richard Eichenberg, *Public Opinion and National Security in Western Europe* (Ithaca: Cornell University Press, 1989).

ity of goals in their foreign policy, but a clear hierarchy among security and nonsecurity goals exists in which the continued independence, territorial integrity, and security of a country from military attack is viewed as a prerequisite for the attainment of other goals such as economic development and the promotion of foreign trade. For example, Waltz argues that "In a self-help [international] system, considerations of security subordinate economic gain to political interest."[13]

From this perspective, the attainment of national security goals assumes primacy over domestic policy issues and political pressures. The territorial integrity of a country and its continued existence as an independent and sovereign state is a prerequisite for the pursuit of all important domestic policy goals. In a realist model political leaders should not be expected to compromise security against external threats due to issues of short-term domestic political gain or loss. Furthermore, the conventional realist approach would predict that political leaders would not use foreign policy and, in particular, security policy to advance their domestic policy programs or political standing. Thus, the resource commitments and attention to the necessities of national security would be expected to override the needs of domestic policy programs or the pressures emanating from competition with counterelites for maintaining positions of political power. Once again, Waltz summarizes the traditional realist position when he states: "In self-help systems the pressures of [international] competition weigh more heavily than ideological preferences or internal political pressures."[14] In essence, the traditional realist position argues that political leaders will, if need be, sacrifice their short-term domestic political standing to protect the greater security interests of their country.

> *Assumption 4.* Domestic political groups consistently seek to shape the domestic and foreign policy choices of state leaders in order to advance their own political and economic interests. These groups are able to exert pressure and influence on political leaders through a variety of channels—the bureaucracy, the military, legislatures, the media, and elections—and they are most active in pressuring the government when they believe that government policies threaten their interests.[15]

---

13. Waltz, *Theory of International Politics*, 107.
14. Kenneth Waltz, "Reflections on *Theory of International Politics*: A Response to My Critics," in Robert Keohane, ed., *Neorealism and its Critics* (New York: Columbia University Press, 1988), 329.
15. Examples of work in the international relations literature with a similar assumption would include Jack Snyder, *Myths of Empire* (Ithaca: Cornell University Press, 1991);

Assumption 5. State leaders believe that a foreign policy setback for their country stemming from a diplomatic retreat or military defeat will impose high domestic costs on them.

Generally the public is not that attentive to foreign policy issues, but if their country does become engaged in a crisis or war, foreign policy becomes much more salient and the public is likely to hold their country's political leadership accountable for the outcome of the international confrontation.[16] The corollary to this assumption is that state leaders will be very sensitive to the potential costs that domestic groups and constituencies might suffer as a result of military conflict or a deterioration in political relations with another country.[17] As a result, decisions

---

Bueno de Mesquita and Lalman, *War and Reason;* Bruce Bueno de Mesquita, David Newman, and Alvin Rabushka, *Forecasting Political Events* (New Haven: Yale University Press, 1985); Robert Putnam, "Diplomacy and Domestic Politics," *International Organization* 42, no. 3 (1988): 427–60; Alan Lamborn, *The Price of Power* (Boston: Unwin Hyman, 1991); James Morrow, "Arms versus Allies," *International Organization* 47, no. 2 (1993): 207–34; Keiseku Iida, "When and How Do Domestic Constraints Matter?" *Journal of Conflict Resolution* 37, no. 3 (1993): 403–26; Jongryn Mo, "Two-Level Games with Endogenous Domestic Coalitions," *Journal of Conflict Resolution* 38, no. 3 (1994): 402–22; Joe Hagan, *Political Opposition and Foreign Policy in Comparative Perspective* (Boulder: Lynne Rienner, 1993).

16. See for example Bruce Bueno de Mesquita and David Lalman, "Domestic Opposition and Foreign War," *American Political Science Review* 84, no. 3 (1990): 747–66 and David Lake, "Powerful Pacifists: Democratic States and War," *American Political Science Review* 86, no. 1 (1992): 24–37.

17. Underlying this assumption is a body of empirical work indicating that political leaders can mobilize public support for a wide range of confrontational foreign policy actions, but this "rally-round-the-flag" effect is limited in duration; particularly in situations in which military force is employed by state leaders. A related body of work, consistent with the thesis that leaders are relatively unconstrained by public opinion only in the short term, is public opinion data on foreign policy issues indicating that aggregate shifts in policy positions are a sensible response to changes in the international environment. Both bodies of literature are summarized in Bruce Russett, *Controlling the Sword* (Cambridge: Harvard University Press), chs. 2, 4. In addition, see Benjamin Page and Robert Shapiro, *The Rational Public: Fifty Years of Trends in American's Policy Preferences* (Chicago: University of Chicago Press, 1991), chs. 5–6; Miroslav Nincic, "The United States, the Soviet Union, and the Politics of Opposites," *World Politics* 40, no. 4 (1988): 452–75; Miroslav Nincic, *Democracy and Foreign Policy* (New York: Columbia University Press, 1992); Ole Holsti, "Public Opinion and Foreign Policy," *International Studies Quarterly* 36, no. 4 (1992): 439–68; and Bradley Lian and John Oneal, "Presidents, the Use of Force, and Public Opinion," *Journal of Conflict Resolution* 37, no. 2 (1993): 277–300. Two empirical studies that identify a clear relationship between the costs and/or defeat in war and the political stability of regimes is Bruce Bueno de Mesquita, Randolph Siverson, and Gary Woller, "War and the Fate of Regimes," *American Political Science Review* 86, no. 3 (1992): 638–46 and Timothy Cotton, "War and American Democracy," *Journal of Conflict Resolution* 30, no. 4 (1986): 616–35.

on security policy are influenced by leaders' estimates of anticipated domestic opposition, and elites can generally count on high levels of public support for confrontational policies with other states only if the direct material and human costs are not high.

A conventional realist model would argue quite differently about the impact of public opinion and interest groups on security policy. The starting point would be that public opinion on security policy is generally not well informed or stable, and most individuals have little interest in foreign policy.[18] The implication then would be that existing public support and anticipated public reactions to security policy decisions do not play a critical role in shaping the policy choices of political leaders on questions of national security. In a traditional realist approach policymakers do not look to an initial base of public support in reaching decisions, and they are not deterred by possible public opposition, calculating that opposition, if it develops, can be effectively undercut. Political leaders believe that they can shape public opinion and generate support for the actions they take. Indeed, Morgenthau argues that leaders may have to ignore public opinion in order to pursue a rational and effective security policy.[19]

Assumption 6. Domestic political institutions structure and induce political elites to resolve conflict in particular ways. In some political systems institutions promote the use or threat of violence and imposition of decisions to settle conflict whereas other systems delegitimize violence and favor compromise to resolve disputes.[20]

---

18. See Russett, *Controlling the Sword,* ch. 4 for a review of much of the literature supporting this assumption.

19. See for example Morgenthau, *Politics among Nations,* 152–54. There is a long tradition of argument dating back to writers such as Machiavelli and de Tocqueville, from which contemporary realists draw, which posits that foreign policy should be conducted by experts and political leaders without the involvement of the general public.

20. Much of the recent literature focuses on the impact of different institutional structures within democratic systems. See for example Kenneth Shepsle, "Institutional Equilibrium and Equilibrium Institutions," in Herbert Weisenberg, ed., *Political Science* (New York: Agathon Press, 1986), 51–81; John Huber, "Restrictive Legislative Procedures in France and the United States," *American Political Science Review* 86, no. 3 (1992): 675–87; G. Bingham Powell, *Contemporary Democracies* (Cambridge: Harvard University Press, 1982); Arend Lijphardt, *Democracies: Patterns of Majoritarian and Consensus Government in Twenty-One Countries* (New Haven: Yale University Press, 1984); Peter Hall, *Governing the Economy* (New York: Oxford University Press, 1986). Examples of works that either compare political institutions and elite behavior across different regime types or examine nondemocratic systems in detail would include classic works such as Zbigniew Brzezinski and Samuel Huntington, *Political Power: USA/USSR* (New York:

Assumption 7. The development of norms and practices by state leaders for resolving domestic political conflict, in turn, affect their approach to the resolution of international conflict.[21]

The corollary to these two assumptions is that if regimes vary in fundamental ways with respect to norms concerning the legitimacy of coercion and compromising in dealing with political opposition, then regime type should be an important factor explaining patterns of international conflict behavior among states. Once again, a conventional realist approach would reject these assumptions and their underlying logic. In the standard realist framework, internal norms and standards for how to resolve political conflict would not have a consistent and significant impact on the resolution of international disputes. Instead, the standard realist position would be that military power and the strategic interests at stake in a dispute would determine the willingness of state leaders to use violence or consider concessions in their relations with other countries.[22]

Viking Press, 1964); Samuel Huntington, *Political Order in Changing Societies* (New Haven: Yale University Press, 1968); and Robert Putnam, *The Comparative Study of Political Elites* (Englewood Cliffs, NJ: Prentice-Hall, 1976). More recent works would include David Collier, ed., *The New Authoritarianism in Latin America* (Princeton: Princeton University Press, 1979); Amos Perlmutter, *Modern Authoritarianism* (New Haven: Yale University Press, 1981); Alfred Stepan, *Rethinking Military Politics* (Princeton: Princeton University Press, 1988); and Barbara Geddes, *Politician's Dilemma* (Berkeley: University of California Press, 1994).

21. This assumption is the foundation for the argument in the "democratic peace" literature that democratic norms of nonviolent conflict resolution affect the foreign policy behavior of democratic states. For works that develop or critically analyze this line of theoretical argument see Bueno de Mesquita and Lalman, *War and Reason;* Michael Doyle, "Liberalism and World Politics," *American Political Science Review* 80, no. 4 (1986): 1151–61; Bruce Russett, *Grasping the Democratic Peace* (Princeton: Princeton University Press, 1993); T. Clifton Morgan and Valerie Schwebach, "Take Two Democracies and Call Me in the Morning," *International Interactions* 17, no. 4 (1992): 305–20; T. Clifton Morgan and Sally Howard Campbell, "Domestic Structure, Decisional Constraints and War," *Journal of Conflict Resolution* 35, no. 2 (1991): 187–211; William Dixon, "Democracy and the Management of International Conflict," *Journal of Conflict Resolution* 37, no. 1 (1993): 42–68; William Dixon, "Democracy and the Peaceful Settlement of International Conflict," *American Political Science Review* 88, no. 1 (1994): 14–32. Another body of work examines the link between internal patterns of political competition among elites and foreign policy behavior. Several studies have focused on the Soviet Union—see Philip Roeder, "Soviet Politics and Kremlin Politics," *International Studies Quarterly* 28, no. 2 (1984): 171–93; James Goldgeier, *Leadership and Soviet Foreign Policy* (Baltimore: Johns Hopkins University Press, 1994); and James Ritcher, *Khrushchev's Double Bind* (Baltimore: Johns Hopkins University Press, 1994).

22. See for example John Mearsheimer, "Back to the Future" for a realist critique of the argument that democratic states should be less prone to use force in resolving conflicts with other democratic states.

Assumption 8. The threat or use of military power is the ultimate recourse for state leaders to resolve disputes with other countries and ensure their security.

This assumption lies at the very basis of any realist model. For example, Waltz states, ". . . the possibility that force will be used by one or another parties looms always as a threat in the background . . . In international politics force serves, not only as the *ultima ratio* [emphasis in original], but indeed as the first and constant one."[23] The primacy of military power as an instrument of foreign policy is underscored by Morgenthau when he argues that ". . . armed strength as a threat or potentiality is the most important material factor making for the political power of a nation."[24] There are two corollaries to this assumption. First, nonmilitary sources of influence and power have only a secondary impact on resolving interstate disputes. Second, foreign policy leaders must be selective in resorting to military threats or the use of force because state resources and military capabilities can be overextended due to an overly expansive definition of what constitutes vital national security interests. Overextension, then, risks undermining a country's underlying base of military power, its capacity to defend vital interests, and military involvement in peripheral conflicts.[25] The threat or use of force should therefore be reserved for those situations in which state leaders believe that compelling issues are at stake.

Assumption 9. State leaders seek to maintain diplomatic and military flexibility in their foreign relations with other states. At

23. Waltz, *Theory of International Politics,* 113.
24. *Politics among Nations,* 31. A wide range of empirical studies can be cited indicating that relative military power plays an important role in shaping the decisions of leaders on questions of war and peace. A sample of quantitative works includes Paul Huth, *Extended Deterrence and the Prevention of War* (New Haven: Yale University Press, 1988); Huth, Gelpi, and Bennett, "The Escalation of Great Power Militarized Disputes"; Bueno de Mesquita, *The War Trap;* William Thompson, *On Global War* (Columbia: University of South Carolina Press, 1988); Henk Houweling and Jan Siccama, "Power Transitions as a Cause of War," *Journal of Conflict Resolution* 32, no. 1 (1988): 87–102; Frank Wayman, J. David Singer, and Gary Goertz, "Capabilities, Allocations, and Success in Militarized Disputes and Wars, 1816–1976," *International Studies Quarterly* 27, no. 4 (1983): 497–515.
25. The problem of overextension for major powers is a central theme in comparative historical studies by Paul Kennedy, *The Rise and Decline of the Great Powers* (New York: Random House, 1987), Robert Gilpin, *War and Change in World Politics* (Cambridge: Cambridge University Press, 1981), and Jack Snyder, *Myths of Empire.* A quantitative analysis of major power overextension is William Thompson and Gary Zuk, "World Power and the Strategic Trap of Territorial Commitments," *International Studies Quarterly* 30, no. 3 (1986): 249–67.

times, however, political leaders will seek agreements or align themselves with other states on security issues in order to advance or protect their country's foreign and domestic policy goals.[26]

There are two corollaries to this assumption. First, state leaders attach considerable importance to maintaining their country's (as well as their own) reputation for honoring international agreements. A general reputation for abiding by international commitments is a very important asset for countries in support of their attempts to exert diplomatic and political influence over other countries in a wide range of security issue areas. Without such a reputation, state leaders would find it more difficult to attract allies to enhance their own security, to deter adversaries from challenging the interests of their allies, and to sustain many forms of security cooperation with opponents based on commitments to respect prior agreements (e.g., arms control measures). In addition, a commitment to abide by international agreements is important to state leaders because their country risks international censure if its foreign policy actions are viewed as illegitimate by many other states. Censure can then lead to international isolation and sanctions that can impose a variety of costs on a country, for example, diminished access to economic aid and loans, curtailment of military arms supplies, or loss of diplomatic influence in international forums.[27]

---

26. See for example the recent literature on the reasons why states enter into military alliances in which the potential tradeoffs between international and domestic policy goals are explicitly analyzed: James Morrow, "Alliances and Asymmetry," *American Journal of Political Science* 35, no. 4 (1991): 904–33; James Morrow, "Alliances, Credibility, and Peacetime Costs," *Journal of Conflict Resolution* 38, no. 2 (1994): 270–97; Morrow, "Arms versus Allies"; Gerald Sorokin, "Alliance Formation and General Deterrence," *Journal of Conflict Resolution* 38, no. 2 (1994): 298–325; Michael Altfeld, "The Decision to Ally," *Western Political Quarterly* 37, no. 4 (1984): 523–44; Steven David, *Choosing Sides* (Baltimore: Johns Hopkins University Press, 1991); Michael Barnett, *Confronting the Costs of War* (Princeton: Princeton University Press, 1992); Stephen Walt, *The Origins of Alliances* (Ithaca: Cornell University Press, 1987). Also see Emerson Niou and Peter Ordeshook, "Alliances in Anarchic International Systems," *International Studies Quarterly* 38, no. 2 (1994): 167–92; Glenn Snyder, "The Security Dilemma in Alliance Politics," *World Politics* 34, no. 4 (1984): 461–95; and Thomas Christensen and Jack Snyder, "Chain Gangs and Passed Bucks," *International Organization* 44, no. 2 (1990): 137–68.

27. There are only a limited number of studies that attempt to test in a systematic and comparative manner what impact legal norms and notions of international legitimacy have on the international conflict behavior of states. See for example Gary Goertz and Paul Diehl, "International Norms and Power Politics," in Frank Wayman and Paul Diehl, eds., *Reconstructing Realpolitik* (Ann Arbor: University of Michigan Press, 1994), 101–22; Charles Kegley and Gregory Raymond, "International Legal Norms and the Preservation

The second corollary is that when we observe states entering into formal alliance agreements with other states, we should expect that there are salient foreign and/or domestic policy gains to be made by the agreement, since such agreements almost invariably entail some constraints on the foreign and defense policy choices of states. States will seek military and diplomatic support from other countries when they believe that their country's foreign policy goals cannot be confidently ensured by relying on their own material and financial resources. Because states often lack the resource capacity and/or political resolve to meet all of their foreign policy goals, security ties and international agreements with other countries are often necessary. Alliances then should not be entered into lightly by states and should indicate that there is a convergence of foreign or domestic policy interests between states.

Now that the assumptions and related corollaries of the modified realist model has been presented, the next step is to derive testable hypotheses from the model. The hypotheses will be directed at each of the following questions: What should be the issues at stake in territorial disputes according to the model? What features of the international political and military environment should affect the challenger's pursuit of territorial gains? How do domestic political conditions constrain or encourage state leaders to dispute territory?

Hypotheses on the Issues at Stake

The first hypothesis is derived from assumption 1, which provides the theoretical foundation for proposing how the challenger would evaluate the saliency of territory and the potential benefits of confronting the target in a territorial dispute. Based on this assumption, I argue that decision makers would assess the utility of challenging the territorial status quo by the extent to which the military security of the country would be enhanced by gaining control of disputed territory. The hypotheses are as follows.

H1.1. There is a positive relationship between the strategic location of bordering territory and (*a*) the probability that a challenger will initiate a territorial dispute, and (*b*) the level of diplomatic

---

of Peace, 1820–1964," *International Interactions* 8, no. 3 (1981): 171–87; Charles Kegley and Gregory Raymond, "Normative Constraints on the Use of Force Short of War," *Journal of Peace Research* 23, no. 3 (1986): 213–27; Herbert Tillema and John Van Wingen, "Law and Power in Military Intervention," *International Studies Quarterly* 26, no. 2 (1982): 220–50; and Arie Kacowicz, "The Problem of Peaceful Territorial Change," *International Studies Quarterly* 38, no. 2 (1994): 219–54.

and military pressure applied by a challenger against a target over disputed territory.

H1.2. There is an inverse relationship between the strategic location of bordering territory and the probability that a challenger will seek a resolution of a territorial dispute through compromise or conciliation.

The logic of these hypotheses is that control over strategically located territory should be of central concern to state leaders responsible for ensuring the military security of their country. Control of strategically located territory would strengthen the military position of the challenger in a number of potential ways. Examples are to enhance power projection capabilities for either defensive or offensive military operations, to establish a military presence in close proximity to narrow choke points or major trade routes on the sea, to extend a defense perimeter around important military bases, or to deny the ability of other states to project their military forces from overseas military bases. Given these potential benefits, leaders should then be more resolute when involved in disputes over such valuable territory, to escalate such disputes to higher levels of conflict in an attempt to coerce the target, and to reject compromise given the potential security gains to be secured by forcing the target to concede.

The second set of hypotheses are derived from assumption 2 and its related corollaries, and assumption 3. These hypotheses focus on the fact that foreign policy makers are also domestic political leaders who seek to remain in power, which should influence their assessment of what salient issues are at stake in a territorial dispute.

H2.1. There is a positive relationship between the location of ethnic minorities within the target along its border who share ties with the predominant ethnic group within the challenger and (*a*) the probability that a challenger will initiate a territorial dispute, and (*b*) the level of diplomatic and military pressure applied by a challenger against a target over disputed territory.

H2.2. There is an inverse relationship between the location of ethnic minorities within the target along its border who share ties with the predominant ethnic group within the challenger and the probability that a challenger will seek a resolution of a territorial dispute through compromise or conciliation.

H3.1. There is a positive relationship between the challenger and target populations sharing common ethnic ties and (*a*) the probability that a challenger will initiate a territorial dispute, and (*b*) the level of diplomatic and military pressure applied by a challenger against a target over disputed territory.

H3.2. There is an inverse relationship between the challenger and target populations sharing common ethnic ties and the probability that a challenger will seek a resolution of a territorial dispute through compromise or conciliation.

The logic supporting these hypotheses consists of two main arguments. First, according to assumption 2 and its corollaries we should expect political leaders to consider not only the military security benefits of changing the territorial status quo but also the potential domestic political payoffs. For state leaders a fundamental concern is whether a foreign policy decision and course of action will generate political support domestically. The utility of challenging the territorial status quo is, therefore, viewed through the lens of whether the leader's domestic political position would be strengthened by confronting its neighbor. In this context, foreign policy issues that appeal to ethnic solidarity are particularly attractive because citizens often feel strong ties of affiliation based on common ethnic backgrounds.

Second, if we extend this logic to the question of territorial disputes, we can argue that appeals to ethnic solidarity and unity would be very effective when minority populations located along the border in a target state share a common background with the largest ethnic group within the challenger. In such a situation, state leaders could legitimize their claim to bordering territory by emphasizing the common linguistic and cultural ties that link the population in the disputed region to their own country. Furthermore, leaders could imply or explicitly charge that the target government was mistreating the minority population. In either case, political leaders within the challenger could portray themselves as championing the rights of self-determination for the minority population within the target.

Appeals to ethnic solidarity and unity could also be invoked when both the challenger and target populations share the same ethnic backgrounds. The logic supporting H3.1 and H3.2 is that cultural and ethnic similarity between challenger and target is also a source of political rivalry and conflict between states. The argument is that ethnic similarity can be expected to promote rivalry and competition *between the political leadership of the challenger and target* for the allegiance and right to rule over the populations of each country. Thus, the attempt by the challenger to achieve political unity coterminous with ethnic boundaries should be strongly resisted by the target. As a result, conflict becomes more likely as the leadership of the challenger seeks to increase its base of political power and support by expanding the territorial size of their country while the leaders within the target seek to protect their domestic position of political power. Furthermore, appeals to national unity can be used by the challenger to sanction and legitimize coercion and violence against the target, and since unification is the goal of the challenger, compromise or accommodation with the target becomes a less acceptable and/or politically attractive policy for leaders within the challenger to pursue.

The final set of hypotheses are derived from assumptions 1 and 2 and their related corollaries as well as assumption 3. These hypotheses focus on the natural resources located within bordering territory and their potential economic and security value to the challenger.

> *H4.1.* There is a positive relationship between the location of known natural resources of economic value within bordering territory and the probability that a challenger will initiate a territorial dispute.
>
> *H4.2.* There is a negative relationship between the location of known natural resources of economic value within bordering territory and the level of diplomatic and military pressure applied by a challenger against a target over disputed territory.
>
> *H4.3.* There is a positive relationship between the location of known natural resources of economc value along the border of the target and the probability that a challenger will seek a resolution of a territorial dispute through compromise or conciliation.

Leaders within the challenger should have domestic political incentives to try to gain control over bordering territory that is rich in economically valuable natural resources. First, the development of such resources would benefit specific industries and sectors of the economy, generating political support for the leadership. Second, increased tax revenues or direct income generated by the export sales of natural resources would contribute to higher levels of state revenue, which could then support expenditures on various domestic programs as well as defense needs. Control over such territory, then, should be particularly attractive to leaders within the challenger since both domestic political as well as military security payoffs can be achieved.

At the same time, however, the challenger can settle a dispute over border territory rich in natural resources without necessarily losing the economic, political, and security benefits of controlling the territory. Specifically, joint projects for the economic development of natural resources along the border can be signed between challenger and target even if the challenger does not have direct control over the territory. Indeed, the target is likely to withhold agreement for joint development until the challenger withdraws its territorial claim. In such a situation, the divisible nature of the benefits associated with disputed territory serves to mitigate high levels of conflict escalation and to promote conflict resolution. Indeed, high levels of tension in the disputed territory risk alienating outside investors—private firms, international institutions, and other states—from supporting projects to develop the resources. In contrast, when strategic or basic issues of political power and popularity are at stake (H1.1–1.2 and H2.1–3.2) the challenger is much more likely to believe that the issues are not divisible, and therefore escalation is more likely while compromise is less attractive to the challenger, that is, the avoidance of conflict and the pursuit of accommodation is unlikely to produce domestic political benefits for the leadership of the challenger.

Hypotheses Regarding the International Context

Assumptions 5 and 8 and their related corollaries provide the theoretical foundation for a series of hypotheses. The first set of hypotheses are as follows.

> *H5.1.* There is a positive relationship between the balance of conventional military forces and (*a*) the probability that a challenger will initiate a territorial dispute, and (*b*) the level of diplomatic and military pressure applied by a challenger against a target over disputed territory.
>
> *H5.2.* There is a negative relationship between the balance of conventional military forces and the probability that a challenger will seek a resolution of a territorial dispute through compromise or conciliation.

The logic of these hypotheses is as follows. The stronger the challenger, the higher the probability that the challenger can overturn the territorial status quo by the use of military force or compel the target to accept its territorial demands backed by the credible threat of force. Conversely, the weaker the challenger, the greater the risk of a diplomatic or military defeat if the challenger confronts a strong target. Military weakness increases the risks of a foreign policy defeat, which, in turn, is a threat to the domestic political position of leaders within the challenger. It follows then that challenger states with greater relative capabilities should be more likely to initiate territorial disputes based on higher expectations of achieving their territorial goals, and more likely to engage in higher levels of coercive pressure in an attempt to force concessions from the target or to take control of disputed territory. The only qualification to H5.1 is that since the data analysis begins in 1950 it is important to control for the fact that if the challenger had been militarily stronger than the target in the past, then there would be a higher likelihood that previous changes in the territorial status quo would have favored the stronger challenger. As a result, the challenger would then have fewer reasons to seek a change in the prevailing territorial status quo in the post–World War II period. As a result, I will include in the equation that tests H5.1 a variable that simply codes whether the challenger had achieved a net gain of territory from the target prior to 1950.[28]

The next set of hypotheses are also derived from assumptions 5 and 8 and related corollaries and focus on the involvement of the challenger in conflicts with other states:

> *H6.1.* There is an inverse relationship between a challenger's involvement in political-military disputes with other states and the level of diplomatic and military pressure applied by a challenger against a target over disputed territory.
>
> *H6.2.* There is a positive relationship between a challenger's involvement in political-military disputes with other states and the probability that a challenger will seek a resolution of a territorial dispute through compromise or conciliation.

If the challenger is engaged in conflicts with other states, it is less likely to be in a strong position to apply diplomatic and military pressure against a target due to the fact that it has already committed or intends to commit some of its available resources to a dispute with another adversary. As a result, the bargaining position of the challenger should be weakened, and thus the probability of the challenger achieving its territorial goals should decrease. The challenger should then avoid escalation of an ongoing dispute with the target and consider a settlement with the target; this policy would focus available resources on the conflict with the other state(s) and avoid the risks of a foreign policy setback in the conflict with the target.

The final set of hypotheses derived from assumptions 5 and 8 are as follows.

---

28. I would like to thank James Morrow for making this point clear to me.

H7. There is a positive relationship between a stalemate in negotiations for the challenger and the subsequent level of diplomatic and military pressure applied by a challenger against a target over disputed territory.

H8.1. There is a positive relationship between target actions to change the political, economic, military status quo within disputed territory and the level of diplomatic and military pressure applied by a challenger against a target over disputed territory.

H8.2. There is an inverse relationship between target actions to change the political, economic, or military status quo within disputed territory and the probability that a challenger will seek a resolution of a territorial dispute through compromise or conciliation.

H9.1. There is a negative relationship between the number of times a challenger has previously suffered a defeat or stalemate in armed conflict with a target and the level of diplomatic and military pressure applied by a challenger against the target over disputed territory.

H9.2. There is a positive relationship between the number of times a challenger has previously suffered a defeat or stalemate in armed conflict with a target and the probability that a challenger will seek a resolution of a territorial dispute through compromise or conciliation.

The logic of H7 is that increased coercive pressure and threats of force by the challenger should be correlated with periods of active diplomacy and ongoing negotiations between challenger and target. Challengers should resort to higher levels of coercive pressure in order to back up their diplomatic position in talks. Since military power is the most important component of a state's bargaining power, the timely threat or use of military power should be used by the challenger to communicate to the target its resolve and the risks of stalemate in the current negotiations.

If we extend this logic further, leaders within the challenger should be more likely to escalate a dispute against the target after the failure of diplomatic efforts and negotiations for two reasons. First, the challenger may resort to increased coercive pressure in order to convince the target that a continued stalemate in negotiations carries with it a heightened risk of armed conflict. Thus, political and military pressure would be designed to compel the target to be more accommodative in future talks. Second, the challenger may turn to coercive pressure and military force as the only viable alternative as a result of having lost confidence in the use of diplomacy and negotiations to change the territorial status quo.

Finally, an additional incentive for the challenger to escalate a dispute after a stalemate in negotiations is that a stalemate can be portrayed by domestic political opposition as a foreign policy setback for the current leadership. As a result, a more confrontational policy may be used by the leaders of the challenger to counter mounting domestic political discontent or to prevent such opposition from arising by taking forceful actions to break the deadlock in the dispute with the target.

The challenger should also respond to actions taken by the target to establish and/or consolidate its control of disputed territory by escalating the dispute to higher levels of diplomatic and military conflict. There are three reasons for this. First, increasing coercive pressure could signal the target that its actions are unacceptable and will be costly to continue, and therefore the target should enter into negotiations. Second, military actions could be initiated in an attempt to disrupt and prevent the target from establishing a new and unfavorable status quo in the disputed territory. Third, the challenger could resort to the large-scale use of force in an attempt to seize the disputed territory based on the belief that the further passage of time would only benefit the target. In sum, H8.1–8.2 posit that when the past policies of the challenger have failed to deter the target from initiating actions that threaten its position in the dispute, the challenger should turn to more coercive policies based on the belief that the threat or use of force is the most important means by which to protect its territorial interests. Finally, as with H7 domestic political concerns could also pressure leaders within the challenger to respond to the actions of the target. In this case, the failure to respond would open the leadership of the challenger to charges of weakness and a foreign policy defeat, which the current leaders would seek to undercut by confronting the target openly and more aggressively.

The logic supporting H9.1–9.2 is that the repeated demonstration of military strength by the target should lead a challenger to avoid high levels of escalation in the future and to moderate its bargaining position in subsequent negotiations with the target. The initial response of the challenger to a defeat may very well be to mobilize internal and external resources in order to build up its military strength and then to confront the target at a later date in an attempt to reverse the previous losses. However, if the target retains the ability to inflict substantial costs on the challenger in subsequent confrontations, then leaders within the challenger should, in accord with assumption 2, acknowledge (however reluctantly) the stronger bargaining position of the target and therefore modify their diplomatic and military policies to reflect better the superior strength of the target.

These hypotheses propose then that decision makers should learn from their country's past failure in military encounters to respect the military strength of their adversary and to avoid escalation against a superior opponent. The adoption of a more prudent and less confrontational policy toward the target, however, would be constrained by the potential for a domestic political backlash following concessions being made to the target. Political opposition within the challenger will undoubtedly portray concessions as a foreign policy defeat and use this against the current leadership. As a result, we would expect that leaders would not be quick to offer far-reaching concessions but to adopt a cautious mixed strategy of maintaining defiant public rhetoric while pursuing an incremental approach toward a settlement in which concessions are discussed behind closed doors. With this strategy the leadership could weaken the position of political opponents while trying to generate support for a basic change in policy over a longer period of time. Whereas in H7 and H8.1–8.2 domestic and international strategic circumstances converge on a common policy for the leadership of the challenger, we find in H9.1–9.2 that domestic and international incentives tend to clash with one another.

The next hypothesis is derived from assumption 8 and is focused on the deterrent role of military allies.

> *H10.* There is an inverse relationship between the target having military allies and the level of diplomatic and military pressure applied by a challenger against a target over disputed territory.

If the target has military allies, then the potential costs and risks of a military confrontation increase for the challenger, while the probability of victory decreases. The deterrent effect of alliances will vary across cases as the challenger estimates how likely it is that allies will come to the defense of the target.[29] Nevertheless, alliance ties should provide

---

29. The literature on the reliability and deterrent value of alliances is quite extensive. See for example Morrow, "Alliances, Credibility, and Peacetime Costs"; Sorokin, "Alliance Formation and General Deterrence"; Fearon, "Signaling versus the Balance of Power and Interests"; Michael Altfeld and Bruce Bueno de Mesquita, "Choosing Sides in Wars," *International Studies Quarterly* 23, no. 1 (1979): 87–112; Alan Ned Sobrasky, "Interstate Alliances: Their Reliability and the Expansion of War," in J. David Singer, ed., *The Correlates of War II* (New York: Free Press, 1980), 161–98; Randolph Siverson and Joel King, "Attributes of National Alliance Membership and War Participation," *American Journal of Political Science* 24, no. 1 (1980): 1–15; Randolph Siverson and Michael Tennefoss, "Power, Alliance, and the Escalation of International Conflict, 1815–1965," *American Political Science Review* 78, no. 4 (1984): 1057–70; Charles Kegley and Gregory Raymond, *When Trust Breaks Down: Alliance Norms and World Politics* (Columbia, SC: University of South Carolina Press, 1990); Paul Huth and Bruce Russett, "Deterrence

some degree of added deterrence, and therefore target states without allies should be confronted by challengers more frequently at higher levels of escalation.

Assumption 9 and related corollaries provide the logical foundation for the following set of hypotheses.

> *H11.1.* There is an inverse relationship between a target and challenger sharing a common adversary and (*a*) the probability that a challenger will initiate a territorial dispute, and (*b*) the level of diplomatic and military pressure applied by a challenger against a target over disputed territory.
>
> *H11.2.* There is a positive relationship between a target and challenger sharing a common adversary and the probability that a challenger will seek a resolution of a territorial dispute through compromise or conciliation.

While the economic, political, or military value of disputed territory establishes the potential benefits to be gained by the challenger, there are also potential costs involved in pursuing a confrontation with a target. If the challenger is engaged in a dispute with a target, it is possible that bilateral relations between the challenger and target will suffer as a result. The logic of assumption 9 implies that leaders will think of potential costs in terms of what the security implications will be of worsening relations with a target.

More specifically, the challenger will consider the contribution that the target can make to its security and foreign policy goals in confrontations that it may have with other states. If the target is viewed as an ally on security and other foreign policy issues, then there is a greater opportunity cost in engaging in a dispute with that country because the target may become a less reliable ally once the challenger presses territorial claims against it. According to assumption 9 states will generally be cautious in forming alliances, and thus they will ally with other states only if there are important foreign policy interests at stake. Thus, we can conclude that a challenger must believe that an ally has considerable value in strengthening its diplomatic and military position in disputes with other states. Convergent security and foreign policy interests between a challenger and target should then provide incentives to the challenger to avoid a dispute with the target, reduce the levels of diplo-

---

Failure and Crisis Escalation," *International Studies Quarterly* 32, no. 1 (1988): 29–45; and Paul Huth, "When Do States Take on Extended Deterrent Commitments?" in Paul Diehl and Frank Wayman, eds., *Reconstructing Realpolitik* (Ann Arbor: University of Michigan Press, 1994), 81–100.

matic and military conflict during a dispute, and conclude a compromise settlement in order to secure the continued support of the target.

The final hypothesis to be presented in this section is derived from assumption 9 and related corollaries and examines the impact of the international norm that states are expected to honor past agreements.

H12. There is an inverse relationship between a challenger agreeing to a border settlement prior to 1950 and the probability that a challenger will initiate a territorial dispute in the postwar period.

One of the basic principles of international law is the commitment of state leaders to abide by the formal agreements that they have entered into, and also to respect agreements that were concluded by their predecessors (*pacta sunt servanda*). The logic of this hypothesis is that if the challenger were to rescind on a prior territorial settlement, that would jeopardize the country's international reputation for honoring commitments. The argument is that state leaders should be very reluctant to do this since a country's pursuit of security and foreign policy goals often requires states to attract allies and to enter into agreements with other states. If other states believe that the challenger is not a reliable partner to international agreements then the challenger should find itself more isolated and unable to draw on the diplomatic and military support of potential allies.

Hypotheses on the Domestic Context

A series of hypotheses are derived from the common logical foundation provided by assumptions 1 through 5 and related corollaries. In each of the hypotheses the focus of attention is the domestic political consequences for the challenger of previous diplomatic and military conflict with the target. The first hypothesis is as follows.

H13. There is a positive relationship between the challenger's involvement in an unsettled territorial dispute with a target prior to World War II and the probability that a challenger will be involved in a territorial dispute in the postwar period.

The logic of this hypothesis is that during the period of prior dispute with the target, political leaders within the challenger will have used the dispute to build internal support by appealing to nationalism. As a result, within the challenger domestic political rhetoric and propaganda would have portrayed the target as an uncompromising adversary and security threat. Furthermore, another consequence of a protracted period of dispute should be that military establishments with the challenger develop a vested interest in maintaining the dispute with the target. For example, an external adversary could be used to justify higher levels of military spending, or to sanction intervention in domestic politics in order to protect the national security interests of the country. The longer-term consequence is that for succeeding regimes there would be real domestic political costs in not maintaining the claim to disputed territory while the political benefits of continuing the dispute would remain.

The next two hypotheses center on the effects of prior crises and militarized conflicts between challenger and target while a third hypothesis addresses the impact of the past outcomes of territorial disputes.

H14.1. There is a positive relationship between the frequency of prior militarized disputes involving the same challenger and target and the level of diplomatic and military pressure applied by a challenger against a target over disputed territory.

H14.2. There is an inverse relationship between the frequency of prior militarized disputes involving the same challenger and target and the probability that a challenger will seek a resolution of a territorial dispute through compromise or conciliation.

H15. There is a positive relationship between the prior loss of territory by a challenger to a target and the probability that a challenger will initiate a territorial dispute.

The logic of the first two hypotheses is quite similar to the argument supporting H13. The domestic political consequence of a prior history of disputes and armed conflict with the target is that political leaders within the challenger will feel less able to be accommodating toward the target and to avoid open confrontation. As a result, higher levels of diplomatic and military pressure can be expected as well as a reluctance to offer concessions in order to settle the dispute.

The logical foundation for H15 is that leaders within the challenger have strong domestic political incentives to appear defiant against a target who has previously gained territory at their country's expense.[30] Political leaders should be able to draw on nationalist support for a policy of contesting the loss of national territory. Political leaders within

---

30. See Gary Goertz and Paul Diehl, *Territorial Changes and International Conflict,* ch. 5 for a related argument about the conditions under which a previous exchange of territory between two states will result in future conflict betwen the same two countries.

the challenger may eventually be able politically to accept the loss of national territory and withdraw the claims in the dispute, but the logic of the assumptions in the model would predict that this would be a slow process of reconciliation to the territorial status quo. Thus, we should expect a clear correlation between the loss of territory prior to 1950 and the maintenance of a claim to the territory after 1950 by challenger states.

One additional hypothesis is derived from assumptions 2 through 4 and draws a connection between post–World War II international norms and domestic politics within developing countries.

> *H16.* There is a positive relationship between the status of the target as a colony or overseas dependency and the probability that a challenger will initiate a territorial dispute.

Decolonization has been one of the central features of international politics since the end of World War II. In developing countries throughout the international system, the principle of self-determination for colonial territories has enjoyed widespread domestic political support. The United Nations Charter—article 1(2)—affirms the right of self-determination for peoples, and in December 1960 the United Nations General Assembly passed a resolution on decolonization declaring that *all colonies* had the right to self-determination (though the resolution also stated that the right of self-determination should not be used to undermine the territorial integrity of existing states).[31] Underlying this General Assembly resolution was the widespread belief among non-Western states that not only were colonial borders often drawn up in a manner violating the principle of self-determination but that the indigenous populations of colonial territories strongly favored independence from their metropole. Thus, political leaders within the challenger, with the expectation of domestic political support, could press claims against the bordering colonial or overseas territory of a target on the grounds of supporting self-determination for the neighboring population. Decolonization then is a foreign policy goal likely to build political support for a leadership within the challenger while carrying very few political risks, that is, domestic elites are not going to be able to use this issue to mobilize political opposition to the leadership.

The final set of hypotheses are derived from assumptions 6 and 7

---

31. This resolution is known as the "Declaration on the Granting of Independence to Colonial Territories and Countries." See United Nations General Assembly Resolution 1514, December 14, 1960.

and their related corollaries and center on the impact of democratic institutions and international conflict behavior.

> *H17.1.* There is an inverse relationship between how democratic the challenger is and the level of diplomatic and military pressure applied by a challenger against a target over disputed territory. *H17.2.* There is a positive relationship between how democratic the challenger is and the probability that a challenger will seek a resolution of a territorial dispute through compromise or conciliation.

The argument is that as political institutions become more democratic in a country, political leaders are less likely to resort to the threat or use of coercion and violence to resolve domestic political conflict. Instead, we should expect that leaders would favor hard-nosed bargaining and compromise on disputed issues. Bargaining and compromise is a feature of competition in all political systems, but the critical point is that the mix of coercive and compromising behavior varies significantly across different political systems. The acceptance of nonviolent means of conflict resolution and the need to compromise with political opponents reflect the structure of incentives produced by democratic institutions. If these democratic institutions are durable and stable in a country over time, we should then expect political elites to accept the legitimacy of compromise and bargaining as the prevalent means by which to resolve political conflict. The implication then for foreign policy is that political elites who have competed for an extended period of time in a democratic system should be less prone to the aggressive use of force to resolve international disputes and more willing to consider some form of compromise as an acceptable solution to a dispute.[32] In sum, norms of

---

32. The principal empirical studies on the war-proneness of democracies include Bueno de Mesquita and Lalman, *War and Reason,* ch. 5; William Domke, *War and the Changing Global System* (New Haven: Yale University Press, 1988), ch. 4; Zeev Maoz and Bruce Russett, "Alliance, Contiguity, Wealth, and Political Stability: Is the Lack of Conflict among Democracies a Statistical Artifact?" *International Interactions* 17, no. 3 (1991): 245–68; Russett, *Grasping the Democratic Peace;* Morgan and Schwebach, "Take Two Democracies and Call Me in the Morning"; Morgan and Campbell, "Domestic Structure, Decisional Constraints and War"; Stuart Bremer, "Dangerous Dyads: Conditions Affecting the Likelihood of Interstate War, 1816–1965," *Journal of Conflict Resolution* 36, no. 2 (1992): 309–41; Stuart Bremer, "Democracy and Militarized Interstate Conflict, 1816–1965," *International Interactions* 18, 3 (1993): 231–50; Dixon, "Democracy and the Management of International Conflict"; Dixon, "Democracy and the Peaceful Settlement of International Conflict"; and Gregory Raymond, "Democracies, Disputes, and Third-Party Intermediaries," *Journal of Conflict Resolution* 38, no. 1 (1994): 24–42.

nonviolent conflict resolution and compromise should not prevent a democratic challenger from disputing territory with a target, but they should influence the pattern of bargaining and negotiation over disputed territory. The willingness of democratic leaders to resort to threats or the use of military force should be reduced, while their propensity to propose a compromise settlement should increase compared to less democratic political systems.

An important point to emphasize is that H17.1–17.2 do not argue that the willingness of democratic leaders to accept nonviolent means of conflict resolution is contingent upon the other country in an international dispute also being governed by democratic leaders. The theoretical basis for this "democratic dyad" proposition is not convincing, though it is common in the scholarly literature. Typically, the argument is that democratic states must adopt the more inflexible and coercive bargaining approaches of nondemocratic states because the reluctance of democratic states to use force and their greater willingness to compromise places them in a weak bargaining position and even leaves them vulnerable to attack.[33]

These conclusions, however, are not well grounded theoretically. Democratic norms of bargaining and conflict resolution closely approximate a general strategy of tit-for-tat and reciprocity in a dispute. As such, democratic leaders are not likely to make unilateral concessions but instead are willing to offer contingent compromise and to reciprocate the intransigence of a bullying adversary. Similarly, democratic norms do not imply that democratic leaders should not be fully prepared to defend themselves if attacked. The defensive use of force and preparations to respond to an attack are fully consistent with democratic norms. Political opposition may indeed arise in democratic systems when the use of force is called for in pursuit of questionable foreign policy goals. However, when national leaders can make a strong case that security interests are at stake, popular and elite support can be mobilized and sustained in democratic countries.[34] In sum, I do not believe that there is a compelling logical argument strongly supporting the conclusion that we should expect leaders of democratic states to be generally bargaining from a position of weakness in international disputes, and therefore they feel compelled to adopt the more coercive bargaining strategies of their nondemocratic opponents. Empirically, studies of crisis bargaining have

---

33. See for example Bueno de Mesquita and Lalman, *War and Reason,* ch. 5 and Russett, *Grasping the Democratic Peace,* chs. 1–2 for a review and analysis of such arguments.

34. Russett, *Controlling the Sword,* ch. 2 reviews much of the literature on this subject.

shown that reciprocating strategies are quite effective in preventing war while protecting the security interests of countries, and democratic states are quite likely to adopt such strategies as well.[35]

Comparing Theoretical Models

In this section I compare and contrast the hypotheses derived from the modified realist model with the propositions that would be generated by a conventional realist approach. There are clearly areas of convergence between the two, but there are also fundamental differences. In table 2 the hypotheses derived from the modified realist model are summarized and compared to the predictions of a conventional realist model. Of the seventeen basic hypotheses derived from the modified realist model, eight could be clearly derived from a conventional realist model. For two of the hypotheses (H4.1–4.3 and H12), it is not clear that a conventional realist model would produce similar predictions, but I think a reasonable argument could be made that many traditional realists would accept these two propositions.[36] All of the remaining seven hypotheses propose that domestic political factors should play a significant role at each stage in the analysis of territorial disputes. Thus, these seven hypotheses predict that domestic-level variables should have a strong impact on the initiation, escalation, and settlement of territorial disputes. A conventional realist approach would reject this set of expectations.

For example, one area of clear difference between the conventional and modified realist models centers on the foreign policy goals of leaders and what conditions lead decision makers to consider the option of diplomatic and military confrontation with a target over territory. The

---

35. See for example Russell Leng, *Interstate Crisis Bargaining Behavior, 1816–1980* (Cambridge: Cambridge University Press, 1993) and Huth, *Extended Deterrence and the Prevention of War*. Furthermore, the conventional wisdom that democratic states are just as likely to use force against nondemocratic states as any other type of state is, in fact, not well established empirically, that is, the results of studies are quite mixed on this question. See James Lee Ray, *Democracy and International Conflict* (Columbia: University of South Carolina Press, 1995), ch. 1 for an excellent review of the empirical literature.

36. The reason for uncertainty is as follows. Economic strength and development certainly can contribute to the military potential of states, and in that sense economics issues are linked to security concerns. However, traditional realists also assert that issues of economic policy are of secondary importance compared to issues of direct military security. If we believe that economic strength is closely linked to military strength, then the argument that military security concerns take precedence over economic issues is problematic. While a traditional realist approach would acknowledge the value of maintaining a reputation for honoring past agreements, it would also argue that the direct security issues at stake in a dispute and the military strength of a country should be the central determinants of whether states abide by existing agreements.

TABLE 2. Summary of Hypotheses to Be Tested and a Comparison with a Conventional Realist Model

Modified Realist Model Hypotheses Relating to	Predicted Relationship to			Would a Conventional Realist Model Predict a Similar Relationship?
	Dispute Initiation	Dispute Escalation	Dispute Settlement	
Issues at Stake				
Strategic location of territory (H1.1–1.2)	+	+	–	Yes
Support for bordering minorities (H2.1–2.2)	+	+	–	No
Political unification (H3.1–3.2)	+	+	–	No
Economic value of territory (H4.1–4.3)	+	–	+	Yes?
International Context				
Balance of military capabilities (H5.1–5.2)	+	+	–	Yes
Disputes with third parties (H6.1–6.2)		–	+	Yes
Stalemate in negotiations (H7)		+	–	Yes
Change in status quo (H8.1–8.2)		–	+	Yes
Defeat in armed conflict (H9.1–9.2)		–	+	Yes
Deterrent alliance ties (H10)		–	+	Yes
Common security ties (H11.1–11.2)	–		+	Yes
Prior settlement (H12)	–		+	Yes?
Domestic Context				
Prior unsettled dispute (H13)	+			No
Prior military conflict (H14.1–14.2)		+	–	No
Prior loss of territory (H15)	+			No
Decolonization norm (H16) *— why not intl*	+			No
Level of democracy (H17.1–17.2)		–	+	No

Note: + means that in statistical tests the coefficient should have a positive sign; – means that in statistical tests the coefficient should have a negative sign.

modified realist model posits that calculations of internal political power and competition with counterelites play a central role in the formation of policy preferences and determine when choices about confrontational foreign policy behavior are placed on the agenda of decision makers. A conventional realist model, in contrast, would argue that the primary goal of state leaders is military security maximization and that strategic interests define the issues at stake in an international dispute over territory. Thus, if one were to ask, What makes territory worth disputing? the modified and conventional realist models would provide different answers. According to a conventional realist model, territorial disputes should center on territory of strategic importance to the states involved. The standard realist model argues that the strategic value of territory should strongly predict whether bordering states become embroiled in territorial disputes, as well as the resolve of state leaders to attain a favorable settlement over disputed territory.

In contrast, according to the modified realist model, territorial disputes will emerge if state leaders expect that a confrontational policy will advance their domestic political position. From this perspective, gaining control of strategically located territory is but one of several issues potentially at stake in a dispute. In addition, the modified realist model would posit that leaders will ask the question, Are the issues at stake salient to, and likely to be supported by, domestic groups? For example, can leaders draw on the power of ethnic solidarity and nationalism to increase their own domestic political standing by portraying themselves as trying to protect the rights of peoples in the disputed territory who share common ethnic ties with the population of their own country? According to the modified realist model, then, the resolve of states engaged in a territorial dispute is positively related to the domestic political benefits that leaders expect to generate from controlling the territory itself and contesting the right of another country to exercise sovereignty over the territory.

Another point of difference between the two models centers on the question of whether the type of political regime has a strong effect on the conflict behavior of states. The conventional realist model would argue that regime type makes little difference, and that instead, the diplomatic positions and the bargaining flexibility of states is largely a function of relative power, strategic interests at stake, and the saliency of disputes with other states. In contrast, the modified realist model posits that the more democratic a political system is, the less likely are its leaders to engage in aggressive foreign policies and to initiate threats or the use of military force to resolve international disputes.

The critical test then for the modified realist model is to see whether

(1) any of the additional seven hypotheses that focus on domestic level variables are supported by the statistical results, and (2) if any of the domestic-level variables are found to have a significant effect, how large is their substantive impact relative to the more conventional realist variables? A conventional realist model would predict that for the seven domestic politics hypotheses, the coefficients would be both statistically insignificant and small, indicating that domestic variables had neither a systematic nor substantively large impact. Findings indicating that one or more of the domestic-level variables had a consistent but limited effect would pose only a minor challenge to the conventional realist approach.

With this understanding of the theoretical underpinnings of the modified realist model and its basic differences with a traditional realist approach, we can begin in the next chapter to conduct systematic empirical tests of the new realist model.[37]

---

37. Before turning to the empirical tests, readers should consult appendix C; the operational measures for each of the seventeen hypotheses derived from the modified realist model are discussed at length.

CHAPTER 4

The Initiation and Persistence
of Territorial Disputes

When and why do neighboring states become involved in territorial disputes with one another? As I argued in chapter 1, territorial disputes have been an enduring feature of international politics for centuries, and in the postwar period 116 interstate borders were disputed between 1950 and 1990. The leaders of most states, however, are not involved in territorial disputes with their neighbors. For example, if we compile a list of all the states that shared borders between 1950 and 1990 and treat each border as potentially subject to a dispute, only about one-third of the borders were disputed.[1] What distinguishes these contested borders from the remaining two-thirds in which there were no territorial disputes? Why do state leaders decide to confront their neighbors with a territorial claim in a relatively small number of situations, whereas in a majority of cases state leaders accept the prevailing territorial status quo? To try and answer these questions I turn to the modified realist model presented in chapter 3 and the hypotheses derived from that model.

This chapter is divided into three sections. I first present the equation to be tested empirically and describe the dataset that will be utilized for the empirical analysis. I then utilize logit analysis to test the equation and discuss the statistical results. To illustrate the general findings of the logit analysis, I also discuss a number of individual cases. I conclude the chapter with a summary of the findings and their theoretical implications.

Equation to be Tested

Based on the hypotheses derived from the modified realist model in chapter 3, the equation listed below will be empirically tested and includes the following variables.

---

1. In total, 116 of 356 borders were disputed. The total number of borders was calculated by adding the 240 borders between 1950 and 1990 that were not contested by neighboring states (see appendix B) to the 116 borders listed in appendix A.

The endogenous variable (y) = the probability in any given year that a challenger state will be involved in a territorial dispute with a target state

c = constant term

The exogenous variables x_1 to x_{11} are specified as follows (for each variable I include the hypothesis that it is associated with from chapter 3 and the expected sign of the coefficient).

Issues at Stake
x_1 = strategic location of bordering territory (H1.1, positive)
x_2 = support for minorities along border of target with ethnic ties to the challenger (H2.1, positive)
x_3 = political unification based on common ethnic background between challenger and target populations (H3.1, positive)
x_4 = economic value of bordering territory (H4.1, positive)

International Context
x_5 = balance of conventional military forces between challenger and target (H5.1, positive)
x_6 = prior gain of territory by challenger (control variable, negative)
x_7 = common security ties between challenger and target (H11.1, negative)
x_8 = prior border agreement signed by challenger (H12, negative)

Domestic Context
x_9 = prior unresolved dispute for challenger (H13, positive)
x_{10} = prior loss of territory by challenger (H15, positive)
x_{11} = support for decolonization when target is a colony or overseas dependency (H16, positive)
u_t = error term

The endogenous variable was coded a value of one for each year that the challenger was involved in a territorial dispute with the target state, and a value of zero was coded for each year that the challenger was not involved in a territorial dispute. The equation is therefore testing hypotheses on the conditions that will lead a challenger state to initiate a territorial dispute and/or to maintain a claim to disputed territory over time.

The coding rules for the identification of a territorial dispute were presented in chapter 2 and the duration of a territorial dispute was determined by the number of years that the challenger maintained a claim to territory that was contested by the target. The beginning and end dates for each dispute and nondispute case are listed in appendixes A and B, while the operational measures for each of the exogenous variables are described in appendix C.

The equation will be tested on 258 dyads of states. One-half of the dyads constitute the 129 cases of territorial disputes described in appendix A, while the remaining dyads were randomly selected bordering states not involved in a territorial dispute at any point between 1950 and 1990. In appendix B, I describe in greater detail the procedures utilized to select the nondispute dyads. Each of the nondispute dyads covers the period between 1950 and 1990, whereas each dispute dyad varies by the number of years that the challenger disputed territory. In total, there are 8,328 observations in the dataset with 5,160 cases (129 * 40) for the nondispute dyads, and 3,039 cases in the set of disputed borders.[2] As a result, in approximately 63.5 percent of the cases (5,160/8,328) there was no territorial dispute between challenger and target, while in the remaining 36.5 percent of the cases (3,039/8,328) there was a dispute.

Statistical Results and Case Analysis

The results of the logit analysis are presented in table 3 with the coefficients, robust standard errors, and significance levels reported.[3] Overall, the findings indicate that the equation provides a good deal of information about the conditions under which challenger states were involved in territorial disputes during the period between 1950 and 1990.[4] Hypotheses that focused on domestic political explanations for territorial disputes generally received considerable support with one exception. Similarly, all but one of the hypotheses that focused on international political and military conditions was supported by the logit results. In total, of the

---

2. See appendix D for a discussion of the logic behind the research design for the dataset.

3. See appendix D for a discussion of issues related to the selection of the statistical estimator utilized in this chapter. The statistical software package SST version 386, developed by Jeffrey Dubin and Douglas Rivers, was utilized to conduct the analysis.

4. The problem of multicollinearity among the exogenous variables was checked for by individually regressing each exogenous variable on all other remaining exogenous variables in the equation in a series of individual ordinary least squares regressions runs (OLS). The resulting r-squared values indicated that high levels of multicollinearity were not present. The r-squared values were below .25 for all of the variables in the equation.

eleven coefficients estimated, ten were in the predicted direction and nine were significant at very high levels. Finally, several of the variables from each level of analysis (domestic and international) had large substantive effects.

With logit coefficients it is quite difficult to draw specific conclusions about the substantive effects of variables in an equation by simply comparing the relative size of coefficients. To assess the impact of each variable a series of additional tables are presented below that provide information about how changes in the values of each variable affect the probability of a territorial dispute. My discussion of the logit findings will be as follows. I begin by examining what were the issues at stake in territorial disputes; then I consider the impact of the international context on decisions to dispute territory; and finally, I discuss the role that domestic political forces played in disputing territory.

The Issues at Stake in Disputing Territory

As we look at the results in table 3 we find that both military security as well as domestic political issues provided reasons for leaders within

TABLE 3.   Logit Estimates of Probability of Territorial Disputes between States, 1950–90

Explanatory Variables	Coefficient	Standard Errors	Significance Level
Constant	−2.152	0.123	<.001
Issues at Stake			
Strategic location of territory	2.637	0.123	<.001
Ties to bordering minority	−0.073	0.010	—
Political unification	1.085	0.099	<.001
Economic value of territory	0.563	0.078	<.001
International Context			
Balance of military forces	0.083	0.166	—
Prior gain of territory	−0.969	0.142	<.001
Common alliance	−2.342	0.114	<.001
Previous settlement	−3.339	0.099	<.001
Domestic Context			
Prior unresolved dispute	3.761	0.099	<.001
Prior loss of territory	2.231	0.102	<.001
Decolonization norm	0.740	0.115	<.001

Note: Number of observations = 8,328.
Log-likelihood = 2,257.9.
Percentage of cases correctly predicted = 87.22.
All significance levels based on one-tailed tests.

challenger states to lay claim to bordering territory. At a broad level of generalization this is consistent with the predictions of the modified realist model. As argued in chapter 3, state leaders are both national security managers as well as domestic politicians seeking to maintain their position of influence and power. As such, the foreign policy goals of state leaders should reflect the pursuit of both external security as well as domestic political gain.

The strongest finding is that the desire of challenger states to gain control over strategically located territory was a powerful predictor of a territorial dispute. In table 3 the coefficient for this variable is, as expected, positive and highly significant (t-ratio = 21.38). The substantive effect of this variable is also very large. When we examine its marginal impact on the probability of a territorial dispute in table 4, we see that if we compare a case in which there is no strategic territory along the border to a case in which there is, there is a 52 percent increase in the likelihood of a dispute emerging. Thus, the logit results provide strong

TABLE 4. The Marginal Impact of Variables Measuring the Issues at Stake on the Probability of Disputing Territory

Change in Value of Explanatory Variable	Change in Probability of Territorial Dispute (%)
Strategic Location of Territory	
Is bordering territory strategically located?	
No vs. Yes	+52.0
Ties to Bordering Minority	
Do bordering minority groups within the target share ties of language and ethnicity with the population of the challenger?	
No vs. Yes	−0.7
Political unification	
Do the populations of challenger and target share ties of a common language and ethnicity?	
No vs. Yes	+15.6
Economic Value of Territory	
Are natural resources with export value located within/ proximate to bordering territory, or would control of bordering territory provide a port outlet to promote trade?	
No vs. Yes	+6.7

Note: The changes in the probability of a territorial dispute were calculated utilizing the coefficients from the equation presented in table 3. The value of a single explanatory variable is changed while all continuous variables in the equation are held at their mean or the modal value for dummy variables. The change in the location on the logistic distribution is then converted into the percentage change in the probability of a territorial dispute. See Gary King, *Unifying Political Methodology* (Cambridge: Cambridge University Press, 1989), 106–8.

support for H1.1. The conclusion to be drawn is that the desire to acquire control over strategically located territory was a powerful motive behind the territorial claims of challenger states. As argued in H1.1, foreign policy leaders should seek to protect the military security of the country, and therefore we should expect that claims to territory would be linked systematically to traditional concerns about the security interests of the country.

As discussed in appendix C, strategic location was coded for any one of the following situations: (1) control of bordering territory would provide an outlet to the sea for an otherwise landlocked challenger; (2) bordering territory provided a desirable location from which the challenger could project military power offshore in close proximity to major shipping lanes; (3) bordering territory was in close proximity to the choke points of narrow straits; (4) the target utilized bordering territory as a military base; (5) naval bases of the challenger were located in close proximity to bordering territory; and (6) control of disputed territory blocked a primary route through which a challenger would attack a target.

In a number of cases leaders from the challenger did, in fact, refer to the strategic location of disputed territory as the primary or as an important reason justifying territorial claims: Argentina vs. Chile in the Beagle Channel and the proximity of disputed islands to an Argentine naval base and concern over Chilean control of passage rights around the Cape Horn; Egypt vs. Israel over the Sinai and the Israeli use of the Sinai as a buffer zone in which a forward defensive position had been established; Syria vs. Israel over the Golan Heights and its strategic value as a location from which to launch an attack on Israel; Iran vs. the United Arab Emirates (UAE) over the Greater and Lesser Tunbs Islands, located in the narrow Straits of Hormuz; Iraqi claims to Kuwaiti islands located in close proximity to an Iraqi naval base; China vs. India and Chinese concerns to gain control of disputed territory bordering on Tibet to ensure reliable year-round routes of access into Tibet; China vs. Taiwan and control over offshore islands both sides desired as bases for military forces; China vs. Vietnam over the Paracel and Spratly Islands located in close proximity to major shipping lanes in the South China Sea; Turkey vs. Greece over Cyprus and Turkish concern that Greek control of the island would threaten their shipping and naval ports. In addition, there are a series of disputes in which challengers viewed foreign military bases on their national territory as a security threat, for example, Cuba vs. United States, Egypt vs. United Kingdom, and Tunisia vs. France.

If we look at the distribution of strategically located territory across dispute and nondispute cases, we see why the logit results are so strong.

There are only six such cases in the nondispute dataset but twenty-five in the population of dispute cases. Thus, twenty-five out of thirty-one times (or about 81 percent) strategically located territory was associated with a territorial dispute. The presence of strategic territory, then, was relatively close to being a sufficient condition for a dispute to exist. At the same time, it is very important to recognize that strategic location was *very often not an issue* in a territorial dispute; less than 20 percent (25/129) of all dispute cases involved strategically located territory. Another way to see that the strategic location of territory was at stake in only a minority of cases is to look at the total number of years of disputed territory in the entire dispute dataset. We find that only about 25 percent of the dispute years (767/3,039) were coded for the presence of strategic territory; strategically located territory is clearly not close to being a necessary condition for a territorial dispute to exist. In sum, strategic issues were salient in a number of dispute cases, but nonmilitary issues were of central concern in a much larger number of cases. This result is quite consistent with the predictions of the modified realist model, that we should expect that the issues at stake will often reflect domestic political incentives to dispute territory.

The second finding to report in table 3 is that economically valuable bordering territory (rich in natural resources with export potential, providing an outlet to the sea to promote trade, or containing scarce water resources) was associated with a higher probability of a territorial dispute. The positive coefficient and large *t*-ratio (7.23) clearly supports H4.1 and indicates that economic incentives did play an important role in explaining why challengers became involved in territorial disputes. According to the results in table 4, bordering territory with economic potential increases the likelihood of a dispute by about 7 percent. These supporting, but not strong, results are reflected in the fact that about 40 percent of all dispute years (124/3,039) include economically valuable territory, while for all of the years in which such territory was coded as present, a territorial dispute existed in about 50 percent of the years (1,224/2,454).

The supportive findings are clearly linked to the fact that in most dispute cases the challenger states were developing countries in which problems of economic development were of critical concern to state leaders and where exports were often concentrated in natural resources and minerals. As a result, when bordering territory was known or suspected to be rich in such resources political leaders had strong incentives to lay claim to the territory in the hope of economically and thus politically benefiting from the development of the resources. Indeed, with few exceptions the challenger in cases where economically valuable territory was in dispute was a developing country (fifty-one of fifty-four cases, or 94 percent).[5] On the other hand, among the thirty nondispute cases in which economically valuable bordering territory was coded as present, we find that in seventeen cases (57 percent) the challenger was not a developing country. The finding that industrial countries were very unlikely to be involved in disputes over economically valuable territory supports the general argument made by scholars that one of the reasons why such states are less likely to be involved in territorial disputes is that for such states continued economic progress is not strongly linked to natural resource endowments or agricultural production of new territory.[6] Economic concerns were also at stake in several disputes in which access to water supplies was the primary issue in contention (Ethiopia vs. Kenya), or outlets for trade via access to rivers or coastal territory (Bolivia vs. Chile or Guatemala vs. United Kingdom/Belize). In either case, economic concerns in the form of supporting agricultural production or promoting foreign trade made the acquisition of bordering territory important to the challenger.

It is also possible to argue that in many cases the economic development of resource-rich bordering territory contributed indirectly to the military capabilities of challenger states. The income and revenue generated by export sales could be used in part to help pay for the costs of arms imports. In most of the dispute cases the challenger was a developing country with, typically, very limited capacities to produce their own armaments. The result was that access to natural resources that might have served as critical inputs into an industrial base for defense production was generally not a primary concern of leaders within the challenger. Instead, these countries relied heavily, if not exclusively, on arms imports from the United States, the Soviet Union, and Western European states such as France and Great Britain. Only since the mid-1970s have a growing number of developing countries acquired the indigenous capacity to produce some of their own weapons.[7] Furthermore, even

---

5. For example, economically valuable territory was at stake in Latin American disputes involving Argentina vs. Uruguay; Ecuador vs. Peru; Nicaragua vs. Honduras; Suriname vs. Guyana; Venezuela vs. Guyana; and in Africa, Morocco vs. Spain; Morocco vs. Algeria; Tunisia vs. Algeria; and Mauritania vs. Spain. In the Middle East most of the disputes among the Persian Gulf states involved access to oil, as did the disputes over the Spratly Islands involving China, Taiwan, Philippines, Malaysia, and Vietnam.

6. See for example Richard Rosecrance, *The Rise of the Trading State* (New York: Basic Books, 1986), ch. 2 and Richard Ullman, *Securing Europe* (Princeton: Princeton University Press, 1991), ch. 2.

7. See for example Michael Brzoska and Thomas Ohlson, *Arms Transfers to the Third World, 1971–1985* (Oxford: Oxford University Press, 1987), 112–19 and Janne Nolan, *Trappings of Power* (Washington, D.C.: Brookings, 1991), ch. 1.

those developing countries such as Argentina, India, Brazil, and South Africa, which have been producing arms since the 1950s or early 1960s, still imported large amounts of arms. Thus, if we examine those territorial dispute cases in which natural resources were located along the border, we see that the challenger sought control over territory containing deposits of oil, coal, iron ore, and phosphates in a large number of cases. Examples would include the claims of Malaysia, the Philippines, and Vietnam against China over the Spratly Islands; Saudi Arabian disputes with many of its Persian Gulf neighbors; Tunisian claims against Algeria; or Moroccan claims to the Western Sahara. In each of these cases the direct interest of the challenger was in the economic value of the natural resource, that is, the use of oil, iron ore, or phosphates for export sales.

In fact, there were only two disputes in which the direct strategic value of natural resources was an important issue at stake. The first case was Libya's occupation of the Aozou Strip along its border with Chad. The territory is believed to be rich in deposits of uranium, which could be used to support a nuclear weapons program. Libyan leader Qaddafi has sought to acquire nuclear weapons for his own country as a counter to Israel's nuclear weapons program. Access to uranium could then be used by Libya to help develop a domestic nuclear program or to acquire a nuclear weapon through cooperation with a nuclear state.[8] The second case involved West Germany's desire to reclaim control from France of the coal and steel producing region of the Saar in the mid-1950s. The region had been vital to the German armaments industry in the past, and West Germany had lost control over the territory after its defeat in World War II.[9]

We don't find explicit and public statements by leaders in these disputes that the income generated by the development of the natural resources would be used to pay for arms imports. As a result, there is little direct evidence that expectations of security gains were a part of the calculations of leaders. At the same time, the connection between the increased national income generated by export sales and the ability of the challenger to pay for arms imports is quite clear. Indirectly, then,

---

8. See Leonard Spector, *Going Nuclear* (Cambridge: Ballinger Publishing Company, 1987), 146–59 and Benyamin Neuberger, *Involvement, Invasion and Withdrawal: Qadhdhafi's Libya and Chad 1969–1981* (Tel Aviv: The Shiloah Center for Middle Eastern and African Studies, 1982), 29, 60.

9. See Jacques Freymond, *The Saar Conflict* (London: Stevens, 1960). The strategic value of the Saar region, however, was not the only reason why West Germany sought to reclaim the territory. In addition, the population was largely German and favored union with West Germany.

a plausible case can be made that military security gains were a contributing factor underlying the challenger's desire to gain control of bordering territory rich in natural resources. A good example would be Saudi Arabia's disputes with most of its neighbors over oil-rich territory (e.g., Kuwait, UAE, Iraq) in which the Saudi's reached agreements to divide up resource-rich bordering territories.[10] Oil exports from these bordering territories have then contributed to the financial capacity of Saudi Arabia to purchase very large amounts of arms from countries such as the United States.[11]

The next finding in table 3 indicates that ties of common language and ethnic background between the general populations of the challenger and target increased the likelihood of a territorial dispute between the two states. The positive coefficient is predicted by H3.1, and it is very significant (t-ratio = 10.95). Furthermore, this variable has an important substantive effect: in table 4 we see that ethnic/cultural similarity increases the probability of a territorial dispute by about 16 percent.

Among the population of territorial disputes there are thirty-six cases in which the challenger and target populations were similar along linguistic and ethnic lines. If we examine these dispute cases we see that because the challenger and target were very similar in cultural terms, they were often part of the same colony or country, which was then subsequently divided either during the period of decolonization since the end of World War I, or as a result of superpower rivalry in the aftermath of World War II. The sources of dispute in the post–World War II period were then linked to the process and manner in which the challenger and target were separated from one another politically.

In the first set of cases the challenger refused to accept the loss of the target and maintained that the two countries should be united into one. This type of case clearly supports the argument advanced in H3.1. The challenger's desire for national unification was based on the lack of legitimacy attached to the independent status of the target either because the target acquired independence quite recently, or it was imposed on the challenger by outside power(s). A number of cases fit this description quite well: North Vietnam's refusal to accept the division of Vietnam; North Korea's goal of unification with South Korea; the Irish Republic's struggle with Great Britain over Northern Ireland; West Germany's desire for reunification with East Germany; Iraq's questioning of

---

10. See for example J. B. Kelly, *Arabia, the Gulf and the West* (London: Weidenfeld and Nicholson, 1980) and S. H. Amin, *International and Legal Problems of the Gulf* (London: Middle East and North African Studies Press Limited, 1981).

11. See Nadav Safran, *Saudi Arabia: The Ceaseless Quest for Security* (Cambridge: Belknap Press, 1985) for a thorough analysis of Saudi defense policy in the post–World War II period.

the legitimacy of Kuwait as an independent state; North Yemen's desire for unification with South Yemen; Morocco's claim to sovereignty over Mauritania and the Western Sahara on the grounds that both were once a province of Morocco; Madagascar's claim to a series of proximate small islands controlled by France on the grounds of historical ties; and China's firm position that Taiwan is an integral part of its country.

In the second set of cases the challenger and target also share a common colonial legacy, but the link between this and the emergence of territorial disputes does not directly support the logic of H3.1. In Latin America, Africa, and the Middle East, there are a number of cases in which the challenger and target were part of the same colonial empire, and the two countries became separate entities when the colonial power established borders between them. For example, countries such as Argentina, Chile, Ecuador, and Peru were all once part of the Spanish empire until the early nineteenth century, while many of the Persian Gulf states were once part of the British empire, and decolonization in Africa during the 1960s resulted in the independence of neighboring former French colonies such as Benin and Niger, Morocco and Algeria, and Tunisia and Algeria. The borders of these countries in many cases were delimited in only quite general and imprecise terms, leaving considerable room for disagreement and alternative interpretations. Hence, when these countries became independent, it was not surprising that in many cases disputes over the location of the border arose.[12]

The interesting puzzle to explain, then, is the absence of territorial conflict among a number of nondisputed borders despite common ethnic and linguistic ties between the challenger and target. If we take a closer look at these cases, they are clustered into two groups. First, there are sixteen cases in Central and South America,[13] and second, there are ten cases in Northern Africa.[14] Within the first set of cases the absence of

---

12. For a description of the treaties and agreements establishing borders between these countries and how imprecise delimitation was in many cases, see Ian Brownlie, *African Boundaries* (Berkeley: University of California Press, 1979); *Workshop on the Role of Border Problems in African Peace and Security* (New York: United Nations, 1993); Husain Albaharna, *The Arabian Gulf States*, rev. 2d ed. (Beirut: Librairie Du Liban, 1975); and Alan Day, ed., *Border and Territorial Disputes*, 2d ed. (London: Longman, 1982), 95–233.

13. The cases as listed in appendix B are the United States vs. Canada; Mexico vs. Guatemala; Guatemala vs. Honduras; Nicaragua vs. Costa Rica; Costa Rica vs. Colombia; Costa Rica vs. Panama; Bahamas vs. Turks and Caicos Islands; Trinidad and Tobago vs. Grenada; Colombia vs. Venezuela; Colombia vs. Peru; Colombia vs. Ecuador; Peru vs. Chile; Bolivia vs. Argentina.

14. Once again, the cases as listed in appendix B are Algeria vs. the Western Sahara; Mauritania vs. Algeria; Algeria vs. Libya; Libya vs. Egypt; Libya vs. Sudan; and Chad vs. Sudan.

conflict in the postwar period was not due to the fact that many of these countries never had border disputes, but because diplomatic and even military conflict over territorial issues had been resolved in the nineteenth and early twentieth centuries. Thus, the period of conflict over territorial unification or separation between challenger and target, as proposed by H3.1, did occur; however settlements were achieved decades before the post–World War II period began.[15] Thus, among these cases questions of legitimacy about the location or even existence of borders with the target were no longer actively debated or politically contentious issues within the challenger. Among the African cases the lack of conflict would seem to stem from the fact that these neighboring countries were ruled by different colonial powers (France, Italy, Spain, and Great Britain), and these colonial powers were more careful in delimiting their borders with other colonial powers than in defining borders within their own colonial empire. Thus, well-defined borders generally existed between these colonial territories, removing an important source of a potential territorial dispute when they became independent states.[16] In addition, another contributing factor that may explain the absence of conflict in these African cases was that despite their common ethnic and linguistic ties, these bordering countries had developed a stronger sense of separate national political identities, the result of decades of rule by different colonial powers who established their own set of political and administrative institutions within their colonies. Thus, the political struggle within the colonies among indigenous political elites in the pre- and postindependence period was directed at taking control of these existing institutions within well-defined borders.[17]

The final result in table 3 is that the presence of a bordering minority within the target with ties of common language and ethnicity to the general population of the challenger did not prove to be strong predictor of whether the challenger would be involved in a territorial dispute. This is a very important finding that runs counter to what is often considered the conventional wisdom, that is, if the location of a large ethnic group is divided by state borders, the minority status of that ethnic group in one country will stimulate irredentist territorial claims by the other state. Indeed, H2.1 argued that the location of such ethnic groups should provide an attractive opportunity for irredentist claims by leaders within

---

15. See for example Gordon Ireland, *Boundaries, Possessions, and Conflicts in South America* (Cambridge: Harvard University Press, 1938).

16. See Brownlie, *African Boundaries*, 26–43, 99–109, 133–40, 617–39.

17. See Saadia Touval, *The Boundary Politics of Independent Africa* (Cambridge: Harvard University Press, 1972), ch. 1 for a discussion of the emergence of political movements and leaders within Africa prior to independence who addressed territorial issues.

the challenger since a foreign policy appealing to ethnic nationalism should be politically popular within the challenger state itself. The coefficient for the ethnic minority variable is essentially zero and the *t*-ratio is very low (-0.76). The substantive impact of this variable is also quite weak. In table 4 we see that the presence of minority groups along the border is associated with a less than 1.0 percent decrease in the likelihood of a territorial dispute. The results in table 4 clearly support the conclusion that irredentist claims were, in fact, *not a primary cause* of territorial disputes between states in the post–World War II period. In only about 29 percent of all dispute years (878/3,039) was there an ethnic minority located along a disputed border, and in less than one-half of all the years (42.5 percent) that an ethnic minority was located along the border was there a territorial dispute between challenger and target (878/2,066).

These findings seem to contradict the fact that some of the most prominent territorial disputes cases in the postwar period (Somalia vs. Ethiopia, Pakistan vs. India, and the Arab-Israeli conflict) have centered around such issues. Furthermore, many of the conflicts in post–cold war Europe seem to center on the treatment of ethnic minorities in bordering states. Examples would include the presence of ethnic Russians in the Ukraine and Baltic states, and the violence among Serbs, Croats, and Muslims as a result of the dissolution of the former Yugoslavia.[18] Nevertheless, the statistical results in table 3 suggest that these highly visible conflicts must be compared to those cases in which minority ethnic groups are located along the border but there is no territorial dispute or ethnic violence.

Among the 129 nonterritorial dispute cases listed in appendix B, there were twenty-nine cases in which minorities were located along the border with the cases distributed across as follows: North and Central America (one); South America (four); Western Europe (eight); Eastern Europe (seven); Africa (four); Middle East (one); Central and South Asia (one); Southeast Asia (three). Among the 129 dispute cases, however, there were only thirty cases of bordering minorities located in disputed territory: North, Central, and South America (three); Europe (eight); Middle East (five); Africa (eight); Central Asia (three); Southeast Asia (three). Thus, there is almost an even

---

18. See for example Ted Hopf, "Managing Soviet Disintegration," *International Security* 17, no. 1 (1992): 44–75; Stephen Van Evera, "Hypotheses on Nationalism and War," *International Security* 18, no. 4 (1994): 5–39; F. Stephen Larrabee, *East European Security after the Cold War* (Santa Monica, CA: RAND, 1993); Jonathan Dean, *Ending Europe's Wars* (New York: Twentieth Century Fund Press, 1994), chs. 4–6; and V. P. Gagnon, "Ethnic Nationalism and International Conflict," *International Security* 19, no. 3 (1994/95): 130–66.

split of bordering minorities across the dispute and nondispute sets of cases. The twenty-nine cases of nondisputed borders, despite the presence of bordering minorities, have not received that much attention by scholars or policymakers because of the lack of conflict, but they are critically important cases to include in any empirical test of H2.1.[19] The findings here suggest that ethnic conflict and self-determination claims are not a principal cause of territorial disputes between states, and therefore we very well may not see an explosion of irredentist claims by states in the post–cold war period.[20] A combination of international pressure and more accommodative policies by state leaders toward their minorities may very well prove effective in managing and limiting the outbreak of such disputes between states.[21]

How can we explain the absence of territorial conflicts among the twenty-nine nondispute cases in which bordering minorities were coded as present? First, just over half of the cases (15/29) were located in Western and Eastern Europe, and in these regions the lack of interstate disputes can be attributed to several reasons. First, democratic states in Western Europe were able to establish a fairly effective regime of rights and protective measures for minorities so that problems of discrimination and repression did not become highly salient political issues attracting attention from neighboring governments. Second, within all Eastern European countries, centralized authoritarian rule discouraged all forms of political protest and rebellion, including ethnic-based movements. However, in several Eastern European countries, state policies were also effective in protecting minorities from various forms of economic and cultural discrimination.[22] Finally, whatever latent conflicts did exist

---

19. This may explain why Robert Mandel ("Roots of the Modern Interstate Border Dispute" *Journal of Conflict Resolution* 24, no. 3 [1980]: 427–54) concludes that ethnicity issues are a primary source of border disputes. Mandel examines sixty-six border disputes between 1945 and 1974 but does not include in his analysis any borders that were not disputed.

20. In contrast, ethnic conflict *within states* seems to be a much more prevalent problem (e.g., the recent outbreak of civil war within Rwanda and the brutal violence between the Hutu and Tutsi populations).

21. A variety of such policies are discussed in Hopf, "Managing Soviet Disintegration"; Van Evera, "Hypotheses on Nationalism and War"; Morton Halperin and David Schefer, *Self-Determination in the New World Order* (Washington, D.C.: Carnegie Endowment for International Peace, 1992), chs. 5–6; and Ted Robert Gurr, *Minorities at Risk* (Washington, D.C.: United States Institute of Peace Press, 1993), ch. 10. The need for more extensive changes in international norms and policies is presented by Gidion Gottlieb, *Nation against State* (New York: Council on Foreign Relations Press, 1993).

22. See Gurr, *Minorities at Risk,* chs. 6–7 in particular for an analysis of how European governments have dealt with ethnic minorities.

between states were kept under tight control by Soviet military dominance in the region.

Outside of Europe, many cases involve developing countries. In these cases a compelling argument could be made that leaders within challengers had good domestic political reasons not to make a major issue of ethnic minorities across the border. The reason why irredentist claims were not raised was that in some cases the challenger itself was not that ethnically homogeneous.[23] As a result, attempts by the largest ethnic group within the challenger to increase its size by annexing the bordering territory of the target populated by the same ethnic group would most likely be a divisive foreign policy issue within the challenger. In ethnically divided countries political stability is often fragile, and a foreign policy that could be credibly viewed by minority ethnic groups as posing a threat to their position of domestic political power and/or autonomy would be likely to spark strong opposition. Among the nondispute cases, examples to which this line of argument could be applied would include the failure of Tanzania, Nigeria, Guinea, Thailand, and Malaysia to press irredentist claims in support of minorities across their borders. In all of these countries there are multiple ethnic and linguistic divisions within the population, and these divisions are an ever present source of political conflict and a threat to political stability. National political leaders in such countries have recognized the dangers in appealing to ethnicity as a basis for legitimizing their policies and instead have attempted to build a sense of nationalism that cuts across the divided ethnic loyalties of the population.[24] In this context, we would not expect national leaders within these countries to appeal to ethnic solidarity as the basis for a territorial claim against another state.

In Africa as well, international opposition from neighboring states may have also reinforced domestic political reasons to avoid raising irredentist claims. As noted in chapter 3, international norms based on the United Nations Charter and resolutions strongly support self-determination in the form of decolonization. However, the United Nations has also taken a clear stand that self-determination for peoples should not threaten the territorial integrity of existing states. For example, the 1960 United Nations resolution on self-determination was limited to challenging the legitimacy of colonial rule and explicitly

---

23. I have drawn largely on the work of Donald Horowitz, *Ethnic Groups in Conflict* (Berkeley: University of California Press, 1985), 281–87 in developing this argument.

24. See for example ibid., Crawford Young, *The Politics of Cultural Pluralism* (Madison: University of Wisconsin Press, 1976), ch. 7, and Gurr, *Minorities at Risk*.

authoritarian or not?

stated that self-determination claims threatening the territorial integrity of sovereign states was inconsistent with the principles of the United Nations Charter.[25] Within Africa, the OAU passed a landmark resolution in 1964 calling on all African states to respect the borders of neighboring states despite the arbitrary way in which the European colonial powers had originally established the borders. In that same year a conference of fifty-five nonaligned states passed similar resolutions making it clear that the legitimacy of self-determination claims was limited to decolonization.[26] Thus, states generally could not expect international support when they disputed the borders of *sovereign states* on the basis of irredentist or self-determination claims, and they may even have risked diplomatic and economic censure by the international community.

In Africa, where borders were often drawn up by colonial powers without regard to the location of ethnic populations, we find that of the thirty-three dispute cases on the continent only eight (about 25 percent) involved irredentist and self-determination claims.[27] Furthermore, of the fifty dispute cases in which the challenger was a state that achieved independence in the post–World War II period (where the political saliency of poorly drawn borders by former colonial powers might be expected to be the greatest), only eleven cases (22 percent) involved irredentist or self-determination claims by the challenger.

In the period between 1950 and 1990 challengers have not received international support in a large majority of cases when they pressed irredentist or self-determination claims in support of minorities against another sovereign state. For example, Somalia has found itself diplomatically isolated within Africa since the early 1960s as a result of its claims against Ethiopia and Kenya, and Pakistan has been unable to generate strong support at the United Nations to pressure India to accept a plebiscite in the disputed territory of Kashmir. Similarly, Afghanistan has not been able to build support at the United Nations or within the nonaligned movement for its dispute with Pakistan over the fate of Pathan tribes along its border.[28] The one clear exception to this pattern has been

---

25. See Halperin and Scheffer, *Self-Determination in the New World Order,* 21.

26. See Touval, *The Boundary Politics of Independent Africa,* 86–93.

27. My findings on the relative unimportance of irredentist claims as the source of conflict in territorial disputes across Africa is similar to the findings in ibid., ch. 2 and J. Barron Boyd, "African Boundary Conflict," *African Studies Review* 23, no. 3 (1979): 1–14.

28. See Touval, *The Boundary Politics of Independent Africa,* chs. 4–5; Sisir Gupta, *Kashmir: A Study in India-Pakistan Relations* (Bombay: Asia Publishing House, 1966); Ravi Nanda, *Indo-Pak Detente* (New Delhi: Lancers Books, 1989); and Kulwant Kaur, *Pak-Afghanistan Relations* (New Delhi: Deep & Deep Publications, 1985).

the ability of Arab states to build support for their claims at the U
Nations in their dispute with Israel.[29]

In sum, the weak support for the hypothesis that ethnic minorities
divided by state borders will often become a source of territorial conflict
reflects the fact that (*a*) treatment of ethnic minorities has been diffused
as a political issue by accommodative state policies, and (*b*) there are
also potential domestic political risks in many developing countries for
state leaders to treat the right to self-determination as a salient issue.

The International Context of Decisions to Dispute Territory

In this section we will examine what impact international political and
military conditions played in the decisions of challenger states to dispute
territory. The answer is that strategic calculations played an important
but not predominant role.

The first important finding is that the balance of conventional military forces between challenger and target *did not* have a powerful effect
on the decisions of the challenger to dispute territory. In table 3 we see
that the coefficient for the balance of forces variable is positive, as
expected by H5.1, but the coefficient is not significant (*t*-ratio = 0.50).
In table 5 the marginal impact of the balance of forces variable is presented, and the results reveal that as the challenger moves from a very
weak to a very strong military position the probability of a territorial
dispute between challenger and target is essentially unchanged. The
unimportance of the military balance in explaining why challengers disputed territory is clearly seen by the fact that only about 10 percent of all
the dispute years (306/3,039) involved challengers who enjoyed clear
military superiority over the target, that is, a four-to-one or greater
advantage in the balance of forces. Furthermore, in only about 26 percent of the years in which the challenger enjoyed such a military advantage did it press a territorial claim against the target (306/1,192). These
findings seem to run *directly counter* to the realist expectation that the
stronger a challenger state is militarily, the more likely the challenger
should confront its weaker neighbor with territorial claims.

---

29. The reluctance of states to challenge the territorial integrity of other states on
the grounds of self-determination is even present among states at war with one another.
The United States, during and after the Gulf War, failed to give strong support to the
Kurds within Iraq who sought to establish an independent Kurdish state for fear that such
support would be too destabilizing for allies such as Turkey, which also has a Kurdish
population. See Lawrence Freedman and Efraim Karsh, *The Gulf Conflict 1990–1991*
(Princeton: Princeton University Press, 1993), ch. 30.

TABLE 5.   The Marginal Impact of Variables Measuring the International Context on the Probability of Disputing Territory

Change in Value of Explanatory Variable	Change in Probability of Territorial Dispute (%)
Balance of Military Forces	
The ratio of challenger to target capabilities varies from 1/9 to 9/1	+0.7
Prior Gain of Territory by Challenger	
Has the challenger attained a net gain of territory at the expense of the target as a result of prior settlements and/or military victory?	
No vs. Yes	−6.4
Common Security Ties	
Are challenger and target military alliance partners?	
No vs. Yes	−9.6
Prior Settlement	
Has the challenger previously signed an agreement that clearly defined its border with the target?	
No vs. Yes	−10.4

Note: See the note to table 4 for a description of how the changes in the probability of a territorial dispute were calculated.

If we examine the population of nondispute dyads in appendix B, we find a number of cases in which powerful states did not advance territorial claims. For example, Brazil did not seek territorial gains against smaller neighbors such as Colombia, Paraguay, or Guyana; the Soviet Union did not dispute its borders with neighbors such as Finland, Afghanistan, or Outer Mongolia; Iraq did not press demands against Jordan; and India did not challenge its border with Burma. Furthermore, in the population of dispute cases we also find a number of examples in which very strong challengers were involved in disputes for only a relatively short period of time, even though the challenger did not compel the weaker target to settle the dispute on terms favored by the challenger: China vs. Afghanistan, Burma, and Nepal, and the Soviet Union vs. Iran and Turkey.

Why is it that powerful challengers in these cases did not exploit a decisive advantage in military capabilities to overturn the territorial status quo? One explanation is that very strong challengers prior to 1950 had already altered the territorial status quo in their favor and as a result were satisfied. Indeed, the control variable for the prior gain of territory by the challenger was included in the equation to take this possibility into account. This control variable, in fact, has a negative and significant coefficient as expected (*t*-ratio = −6.84) and in table 5 we see that the probability of a dispute decreases by about 6 percent when the challenger had previously gained territory.[30] The absence of a prior gain of territory is quite close to being a necessary condition for a dispute in the postwar period. Approximately only 6 percent of all the dispute years involved challengers who had previously gained territory from the target (193/3,039) and close to 90 percent of all years coded as a prior gain for the challenger were nondispute years. There were only a handful of cases in which the challenger had previously gained territory from the target but continued to press for more territorial gains: Dutch claims against West Germany in the early 1950s despite prior gains in 1949; Morocco's continuing claims to Spanish enclaves and islands despite the Spanish surrender of the Western Sahara in 1975; Somalia's claims against Kenya despite prior gains in a 1924 agreement between Italy and the British; Somalia's claims against Djibouti despite territorial gains secured in 1935; and Soviet claims against Iran despite gains achieved in 1828.[31]

If we examine the nondispute cases in which the challenger had previously gained territory, we do find a number of challengers who were in fact much stronger than the target: Brazil vs. Paraguay, Venezuela, and Colombia; Argentina vs. Paraguay; the Soviet Union vs. Finland and Czechoslovakia; United Kingdom (Sierra Leone) vs. Liberia; Turkey vs. Syria; India vs. Burma; and UK (Malaysia) vs. Thailand. Thus, one important reason why there is not a stronger correlation between military strength and territorial disputes is that powerful challengers have already secured a change in the territorial status quo to their favor.[32]

This, however, does not provide a complete explanation for the weak findings. It is not possible to construct a convincing realist type explanation for why we find many examples of very weak states disputing the borders of their powerful neighbors. The logic of H5.1 clearly predicts that weak states should be deterred from initiating disputes since they lack the credible threat of force to back up their territorial

---

30. The modest marginal impact for this variable to a large extent is a reflection of the fact that in the marginal impact analysis the baseline probability of a challenger being involved in a territorial dispute is only about 11 percent. Thus, it is difficult for variables that *reduce* the likelihood of a dispute to have large substantive effects when the probabilities are so low to begin with. This caveat, therefore, applies equally well to the results concerning common security ties and prior agreements discussed below.

31. See Gary Goertz and Paul Diehl, *Territorial Changes and International Conflict* (New York: Routledge, 1992), 149–59.

32. See ibid., and Ireland, *Boundaries, Possessions, and Conflicts in South America,* 109–15, 117–23, 138–44.

claims. Nevertheless, we find in Central America and the Caribbean that states such as Honduras, Nicaragua, Panama, and Cuba all had (or continue to have) claims against territory held by the United States. In Europe, Ireland has demanded that the British withdraw from Northern Ireland, while off the coast of Africa states such as Comoros, Madagascar, Mauritius, and Seychelles have all challenged French control of various islands, and Lesotho has claimed large sections of South African territory. In all of these cases the challenger state did not have a credible military option to threaten the target's control of territory but nevertheless initiated disputes.

A common thread linking many of these cases is that the challenger was disputing colonial or overseas territory of the target state. This suggests that challenger beliefs about the international as well domestic political legitimacy of their territorial claims, that is, support for decolonization and/or the termination of "unequal" treaties, often took precedence over strategic assessments of relative bargaining power based on comparative military strength. Indeed, as I describe below, challengers frequently sought to legitimize their territorial claims by asserting that their actions supported the goal of decolonization.

The second result in table 3 is that a military alliance between challenger and target was associated with a lower probability of a territorial dispute. This inverse relationship is consistent with H11.1 and suggests that the challenger's desire to maintain the diplomatic and military support of its ally provided an incentive for the challenger to avoid actions likely to be viewed by the ally as hostile. The negative coefficient is highly significant (t-ratio $= -20.45$) and has a moderate substantive effect in the marginal impact analysis. In table 5 we see that shared alliance ties reduce the likelihood of a territorial dispute by almost 10 percent. The absence of an alliance between challenger and target was not a necessary condition for a dispute to exist, but in almost 72 percent of all dispute years there were no alliance ties between the two countries (2,173/3,039). At the same time, in about 77 percent of all the years that the challenger and target were military allies there was no territorial dispute between the two states (2,890/3,756).

Common alliance ties seem most important in explaining the relative absence of conflict among Western European NATO member states and among members of the Arab League who were front-line states in the conflict with Israel (Syria, Jordan, Iraq, and Lebanon). In these regions, alliance partners were not involved in a large number of disputes and when they were, many were relatively short-lived. Warsaw Pact members from Eastern Europe were also not involved in territorial disputes with one another, but the explanation for the absence of conflict should be attributed largely to Soviet military hegemony and not the strong security interests linking the Eastern European states to one another.[33]

In contrast, common alliance ties in Latin America did not seem to act as a strong deterrent to a challenger confronting its neighbor: allied states in the region were roughly divided between dispute and nondispute cases. The differences between the Western European and Arab cases and the Latin American cases point to a general finding. Shared alliance ties were less likely to prevent conflict if the challenger and target did not face what was perceived to be a common and threatening adversary. In Latin America the Rio Pact was originally designed to counter hostile intervention from major powers outside the region, and in the postwar period there was no credible threat of such intervention.[34] The primary security threats came from within the region itself where, in some cases (Argentina vs. Chile and Ecuador vs. Peru) allies were likely to view *one another* as primary security threats (a similar situation applied to Turkey and Greece within NATO), or states would support rebel groups seeking to overthrow neighboring governments (e.g., Cuba's support for the overthrow of conservative dictatorships in Central America). In either case, formal allies within the region were not that important to a challenger in responding to the security threats that it may have faced. Instead, the United States, as the dominant power within the alliance, was the one state that leaders from Central and South America generally turned to for security assistance if it was requested.[35]

Among allies within Western Europe or the Middle East, however, there was a much stronger perception of a security threat, providing a more compelling reason for allies to cooperate and avoid protracted

33. See for example David Holloway and Jane Sharp, eds., *The Warsaw Pact: Alliance in Transition?* (Ithaca: Cornell University Press, 1984) and Jan Triska, ed., *Dominant Powers and Subordinate States* (Durham: Duke University Press, 1986).

34. Prior to World War II the United States had been primarily concerned with preventing intervention by the major European powers (Germany, France, and Britain). However, after 1945, as a result of the cold war, the primary outside threat to the region as perceived by the United States was the Soviet Union. The Soviet Union, however, lacked the capacity to project its military capabilities in Central and South America. Cuba could have become the local base from which the Soviets could have developed such a capacity, but in the resolution of the Cuban Missile Crisis in 1962 the Soviets agreed not to deploy or station offensive military forces in Cuba.

35. See for example Jerome Slater, *The OAS and United States Foreign Policy* (Columbus: Ohio State University, 1967); Ivan Musicant, *The Banana Wars: A History of United States Military Intervention in Latin America from the Spanish-American War to the Invasion of Panama* (New York: Macmillan, 1990); and Stephen Rabe, *Eisenhower and Latin America* (Chapel Hill: University of North Carolina Press, 1988).

conflict among themselves. Within Western Europe the threat of the
Soviet Union served in part to promote economic and military cooperation among NATO allies. Within the Middle East, intra-Arab divisions
certainly existed—Syria vs. Jordan, Syria vs. Iraq, and Egypt vs. Saudi
Arabia—but one of the few issues that at times compelled the Arab
countries to cooperate with one another was their hostility and opposition to Israel. For example, analysts have argued that irredentist senti-
ments in support of a Greater Syria have been prevalent in Syria for
decades, but the struggle against Israel has pressured Syrian leaders like
Asad to subordinate interests in a Greater Syria to the more immediate
strategic goal of trying to form a unified Arab coalition to oppose Israel
diplomatically and militarily.[36]

The territorial disputes that did exist between NATO members or
within the Arab League further illustrate the point that within large
multilateral defense pacts the cohesion of the alliance very much de-
pends on the strength of bilateral security relationships. Common membership in NATO has not prevented Greece and Turkey from escalating
their rivalry over Cyprus to the brink of war on several occasions since
the 1960s. The reason is that neither country looks to the other for
support against security threats. For example, Turkey viewed the Soviet
Union as a security threat, but in any scenario in which Turkey would
find itself confronted with some form of Soviet military action, the military response of Greece would be of little importance compared to the
support of NATO allies like the United States, Britain, or France. Thus,
Turkish leaders did not face a dilemma in choosing between competition
with Greece over Cyprus and the loss of a valuable ally. The same
argument can be applied to Iraq's dispute with Kuwait. Kuwait was not
at all important to Iraq as a military ally; it could offer no military
support in the event of armed conflicts with Iran or Israel. Thus, provok-
ing the hostility of Kuwait in a territorial dispute did not affect Iraq's
security position in disputes with other states.

The final hypothesis tested in this section was whether challengers
were less likely to confront a target if, prior to 1950, they had agreed to a
compromise settlement of a border dispute formalized in a written agree-

---

36. For a general discussion of rivalries within the Arab world see for example
Malcom Kerr, *The Arab Cold War* (New York: Oxford University Press, 1970) and Tawfig
Hasou, *The Struggle for the Arab World* (London: KPI Limited, 1985). For an analysis of
the Syrian case in more detail see Moshe Ma'oz and Avner Yaniv, eds., *Syria under Asad*
(New York: St. Martin's Press, 1986); Alasdair Drysdale and Raymond Hinnebusch, *Syria
and the Middle East Peace Process* (New York: Council on Foreign Relations Press, 1991);
ch. 3, Daniel Pipes, *Greater Syria* (New York: Oxford University Press, 1990); and Moshe
Ma'oz, *Asad* (New York: Grove Weidenfeld, 1988), chs. 9–10.

ment and/or had signed agreements resulting in a clearly delimited border. Thus, the question is whether the challenger would be willing to repudiate a signed agreement in an attempt to overturn the territorial status quo due to the desire to redress past losses, or as a response to new domestic or international circumstances that provide the opportunity or the incentive to change the territorial status quo. The results in table 3 indicate that states generally did honor past agreements (as predicted by H12) despite many potential reasons to contest them, for example, changes in military capabilities, a change in regimes and leaders with new priorities and problems, or the discovery of natural resources with economic potential. The negative coefficient for this variable is highly significant (t-ratio $= -33.56$), and in table 5 we see that the likelihood of a dispute decreases by about 10 percent given a prior formal settlement.[37] These results then provide strong support for H12 and the argument that states place considerable value on maintaining a reputation for honoring international agreements in order to support foreign policy goals in the future.[38] We find very strong patterns in the data when we look for necessary and sufficient conditions. Only about 10 percent of all dispute years involved challengers disputing territory despite the existence of a prior agreement that had clearly settled a dispute or defined the location of the border (311/3,039). Similarly, in less than 9 percent of all the years coded with a prior settlement in place was there a territorial dispute (311/3,673).

Among the 129 dispute cases there are only fifteen instances in which a challenger repudiated earlier agreements in pressing its territorial claim against the target. In almost all of these cases the challenger sought to justify its territorial claims by questioning either the legitimacy of the original agreement or by charging that the target had failed to abide by the terms of the original agreement. For example, in cases such as Morocco vs. Mauritania, Togo vs. Ghana, and Uganda vs. Tanzania the challenger questioned the agreement since it had originally been signed by its former colonial ruler, weakening its commitment to abide by it since it had little influence over the terms of the original agreement. In six other cases the challenger charged that the earlier agreements had been signed under conditions of coercive pressure, undercutting their validity (Cuba vs. United States, Nicaragua vs. Colombia, Ecuador vs. Peru, Venezuela vs. Guyana, China vs. the Soviet Union, Afghanistan

---

37. Once again, the size of the substantive effect for this variable is limited by the model's very low baseline prediction of how likely a challenger is to be involved in a territorial dispute.

38. Similar findings are reported by Stephen Kocs, "Territorial Disputes and Interstate War, 1945–1987," *Journal of Politics* 57, no. 1 (1995): 159–75.

vs. Pakistan, and the Soviet Union vs. Turkey). For example, Venezuela in its dispute with Guyana denounced in 1962 an earlier settlement based on a ruling by a court of arbitration in 1899. Venezuela claimed that the original award, which favored Guyana, was not valid in part because the United States coerced Venezuela into accepting the award and because the integrity of the tribunal was compromised by political deals involving the British.[39] China has disputed its border with the Soviet Union on the grounds that previously signed agreements were invalid because they were "unequal treaties" imposed on China by an imperialistic Russia.[40] Finally, Iran in 1969 renounced a 1937 agreement on the Shatt-al-Arab Waterway and justified its actions as a response to the failure of Iraq to respect the terms of the original agreement.[41]

If we examine the nondispute cases, however, we find eighty-two instances in which challengers had signed and were abiding by an agreement to establish a border or settle a territorial dispute with the target. In total, then, 85 percent (82/97) of the territorial or border settlements signed by the challenger before 1950 were still in force and adhered to by the challenger through the end of 1990.

As an extension of these findings on the importance of prior agreements in preventing disputes from reemerging, we can also look at all agreements reached to settle territorial disputes during the period between 1950 and 1990. Forty-five such agreements were concluded, and in only one case did the challenger subsequently repudiate a previously signed agreement: the decision by the Iraqi leader Saddam Hussein in September 1980 to abrogate the 1975 Algiers Accord settling the dispute with Iran over the Shatt-al-Arab Waterway. Even in this case, however, the renunciation of the agreement was justified as a response to the alleged failure of Iran to adhere to the terms of the 1975 Accord. In particular, Iran was charged with continuing to occupy territory that it was obligated to withdraw from and supporting the Kurdish rebellion within Iraq.[42] In total, then, between 1816 and 1990 142 border pacts and territorial dispute settlements were concluded, and in 1995, 126 of those agreements (or about 89 percent) remained in force with the former challenger state honoring the terms of the agreement.

39. See Jacqueline Anne Braveboy-Wagner, *The Venezuela-Guyana Border Dispute* (Boulder: Westview Press, 1984), ch. 6.

40. See Day *Border and Territorial Disputes,* 261.

41. See J. M. Abdulghani, *Iraq and Iran: The Years of Crisis* (Baltimore: Johns Hopkins University Press, 1984), 51 and S. H. Amin, *International and Legal Problems of the Gulf* (London: Middle East and North African Studies Press Limited, 1981), 75–80.

42. See Abdulghani, *Iraq and Iran,* 202–4.

The Domestic Context of Decisions to Dispute Territory

In this section I summarize the results of the logit analysis regarding what impact the domestic political setting of the challenger had on dispute behavior. The results in table 3 provide very strong support for the conclusion that a past history of conflict with the target generates strong domestic political incentives for leaders to remain involved in territorial disputes with their historical adversary.

When territorial disputes become protracted and intractable, leaders within the challenger have very few political incentives to try to break out of a deadlock with the target. Thus, a history of an unresolved territorial dispute with the target prior to World War II was strongly associated with a dispute between the two countries in the post-1950 period, as predicted by H13. The coefficient is large and highly significant (*t*-ratio = 30.90). In table 6 we see that a prior history of an unresolved dispute increased the likelihood of a territorial dispute by a dramatic 73 percent. About one-half of all dispute years post-1950 were preceded by unresolved territorial conflict between challenger and target (1,537/3,039) and in 90 percent of all years in which a prior dispute was coded as existing there was a dispute in the post–World War II period (1,337/1,701). In the dataset there were fifty-eight cases coded for the presence of prior unresolved dispute prior to World War II, and

TABLE 6. The Marginal Impact of Variables Measuring the Domestic Context on the Probability of Disputing Territory

Change in Value of Explanatory Variable	Change in Probability of Territorial Dispute(%)
Prior Unsettled Dispute	
Was challenger involved in an unresolved territorial dispute with the target prior to World War II?	
No vs. Yes	+73.0
Previous Loss of Territory by Challenger	
Has the challenger suffered a net loss of territory to the target as a result of prior settlements and/or military defeats?	
No vs. Yes	+42.2
Decolonization Norm	
Is the territory of the target a colony or overseas dependency?	
No vs. Yes	+9.4

Note: See the note to table 4 for a description of how the changes in the probability of a territorial dispute were calculated.

in fifty-four cases (or 93 percent) there was a dispute in the post-1950 period. Thus, an unresolved dispute prior to World War II was quite close to being a sufficient condition for a dispute after 1950.[43]

It is important to emphasize that this variable attempts to capture what impact a *history of territorial conflict has on the behavior of political leaders within the challenger state.* Other variables in the equation, as discussed previously, attempt to measure more directly the economic, political, and military issues at stake in disputing territory. The variable for a past unresolved conflict, however, attempts only to measure the domestic political impact that a past dispute has independent of the strategic, economic, or political issues at stake in the dispute over territory. The argument of H13 is that once a territorial dispute emerges, irrespective of the initial issues at stake, it will become part of the domestic political debate and discourse and a foreign policy issue that leaders will package to advance their own domestic political standing and hold on office. In a very important sense, then, the issues at stake in a dispute will evolve to include salient domestic political concerns for leaders within the challenger distinct from the specific justifications and motives behind the original emergence of the conflict.

The strong findings reflect the fact that many postwar territorial disputes have a history of conflict extending back into the interwar period and as far back as the early nineteenth century for a smaller number of cases. It is essential that this historical context be taken into account, since the argument of H13 is that territorial disputes can become self-sustaining because of domestic political forces favoring continued conflict created by years of adversarial relations. Thus, once the dispute with the target has become an important foreign policy issue, the next generation of political leaders find it in their interest to maintain the dispute.

When we examine the fifty-four dispute cases with a history of an unresolved territorial conflict, we find two sets of political forces within the challenger strongly favoring the continuation of territorial disputes over time: (1) broadly based support within the population for the territorial claims against the target, based in part on prior mobilization of the population by the political leadership, and (2) more narrowly based but still politically powerful support within key political actors such as the military, the foreign policy bureaucracy, or the ruling political elite.

---

43. The cases that do not support the hypothesis are: (1) Haiti vs. United States over Navassa Island, (2) Argentina vs. Paraguay over the delimitation of a short section of the border along the Polcomayo River, (3) Czechoslovakia vs. Poland over the Teschen region annexed by Poland in 1938, and (4) Bulgaria vs. Romania over the southern Dobrudja region ceded to Romania in 1913.

For example, a history of past conflict and unresolved territorial disputes was particularly evident for cases in Latin America. In this region several postwar disputes had a history of conflict dating back to the nineteenth century: Argentina vs. Chile and Great Britain; Ecuador vs. Peru; Bolivia vs. Chile; Guatemala vs. Great Britain; and Honduras vs. El Salvador. Over this protracted period of dispute, numerous diplomatic and militarized confrontations between challenger and target had taken place, including several wars.[44] The domestic political consequence was that the territorial dispute with the target became a politically charged issue within the challenger. Against this backdrop, in countries such as Argentina, Ecuador, Bolivia, Honduras, and Guatemala, the failure to maintain a claim to territory would have been portrayed by political opposition as a major foreign policy setback for the current regime in power.[45]

Another region where a prior history of conflict was quite important was the Middle East. In the interwar period the Arab-Israeli conflict emerged as a very contentious and politicized issue within the Arab world as Great Britain struggled to devise an acceptable plan for the future status of Palestine. By the time Israel declared its independence in 1948, Arab leaders in countries such as Egypt, Syria, Jordan, Lebanon, and Iraq could depend on strong domestic political support for a policy of confrontation and hostility.[46] The other set of Middle

---

44. For example, Argentina and Chile were involved in multiple militarized disputes short of war dating back to the late nineteenth century; Chile and Bolivia fought against one another in the Pacific War from 1879–1883; Nicaragua and Honduras were adversaries in the Central American War of 1907; and the long-standing territorial dispute between Ecuador and Peru escalated to large-scale armed conflict in 1941.

45. See for example Peter Calvert, *Boundary Disputes in Latin America* (London: Institute for the Study of Conflict, 1983); Ireland, *Boundaries, Possessions, and Conflicts in South America;* William Bianchi, *Belize: The Controversy between Guatemala and Great Britain over the Territory of British Honduras in Central America* (New York: Las Americas Publishing Co., 1959); Anthony DeSoto, *Bolivia's Right to an Access to the Sea* (Pasadena: Jensen Publishing Co., 1962); David Zook, *Zarumilla y Maranon: The Ecuador-Peru Dispute* (New York: Bookman Associates Inc., 1964); William Krieg, *Ecuadorean-Peruvian Rivalry in the Upper Amazon,* 2d ed. (Bethesda, MD: William Krieg, 1986); Heraldo Munoz and Joseph Tulchin, eds., *Latin American Nations in World Politics* (Boulder: Westview, 1984); Elizabeth Ferris and Jennie Lincoln, eds., *Latin American Foreign Policies* (Boulder: Westview, 1981); Elizabeth Ferris and Jennie Lincoln, eds., *The Dynamics of Latin American Foreign Policies* (Boulder: Westview, 1984).

46. A concise history of the emerging Arab-Israeli conflict in the interwar period is presented in Ritchie Ovendale, *The Origins of the Arab-Israeli Wars,* 2d ed. (London: Longman, 1992), chs. 1–7 and Mark Tessler, *A History of the Israeli-Palestinian Conflict* (Bloomington: Indiana University Press, 1994), chs. 3–4. Also see Pipes, *Greater Syria,* ch. 2 and Ma'oz, *Asad,* 45–48.

East dispute cases with a history of prior conflict involved the multiple claims of Saudi Arabia to the territory of its neighbors dating back to the 1920s and 1930s. In these cases there is less evidence of territorial disputes becoming an issue around which political leaders attempted to mobilize broad political support. Given the very closed nature of the Saudi political system and the lack of military strength, conflict with the British over territory was largely confined to the diplomatic level and was not highly publicized by the government (though militarized confrontations with the local armed forces of neighboring territories did take place frequently in the 1920s and 1930s). Certainly within the leadership of Saudi Arabia, however, the legitimacy and rationale for pressing territorial claims developed in the interwar period was widely accepted and served as the basis for Saudi territorial claims in the post–World War II period.[47]

One very important consequence of a history of conflictual relations with the target was that military establishments within challenger states often become strong supporters of claims to disputed territory advanced by their country's political leadership. For example, throughout much of South America, military establishments have utilized theories of geopolitics to support their country's claim to disputed territory in cases such as Argentina vs. Chile and Great Britain, Bolivia vs. Chile, Ecuador vs. Peru, and Venezuela vs. Guyana.[48] The characterization of the target as an adversary who unjustly controlled disputed territory also provided a convincing rationale for the military to argue for large defense budgets. Furthermore, a threatening international environment could be used by the military to justify a crackdown on domestic political opposition. The result was that in many countries the armed forces had strong institutional incentives to support a firm policy of continued opposition to the target, and in many territorial dispute cases the military had a history of extensive involvement in domestic politics, for example, China, Argentina, Pakistan, Greece, Turkey, Egypt, and Syria.[49]

---

47. The history of Saudi claims and negotiations with the British presented in J. B. Kelly, *Arabia, the Gulf and the West* (London: Weidenfeld and Nicholson, 1980), and Albaharna, *The Arabian Gulf States*. Also see Safran, *Saudi Arabia*, ch. 3.

48. See Jack Child, *Geopolitics and Conflict in South America* (New York: Praeger, 1985).

49. There is a very large literature on civil-military relations within developing countries. The principal works that focus on the role of the military in challenger states involved in territorial disputes includes Raymond Hinnebusch, *Egyptian Politics under Sadat* (Cambridge: Cambridge University Press, 1985), 12–17, 99–111, 125–31; Raymond Baker, *Egypt's Uncertain Revolution under Nasser and Sadat* (Cambridge: Harvard University Press, 1978), 48–60, 158–61; Drysdale and Hinnebusch, *Syria and the Middle East Peace Process*, ch. 2, 4; Ma'oz, *Asad*, ch. 5; Hasan-Askari Rizvi, *The Military and Politics*

This line of argument can also be extended to include those territorial disputes with a history of protracted conflict since the end of World War II, since even one or two decades of adversarial relations with a target can have significant domestic political ramifications within the challenger. Thus, if we examine data on military expenditures from the early 1960s to late 1980s for challenger states who have been engaged in protracted and conflictual territorial disputes with target states, both before and after World War II, we find that levels of military spending are quite high. In cases such as Argentina vs. Chile; Greece vs. Turkey; Syria and Egypt vs. Israel; Pakistan vs. India; Somalia vs. Ethiopia; China vs. India, the Soviet Union, and Vietnam; and North Korea vs. South Korea we find that military expenditures are consistently high for challenger (as well as target) states. The ratios of military expenditures to gross national product or total government spending for these states are always above the regional average, typically about twice as high and sometimes six to seven times greater.[50]

Political leaders in many challenger countries, then, risked the opposition of the military if they did not maintain a territorial claim against the target, and in many authoritarian regimes the risk for political leaders included the threat of a coup supported by the military to remove them from power. In sum, viewed from the perspective of domestic politics within the challenger, the status quo position of maintaining a

in Pakistan 1947–86, 3d ed. (Lahore: Progressive Publishers, 1986); Mohammad Asghar Khan, *Generals in Politics, Pakistan 1958–1982* (New Delhi: Vikas, 1983); Stephen Cohen, *Pakistan Army* (Berkeley: University of California Press, 1984); Richard Clogg and George Yannopoulos, eds., *Greece under Military Rule* (New York: Basic Books, 1972); C. M. Woodhouse, *The Rise and Fall of the Greek Colonels* (London: Granada, 1985); Constantine Danopoulos, *Warriors and Politicians in Modern Greece* (Chapel Hill: Documentary Publications, 1985); David Rock, *Authoritarian Argentina* (Berkeley: University of California Press, 1993), ch. 7; Gary Wynia, *Argentina: Illusions and Realities* (New York: Holmes & Meier, 1992), ch. 4; Karen Remmer, *Military Rule in Latin America* (Boston: Unwin Hyman, 1989); Amos Perlmutter, *The Military and Politics in Modern Times* (New Haven: Yale University Press, 1977), chs. 5–6; Edward Olsen and Stephen Jurika, eds., *The Armed Forces in Contemporary Asian Societies* (Boulder: Westview, 1986); Stephanie Neuman, ed., *Defense Planning in Less-Industrialized States* (Lexington, MA: Lexington Books, 1984); Michael Swaine, *The Military and Political Succession in China* (Santa Monica: RAND, 1992); A. Doak Barnett, *The Making of Foreign Policy in China* (Boulder: Westview, 1985), 96–104.

50. See *World Military Expenditures and Arms Transfers 1963–1973* (Washington, D.C.: United States Arms Control and Disarmament Agency, 1974); 14–66, *World Military Expenditures and Arms Transfers 1986* (Washington, D.C.: United States Arms Control and Disarmament Agency, 1987), 59–100; and *World Military Expenditures and Arms Transfers 1990* (Washington, D.C.: United States Arms Control and Disarmament Agency, 1991), 47–88.

territorial dispute with a target was an attractive policy for leaders to follow, carrying with it far fewer risks than having to justify, in the face of likely strong opposition, why a territorial claim should not be maintained in the postwar period.

The second major finding in table 3 regarding the domestic political setting is that if the challenger had previously lost territory to the target, the challenger was very likely to seek the recovery of that territory by disputing its border with the target (as proposed by H15). The coefficient for the loss of territory variable is positive and highly significant (t-ratio = 21.77), and it has a very potent impact on the probability of a territorial dispute. In table 6 we see that the challenger is 42 percent more likely to be in a dispute if it had previously suffered a loss of territory at the hands of the target. Thus, regardless of what the more tangible and direct value of disputed territory may be, the desire of political leaders to show their commitment to the goal of recovering lost national territory is a foreign policy goal that will be certain to generate domestic political support and an issue on which it would be difficult for political opponents to contest the existing leadership.

In total, there were fifty-eight dispute cases in which the challenger was seeking to redress past territorial losses, while there were only twenty-four nondispute cases in which the challenger did not protest the loss of territory. When these fifty-eight cases are examined in more detail, we can see the political dynamics predicted by H15. In case after case, political leaders in the challenger state made repeated references to the injustice suffered by their country in the past and the need to restore national honor by the return of the disputed territory. In adopting such a policy of confrontation with the target, political leaders within the challenger consistently mobilized the support of the general population as well as key groups such as the military. This general pattern of elites generating domestic support by appealing to nationalism and patriotism was evident in a broad range of cases from South America to the Far East. In South America examples would include the Argentine claim to the Falkland/Malvinas Islands, which the British have occupied since the early nineteenth century, Bolivia's long-standing claim to the coastal territory of Chile stemming from its defeat in the Pacific War of 1879–1884, and Ecuador's rejection of the Rio Protocol, which required Ecuador to make territorial concessions following its military defeat at the hands of Peru in 1941.[51] In Europe, West Germany was reluctant to

---

51. See for example Krieg, *Ecuadorean-Peruvian Rivalry in the Upper Amazon;* DeSoto, *Bolivia's Right to an Access to the Sea;* and Douglas Kinney, *National Interest/ National Honor: The Diplomacy of the Falklands Crisis* (New York: Praeger, 1989).

accept the loss of German territory to Poland along the Oder-Neisse Line as a result of Germany's defeat in World War II,[52] while in the Middle East the Israeli occupation of the Golan Heights following the Six Day War of 1967 has been stridently opposed by President Asad within Syria.[53] Finally, in the Far East, Japan has refused to accept the loss of islands to the Soviet Union following defeat in World War II.[54]

The final result in table 3 to be discussed is that when leaders could portray their territorial claims as supporting decolonization and self-determination, a dispute with the target was more likely. As predicted by H16, colonial and overseas borders were quite likely to be disputed by leaders of developing countries who could consistently rally strong domestic political support for such territorial claims given the widespread support for the norm of decolonization in the postwar period. The large coefficient and strong *t*-ratio (6.45) provides firm support for H16. In table 6 we see that the likelihood of a territorial dispute increases by about 9 percent when there is a colonial border. Interestingly, the supportive results here contrast with the earlier finding that irredentist or self-determination claims against sovereign states in support of ethnic minorities was not a strong predictor of territorial disputes in the postwar period. In total, about 32 percent of all dispute years involved colonial borders (965/3,039), while close to 71 percent of all years coded for the presence of colonial borders were disputed (965/1,365).

Challengers who have disputed colonial territory have rarely encountered active opposition from the international community, and such a policy has consistently worked to the leaders' domestic political advantage. For example, the United Nations failed to even sanction India for using military force to wrest control of Goa from Portugal in 1961, and the decision to use force was strongly supported within India.[55] The typical pattern was that challengers either received international support for their claims, or the United Nations and regional organizations failed to become actively involved in the dispute. The United Nations would only take a neutral stance when it believed there was evidence that the

---

52. See for example Wolfram Hanrieder, *Germany, America, Europe: Forty Years of German Policy* (New Haven: Yale University Press, 1989), chs. 6–7.

53. See Drysdale and Hinnebusch, *Syria and the Middle East Peace Process,* chs. 3–4 and Ma'oz, *Asad,* ch. 8.

54. See Rajendra Jain, *The USSR and Japan, 1945–1980* (Atlantic Highlands, NJ: Humanities Press, 1981); William Nimmo, *Japan and Russia* (Westport, CT: Greenwood Press, 1994); and Donald Hellmann, *Japanese Foreign Policy and Domestic Politics* (Berkeley: University of California Press, 1969).

55. See Leo Lawrence, *Nehru Seizes Goa* (New York: Pageant Press, 1963), ch. 8 and Arthur Rubinoff, *India's Use of Force in Goa* (Bombay: Popular Prakashan, 1971), 94–99.

population of the target did not desire unification with the challenger. For example, in the British-Argentine dispute over the Falklands, the United Nations consistently encouraged both parties to negotiate a settlement respecting the rights of the local population, while within Argentina opposition to British control of the islands was an issue generating widespread support across the entire political spectrum.[56] In the Guatemalan dispute with the British over Belize, Guatemalan governments increasingly found themselves isolated regionally and at the United Nations from the mid-1970s onwards, but political opposition within Guatemala did not challenge ruling governments on the basis of their policy toward Belize.[57] The norm of decolonization was also openly used by political leaders to legitimize attacks on the right of states to maintain foreign military bases in cases such as Cuba vs. the United States over Guantanamo Bay, Egypt vs. the United Kingdom over the Suez Canal, or Tunisia vs. France and the Bizerte Naval Base. Once again, in each of these cases we find widespread domestic political support within the challenger for confronting the target.[58]

Conclusion

We began this chapter by asking the simple question, Why do the leaders of states become involved in territorial disputes with their neighbors? To answer this question I turned to a set of hypotheses derived from the modified realist model presented in chapter 3. Statistical tests were then utilized to assess the relative explanatory power of the hypotheses, and overall the results produced considerable support for the modified realist model.

The modified realist model draws on the basic insights of a traditional realist approach by examining the military security interests of states in disputing territory and the ability of state leaders to pursue those interests given their country's international political-military situation. The empirical results clearly indicate that state leaders seek to gain control of territory that will strengthen their country's security position,

---

56. See Kinney, *National Interest/National Honor;* T. V. Paul, *Asymmetric Conflicts: War Initiation by Weaker Powers* (Cambridge: Cambridge University Press, 1994), ch. 8; and Michael Charlton, *The Little Platoon: Diplomacy and the Falklands Dispute* (New York: Blackwell, 1989).

57. See Day, *Border and Territorial Disputes,* 346–63 and Zammit, *The Belize Issue.*

58. See Peter Mansfield, *The British in Egypt* (New York: Holt, Rinehart, Winston, 1971), 295–312; Robert Butterworth, *Managing Interstate Conflict, 1945–74* (Pittsburgh: University Center for International Studies, University of Pittsburgh, 1976), 314–16; and Day, *Border and Territorial Disputes,* 363–67.

and they are also sensitive to the security costs of disputing the territory of allies and rejecting prior international agreements establishing borders with its neighbors.

The modified realist model, however, extends beyond the confines of the traditional realist approach by incorporating in a systematic way the impact of domestic politics on the decision to dispute territory. The inclusion of domestic politics into the model improves its explanatory power significantly. Individually, the coefficients for domestic-level variables were consistently significant and often had large substantive effects. Specifically, domestic politics provided three basic reasons for political leaders to be involved in territorial disputes: (1) to try to gain control over valuable natural resources for their economic potential and development, (2) to protest the prior loss of national territory and to generate popular support with a policy of seeking to recover the lost territory, and, most importantly, (3) to avoid the political controversy of not maintaining a territorial claim in the context of a long-standing dispute with a neighboring state over a disputed border.

Collectively, the added insight provided by the inclusion of the domestic-level variables can be assessed by removing these variables from the equation tested and then rerunning the analysis with only variables from a traditional realist model. If the domestic-level variables collectively make an important contribution to explaining decisions to dispute territory, then the log-likelihood values for the two equations should be significantly different. In table 7 the logit results for the traditional realist model are reported, and if we compare the log-likelihood value from this equation with the comparable value for the equation reported in table 3, we find that the values are significantly different ($v = 2244.6$, $df = 5$, $p < .001$).[59]

The point of this comparison is not to determine whether domestic-level variables are more or less powerful in explaining decisions to dispute territory than variables that measure international conditions. Rather, the comparison is meant to reinforce the underlying theoretical foundation of the modified realist model, that is, the most powerful explanations of foreign policy will be premised on the recognition that state leaders are simultaneously engaged in a two-level game of strategic interaction with both foreign adversaries and domestic political opponents. The empirical

---

59. The following formula was utilized to determine significance levels: $v = -2$ [log-likelihood function value x_1 − log-likelihood function value x_2] with $x_2 - x_1$ degrees of freedom and where x_1 and x_2 represent equation 1 and 2 respectively. The significance level of the calculated value was then checked on a chi-square distribution. See G. S. Maddala, *Limited-Dependent and Qualitative Variables in Econometrics* (Cambridge: Cambridge University Press, 1983), 39–40.

CHAPTER 5

Political and Military Conflict
over Disputed Territory

In this chapter I empirically analyze the conflict behavior of states that
were involved in territorial disputes between 1950 and 1990. Hypotheses will be tested on what domestic and international conditions lead a
challenger state to engage in high versus low levels of diplomatic and
military conflict over disputed territory. If we examine levels of conflict
in territorial dispute cases, we find that challenger states are typically
not engaged in high levels of confrontation; over 50 percent of the
annual observations are characterized by low levels of diplomatic conflict. Indeed, in approximately one-half of the 129 territorial dispute
cases the challenger state did *not even once* threaten or resort to the
use of military force in an attempt to gain control of disputed territory.
Aggressive diplomatic and political behavior by the challenger
state accounts for about 32 percent of the annual observations and
includes actions such as restrictions on economic and diplomatic relations, hostile propaganda and rhetoric, as well as attempts to destabilize the regime of the target. Militarized confrontations, in which the
challenger issues verbal threats and/or engages in the movement and
buildup of military forces, constitute about 11 percent of the annual
observations. These militarized confrontations are concentrated in disputes over a relatively small number of borders—approximately twenty
cases.
The puzzle then is to try and differentiate between those conditions
that promote relatively stable and peaceful relations and those that
prompt leaders to pursue territorial claims in an aggressive and confrontational manner. This is the central question I address in this chapter. As
in the previous chapter, I first describe the equation to be tested as well
as the research design for empirical analysis. I then present the results of
the statistical analysis and examine a number of individual cases to help
illustrate the statistical findings. I conclude the chapter with a discussion
of the added explanatory power provided by the modified realist model
in comparison to a traditional realist model.

Equation to Be Tested

From the modified realist model presented in chapter 3 a number of testable hypotheses were derived to explain the level of diplomatic and military conflict over disputed territory. The empirical findings from chapter 3 indicated that the potential for strategic and economic gains or the avoidance of domestic political losses were the primary factors explaining why challengers were involved in territorial disputes. In this chapter, however, the potential military and international political costs of escalating a dispute play a greater role, and the modified realist model in this chapter portrays the decisions of a challenger as involving a more complex interplay of cost-benefit calculations. This is particularly true regarding the effects of the international environment on challenger decisions. For example, in the previous chapter only four hypotheses were tested concerning the impact of international-level variables. In contrast, in this chapter, seven international-level hypotheses are tested with each of the additional hypotheses centering on the timing or prospects for successfully escalating a territorial dispute. At the same time, there are also a number of hypotheses regarding the role that domestic political factors can play in the escalation of disputes. The broad expectation then is that both domestic and international-level variables should produce strong and consistent effects in the statistical analysis.

The equation to be tested in this chapter is listed below. For each variable in the equation I include the hypothesis number and expected sign of the coefficient.

The endogenous variable y = the level of diplomatic and military conflict initiated by a challenger against a target over bordering territory

c = constant term

The exogenous variables x_1 to x_{14} are specified as follows.

Issues at Stake

x_1 = strategic location of bordering territory (H1.1, positive)

x_2 = support for minorities along border of target with ethnic ties to the challenger (H2.1, positive)

x_3 = political unification based on common ethnic background between challenger and target populations (H3.1, positive)

x_4 = economic value of bordering territory (H4.2, negative)

International Context

x_5 = the balance of conventional military capabilities between challenger and target (H5.1, positive)

x_6 = challenger dispute involvement with other states (H6.1, negative)

x_7 = stalemate in negotiations (H7, positive)

x_8 = target attempt to change status quo (H8.1, positive)

x_9 = defeat in armed conflict for challenger (H9.1, negative)

x_{10} = deterrent alliance ties of target (H10, negative)

x_{11} = common security ties between challenger and target (H11.1, negative)

Domestic Political Context

x_{12} = prior militarized disputes between challenger and target (H13, positive)

x_{13} = democratic norms of challenger (H17.1, negative)

x_{14} = selection effects

u_t = error term

The endogenous variable (y) was coded on a three-point scale of diplomatic and military conflict initiated by the challenger over the disputed territory of the target. The scale is as follows.

0 = minimal or no diplomatic/political conflict over disputed territory. The challenger is involved in a territorial dispute, but there is very limited evidence of public confrontation over territory, and the dispute has no apparent adverse affect on bilateral relations between challenger and target. In such cases a challenger is either not actively pressing its claim against a target, or diplomatic interactions and negotiations over disputed territory are conducted without much publicity or conflict.

1 = moderate to high levels of diplomatic and political conflict over disputed territory. A challenger actively confronts a target over disputed territory, and the actions of a challenger include one or more of the following: (*a*) hostile rhetoric and public recriminations, (*b*) soliciting of third-party support in order to pressure a target into making concessions, (*c*) use of sanctions or restrictions on bilateral diplomatic, economic, or military ties as a result of the territorial dispute, and (*d*) efforts to overthrow or destabilize the government of a target in an attempt to induce a change in target policy over disputed territory.

2 = high levels of diplomatic pressure are coupled with militarized confrontations over disputed territory. A challenger, in addition to active and confrontational diplomatic actions, threatens or resorts to the use of military force against a target.

Each case was coded on an annual basis according to this three-point scale, and multiple sources were consulted to create a chronology of actions taken by the challenger related to the territorial dispute. When a militarized confrontation occurred a value of two was coded regardless of the level of conflict prior to or after the confrontation. If no such confrontation took place, however, then the case was coded according to which level of conflict occurred for the majority of the months during the year. The distribution of values on the endogenous variable was: approximately 57 percent of the cases (1,735) equaled zero, 32 percent of the cases (969) equaled one, and 11 percent of the cases (335) equaled two. Conflict and cooperation between challenger and target over *non*territorial issues were not included in the chronology. The principal sources relied upon to code the endogenous variables are listed in the bibliography at the end of appendix A. The operational measures for each of the exogenous variables are discussed in appendix C.

The dataset for this chapter consists of the 129 territorial disputes listed in appendix A. The dataset consists of 3,039 years of observations in which the challenger was disputing territory with a target, and the data on the endogenous and exogenous variables was collected on an annual basis for each of the dispute cases.[1]

Statistical Results and Case Analysis

An ordered probit model was used to test the equation, and the potential effects of selection bias were taken into account in the estimation.[2] The coefficients, robust standard errors, and significance levels for the probit analysis are presented in table 8.[3] Overall, the results provide substantial insight regarding what conditions play an important role in the decisions of a challenger state to apply diplomatic and military pressure against a target in a territorial dispute. Across domestic as well as international-level variables the estimated coefficients are uniformally in the predicted direction, a number of variables have large substantive effects, and the significance levels are quite high for many variables as well.

---

1. See appendix D for a more detailed discussion of the research design for the dataset utilized in this chapter.

2. See appendix D for a discussion of issues related to the estimation of the equation, including corrections for selection bias.

3. I checked for multicollinearity among the variables in the equation by regressing each of the exogenous variables on all of the remaining exogenous variables in a series of individual OLS runs. The r-squared values for each equation were then relied upon to assess to what extent multicollinearity was present. The r-squared values were not high indicating that multicollinearity was not a problem in the estimation of the equation. The r-squared values were between 0 and .20 for ten of the variables, between .2 and .3 for two variables, and between .3 and .4 for another two variables.

As in the previous chapter, additional tables are presented below (tables 9–11) to aid in the interpretation of the substantive effect of the coefficients in table 8. Each table provides information on how changes in the value of an exogenous variable are related to changes in the probability of low levels of diplomatic conflict ($y = 0$), high levels of diplomatic and political confrontation ($y = 1$), and the resort to the threat or use of military force ($y = 2$).

The discussion of the results will be divided into three sections. In the first section I consider how the underlying issues at stake in a territorial dispute were related to escalation. I then broaden the analysis in the next two sections to examine more fully the impact that international and domestic conditions had on the challenger's willingness to escalate the dispute with the target.

The Issues at Stake and the Escalation of Disputes

Hypotheses focusing on the military security and domestic political issues at stake were tested, and the results provided support for all of the

TABLE 8.   Ordered Probit Estimates of Level of Conflict among Territorial Dispute Cases, 1950–90

Explanatory Variables	Coefficient	Standard Errors	Significance Level
Constant	−0.139	0.147	—
Selection effects	−0.617	0.120	<.001
Issues at Stake			
Strategic location of territory	0.420	0.059	<.001
Ties to bordering minority	0.794	0.062	<.001
Political unification	0.745	0.063	<.001
Economic value of territory	−0.233	0.050	<.001
International Context			
Balance of military forces	0.808	0.104	<.001
Challenger disputes	−0.119	0.016	<.001
Stalemate in negotiations	0.689	0.063	<.001
Attempt to change status quo	0.397	0.061	<.001
Defeat in armed conflict	−0.198	0.034	<.001
Deterrent alliance	−0.069	0.054	<.10
Common security ties	−0.726	0.060	<.001
Domestic Context			
Prior militarized disputes	0.035	0.003	<.001
Democratic norms	−0.011	0.004	<.001

Note: Number of observations = 3,039; Log-likelihood = −2,300.7; Percentage of cases correctly predicted = 64.5; All significance levels based on one-tailed tests.

hypotheses though the results are stronger for the domestic-level hypotheses. Territorial disputes involving issues of ethnic irredentism or national unification were the most likely to escalate to high levels of diplomatic and military conflict. In contrast, for disputes in which economic issues were at stake the likelihood of escalation was far lower. Finally, disputes involving military security issues were likely to escalate, but they were not as dangerous as disputes in which ethnic irredentism and national unification were the issues at stake. Overall then the results clearly support the modified realist model and demonstrate the limits of a traditional realist approach. A traditional realist model was only partially supported even though a consistent relationship was found to exist between security issues and escalation. The reason is that a traditional realist model would predict that disputes involving security issues should be the *most conflictual,* but the results clearly indicate that certain disputes defined in terms of domestic political issues were prone to higher levels of escalation.

The first result in table 8 to examine in greater detail is that strategically valuable bordering territory was associated with an increased likelihood of conflict escalation by the challenger. The positive coefficient and strong t-ratio (7.11) for this variable indicate firm support for H1.1. In table 9 we see that this variable produces about a 15 percent increase in the probability of escalation to high levels of diplomatic and/or military conflict ($y = 1$ or 2).

In the previous chapter we found that the strategic location of bordering territory was a strong predictor of whether a challenger would become involved in a territorial dispute. The findings of this chapter build on these results by arguing that when strategic issues are at stake in territorial disputes, challenger states are more likely to adopt coercive diplomatic and military policies in an attempt to gain control of the disputed territory.

In total, there were twenty-five cases in which disputed territory was strategically located, and in about two-thirds of the cases the challenger did resort to generally high levels of diplomatic or military pressure. Examples would include the use of force by Iran to take control of the islands of Abu Masu and the Greater and Lesser Tunbs in 1971,[4] Iraqi diplomatic and military pressure on Kuwait to gain control of Warbah and Bubiyan Islands,[5] Argentina's military pressure against

---

4. See Rouhollah Ramazani, *Iran's Foreign Policy 1941–1973* (Charlottesville: University Press of Virginia, 1975), 415–35.

5. See David Finnie, *Shifting Lines in the Sand* (Cambridge: Harvard University Press, 1992), ch. 10 and Lawrence Freedman and Efraim Karsh, *The Gulf Conflict 1990–1991* (Princeton: Princeton University Press, 1993), chs. 1–3.

TABLE 9.   The Marginal Impact of Variables Measuring the Issues at Stake on the Level of Conflict over Disputed Territory

	Probability of Alternative Levels of Conflict (%)		
Change in Value of Explanatory Variable	$y = 0$	$y = 1$	$y = 2$
Strategic Location of Territory			
Is bordering territory strategically located?			
No vs. Yes	−15.1	+11.5	+3.6
Ties to Bordering Minorities			
Do bordering minority groups within the target share ties of language and ethnicity with the population of the challenger?			
No vs. Yes	−30.0	+20.5	+9.5
Political Unification			
Do the populations of challenger and target share ties of a common language and ethnicity?			
No vs. Yes	−28.0	+19.5	+8.5
Economic Value of Territory			
Are natural resources with export value located within/ proximate to bordering territory, or would control of bordering territory provide a port outlet to promote trade?			
No vs. Yes	+7.0	−5.9	−1.1

Note: The change in the probability of dispute escalation were calculated utilizing the coefficients from the equation presented in table 8. The value of a single explanatory variable is changed while all continuous variables in the equation are held at their mean or the modal value for dummy variables. The change in the location on the cumulative normal distribution is then converted into the percentage change in the level of conflict over disputed territory. See Gary King, *Unifying Political Methodology* (Cambridge: Cambridge University Press, 1989), 106–8.

Chile over disputed islands in the Beagle Channel during the late 1970s,[6] and the Egyptian and Syrian decisions to go to war in 1973 in an attempt to regain the lost territories of the Sinai and the Golan Heights.[7] In addition, the one clear case in which the challenger resorted to the use of military force to gain control of minerals of strategic value was the Libyan occupation of the uranium-rich Aozou Strip in 1972.[8] In the

6. See Alan Day, ed., *Border and Territorial Disputes,* 2d ed. (London: Longman, 1982), 335–37.

7. See for example Chaim Herzog, *The War of Atonement* (Boston: Little, Brown, 1975); Mohammed Heikal, *The Road to Ramadan* (New York: Ballantine Books, 1975); and Alasdair Drysdale and Raymond Hinnebusch, *Syria and the Middle East Peace Process* (New York: Council on Foreign Relations Press, 1991), 103–8.

8. See Benyamin Neuberger, *Involvement, Invasion and Withdrawal* (Tel Aviv: The Shiloah Center for Middle Eastern and African Studies, 1982), ch. 4.

remaining one-third of the cases the challenger did not escalate the dispute for a majority of years, and the explanation in many situations is the challenger's lack of military capabilities to threaten force against the target. For example, Bolivia's dispute with Chile has only sporadically escalated to the level of sharp diplomatic conflict, and Bolivia did not once threaten or resort to the use of military force.[9] Similarly, all of the countries with competing claims to the Spratly Islands had limited naval capabilities for projecting military power into the South China Sea, and this helps to account for the low frequency of military clashes over the disputed islands despite periodic diplomatic protests and conflicts over the islands (only one confrontation between Chinese and South Vietnamese forces in early 1974 and then several in the 1980s between China and Vietnam).[10]

If we turn to the hypotheses targeted at domestic politics, we find strong results for two variables. First, the presence of minority groups along the border of the target with common ethnic ties to the general population of the challenger increased the likelihood of escalation. The positive and very significant coefficient (t-ratio = 12.91) strongly supports H2.1. In table 9 we see that the presence of minority groups produces a 30 percent increase in the likelihood of escalation ($y = 1$ or 2).[11] These statistical findings converge with the conventional wisdom that when ethnic irredentism and support for national self-determination for an ethnic group are the issues at stake in a territorial dispute, acute conflict and violence are more likely. A number of exam-

---

9. See for example John Allcock, Guy Arnold, Alan Day, D. S. Lewis, Lorimer Poultney, Roland Rance, and D. J. Sagar, *Border and Territorial Disputes,* rev. 3d ed. (London: Longman, 1992), 573–77; Douglas Shumavon, "Bolivia: Salida al Mar," in Elizabeth Ferris and Jennie Lincoln, eds., *Latin American Foreign Policies* (Boulder: Westview, 1981), 179–90; and Waltraud Quesiser Morales, "Bolivian Foreign Policy: The Struggle for Sovereignty," in Jennie Lincoln and Elizabeth Ferris, eds., *The Dynamics of Latin American Foreign Policies* (Boulder: Westview, 1984), 171–91.

10. For an analysis of the dispute over the Spratly Islands in the postwar period see Allcock et al., *Border and Territorial Disputes,* 542–44; Chi-kin Lo, *China's Policy towards Territorial Disputes: The Case of the South China Sea Islands* (New York: Routledge, 1989); and Marwyn Samuels, *Contest for the South China Sea* (New York: Methuen, 1982). For more recent assessments of the dispute along with an analysis of the balance of naval and air power among the disputants, see Desmond Ball, "Arms and Affluence: Military Acquisitions in the Asia-Pacific Region," *International Security* 18, no. 3 (1993/94): 78–112; Denny Roy, "Hegemon on the Horizon? China's Threat to East Asian Security," *International Security* 19, no. 1 (1994): 149–68; and Michael Gallagher, "China's Illusory Threat to the South China Sea" *International Security* 19, no. 1 (1994): 169–94.

11. A similar finding is reported in Robert Mandel, "Roots of the Modern Interstate Border Dispute," *Journal of Conflict Resolution* 24, no. 3 (1980): 427–54, who found that border disputes involving ethnic issues were more likely to escalate to armed conflict.

ples illustrate these findings: the dispute between Pakistan and India over Kashmir, the Arab-Israeli conflict and the conflict over the rights of the Palestinians to a homeland, and Somalia's conflict with Ethiopia over the ethnic Somali population located in the Ogaden.

If we compare these results on bordering minorities with those from the previous chapter, an interesting contrast is apparent. The results in chapter 4 indicated that irredentist claims and support for the self-determination rights of minority groups were not a strong predictor of why challengers became involved in territorial disputes. One contributing factor was that prevailing international norms in the post–World War II period have not supported the rights of national groups or states to self-determination when it threatened the territorial integrity of sovereign states. The results in this chapter suggest that precisely because this international norm is generally respected, only states that have strong domestic political forces favoring conflict with the target will become involved in territorial disputes over irredentist or self-determination claims. Therefore, higher levels of escalation should be expected.

In many cases, then, the domestic political incentives for leaders to dispute territory offset the lack of international support for such claims. Examples would include Somalia's claims against Ethiopia, Pakistan's dispute with India over Kashmir, Afghanistan's conflict with Pakistan over the Durand Line, and Turkey's confrontation with Greece over the fate of Turkish Cypriots since the 1974 invasion. In each of these cases the challenger was not able to generate diplomatic support for its position within either regional organizations or the United Nations, and, in some cases, these international organizations openly opposed the challenger's claims (i.e., the OAU and Somalia and the United Nations and Turkey). Nevertheless, political leaders in the challenger states persisted in their claims, maintained very firm diplomatic positions, resorted to the threat or use of military force, or continued to occupy disputed territory.[12]

The second strong finding was that disputes in which the challenger sought political unification with the target held a high likelihood of escalation. In table 8 the ethnic similarity variable is positive and very significant (*t*-ratio = 11.78), which strongly supports H3.1. In table 9 the marginal impact analysis reveals that when the populations of the challenger and target share the same ethnic and linguistic background the probability of escalation increases by 28 percent.

---

12. See Saadja Touval, *The Boundary Politics of Independent Africa* (Cambridge: Harvard University Press, 1972), 83–89, 111-18, 133–53; Allcock et al., *Border and Territorial Disputes,* 48–63, 411–26, 474–88; and Tozun Bahcheli, *Greek-Turkish Relations since 1955* (Boulder: Westview Press, 1990), ch. 4.

Cases such as North vs. South Vietnam; North vs. South Korea; China vs. Taiwan; Iraq vs. Kuwait; North vs. South Yemen; India vs. Portugal over Goa; and Morocco vs. Spain and the Western Sahara all illustrate how challengers who sought political unification with the target often turned to the threat or use of military force. The Moroccan case is particularly revealing because King Hassan of Morocco did not favor independence for the territory of the Western Sahara but instead desired to absorb the territory as a part of Morocco. Nevertheless, he portrayed his country's position as one supporting self-determination in order to avoid international opposition during the 1960s and early 1970s. However, when the ICJ issued a ruling in 1975 that did not support Morocco's claim of historical ties to the disputed territory, Hassan had to choose between a policy that was domestically supported—the annexation of Western Sahara—and one that was supported internationally—the right to independence for the population within the territory—and he selected the former.[13]

Despite the strong findings for the ethnic similarity variable, there are cases in which the challenger did not escalate disputes to high levels of diplomatic and military conflict. Interestingly, in only one of these cases—West vs. East Germany—did the challenger question the very sovereignty of the target. In the cases that did not support H3.1 the disputes often centered on relatively small sections of territory along a border that otherwise had been recognized by both parties. In Central and South America examples would include the disputes between Nicaragua and Honduras and between Argentina and Uruguay while, in Africa, the disputes between Benin and Niger and between Tunisia and Algeria are good examples. Finally, in the Middle East relevant cases would involve the dispute between Jordan and Saudi Arabia or among the smaller Persian Gulf states.

The final result to discuss is that the presence of economically valuable bordering territory was negatively related to escalatory actions by the challenger, as predicted by H4.2. It was hypothesized that disputes centering on economic issues, compared to other issues at stake in a dispute, should be the least likely to escalate, and the results do support this prediction. Indeed, the hypothesis posits that economic issues should be systematically related to *low* levels of conflict, and the probit results are moderately supportive. The coefficient for this variable in table 8 is negative with a very respectable t-ratio of 4.70. On the other hand, the marginal impact results in table 9 show that the presence of

13. See Tony Hodges, *Western Sahara* (Westport, CT: Lawrence Hill & Company, 1983), chs. 27–28.

economically valuable territory is associated with a modest 7 percent reduction in the probability of escalation.

A closer examination of individual cases helps to explain the lack of stronger results for this variable. Consistent with H.4.2, there are fifty-four cases in which economically valuable territory was in dispute, and in about forty cases (or about 74 percent) levels of conflict were low. For example, a cluster of disputes among states involving access to oil rights generally did not escalate beyond hard-nosed negotiations or small-scale shows of force (Argentina vs. Uruguay, Tunisia vs. Algeria, Iran vs. Saudi Arabia, Oman vs. UAE, Qatar vs. Bahrain, Saudi Arabia vs. Iraq, and Saudi Arabia vs. Kuwait). There are, however, fourteen cases in which a majority of the dispute years were coded with high levels of diplomatic or military conflict ($y = 1$ or 2).[14] Among these disputes, however, political and security as well as economic issues were at stake, and generally the more zero-sum nature of the political and security issues (ethnic irredentism, national unification, and strategic location of territory) overwhelmed the moderating effects of potential cooperation on the joint development of economic resources. Thus, *when only economic issues were the primary issues at stake,* the likelihood of escalation was quite low. This pattern of behavior suggests that leaders were generally not willing to sacrifice salient domestic political or security concerns for the opportunity to secure economic gains. When there was a potential trade-off between political and economic gains, the former typically prevailed.

The International Context of Decisions to Escalate

In this section we consider the impact that international political and military conditions had on decisions by the challenger to escalate. The results in table 8 for the international-level variables are generally quite strong. The results in this chapter, then, provide an interesting comparison with the findings from the previous chapter. While the pursuit of military security gains was often not a motive behind decisions to become involved in territorial disputes, calculations concerning the security consequences of escalating disputes seemed to be quite salient to leaders within challenger states.

If we turn to the first set of findings in table 8, we see that the

---

14. The cases are: Panama vs. the United States; Venezuela vs. the United Kingdom/Guyana; West Germany vs. East Germany; Iran vs. Iraq; North Yemen vs. the United Kingdom/South Yemen; Saudi Arabia vs. the United Kingdom/UAE; Chad vs. Libya; Morocco vs. Algeria, Mauritania, and Spain; Somalia vs. Ethiopia; China vs. Soviet Union; China vs. Vietnam; Japan vs. Soviet Union.

conventional balance of forces variable has a positive and significant coefficient (t-ratio = 7.80), as predicted by H5.1. This result indicates that challenger states were more likely to engage in higher levels of diplomatic and military pressure against a target as their relative military position improved. In table 10 the marginal impact of the balance of forces is reported, and we find that a change in the balance of forces from a one-to-nine disadvantage to a nine-to-one advantage for the challenger is associated with about a 22 percent increase in the likelihood of conflict escalation (y = 1 or 2).

If we examine the cases in more detail, we see that the effects of the military balance are, in fact, somewhat curvilinear. That is, very weak as well as very strong challengers were less likely to engage in high levels of escalation compared to challengers who were closer to parity in military capabilities. Very weak challengers lacked the military means to pose a credible threat to the target and therefore seldom initiated militarized confrontations. Conversely, very strong challengers certainly had the military capabilities to seize disputed territory, but they often did not resort to the use of force since vital security interests were unlikely to be at stake. The reason is that because the challenger had such a decisive military advantage, the control over disputed territory was only of minimal strategic importance; the target did not pose a military threat.

In the twenty-six cases in which the challenger faced on average a three-to-one or worse disadvantage in the balance of forces, the proportion of years in which the challenger was involved in a militarized confrontation was less than 2 percent. For example, successive Bolivian governments failed to threaten Chile despite a strong desire to gain direct access to the Pacific, Spanish governments did not attempt to use military force to dislodge the British from Gilbralter, and Japan did not contest with military force Soviet control of the disputed Kurile Islands. In each of these cases, challenger governments maintained a very firm policy of diplomatic opposition, but their military weakness required that they be very cautious about becoming involved in any armed confrontations.[15] Indeed, there are numerous examples of relatively weak states adopting quite tough and inflexible negotiating positions regarding their territorial demands, but they rarely escalated the conflict to the military level despite the refusal of the much stronger target to make

---

15. See for example Shumavon, "Bolivia: Salida al Mar"; Morales, "Bolivian Foreign Policy"; Anthony DeSota, *Bolivia's Right to an Access to the Sea* (Pasadena: Jensen Publishing Co., 1962); Howard Levie, *Gibraltar* (Boulder: Westview, 1983); William Nimmo, *Japan and Russia* (Westport, CT: Greenwood, 1994), chs. 1–2; and Rajendra Jain, *The USSR and Japan, 1945–1980* (Atlantic Highlands, NJ: Humanities Press, 1981).

TABLE 10. The Marginal Impact of Variables Measuring the International Context on the Level of Conflict over Disputed Territory

Change in Value of Explanatory Variable	Probability of Alternative Levels of Conflict (%)		
	$y = 0$	$y = 1$	$y = 2$
Balance of Military Forces			
The ratio of challenger to target capabilities varies from:			
1/9 to 1/3	−3.4	+3.0	+0.4
1/3 to 1/1	−6.5	+5.3	+1.2
1/1 to 3/1	−7.2	+5.6	+1.6
3/1 to 9/1	−4.6	+3.3	+1.3
Challenger Dispute Involvement			
In how many other territorial disputes is the challenger involved?			
0 vs. 1	+4.1	−3.3	−0.8
1 vs. 2	+3.9	−3.2	−0.7
2 vs. 5	+9.6	−8.4	−1.2
5 vs. 10	+9.6	−8.9	−0.7
Stalemate in Negotiations			
Did negotiations and diplomatic initiatives fail to produce concessions from the target in the previous year?			
No vs. Yes	−25.8	+18.2	+7.6
Challenge to Status Quo			
Did the target engage in actions to establish or consolidate control over disputed territory?			
No vs. Yes	−14.3	+10.9	+3.4
Defeat in Armed Conflict			
How many times has the challenger suffered a defeat/stalemate in previous armed confrontations with the target?			
0 vs. 1	+6.2	−5.2	−1.0
1 vs. 2	+5.3	−4.6	−0.7
2 vs. 3	+4.3	−3.9	−0.4
3 vs. 4	+3.4	−3.2	−0.2
Deterrent Alliance Ties			
Do other states have defense commitments to the target based on military alliance ties?			
No vs. Yes	+2.2	−1.8	−0.4
Common Security Ties			
Are challenger and target military alliance partners?			
No vs. Yes	+17.5	−15.3	−2.2

Note: See the note to table 9 for a description of how the changes in the probability of conflict levels were calculated.

territorial concessions. Cuba, for example, has maintained a policy of unyielding opposition to the U.S. military base at Guantanamo Bay for decades, but Cuba has not attempted to compel the United States to withdraw by militarily challenging the U.S. forces positioned there.[16]

In eleven cases the challenger enjoyed on average a three-to-one or greater advantage in the balance of forces, and the number of militarized disputes initiated per year was still only less than 20 percent. For example, China did not rely on coercive pressure against neighbors such as Afghanistan, Burma, and Nepal, and the Soviet Union did not resort to military pressure to force Iran to make territorial concessions. In each of these cases the challenger had an overwhelming military advantage and only relatively small sections of territory were in dispute. Therefore, the strategic issues at stake were quite limited for the challenger.

In contrast, if we look at those eighteen disputes with the highest frequency of years coded for the threat or use of force, we find that in two-thirds of these cases (twelve) the challenger and target either possessed roughly equal military capabilities, or the challenger enjoyed a clear but not overwhelming advantage. For these eighteen cases, the ratio of challenger to target forces averaged about 1.3/1.0, and the frequency of militarized disputes initiated per year was approximately 40 percent.[17] Furthermore, if we look at the seventeen crises in which the challenger resorted to the large-scale use of military force that in many cases led to the outbreak of war with the target,[18] the challenger had a clear military advantage in only six cases.[19] In the remaining twelve cases the challenger was evenly matched or slightly inferior to the target.

In fact, a closer examination of the cases in which the challenger attacked the target even though the balance of forces did not favor the

---

16. See Allcock et al., *Border and Territorial Disputes*, 582–85.

17. The cases are: (1) Argentina vs. Chile (2) Argentina vs. Great Britain (3) Ecuador vs. Peru (4) Venezuela vs. United Kingdom/Guyana (5) Turkey vs. Greece (6) Egypt vs. Israel (7) Iran vs. United Kingdom/UAE (8) Iran vs. Iraq (9) Syria vs. Israel (10) Libya vs. Chad (11) Somalia vs. Ethiopia (12) China vs. India (13) India vs. Portugal (14) Pakistan vs. India (15) North vs. South Vietnam (16) China vs. Vietnam (17) South Vietnam/Vietnam vs. Cambodia (18) Thailand vs. Cambodia.

18. The cases are: (1) Argentina vs. United Kingdom in 1982 (2) Turkey vs. Greece in 1974 (3) Egypt vs. Israel in 1967, 1970, and 1973 (4) Iraq vs. Iran in 1980 (5) Iraq vs. Kuwait in 1990 (6) Jordan vs. Israel in 1967 (7) Syria vs. Israel in 1967 and 1973 (8) Somalia vs. Ethiopia in 1977 (9) Uganda vs. Tanzania in 1978 (10) China vs. India in 1962 (11) India vs. Portugal in 1961 (12) Pakistan vs. India in 1965 (13) Indonesia vs. Malaysia in 1964 (14) North Korea vs. South Korea in 1950 (15) North Vietnam vs. South Vietnam in 1965 (16) Vietnam vs. Cambodia in 1977 (17) China vs. Vietnam in 1979.

19. The cases are Turkey vs. Greece in 1974; China vs. India in 1962; India vs. Portugal in 1961; China vs. Vietnam in 1979; North Korea vs. South Korea in 1950; and Vietnam vs. Cambodia in 1977.

challenger reveals that challengers often had limited aims strategies designed to seize and then hold relatively small sections of territory (e.g., Pakistan vs. India in 1965, Egypt and Syria vs. Israel in 1973, or Argentina vs. Great Britain in 1982). As a result, the military calculation of greatest concern to the challenger was not the capacity of the target to fight a large-scale war along an entire border, but the ability of the target to compel the challenger to withdraw from the territory it had seized and in which it had established a strong defensive position.[20] Furthermore, a decisive military victory was not the expected outcome for the challenger. Instead, the goal was to achieve a fait accompli or force a stalemate on the battlefield, which would then strengthen the challenger's position at the negotiating table. The implication for the statistical analysis is that the operational measure of relative military strength employed in testing H5.1 probably *overstates the disadvantage* that the challenger faced in many cases in a decision to use military force against the target. A more refined measure of military capabilities might very well produce results stronger than those reported in tables 8 and 10.

The importance of the balance of forces is apparent not only when we compare across cases but also within cases over time. In several disputes the challenger's use or threat of force is correlated with significant shifts in the relative balance of military strength. For example, it was not until late 1971, after the British had almost completely withdrawn militarily from the Persian Gulf, that Iran used military force to occupy and take control of the disputed islands of Abu Musa, Greater Tunb, and Lesser Tunb from the United Arab Emirates. For decades prior to 1971 Iran had claimed sovereignty over the islands but had not attempted to challenge British control directly.[21] In a similar case, Iraq had territorial claims against Kuwait dating back to the 1930s, but Iraq refrained from any military threats against Kuwait while it was a British colonial possession. However, once Kuwait became independent in 1961 and the British no longer maintained a military presence on Kuwaiti territory, then Iraq adopted a more coercive diplomatic and military position in the dispute and finally in 1990 invaded Kuwait.[22] Finally, prior to the French withdrawal from Algeria in 1962 Morocco had only pursued diplomatic means in its claim to the disputed Tindouf area.

---

20. See for example T. V. Paul, *Asymmetric Conflicts: War Initiation by Weaker Powers* (Cambridge: Cambridge University Press, 1994), chs. 6–8.

21. See for example Allcock et al., *Border and Territorial Disputes,* 381–84 and Husain Albaharna, *The Arabian Gulf States,* rev. 2d ed. (Beirut: Librairie Du Liban, 1975), 337–48.

22. See Finnie, *Shifting Lines in the Sand* and Freedman and Karsh, *The Gulf Conflict.*

However, in 1963 Morocco resorted to the use of military force to back its claim, and armed clashes along the border almost escalated to the outbreak of war.[23]

In sum, assessments of relative military strength seem to be one important component of a challenger's decision to threaten or resort to the use of military force. Challengers did not resort to the large-scale use of military force against powerful targets, and when weaker challengers did threaten the use of force against stronger targets they did so through limited military actions designed to probe the resolve of the target. As a result, the challenger could pull back from further escalation if the target responded in a forceful manner.[24] Nevertheless, in a number of territorial disputes the credibility of deterrence was open to greater question since the target did not possess a clear military advantage. Under these conditions of greater uncertainty about the likely outcome of armed conflict, it seems likely that military calculations were not decisive for the challenger.[25] Military assessments were important to the extent that they did not preclude the option of possibly using force; however, nonmilitary considerations were more likely to have been critical in tipping the decision for or against escalation under these conditions of greater military risk.[26]

The second finding in table 8 is that alliance ties had only a very limited extended deterrent value for the target. The negative coefficient

---

23. See Touval, *The Boundary Politics of Independent Africa,* 112–15.

24. A couple of examples illustrate this point: (1) Saudi Arabia occupied disputed territory in Abu Dhabi during the fall of 1952 but eventually withdrew the forces following a blockade by the British and the threat of further military action. (2) Ecuadorean forces occupied disputed Peruvian territory in the fall of 1980 but when superior Peruvian forces discovered the Ecuadorean forces in January 1981, Ecuador was quick to withdraw when threatened with a large-scale clash. On the Saudi case see Robert Butterworth, *Managing Interstate Conflict, 1945–1974* (Pittsburgh: University Center for International Studies, University of Pittsburgh, 1976), 128–29. The Ecuadorean case is analyzed by William Krieg, *Ecuadorean-Peruvian Rivalry in the Upper Amazon,* 2d ed. (Bethesda: William Krieg, 1986), 266–330.

25. Russell Leng, *Interstate Crisis Behavior, 1816–1980* (Cambridge: Cambridge University Press, 1993), ch. 5 reaches a similar conclusion about the importance of the balance of military forces in his study of forty crises from 1816–1980 as does Paul, *Asymmetric Conflicts,* chs. 6–8 in his study of Pakistan's attack in 1965, Egypt's in 1973, and Argentina's in 1982.

26. This helps explain why in a previous study I found that the military balance had little impact on conflict escalation—see Paul Huth and Bruce Russett, "General Deterrence between Enduring Rivals," *American Political Science Review* 87, no. 1 (1993): 61–72. In that study we only analyzed territorial disputes with a high frequency of militarized confrontations in which the military balance did not decisively favor the challenger. In contrast, the population of cases analyzed here includes much greater variance in the frequency of militarized disputes and the balance of military forces.

for the alliance variable indicates that alliance ties did act as a deterrent (consistent with H10) but the coefficient's significance is questionable. The *t*-ratio is only −1.28, and in table 10 we see that a low level of diplomatic conflict ($y = 0$) is only about 2 percent more likely when the target has military allies. These weak probit results reflect the fact that in only about 56 percent of the observations in which the challenger had an ally did the challenger avoid higher levels of diplomatic or military conflict (474/847). The limited deterrent effect of alliance ties, when compared to the effects of the conventional balance of forces between challenger and target, suggests that in many territorial disputes challenger states were likely to discount the potential support of the target's allies when escalating the dispute.

The explanation for this finding is that in most of the cases in which a plausible threat to use military force existed, the allies of the target did not have military forces of their own on the territory of the target. Allies, therefore, were generally not in a position to provide on short notice direct military support to a target threatened with attack. A clear exception to this generalization, however, was the presence of U.S. armed forces on the territory of South Korea, which certainly bolstered the credibility of the U.S. defense commitment to that country. Challengers, however, were frequently not threatening large-scale offensives to invade the target but were instead considering more limited military actions designed to seize specific sections of disputed territory. Previous studies have shown that the strongest deterrent to a potential aggressor is a credible threat to respond quickly with sizable forces at the point of attack.[27] The allies of the target were simply not capable of doing this in most of the cases, given the limited territorial goals of the challenger. As a result, alliance ties were a weak substitute for the target possessing relatively strong conventional forces of its own.

The propensity of the challenger to escalate a dispute was strongly influenced by its involvement in conflicts with other states. In particular, the challenger was less likely to escalate against a target if it was involved in territorial disputes with other states. The negative coefficient for this variable is quite significant (*t*-ratio = −7.55), which strongly supports H6.1.[28] In table 10 the results indicate that as the number of

27. See Paul Huth, *Extended Deterrence and the Prevention of War* (New Haven: Yale University Press, 1988) and John Mearsheimer, *Conventional Deterrence* (Ithaca: Cornell University Press, 1983).

28. When the alternative measure of the challenger's dispute involvement—the number of months in each year that the challenger was involved in militarized disputes with other states—was substituted into the equation, supportive but weaker results were produced. The coefficient was negative ($b = -0.030$) and significant (*t*-ratio = −5.01),

other territorial disputes for the challenger increases from zero to ten, the likelihood of low levels of diplomatic conflict increases by about 27 percent.

A number of examples illustrate these general findings. China was involved in multiple disputes throughout the 1950s and 1960s. In the late 1950s China was a party in ten disputes involving India, Pakistan, Burma, Nepal, Afghanistan, Taiwan, the Soviet Union, South Vietnam, Japan, and the Philippines. During the late 1950s and early 1960s, however, China only pursued an active and confrontational policy toward India and Taiwan.[29] Saudi Arabia had simultaneous disputes with Jordan, Iraq, Iran, Kuwait, and the British but pursued a tough diplomatic policy only toward the British in the disputes over Abu Dhabi and Qatar.[30] In the 1960s Morocco had disputes with Spain, Algeria, and Mauritania but was careful to avoid escalation of all three disputes at the same time. For example, a sharp deterioration in relations with Algeria in the early to mid-1960s was accompanied by relatively stable relations with both Spain and Mauritania. However, when Morocco adopted a more active and confrontational policy toward Spain in the early 1970s, it had already settled its disputes with Algeria and Mauritania.[31] Somalia had territorial claims against Ethiopia, Kenya, and Djibouti, but after a period of high levels of conflict with Ethiopia and Kenya in the early 1960s, Somalia deescalated its dispute with Kenya while maintaining a more confrontational policy toward Ethiopia.[32] Conversely, Ethiopia

---

and the marginal impact was to decrease the likelihood of escalation by a maximum of about 11 percent.

29. On Chinese relations with India see Allen Whiting, *The Chinese Calculus of Deterrence* (Ann Arbor: University of Michigan, 1975), ch. 1; Nancy Jetly, *India China Relations, 1947–1977* (New Delhi: Radiant Publishers, 1979); Bhim Sandhu, *Unresolved Conflict, China and India* (New Delhi: Radiant Publishers, 1988); and Steven Hoffmann, *India and the China Crisis* (Berkeley: University of California Press, 1990). Chinese policy toward Taiwan is examined in Simon Long, *Taiwan: China's Last Frontier* (New York: St. Martin's Press, 1991); Thomas Stolper, *China, Taiwan, and the Offshore Islands* (Armonk, NY: M. E. Sharpe, 1985); and Shu Guang Zhang, *Deterrence and Strategic Culture* (Ithaca: Cornell University Press, 1994).

30. See Albaharna, *The Arabian Gulf States*, 196–238 and 261–63.

31. See Touval, *The Boundary Politics of Independent Africa*, 255–69 and Hodges, *Western Sahara*, ch. 11.

32. In 1967 the new regime of President Abdirashid Ali Sharmarke in Somalia sought improved relations with both Ethiopia and Kenya. The Arusha Accords signed in October 1967 between Kenya and Somalia marked the beginning of a detente in relations, which was generally maintained through the 1970s and early 1980s. Detente with Ethiopia, however, was never as firmly established and collapsed by the mid-1970s. See Touval, *The Boundary Politics of Independent Africa*, ch. 9 and Day, *Border and Territorial Disputes*, 114–18, and 131–36.

was more accommodative in its disputes with Kenya and Sudan while very firm in opposing the claims of Somalia.[33]

Two related reasons explain why challengers in these cases were less likely to escalate when they were involved in multiple territorial disputes. First, challengers lacked the military capabilities to project their military forces across several borders simultaneously. If a state was a challenger in multiple disputes it could not generally pose a credible threat of attack on multiple fronts. Thus, Somalia could not expect to defeat both Ethiopia and Kenya, while Morocco could not credibly threaten both Spain and Algeria. Conversely, if a state was both a challenger and target in different cases, it had to worry that if it escalated a dispute with one state it would risk weakening its defensive position along its other borders and therefore undercut its ability to deter potential challengers (i.e., Ethiopia's primary concern was the threat of Somalia, and therefore it did not aggressively press its claims against Sudan or Kenya).

Second, challengers involved in multiple disputes had incentives to avoid confrontation with some states and thereby convince those states to support their claims in a dispute with another adversary. For example, China in part sought cooperative relations with Pakistan in the hope that Pakistan would support China in its dispute with India, and an accommodative policy toward Japan in the 1970s over the disputed Senkaku Islands was linked to the goal of trying to induce Japan to form an anti-Soviet coalition in the Far East.[34] Similarly, Morocco normalized its relations with Mauritania and Algeria in return for their support of Morocco's claims against Spain, and Mauritania made concessions to Mali in order to convince Mali to not support Morocco's claim against Mauritania.[35] Finally, Iran in December 1970 retreated from its claim to Bahrain in an attempt to secure support from Saudi Arabia and other Persian Gulf states for its claim to the islands of Abu Musa and the Greater and Lesser Tunbs, which it occupied in November 1971.[36] As an

33. See Touval, *The Boundary Politics of Independent Africa,* 133–53, 212–26, and 246–49 for a discussion of Ethiopia's relations with its neighbors.

34. See Anwar Hussain Syed, *China and Pakistan: Diplomacy of an Entente Cordiale* (Amherst: University of Massachusetts Press, 1974); Rasul Rais, *China and Pakistan: A Political Analysis of Mutual Relations* (Lahore: Progressive Publishers, 1977); Yaacov Vertzberger, *The Enduring Entente: Sino-Pakistani Relations 1960–1980* (New York: Praeger, 1983); A. Doak Barnett, *China and the Major Powers in East Asia* (Washington, D.C.: Brookings, 1977), ch. 2; and Rajendra Jain, *China and Japan 1949–1980,* rev. 2d ed. (London: Martin Robertson, 1980), chs. 6–7.

35. See Touval, *The Boundary Politics of Independent Africa,* 131, 166, 249–51, 267–68, and Hodges, *Western Sahara,* ch. 11.

36. See Ramazani, *Iran's Foreign Policy,* 411–15.

extension of this second point, challengers also pursued accommodative policies in disputes with some states in order to foster an image of reasonableness and peaceful intentions, so as to build greater international support for their territorial claims in other disputes. An excellent example was China's policy of accommodation toward Afghanistan, Burma, and Nepal in the early 1960s. Chinese leaders believed that peaceful and friendly relations with many of its neighbors would help to convince other states that the failure of China to reach a settlement with India was due to India's intransigence and thereby would isolate India diplomatically.[37]

The next set of findings center on the effects of variables that measure common security interests between challenger and target. In table 8 we see that if the challenger had military alliance ties with the target, it was less likely to escalate. As predicted by H11.1, the negative coefficient is quite significant (t-ratio $= -12.05$) and in table 10 we see that low levels of conflict are almost 18 percent more likely between allies. Similar, but somewhat weaker, results are produced when the alternative measure of common security interests—the challenger and target were involved in a territorial dispute with a common adversary—was substituted into the equation. The coefficient is negative ($b = -0.42$) and significant (t-ratio $= -6.42$) and is associated with about an 11 percent decrease in escalation ($y = 1$ or 2).

A number of examples illustrate the effects of common security interests between challenger and target. In Western Europe, NATO allies were involved in several territorial disputes (France vs. the United Kingdom, Netherlands vs. Belgium and West Germany, and West Germany vs. France), but all of the disputes were short lived and in none of the cases did the challenger resort to high levels of diplomatic or military pressure. The common perception of a threat posed by the Soviet Union and the Warsaw Pact undoubtedly contributed to the belief among the allies that their disputes should not drive a serious wedge between them and thus weaken the ability of NATO to oppose the Warsaw Pact. In the Middle East, Iran and Saudi Arabia were involved in a dispute from 1950 to 1968, but neither side engaged in high levels of diplomatic or military pressure. The avoidance of conflict can in part be attributed to a shared interest in confronting their common adversaries of Iraq and Great Britain, with whom they both had territorial disputes. Similarly,

---

37. See Ralph Pettman, *China in Burma's Foreign Policy* (Canberra: Australian National University Press, 1973); Asad Husan and Asifa Anwar, *Conflict in Asia: A Case Study of Nepal* (New Delhi: Classical Publications, 1979); and T. R. Ghoble, *China-Nepal Relations and India* (New Delhi: Deep & Deep Publications, 1986).

Saudi Arabia and Kuwait had a common interest in avoiding serious conflict in their territorial disputes so that their powerful neighbor Iraq could not play one off against the other in pursuit of its own territorial claims.[38] In Africa, the common threat of Somali irredentism provided the impetus for Ethiopia and Kenya to form a military alliance and to develop and maintain close cooperative relations.[39] Finally, in Central Asia China and Pakistan avoided conflict in their territorial dispute as part of a general policy of diplomatic and military cooperation against their common adversary of India. China, for example, provided substantial amounts of conventional arms to Pakistan beginning in the mid-1960s and is believed to have provided assistance to Pakistan's nuclear weapons program.[40]

While common security ties generally served to mitigate conflict between challenger and target, there are several examples in which such ties did not deter the challenger from high levels of diplomatic and military escalation: (1) common alliance ties within NATO did not prevent Greece and Turkey from actively competing for influence and control over Cyprus, (2) despite their common membership in the Rio Pact, Argentina frequently resorted to military threats against Chile, and (3) Iraq pursued a confrontational policy toward Kuwait even though they were both members of the Arab League. As argued in chapter 4, in each of these cases the target was a relatively weak ally who could provide little in the way of military aid to support the challenger in conflicts with other states. As a result, there were minimal security risks associated with the loss of the target as a potential military ally. For example, Iraq's primary security threat was Iran, but Kuwait was not capable of posing a military threat to Iran. Similarly, the Soviet Union was a security concern for Turkey, but Greece could do little to assist Turkey in the event of a military confrontation with the Soviet Union.

A different logic applies to cases in which, despite a common territorial dispute adversary, the challenger engaged in high levels of escalation against a target. In a number of cases the common adversary was less of a security threat to the challenger than the target itself. As a result, the challenger was not willing to make concessions to obtain the support of

38. See Gholam Razi "Relations in the Persian Gulf," in Abid Al-Marayati, ed., *International Relations of the Middle East and North Africa* (Cambridge: Schenkman Publishing Co., 1984), 406-10; Ramazani, *Iran's Foreign Policy,* 398–99, 406, 409–14; and J. M. Abdulghani, *Iraq and Iran: The Years of Crisis* (London: Croom Helm, 1984), 80, 86–87.

39. See Touval, *The Boundary Politics of Independent Africa,* 141–42, 248–49.

40. See Rais, *China and Pakistan,* 99–106; Syed, *China and Pakistan,* 139–44; Vertzberger, *Enduring Entente,* 88–90; and Leonard Spector, *Going Nuclear* (Cambridge: Ballinger, 1987), 105.

the target, since the challenger was in a favorable position to apply diplomatic and military pressure against the common adversary without the support of the target. For example, Iran and Iraq both had disputes with Saudi Arabia, but that did not lead Iran to seek Iraqi support in opposition to Saudi Arabia. India and China both had disputes with Pakistan, but neither sought to accommodate the other in order to gain their support against Pakistan. Japan did not seek to cooperate with the Soviet Union in an attempt to improve its bargaining position against their common adversary of China. Finally, China was not willing to be conciliatory toward the Soviet Union in order to be in a stronger position to confront Japan.

Common security interests can be a powerful force pushing the challenger to avoid conflict with a target. The statistical findings understate this effect because the degree of common security interests represented by alliance ties and the same territorial dispute adversary varies considerably across cases and is not adequately captured by a measure that only codes the presence of alliance ties or a common territorial dispute adversary. The estimated coefficient reflects the general effect of this variable and therefore includes cases in which the challenger's likely estimate of the value of the target as a military and diplomatic ally was only moderate if not low. However, when a challenger viewed a target as a valuable ally, then common security interests provided strong incentives for the challenger to avoid escalation of the dispute with the target. As a result, if a more refined measure could have been developed, capturing more accurately the degree of common security interests, then stronger statistical findings most likely would have been produced.

The next finding to discuss is what impact prior military defeats for the challenger had on the subsequent probability of escalation by the challenger. The hypothesis (H9.1) is that the likelihood of escalation should decrease following military setbacks at the hands of the target, and the results in table 8 are supportive. The coefficient is negative and significant (t-ratio = 5.75), and the substantive effect of the variable is important. The marginal impact results in table 10 show that as the number of prior defeats increases, the probability of escalation decreases by as much as 19 percent.[41]

---

41. These findings do not converge with those of Russell Leng who reported that states tend to adopt more coercive bargaining strategies following past diplomatic or military setbacks. A possible explanation is that Leng restricts his empirical analysis to only a limited number of dyads involved in recurrent crises and eventually war, whereas my dataset includes some dyads not involved in multiple crises beyond an initial armed conflict. Furthermore, my dataset is structured as a time series of annual observations of conflict behavior while the unit of analysis for Leng is a specific crisis. See Russell Leng,

An examination of the cases reveals the expected struggle for state leaders within the challenger between recognizing their country's military weakness and the desire to avoid being charged with appeasement by domestic opposition for not continuing to confront the target militarily. For example, in most of the cases political and military leaders did learn from the previous military setbacks to respect the military strength of the target. At the same time, political leaders did feel constrained by the expectation of domestic political opposition and the potential loss of political support if they did not publicly maintain a tough and defiant posture toward the target. The result was that in a majority of disputes, the challenger formally maintained a policy of opposition and employed hostile rhetoric toward the target following a military setback but at the same time became more cautious in resorting to the further use of military force. As a result, the overall effect is that levels of diplomatic and political conflict remain high following a military defeat, but continued escalation to large-scale armed conflict becomes much less frequent.

Several examples illustrate this pattern. Successive Greek governments adamantly opposed Turkish control of Cypriot territory following the Turkish invasion in 1974, but no attempt has been made by Greek governments to compel Turkey to withdraw by the threat or use of military force. Instead, Greece has employed diplomatic means to oppose the Turkish partition of Cyprus and has been active at the United Nations in trying to build support for its position.[42] Following their military defeat at the hands of China in 1962, India has maintained a very stiff diplomatic policy of refusing to consider a compromise settlement or to accept the Chinese occupation of disputed territory, but no attempts have been made by India militarily to challenge the territorial status quo established by the Chinese victory in 1962.[43] Pakistan suffered a military defeat at the hands of India in 1971 but has maintained its firm support for the principle of self-determination over the disputed Kashmir territory.[44] Nevertheless, Pakistan has not resorted to the large-scale

---

"When Will They Ever Learn?: Coercive Bargaining Strategies in Recurrent Crises," *Journal of Conflict Resolution* 27, no. 3 (1983): 379–419.

42. See for example Bahcheli, *Greek-Turkish Relations since 1955*, ch. 4 and Constantine Danopoulos, *Warriors and Politicians in Modern Greece* (Chapel Hill: Documentary Publications, 1985), ch. 6.

43. See Jetly, *India China Relations*, chs. 8–10 and Sandhu, *Unresolved Conflict*, ch. 8.

44. For example in the Simla Agreement signed in July 1972 following Pakistan's military defeat in December 1971, Pakistan pledged, as it had on numerous other occasions, to settle all disputes with India peacefully, but no concessions were offered on Kashmir itself. See Syed, *China and Pakistan*, 156 and Allcock et al., *Border and Territorial Disputes*, 474–88.

use of military force in an attempt to overturn the status quo in Kashmir since 1971 (though a number of border clashes and militarized disputes have occurred in the 1980s and 1990s).[45] Finally, Argentina's attempt to seize the Falklands Islands failed in 1982 when British military forces in a counterattack defeated Argentine forces deployed on the islands. Since 1982 there have been no Argentine military moves or threats against the Falklands, but at the same time Argentine governments have steadfastly maintained their country's claims to the islands.[46]

There are cases, however, in which the challenger did become involved in large-scale military conflicts following earlier military defeats. For example, Egypt went to war against Israel in 1969–70 and 1973, and Syria in 1973 as well, despite their clear defeats in 1948 and 1967, and Somalia became embroiled in a large-scale armed conflict with Ethiopia in 1977 despite earlier setbacks in the 1960s. In the latter case, Somalia had improved its military position considerably by the mid-1970s compared to its relative strength a decade earlier, and therefore subsequent escalation in the 1970s is not puzzling.[47] The explanation for the Arab attack in 1973, however, is not as straightforward. It is true that both Egypt and Syria had improved their relative military capabilities since their defeat in 1967 through large arms imports from the Soviet Union. Egypt for example had imported over eight billion dollars' worth of arms between 1968 and 1972 and Syria about two billion. Israel over the same period imported close to five billion dollars in arms largely from the United States.[48] As a result, by 1973 Egyptian leaders had regained some of their lost confidence in their country's ability to confront Israel on the battlefield. However, that greater confidence was also a function of Sadat and the military leadership adopting more conservative and less ambitious military goals against Israel, that is, a limited aims strategy of regaining control of Israeli-occupied territory in the Sinai. Thus, the past defeats of Egypt at the hands of Israel compelled Egyptian military and

45. See for example Robert Wirsing, *Pakistan's Security under Zia, 1977–1988* (New York: St. Martin's Press, 1991), ch. 4.

46. See John Allcock et. al., *Border and Territorial Disputes*, 557–61.

47. Between 1973 and 1975 Somalia received an estimated 486 million dollars (constant 1985 dollars) worth of imported arms whereas Ethiopia imported only 172 million dollars of arms during the same period. During the period from 1960 to 1972 Somalia imported in total only about 130 million dollars of arms. See Michael Brzoska and Thomas Ohlson, *Arms Transfers to the Third World, 1971–85* (New York: Oxford University Press, 1987), 332–35 and Raymond Garthoff, *Detente and Confrontation* (Washington, D.C.: Brookings, 1985), 630–53.

48. See Brzoska and Ohlson, *Arms Transfers to the Third World, 1971–85*, 332–35 and Paul, *Asymmetric Conflicts*, 134–39.

political leaders to be more cautious in the future use of force and to accept more conservative estimates of what could be achieved on the battlefield. Syria, for its part, was only willing to attack if Egypt was also prepared to do so, recognizing that it could not confront Israel by itself, and its military goals were limited to retaking the occupied Golan Heights. Syria, however, failed in its attempt to retake the Golan Heights in 1973, and since that time there have only been a very few minor border clashes in the disputed territory.[49]

In sum, political and military leaders within challenger states have generally been reluctant to moderate their opposition to the target because of the failure to achieve their territorial goals by the threat or use of force. The hard realities of defeat on the battlefield, however, have compelled leaders heavily pressured by domestic political forces to remain belligerent to seek a middle course between war and retreat. A very accommodative diplomatic policy following a military setback would risk the credibility of the leadership's international reputation as well as its position of domestic political influence and power. For example, several scholars have argued that President Nasser of Egypt favored some type of accommodation with Israel as far back as the early 1950s but was very cautious in openly moving toward a peace settlement for fear that Egypt's standing as the leader of the Arab world would be undermined, as would his own position of influence and power within his own country and among other Arab leaders.[50] Another example is the policies of Syrian President Asad following the 1973 and 1982 wars with Israel. Scholars have argued that Asad has been interested in a peace settlement since the end of the October War, but he has been very cautious in moving forward on such a policy in order to protect his position of regional influence and leadership within the Arab world as well as his own domestic power base. As a result, Asad has insisted that

---

49. See Heikal, *The Road to Ramadan;* Saad al-Shazli, *The Crossing of the Suez* (San Francisco: American Mideast Research, 1980); Jonathan Shimshoni, *Israel and Conventional Deterrence* (Ithaca: Cornell University Press, 1988); Janice Gross Stein, "Calculation, Miscalculation, and Conventional Deterrence I" in Robert Jervis, Richard Ned Lebow, and Janice Gross Stein, *Psychology and Deterrence* (Baltimore: Johns Hopkins University Press, 1985), 34–59; Paul, *Asymmetric Conflicts,* ch. 7; Elli Lieberman, "The Rational Deterrence Theory Debate," *Security Studies* 3, no. 3 (1994): 384–427; and Drysdale and Hinnebusch, *Syria and the Middle East Peace Process,* 103–7.

50. See Robert Stephens, *Nasser: A Political Biography* (London: Allen Lane, The Penguin Press, 1971), 437–54, 522–28; Anthony Nutting, *Nasser* (London: Constable, 1972), chs. 19–22; Mark Tessler, *A History of the Israeli-Palestinian Conflict* (Bloomington: Indiana University Press), 338–39, 389, 410–11; and Ben Mor, *Decision and Interaction in Crisis* (New York: Praeger, 1993), 116–18, 127.

there can be no territorial compromise over the Golan Heights in any settlement with Israel, while supporting a significant buildup of Syrian military power in an attempt to put greater pressure on Israel to make concessions.[51] The peace initiatives of Anwar Sadat toward Israel in the late 1970s were therefore quite exceptional given the hostile attitude of the Arab world to such a policy as well as the opposition of the military within Egypt itself.[52]

The final two sets of probit results focus on the timing of escalatory behavior in response to the prior actions of the target. The first hypothesis tested was whether the challenger was more likely to escalate the dispute if in the previous year negotiations had ended in stalemate (H7). In table 8 we see that the coefficient for this variable is positive and quite significant (t-ratio = 10.86), which strongly supports H7. The marginal impact of this variable is also quite large. In table 10 we see that high levels of diplomatic and military conflict are about 26 percent more likely following a stalemate in negotiations. Another way to see that the results are quite strong is that of the eighty-six disputes in which negotiations were coded as ending in stalemate one or more times, high levels of diplomatic and military conflict followed in the next year in sixty-six disputes, or 77 percent of the cases.

When we examine the individual cases, these strong findings are caused by a combination of domestic political as well as military strategic calculations. The hypothesis is that escalation is likely as a strategic move by the challenger to convince the target that the alternative to a diplomatic stalemate is the threat of war and armed conflict. The hypothesis then frames the question from the perspective of interstate bargaining and the use of diplomatic and military pressure to force concessions from the target. On the other hand, a domestic politics perspective focuses on the political pressures on leaders to escalate the dispute to avoid charges by political opponents of a foreign policy setback. The two lines of argument, in fact, are not incompatible and can be viewed as mutually reinforcing the decision of leaders to escalate a dispute.

---

51. See Drysdale and Hinnebusch, *Syria and the Middle East Peace Process,* chs. 3–4.

52. See for example Ismail Fahmy, *Negotiating for Peace in the Middle East* (Baltimore: Johns Hopkins University Press, 1983), chs. 6, 11–14; Melvin Friedlander, *Sadat and Begin: The Domestic Politics of Peacemaking* (Boulder: Westview, 1983), chs. 3–5, 7; Martin Indyk, *"To the Ends of the Earth": Sadat's Jerusalem Initiative* (Cambridge: Harvard University, Center for Middle Eastern Studies, 1984), 5–11, 51–52; and Raymond Hinnebusch, *Egyptian Politics under Sadat* (Cambridge: Cambridge University Press, 1985), 66–75.

When individual cases are examined in more detail, both perspectives provide a good deal of insight. For example, in the Middle East, the decisions by Egypt to launch the War of Attrition between 1969 and 1970 and then the October War in 1973 were motivated by the desire of Nasser and then Sadat to break the diplomatic deadlock in negotiations with Israel and to convince Israel to be more forthcoming in future negotiations. At the same time, both presidents faced considerable domestic political pressures to take more forceful actions against Israel.[53] In the case of the Argentine invasion of the Falkland Islands in April 1982, negotiations were stalemated by the end of 1981, and a further round of talks in February 1982 had failed to make any progress. Argentina, in fact, had already begun active preparations for an invasion in late December 1981, and the military leadership was waiting for the right time to launch the attack. Two basic reasons can be advanced for the decision to occupy the islands by the leadership of Argentina. First, there was considerable domestic political support for the regime's opposition to continued British control of the islands, and the leadership believed therefore that a successful occupation of the islands would bolster their declining legitimacy due to worsening economic conditions. Second, the invasion was intended not as a substitute for negotiations but as a means to bargain from a position of strength. The Argentine plan was to occupy the islands and then resume negotiations with the British, with the goal being to compel the British to cede sovereignty of the islands.[54] Finally, the Pakistani attack against Indian-controlled sections of Kashmir in 1965 was motivated by deep concern that the stalemate over Kashmir, reflected in the failure of negotiations with India in previous years, threatened to become permanent as India consolidated its control over Kashmir. Thus, the decision to resort to military force reflected a desire to break the current diplomatic stalemate and to pressure India into returning to the negotiating table. Once again, however, Pakistani leaders also felt domestic pressures to act, and they were confident that a policy of armed confrontation would be supported domestically.[55]

---

53. See Shimshoni, *Israel and Conventional Deterrence*, ch. 4; Heikal, *The Road to Ramadan;* Mahmoud Riad, *The Struggle for Peace in the Middle East* (London: Quartet Books, 1981); al-Shazli, *The Crossing of the Suez;* Paul, *Asymmetric Conflicts,* 130–34, 141–44; Stein, "Calculation, Miscalculation, and Conventional Deterrence I"; Yaacov Bar-Siman-Tov, *The Israeli-Egyptian War of Attrition, 1969–1970* (New York: Columbia University Press, 1980); Lawrence Whetten, *The Canal War* (Cambridge: MIT Press, 1974).

54. See Paul, *Asymmetric Conflicts,* 146–66 and Douglas Kinney, *National Interest/ National Honor: The Diplomacy of the Falklands Crisis* (New York: Praeger, 1989), 59–71.

55. See Paul, *Asymmetric Conflicts,* 107–25 and Russell Brines, *The Indo-Pakistani Conflict* (London: Pall Mall Press, 1968), chs. 2–5. The underlying logic of H7 could

The second hypothesis to be tested was whether the challenger was more likely to escalate a dispute in response to political, economic, or military actions taken by the target to alter the prevailing status quo within the area of disputed territory (H8.1). The results in table 8 are as expected: the coefficient is positive and quite significant (*t*-ratio = 6.49), and the variable produces about a 14 percent increase in the chances of escalation according to the marginal impact results in table 10. In total, there were 585 dispute years in which the target undertook actions to alter the status quo, and in 71 percent of the years (416) the challenger responded with high levels of diplomatic or military conflict.

When we examine the individual cases in more detail we see that, as with the findings for stalemated negotiations, both domestic political as well as military strategic incentives supported the decision of the leaders within the challenger to adopt more confrontational policies. There are over forty disputes in which the target undertook actions to challenge the status quo, and in many of these disputes we find evidence that actions by the target were characterized by the challenger as illegitimate. Therefore, the challenger argued that an escalatory response was justified. In these cases political leaders felt the need to respond to the actions of the target in a confrontational manner due to domestic political pressures. However, in numerous cases the threat or use of military force by the challenger was initiated with the intent of pressuring the

possibly be extended to include the hypothesis that challengers should be expected to resort to higher levels of diplomatic and military escalation either just prior to or during periods of ongoing negotiations in an attempt to induce the target to make concessions. This would be consistent with the notion that the strategic use of coercive pressure is a central feature of interstate bargaining. Several examples can be cited to support this proposition. In the case of the Argentine invasion of the Falklands in April 1982, a round of talks had been completed between the two countries in February, and a further round of talks was planned for later that year. As already described, the objective behind the Argentine invasion was to gain control of the islands so that when talks resumed, Britain would find itself in such a weak position that it would make far-reaching concessions. In Africa, the armed confrontation initiated by Morocco against Algeria in 1963 was designed to pressure Algeria to be more accommodating in the context of the latest round of negotiations initiated in the previous year. Similarly, Mali's support for an insurgency movement within Mauritania in the early 1960s was directed at putting pressure on Mauritania to make concessions in the ongoing negotiations over their disputed border. In the Persian Gulf Iran engaged in military clashes along the Iraqi border as well as providing support for the Kurdish rebellion within Iraq during the period of negotiations leading to the 1975 Algiers Accord. Indeed, the primary reason why Iraq made concessions to Iran in the 1975 agreement was to induce Iran to end its support for the Kurdish rebellion. Finally, against the backdrop of intermittent rounds of border talks both China and India during the period from late 1959 until the fall of 1962 were engaging in the buildup and show of military forces within disputed border regions in an attempt to show their resolve and strengthen their bargaining position in the negotiations.

target so that it would reconsider its policies and possibly make concessions in future talks.

For example, in many of these cases the actions of the target provoked a strong response from the challenger, and their opposition was
clearly communicated to the broader international community via international forums such as the United Nations and regional organizations
such as the Arab League, the OAU, or the OAS (Organization of American States). In protesting and condemning the behavior of the target,
the leaders of the challenger argued that the actions of the target were
illegitimate and often issued either veiled or explicit warnings of future
reprisals against the target. At the same time, challenger leaders also
clearly conveyed to their own domestic political audience their opposition to the actions of the target. Domestically, within the challenger,
opposition and hostility toward the target were already well established
and supported by the population. As a result, political leaders *did not
need to justify* to their domestic political audience more coercive actions.
Nevertheless, domestic pressures to stand up and oppose the actions of
the target provided clear incentives for leaders within the challenger to
adopt more belligerent policies. Reprisals by the challenger typically
included an increase in diplomatic and economic pressure against the
target through actions such as restrictions on trade or aid, and the sever-
ing of diplomatic ties. Furthermore, in some cases the challenger would
extend greater material or financial support to rebel groups operating in
the disputed territory, but the use of military force to compel or punish
the target was less frequent.

The Arab-Israeli conflict illustrates many of these points quite
well. For example, in the 1950s and early 1960s Israeli plans to divert
water sources from the Jordan River provoked strong opposition from
the Arab states, who brought the case before the United Nations and
argued that Israeli plans were a threat to their own economic security
and violated international law. Furthermore, military action was threatened on several occasions, and border raids and small-scale armed
clashes were initiated by Syria. At a crucial meeting of the Arab
League in January 1964, however, Syria could not convince Egypt and
other Arab states to go to war over this issue and, as a result, the Arab
League did not sanction the option of resorting to the large-scale use of
force against Israel.[56] Similarly, following the Six Day War of 1967,

---

56. On the dispute over the waters of the Jordan river see Samir Saliba, *The Jordan
River Dispute* (The Hague: Nijhoff, 1968); Yoram Nimrod, "Conflict over the Jordan–Last
Stage," *New Outlook* 8, no. 6 (1965): 5–18; G. H. Jensen, "The Problem of the Jordan
Waters," *World Today* 20, no. 2 (1964): 60–68; and Lieberman, "The Rational Deterrence
Theory Debate," 398–400. Regarding the larger question of Israel's ability to deter mili-

Israeli development of settlements in the occupied West Bank was condemned repeatedly by the Arab states and brought to the United Nations for consideration. Additionally, border raids into the West Bank were initiated by PLO forces, but a direct military challenge by Arab armies to the Israeli occupation in the West Bank was not attempted. Similarly, PLO raids from bases in Lebanon were supported by Syria, and the goal was to make clear to Israel the continuing costs of holding onto occupied territories. Syria, however, was also cautious in escalating the tensions along the Lebanese border to a major military confrontation. The Syrian desire to put military pressure on Israel and to inflict casualties was tempered by the recognition of Israeli military strength.[57]

The Domestic Context of Decisions to Escalate

In this section I discuss the results for two hypotheses that were tested. In the discussion of the findings in the previous section I noted that the predominant impact of domestic politics was to encourage leaders to remain on a course of confrontation with the target following diplomatic and military conflict. The first hypothesis tested in this section also presents supporting evidence for the argument that confrontational policies often rallied domestic support behind the regime, and therefore the response of political leaders within the challenger to prior conflict with the target was to charge the target with aggressive and unyielding behavior. This type of rhetoric and public posturing, in turn, supported the arguments of hard-line groups within the challenger favoring continued confrontation and further escalation. Political leaders then would receive domestic political support for maintaining confrontational policies toward the target. In many respects domestic politics within the challenger reinforced the adversarial nature of interstate relations between the challenger and target.

The first strong finding then is that a past history of militarized

---

tary attacks and the operation of guerrilla forces along the border see Shimshoni, *Israel and Conventional Deterrence* and Brad O'Neill, *Armed Struggle in Palestine* (Boulder: Westview Press, 1978).

57. See for example O'Neill, *Armed Struggle in Palestine*, 43–46, 65–66, 94–97, 126–34, 215–29; Shimshoni, *Israel and Conventional Deterrence;* Yair Evron, *War and Intervention in Lebanon* (Baltimore: Johns Hopkins University Press, 1987), chs. 4, 6; Zeev Schiff and Ehud Ya'ari, *Israel's Lebanon War* (New York: Simon & Schuster, 1984), chs. 2–7, 11; Itamar Rabinovich, *The War for Lebanon, 1970–1985,* rev. ed. (Ithaca: Cornell University Press, 1985), 127–31, 143–47, 155; William Harris, *Taking Root: Israeli Settlements in the West Bank, the Golan, and Gaza-Sinai, 1967–1980* (New York: John Wiley & Sons, 1980); and Tessler, *A History of the Israeli-Palestinian Conflict,* 466–74, 489–507, 519–31, 539–68.

disputes with the target increased the likelihood of subsequent escalation by the challenger. In table 8 we see that the coefficient for this variable is positive and very significant (t-ratio = 10.17), which clearly supports H14.1. The substantive effect for this variable is large as well. In table 11 the marginal impact analysis indicates that a change from no militarized disputes to as many as forty such disputes since 1900 increases the likelihood of challenger escalation (y = 1 or 2) by about 51 percent. These results are consistent with the argument of H14.1 that when political leaders confront an adversary with whom there is a long-term history of past conflict, they are likely to have a strong base of domestic political support for continuing to pursue territorial claims by a combination of confrontational diplomatic and/or military policies. Similar results are obtained when we consider the more short-term history of past militarized confrontations between challenger and target. Thus, when we substitute into the equation the variable measuring the number of militarized disputes between the challenger and target in the previous year, the coefficient is positive and significant (b = 0.64, t-ratio = 11.84), and the marginal impact of the variable produces an approximate 47 percent

TABLE 11. The Marginal Impact of Variables Measuring the Domestic Context on the Level of Conflict over Disputed Territory

Change in Value of Explanatory Variable	Probability of Alternative Levels of Conflict (%)		
	$y = 0$	$y = 1$	$y = 2$
History of Conflict			
How many militarized disputes were challenger and target involved in since 1900?			
0 vs. 5	−5.3	+4.5	+0.8
5 vs. 10	−5.9	+4.8	+1.1
10 vs. 20	−13.3	+9.7	+3.6
20 vs. 30	−14.0	+7.9	+6.1
30 vs. 40	−13.0	+4.0	+9.0
Democratic Norms			
For how many years has the challenger been democratic in the past twenty-five years?			
0 vs. 5	+1.8	−1.4	−0.4
5 vs. 10	+1.7	−1.4	−0.3
10 vs. 15	+1.7	−1.4	−0.3
15 vs. 20	+1.6	−1.3	−0.3
20 vs. 25	+1.5	−1.3	−0.2

Note: See the note to table 9 for a description of how the changes in the probability of conflict levels were calculated.

increase in the probability of escalation. In sum, the domestic political consequences of past conflict with the target have both short- and long-term effects, which act to perpetuate the adversarial relationship between the two states.

A number of examples illustrate these statistical results quite well. In South America political leaders within Argentina have drawn on nationalist support to confront their historical adversary of Chile, while in Ecuador political elites have received strong domestic support for a policy of confrontation with Peru. In the case of Ecuador, the previous defeat of their country in armed conflict at the hands of Peru and the resulting loss of national territory provided the domestic political foundation for leaders to challenge the territorial status quo with a policy that sought to redress prior setbacks, based on the premise that Peru had acted aggressively in the past. Furthermore, in both Argentina and Ecuador diplomatic and militarized confrontations in the postwar period with their historical adversaries were accompanied by political leaders mobilizing popular support for their policy of opposition and, in turn, domestic political pressures were exerted on leaders to maintain a confrontational policy toward the target.[58] In the Far East the long history of military conflict involving both Japan and China against the Soviet Union contributed to a deep sense of mistrust within the Chinese political and military leadership, which, in turn, supported unyielding diplomatic positions and cool and even at times hostile bilateral relations between the countries.[59]

In the Mediterranean, a history of armed conflict between Greece and Turkey ensured that foreign policy leaders within both countries could count on strong domestic political support for a policy of competition and rivalry over Cyprus. Furthermore, public opinion in both coun-

---

58. See Peter Calvert, *Boundary Disputes in Latin America* (London: Institute for the Study of Conflict, 1983); Oscar Moraga, *El Precio dela Paz Chileno-Argentina, 1810–1969*, vol. 3 (Santiago: Editorial Naccimeuto, 1969); Juan Lanus, *De Chapultepec al Beagle: Politica Exterior Argentina, 1945–1980* (Buenos Aires: Emece Editores, 1984); David Zook, *Zarumilla y Maranon: The Ecuador-Peru Dispute* (New York: Bookman Associates Inc., 1964); and Krieg, *Ecuadorean-Peruvian Rivalry in the Upper Amazon.*

59. On Japanese relations with the Soviet Union see William Nimmo, *Japan and Russia* (Westport, CT: Greenwood Press, 1994), chs. 1–2 and Donald Hellmann, *Japanese Foreign Policy and Domestic Politics* (Berkeley: University of California Press, 1969). The history of diplomatic and military conflict between China and the Soviet Union is presented in Tsien-hua Tsui, *The Sino-Soviet Border Dispute in the 1970s* (Oakville: Mosaic Press, 1983), ch. 1; Henry Wei, *China and Soviet Russia* (Princeton: D. Van Nostrand, 1956); Sow-Theng Leong, *Sino-Soviet Diplomatic Realtions, 1917–1926* (Canberra: Australian National University Press, 1976); Tai Sung An, *The Sino-Soviet Territorial Dispute* (London: Westminster, 1973).

tries at times pressured governments to adopt forceful policies in response to the perceived aggressive actions of each state.[60] In Africa, the hostile relations between Morocco and Algeria in the early 1960s were used by Moroccan leaders to bolster their domestic political standing. However, this policy of opposition to Algeria had the longer-term effect of compelling Moroccan leaders in the mid- to late 1960s to persist in confrontational policies even after a change in policy was deemed desirable.[61] Finally, in the Middle East, confrontational policies toward Israel were always good domestic politics for leaders within Arab countries such as Jordan, Syria, and Egypt, particularly after a recent escalation in political and military conflict with Israel. Analysts have argued for example that confrontations with Israel in the 1960s were used by Syrian leaders to try and build political support for the regime.[62]

An example involving Egypt and Israel in the 1950s nicely captures the dynamics summarized above. In February 1955 Israeli forces carried out a large-scale retaliatory strike against guerrilla forces and military targets in the Gaza Strip, resulting in close to 100 Egyptian casualties. Within Egypt the Israeli raid created an uproar, and there was strong domestic political pressure on President Nasser to respond forcefully. Prior to the raid Israeli and Egyptian officials had held several secret meetings to explore the possibilities of a peace settlement, but the Israeli strike scuttled any further talks.[63] The response of President Nasser, as one analyst argued, was to "put Israel and Egypt on a collision course. Its consequences were inexorable: Nasser's decision to mount *fedayeen* guerrilla-type reprisals, the succession of raids and reprisals; the expanding arms race; and, finally, the Sinai War."[64] In sum, a history of adversarial relations created a domestic political environment in which elites within the challenger could expect strong support for a confrontational policy toward the target. At times such support actually pressed leaders to adopt hard-line policies when they themselves favored

60. See for example Bahcheli, *Greek-Turkish Relations,* 27–28, 34–41, 62–73, 87–90, 107–13, 121–24, 133; Christopher Hitchens, *Cyprus* (London: Quartet Books, 1984), 31–32, 39–47, 53–57, 105–19, 133–39, 151, 155; and Polyvios Polyviou, *Cyprus: Conflict and Negotiation 1960–1980* (London: Duckworth, 1980), 13–15, 36, 40–45, 67–69, 102–4, 122–31, 147–48, 154–57, 168–69, 190–98, 205–13.

61. See Touval, *The Boundary Politics of Independent Africa,* 255–69.

62. See for example Tessler, *A History of the Israeli-Palestinian Conflict,* 360, 365–67, 378; Adeed Dawisha, "Arab Regimes: Legitimacy and Foreign Policy," in Giacomo Luciani, ed., *The Arab State* (Berkeley: University of California Press, 1990), 284–99; and Yaacov Bar-Siman-Tov, *Linkage Politics in the Middle East* (Boulder: Westview, 1983).

63. See Tessler, *A History of the Israeli-Palestinian Conflict,* 338–46.

64. See Robert Bowie, *Suez: International Crises and the Role of Law* (New York: Oxford University Press, 1974), 10.

more accommodative policies. Nevertheless, a domestic political consensus within the challenger in support of a hard-line position was generally tempered by the leader's awareness of their country's military weakness. Thus, Japan did not attempt militarily to challenge the Soviet Union's control over the disputed northern Kurile Islands, Greece was not willing to confront Turkey in a direct military confrontation in several crises over Cyprus,[65] and Ecuador engaged only in low-level militarized probes along the disputed border with Peru.[66]

Up to this point, when domestic politics have been discussed I have emphasized how domestic political support has generally favored continued conflict and confrontation with a target state. The final set of findings, in contrast, focus on domestic political factors predicted to promote cooperation between the challenger and target and to reduce the incentives of the challenger to escalate a dispute. In H17.1 it was hypothesized that democratic challengers were less likely to engage in escalatory actions against the target. In table 8 the coefficient for the democratic norms variable is negative as expected and significant (the t-ratio = 3.01). The substantive effect of this variable, however, is not that large, as indicated by the results in table 11. We see there that as we move from a case in which the challenger has no history of democratic rule to one in which the challenger has been democratic for the past twenty-five years, the likelihood of high levels of diplomatic and military conflict decreases by about 8 percent.

If we examine the cases in more detail we find an interesting pattern. Among the forty-one disputes with relatively high levels of escalation,[67] only one (India vs. Portugal) involved challenger states with a well-established pattern of democratic rule (at least fifteen years of prior democratic rule for a majority of the years in dispute). Thus, in about 98 percent of the cases (40/41) with very high levels of escalation, the challenger was nondemocratic, clearly supporting H17.1. Furthermore, if we consider only those disputes in which the challenger had high democracy scores, the percentage of cases with relatively high levels of

---

65. Since 1960 there have been three major international crises over Cyprus involving Greece and Turkey. In both 1964 and 1967 Greek governments accepted diplomatic settlements favored by Turkey under the threat of Turkish military intervention, and in 1974 Greece did not intervene to oppose the Turkish invasion of Cyprus. See Bahcheli, *The Greek-Turkish Dispute,* and Polyviou, *Cyprus.*

66. In 1953, 1954, and 1955 small-scale military troop movements along the border occurred, and in 1977 and 1981–1982 limited armed clashes took place. See Zook, *Zarumilla y Maranon* and Krieg, *Ecuadorean-Peruvian Rivalry in the Upper Amazon.*

67. These cases are defined as having a value of 1 or 2 on the exogenous variable for a majority of the years that a dispute existed, including at least two militarized disputes.

escalation is quite low (2/20 or only 10 percent). Once again, H17.1 receives support. However, when one examines the population of dispute cases in which the challenger had a low democratic norms coding, less than one-half of the disputes were characterized by relatively high levels of escalation. Thus, there are a substantial number of cases in which nondemocratic states did not resort to high levels of diplomatic or military pressure, contrary to the expectations of H17.1. The modest results in tables 8 and 11 therefore are not a reflection of the fact that democratic states often engaged in high levels of escalation but that a good number of nondemocratic states failed to do so.

If we then examine those cases in which nondemocratic challengers did not engage in high levels of escalation, the one common feature is that the challenger in a large number of cases faced more pressing security threats from states other than the target. As a result, the challenger either gave a low priority to the dispute with the target and therefore was not very active in pursuing its claim, or the challenger and target shared a common adversary and the challenger decided to build friendly relations with the target in an attempt to solidify the target's support as an ally. For example, in the dispute between Iran and Saudi Arabia both countries were entangled in more confrontational territorial disputes with other states, and therefore they shared a mutual interest in avoiding high levels of escalation in their own conflict. Similarly, Ethiopia's conflict with Somalia provided a strong impetus for Ethiopia to pursue accommodative policies toward its other neighbors, Kenya and Sudan. Both of these examples illustrate the more general point that external security considerations often seemed to be pivotal in determining how flexible and accommodative the challenger was, despite the presence of opposing domestic political forces.

The final result in table 8 to report is that the variable included in the equation to capture the potential effects of selection bias had a negative coefficient that was significant (t-ratio $= -5.15$) and, though not presented in a table, produced about a 9 percent decrease in the likelihood of escalation. The substantive interpretation of the negative coefficient for this variable is that the more likely a challenger was to be involved in a territorial dispute, the less likely it was to escalate the dispute to high levels of diplomatic and military conflict. This may seem counterintuitive at first, that is, we should expect that the more resolved a state is to dispute territory, the more likely it would be to escalate the dispute. This inverse relationship, however, makes sense when the results from chapter 4 are considered carefully. Remember that the challengers most likely to be involved in territorial disputes were those states that: (1) had previously lost territory to the target, (2) had disputed territory for a protracted period of time, and (3) were pressing the target to decolonize. In many of these cases, a common attribute of the challenger was its *lack of military strength*. For example, the reason why the challenger had lost territory previously was often due in part to a weak military position. Similarly, one reason why challengers were involved in long-standing disputes was their inability to force the target by the credible threat of force to make territorial concession. Finally, in most cases challengers who were pressing for decolonization were developing countries, and the target was a much stronger military power such as France, Great Britain, or the United States. Thus, in these types of cases even though these challengers were strongly motivated to dispute territory, they often lacked the military means to back up their claims. Of the twenty-six cases in which the challenger previously lost territory and was involved in a dispute with the target prior to World War II, the challenger had a favorable balance of forces in only three cases (about 12 percent). In the remaining twenty-three cases (88 percent) the challenger's military position was moderately to very weak compared to the target. The military weakness of the challenger is even more apparent when we examine the fifty cases in which the challenger was disputing colonial/overseas territories of the target. In only three cases (6 percent) did the challenger enjoy a military advantage, while in the remaining forty-seven cases (94 percent) the challenger was at a disadvantage. Furthermore, in thirty-nine cases (78 percent) the ratio of challenger to target military capabilities was one-to-four or less. Thus, it is not a contradiction to find that challengers who are the most likely to dispute territory are actually less capable of escalating the dispute. At the same time, the substantive impact of this variable is relatively modest, reflecting the fact that there are a number of factors that shape patterns of challenger escalation within a dispute but are not predictors of whether a dispute is initiated to begin with (e.g., dispute involvement with other states, defeat in armed conflict, stalemate in negotiations). As a result, a prior understanding of the propensity for a challenger to issue a claim to territory is helpful but not decisive in understanding the dynamics of escalation over disputed territory.

Conclusion

In this chapter I empirically tested the power of the modified realist model to explain levels of diplomatic and military conflict over disputed territory. The statistical results, coupled with the more detailed examination of individual cases, revealed that decisions by challenger states to escalate

TABLE 12. Conventional Realist Model and Ordered Probit Estimates of Level of Conflict among Territorial Disputes, 1950–90

Explanatory Variables	Coefficient	Standard Errors	Significance Level
Constant	−0.304	0.145	<.025
Selection effects	−0.195	0.113	<.05
Issues at Stake			
Strategic location of territory	0.562	0.058	<.001
Economic value of territory	−0.164	0.047	<.001
International Context			
Balance of military forces	0.998	0.098	<.001
Challenger disputes	−0.115	0.015	<.001
Stalemate in negotiations	0.775	0.060	<.001
Attempt to change status quo	0.444	0.058	<.001
Defeat in armed conflict	−0.095	0.024	<.001
Deterrent alliance	−0.019	0.052	—
Common security ties	−0.625	0.054	<.001

Note: Number of observations = 3,039; Log-likelihood = −2463.1; Percentage of cases correctly predicted = 61.8; All significance levels based on one-tailed tests.

disputes were shaped by a complex interplay of domestic and international factors. Hypotheses cast at each level of analysis received varying degrees of empirical support and, thus, the principal claim of the modified realist model—the necessity to consider carefully both domestic and international factors in the study of security policy—is strongly supported by the evidence. Once again, if I compare the statistical performance of a traditional realist model with the modified realist model tested in this chapter, I find that the latter model adds considerable explanatory power. In table 12 I report the probit results for an equation that only includes traditional realist variables, and if the log-likelihood value for this equation is compared to the same value for the modified realist equation tested in table 8, we find that the difference in the log-likelihood values are significantly different ($v = 324.8$, $df = 4$, $p < .001$).[68]

One of the most interesting overall findings in this chapter was that the international political and military position of challenger states played a key role in explaining patterns of escalation, but in the previous chapter similar variables did not produce strong results when the focus was to explain the reasons why states were involved in territorial disputes. These contrasting results indicate that while state leaders are often not driven by

68. See footnote 58 in the conclusion to chapter 4 for a discussion of how the significance levels are calculated.

the goal of strategic gains or constrained by the balance of military power to dispute territory, they nevertheless do act strategically in their decisions as to when and to what level they will escalate a conflict over disputed territory.

A second central finding was that domestic politics within challenger states often acted as a force supporting and, in some cases, pushing leaders toward escalatory behavior. In most cases when the domestic political incentives to pursue a confrontational policy conflicted with international political opinion favoring accommodation, leaders decided on a course of action that was supported domestically but risked censure internationally.

The third major finding of this chapter was that while domestic political incentives often favored international conflict over accommodation, the domestic political incentives to escalate a dispute were tempered by calculations of relative military strength and the larger strategic context facing the leaders of challenger states.

CHAPTER 6

The Peaceful Resolution of Territorial Disputes

In the previous two chapters we have tested the ability of the modified realist model to explain the initiation and escalation of territorial disputes. In this chapter we shift the theoretical and empirical analysis to the outcomes of territorial disputes and attempt to explain when a challenger state will seek a peaceful resolution of a territorial dispute through compromise or conciliation.

Of the 129 cases of territorial disputes between 1950 and 1990, fifty-three cases (about 41 percent) were settled peacefully by the challenger through compromise or conciliation; in another fifty-seven cases (about 44 percent) the disputes were stalemated; and in the remaining nineteen cases (15 percent) the disputes were settled on terms favorable to the challenger, that is, by the occupation of disputed territory or capitulation by the target in a signed agreement. In a majority of cases (seventy-six or 59 percent), then, challengers were not willing to compromise on their territorial claims. Nevertheless, there were a substantial number of cases in which the challenger did in fact pursue a peaceful resolution of the dispute. The central question then is, What are the conditions associated with such peaceful outcomes? The purpose of this chapter is to use empirical tests to determine whether the hypotheses derived from the modified realist model can provide a compelling answer to this question.

As with chapters 4 and 5, I begin by presenting the equation to be tested and the research design for empirical analysis. Probit analysis is then used to test the equation, and the results are discussed and individual cases are examined to illustrate the statistical findings. In the concluding section I summarize the findings and their general theoretical implications.

Equation to Be Tested

The reasons why a challenger state would seek the resolution of a territorial dispute by compromise could be driven by both domestic as well international conditions. One set of hypotheses to be tested posit that foreign policy leaders will reach decisions largely on the basis of strategic priorities in a changing international political-military environment. The incentives to compromise increase when pressing conflicts emerge with other states and the target's support as an ally is deemed valuable; compromise is less attractive if the territory in dispute is of strategic value. On the other hand, the modified realist model also pays close attention to domestic politics within the challenger, and accordingly a number of hypotheses will be tested arguing that compromise with a target state is very often a difficult political move for leaders to pursue and thus the domestic political benefits of settling a dispute are often weak. Initiatives to settle, however, should be more likely among democratic challengers and when economic issues are at stake in the disputed territory.

The equation to be tested includes the following variables.

The endogenous variable y = the likelihood that a challenger will favor a peaceful resolution of a territorial dispute.

c = constant

The exogenous variables x_1 to x_{12} are specified as follows.

Issues at Stake
x_1 = strategic location of bordering territory (H1.2, negative)
x_2 = support for minorities along border of target who share ties of common language and ethnicity with challenger (H2.2, negative)
x_3 = political unification based on common language and ethnic background between populations of challenger and target (H3.2, negative)
x_4 = economic value of bordering territory (H4.3, positive)
International Context
x_5 = balance of conventional military forces between challenger and target (H5.2, negative)
x_6 = challenger dispute involvement with other states (H6.2, positive)
x_7 = target attempt to change status quo (H8.2, negative)
x_8 = defeat or stalemate in armed conflict (H9.2, positive)
x_9 = common security ties between challenger and target (H11.2, positive)
Domestic Context
x_{10} = prior militarized disputes with target (H14.2, negative)
x_{11} = democratic norms of challenger (H17.2, positive)
x_{12} = selection bias effect
u_t = error term

The endogenous variable (y) measures the willingness of a challenger to accept the location of a border on terms favored by the target. A three-point scale is utilized.

0 = the challenger refuses to compromise or withdraw its territorial claim and either (a) resorts to the use of military force in an attempt to seize disputed territory or (b) occupies disputed territory and refuses to withdraw despite the target's demand that it do so.

1 = the challenger refuses to make concessions over disputed territory, but conflict with the target is limited to diplomatic and nonmilitary actions.

2 = the challenger either proposes or agrees to territorial concessions by (a) offering to reduce its claims during negotiations with the target, (b) agreeing to a settlement in which disputed territory is divided, or (c) agreeing to accept the territorial status quo favored by the target.

The equation to be tested attempts to predict when a challenger state will seek and then agree to a territorial settlement through compromise and accommodation.[1] To code the outcome of each territorial dispute on an annual basis, multiple sources (listed in the bibliography at the end of appendix A) were consulted to create a yearly chronology of diplomatic and military (non)actions taken by the challenger with respect to the disputed territory of a target. If the challenger resorted to the use of military force (including the occupation of territory) during a given year and did not propose or agree to any territorial concessions, a value of zero was coded. When the challenger did not use military force, the endogenous variable was coded on the basis of the challenger's diplomatic and negotiating position over disputed territory at the end of any given year. The operational measures for each of the exogenous variables are summarized in appendix C.

The dataset to be analyzed in this chapter consists of the 129 territorial dispute cases listed in appendix A. Across the duration of each dispute, data was collected annually for all of the variables in the equation.[2] In total, there are 3,039 observations with close to 11 percent of

---

1. For the remainder of this chapter I will use the term *compromise by the challenger* to refer to the range of accommodative behavior coded as a value of 2 on the endogenous variable. Thus, compromise by the challenger includes the renunciation or withdrawal of claims to disputed territory.

2. In appendix D I discuss at greater length questions of research design in the construction of the dataset for this chapter.

the cases (317) coded a zero on the endogenous variable, while about 73 percent of the cases (2,224) were coded a value of one, and the remaining 16 percent of the cases (498) were coded a value of two.

Statistical Results and Case Analaysis

An ordered probit model was utilized to test the equation and, as in chapter 5, the potential effects of selection bias were taken into account in the estimation procedure.[3] The results of the probit analysis are presented in table 13 with the coefficients, robust standard errors, and significance levels reported. Overall, the results indicate that domestic as well as international factors play important roles in explaining when a challenger state is likely to seek and agree to a compromise settlement of a territorial dispute. The findings indicate that domestic political factors generally pressured leaders to avoid offering concessions. On the other hand, changing assessments of a country's strategic position and military strength were the primary forces that compelled leaders to seek a settlement despite domestic political obstacles. In the equation all of the estimated coefficients have the correct predicted sign, and all of them are significant with some variables producing large substantive effects. Based on these results a number of interesting comparisons can be made with the findings from the previous chapters.[4] To facilitate the interpretation of the substantive impact of each of the coefficients in table 13, a series of additional tables (14–16) are presented below reporting how changes in the value of an explanatory variable are associated with a change in the probability of a compromise settlement.

The presentation of the results will be divided into the same three sections as in the previous chapters. We will begin with the issues at stake and then consider in turn the international and domestic contexts of decisions to settle territorial disputes.

---

3. To correct for selection effects a two-stage estimation procedure was employed in which the selection equation first estimated the probability that bordering states would become involved in a territorial dispute. The outcome equation then estimated the probability that a challenger would seek a compromise settlement of a territorial dispute. See appendix D for a more complete description of the steps taken to correct for selection bias and a more general discussion of the statistical issues involved in the empirical analysis for this chapter.

4. Multicollinearity among the exogenous variables was tested for by regressing each exogenous variable on all other exogenous variables in a series of OLS runs. As with tests in chapters 4 and 5, the r-squared values from the OLS runs indicate that multicollinearity was not a problem with eight r-squared values less than .20, two values between .2 and .3, and the remaining two between .30 and .40.

The Issues at Stake and the Settlement of Disputes

The probit results for the variables measuring the issues at stake reveal an interesting pattern. All of the coefficients for the variables have the correct sign and are statistically significant. Nevertheless, none of the variables have large substantive effects in either promoting or blocking the settlement of disputes. The lack of stronger results points to a very important theme that is derived from the results of chapter 4: once a territorial dispute becomes a salient domestic political issue within the challenger, there are few political incentives for leaders to make concessions to settle a dispute. As a result, such territorial disputes often persist for a protracted period of time regardless of the specific issues at stake in the conflict. As will be discussed below, the generally modest findings for the issues at stake variables were not produced by the lack of a strong empirical relationship between the presence of a given variable and the expected pattern of compromise/no-compromise. Rather, the empirical pattern obtained was such that even when a variable was not present, the overall rate of compromise did not change very much; this reflects, I believe, the immobilism introduced by domestic politics toward the settlement of many disputes. The conclusion then is that no

TABLE 13. Ordered Probit Estimates of Probability of Peaceful Settlement of Territorial Disputes, 1950–90

Explanatory Variables	Coefficient	Standard Errors	Significance Level
Constant	1.275	0.154	<.001
Selection effects	0.068	0.117	—
Issues at Stake			
Strategic location of territory	−0.287	0.064	<.001
Ties to bordering minority	−0.217	0.055	<.001
Political unification	−0.172	0.059	<.005
Economic value of territory	0.147	0.045	<.001
International Context			
Balance of military forces	−0.165	0.091	<.05
Challenger disputes	0.038	0.012	<.001
Attempt to change status quo	−0.165	0.068	<.01
Defeat in armed conflict	0.357	0.045	<.001
Common security ties	0.571	0.060	<.001
Domestic Context			
Prior militarized disputes	−0.025	0.004	<.001
Democratic norms	0.018	0.004	<.001

Note: Number of observations = 3,039; Log-likelihood = −2,150; Percentage of cases correctly predicted = 73.02; All significance levels based on one-tailed tests.

particular set of issues are fundamentally more or less prone to compromise than others.

The first result in table 13 to discuss is for the hypothesis that a challenger should be less likely to seek a compromise settlement when disputed territory is of strategic value (H1.2). The coefficient for this variable is negative as expected and is significant with a t-ratio of 4.50. In the marginal impact analysis in table 14 we see that the presence of strategic territory decreased the likelihood of a settlement by close to 6 percent.

The conclusions that should be drawn from these findings need to be stated very carefully, however. When the data is examined in more detail we find that challengers, in fact, *do not compromise* in disputes in which strategic territory is at stake as predicted by H1.2. In total, there

TABLE 14.   The Marginal Impact of Variables Measuring the Issues at Stake on the Probability of the Challenger Compromising

	Probability of Challenger Compromising (%)		
Change in Value of Explanatory Variable	$y = 0$	$y = 1$	$y = 2$
Strategic Location of Territory			
Is bordering territory strategically located?			
No vs. Yes	+5.5	+0.0	−5.5
Ties to Bordering Minorities			
Do bordering minority groups within the target share ties of language and ethnicity with the population of the challenger?			
No vs. Yes	+4.0	+0.4	−4.4
Political Unification			
Do the populations of challenger and target share ties of a common language and ethnicity?			
No vs. Yes	+3.1	+0.5	−3.6
Economic Value of Territory			
Are natural resources with export value located within/ proximate to bordering territory, or would control of bordering territory provide a port outlet to promote trade?			
No vs. Yes	−2.1	−1.5	+3.6

Note: The changes in the probability of a dispute settlement were calculated utilizing the coefficients from the equation presented in table 13. The value of a single explanatory variable is changed while all continuous variables in the equation are held at their mean or the modal value for dummy variables. The change in the location on the cumulative normal distribution is then converted into the percentage change in the probability of compromise by the challenger. See Gary King, *Unifying Political Methodology* (Cambridge: Cambridge University Press, 1989), 106–8.

are twenty-five disputes involving strategic territory, and in twenty cases the rate of compromise is low. Thus, it would seem that 80 percent of the cases support the hypothesis. Put differently, in about 90 percent of the dispute years coded for the presence of strategically located territory, the challenger did not compromise or offer concessions (691/767).

A number of examples illustrate how challenger states were reluctant to make significant concessions over strategic territory in order to achieve a settlement: (1) Iran vs. UAE over the islands of Abu Musa and the Greater and Lesser Tunbs, (2) Iraq vs. Kuwait over the islands of Warba and Bubiyan, (3) China vs. Vietnam over the Spratly and Paracel Islands, (4) Syria vs. Israel over the Golan Heights, (5) Libya vs. Chad over the Aozou Strip, (6) Egypt vs. the United Kingdom over the Suez Canal, (7) Cuba vs. the United States over Guantanamo Bay, (8) Argentina vs. Chile over islands in the Beagle Channel, (9) the Spanish-British dispute over Gibraltar, and (10) China vs. India. In none of these cases did the challenger withdraw its territorial claim or offer one-sided concessions to meet the demands of the target. In only two cases—Argentina vs. Chile in 1984 and Libya vs. Chad in 1994—have compromise settlements been reached. In several of these cases challengers, despite regional opposition and isolation, persisted in their claims to the disputed territory. Iran, for example, has been widely criticized by other Persian Gulf states for its occupation of the disputed islands since 1971 but has not withdrawn. The OAU had called for the withdrawal of Libya from the Aozou Strip since the mid-1970s, but it was only after Libya had suffered heavy military losses in fighting within Chad in 1987 that Qadaffi agreed to submit the dispute to the ICJ.[5] Argentina, after decades of contesting Chilean rights to islands in the Beagle Channel, finally conceded them to Chile in a treaty signed in 1984. Even though Argentina did make territorial concessions in the treaty, security concerns were by no means abandoned by the new civilian government in reaching a settlement. As discussed below, the Argentine military was a vocal opponent of the treaty on the grounds that it compromised the country's national security, particularly maritime control over access to and from the Atlan-

---

5. See John Allcock, Guy Arnold, Alan Day, D. S. Lewis, Lorimer Poultney, Roland Rance, and D. J. Sagar, *Border and Territorial Disputes*, rev. 3d ed. (London: Longman, 1992), 232–34, 383–84; Colin Legum and Marion Doro, eds., *Africa Contemporary Record 1987–1988* (New York: African Publishing Co., 1989), 180–84; Rene Lemarchand, ed., *The Green and the Black* (Bloomington: Indiana University Press, 1988), ch. 6; and J. M. Abdulghani, *Iraq and Iran: The Years of Crisis* (London: Croom Helm, 1984), 89–92. For a summary of the ICJ ruling issued in February 1994 see *Keesing's Record of World Events 1994* (London: Longman, 1994), 39849.

tic. President Alfonsin, however, was aware that he had to be able to make a credible case to the Argentine public that important security interests were protected in the agreement. Thus, while Alfonsin did agree to a major concession by recognizing Chilean sovereignty over the disputed islands in the Beagle Channel, he also addressed basic security concerns by insisting that Chile accept tight restrictions on its maritime rights to the Atlantic. As a result, Alfonsin argued that the security interests of Argentina were protected by the Treaty.[6]

There are also a number of disputes in which challengers were more willing to accept compromise settlements with other neighboring states when disputed territory was not strategically important to them. For example, China concluded agreements in the early 1960s over small sections of disputed territory with neighboring countries such as Afghanistan, Nepal, Burma, and Pakistan. Furthermore, China has been more accommodative with both Malaysia and the Philippines over the Spratly Islands since neither country is viewed as a regional adversary, and therefore a presence by these countries among the islands to develop their economic potential is not viewed as a threat. In contrast, China has been very concerned about the security implications of Vietnamese control of the Spratly and Paracel Islands.[7] Other examples would include Iran settling a dispute with Saudi Arabia over several offshore islands and Argentina reaching an agreement with Uruguay over the boundary along the Rio de la Plata river. In each of these cases the lack of security issues at stake seemed to have contributed to compromise settlements.[8] Nevertheless, across the entire dataset of

---

6. See James Garrett, "The Beagle Channel Dispute," *Journal of Inter-American Studies and World Affairs* 27, no. 1 (1985): 81–109; Jack Hopkins, *Latin America and Caribbean Contemporary Record 1984–1985* (New York: Holmes & Meier, 1986), 229–42; Abraham Lowenthal, *Latin America and Caribbean Contemporary Record 1985–1986* (New York: Holmes & Meier, 1988), B3–B21.

7. See for example Anne Gilks, *The Breakdown of the Sino-Vietnamese Alliance, 1970–1979* (Berkeley: Institute of East Asian Studies, 1992), 112–15 and Chi-kin Lo, *China's Policy towards Territorial Disputes* (London: Routledge, 1989).

8. In these two cases documentary evidence of the decisions to reach settlements is very limited, and therefore any conclusions about these cases are tentative. Nevertheless, the relative ease with which agreements were reached and the lack of reference to strategic issues in these disputes contrasts sharply with the behavior of Iran and Argentina in other disputes in which concern over the strategic value of territory was expressed by political and military leaders—for example, the Argentine claim to islands in the Beagle Channel or the Iranian claims to islands in the Strait of Hormuz. On the settlement of the Saudi-Iranian dispute see S. H. Amin, *International and Legal Problems of the Gulf* (London: Middle East and North African Studies Press Limited, 1981), 101–6 and Rouhallah Ramazani, *Iran's Foreign Policy 1941–1973* (Charlottesville: University Press of Virginia, 1975), 413–14. The Argentina dispute with Uruguay is summarized in Robert Butterworth, *Managing Interstate Conflict, 1945–74* (Pitts-

dispute cases, whether strategic territory was in dispute did not seem to make a very large difference in the likelihood of compromise by the challenger. The lack of stronger results in the probit analysis, then, reflects the fact that even when strategic issues were not at stake, the likelihood of compromise by the challenger was generally not very high, that is, the presence of strategic territory was far from being a necessary condition for the challenger to adopt an inflexible diplomatic and negotiating position. Thus, of the 2,541 dispute years in the dataset in which the challenger refused to compromise ($y = 0$ or 1), only about 27 percent (or 691 years) were correlated with the presence of strategic territory.

The next finding in table 13 is that the challenger was less likely to compromise when issues of political and national unification were intertwined in the dispute over territory. The negative coefficient for the ethnic/cultural similarity variable was in the predicted direction (H3.2), and it is significant with a t-ratio of -2.95. In table 14 we find that this variable decreases the likelihood of a compromise settlement by approximately a modest 4 percent. Once again, the lack of stronger results is due to the fact that a common ethnic background between challenger and target was by no means a necessary condition for the challenger to adopt an unyielding position in its claims to territory. For example, of the 2,541 dispute years in which the challenger did not compromise, only 27 percent of those years (691) involved disputes in which both challenger and target shared common ethnic and linguistic ties. On the other hand, almost 82 percent of the time when the common ethnic background variable was coded as present, there was no compromise by the challenger (691/844).

If we examine individual cases we find a number of examples supporting the general logic of H3.2. Across these cases we find that challengers were often not willing to withdraw claims to territory that was once part of their national territory and which they believed should be reclaimed by their country. Indeed, in some cases the challenger sought complete unification with the target. For example, there were nine such cases in which the challenger sought political unification with the target, and in only one case (Morocco vs. Mauritania in 1970) did the challenger formally withdraw all territorial claims in a treaty.[9] In two other cases (Egypt vs. Sudan in 1956 and Iraq vs. Kuwait in 1963) the challenger recognized the independence of the target but claims to more limited

burgh: University Center for International Studies, University of Pittsburgh, 1976), 430–31.

9. See Saadia Touval, *The Boundary Politics of Independent Africa* (Cambridge: Harvard University Press, 1972), 255–69 and Tony Hodges, *Western Sahara: The Roots of Desert War* (Westport, CT: Lawrence Hill & Company, 1983), ch. 11.

sections of territory remained.[10] In the remaining six cases the challenger remained committed to unification and therefore did not compromise on this basic goal (though concessions were offered on the terms of unification): North vs. South Vietnam; North vs. South Korea; China vs. Taiwan; North vs. South Yemen; Ireland vs. the United Kingdom; and West vs. East Germany.[11] Challengers were also reluctant to compromise when they sought the recovery of territory lost as a result of defeat in war with neighboring states. In South America, Bolivia has sought the return of coastal territory lost in the Pacific War of 1879–1884, and Ecuador has refused to recognize the loss of territory to Peru (formalized in the Rio Protocol signed in 1942) following its defeat in armed conflict in 1941.

Several of these cases involved the loss or division of territory in agreements signed during the period of colonial rule and since the end of World War I. As a result, the political legitimacy of the territorial status quo established by these agreements was often questioned by the challenger. In many of these cases leaders within the challenger believed that their country had the right to extend its political rule over the territory of the target and that the extension of their country's borders would enhance their own domestic political power and prestige.

There are a number of cases, however, in which issues of territorial unification or annexation did not seem to play much of a role, and challengers therefore settled disputes through compromise. Examples would include Argentina vs. Uruguay, Netherlands vs. Belgium, Jordan vs. Saudi Arabia, Saudi Arabia vs. Kuwait, and Tunisia vs. Algeria. In each of these cases the disputed territory was not heavily populated and was quite limited in size, and that seems to have had the important consequence of reducing its domestic political saliency within the challenger. Furthermore, in several cases territorial control was not necessary for the challenger to achieve tangible benefits in a settlement. That is, oil deposits were located within the disputed territory, and the most important issue for the challenger was to capture some portion of the

---

10. See Touval, *The Boundary Politics of Independent Africa,* 194–96; Hussein Zulfakar Sabry, *Sovereignty for Sudan* (London: Ithaca Press, 1982); Graham Thomas, *Sudan, 1950–1985* (London: Darf Publishers LTD., 1990), chs. 2–3; and David Finne, *Shifting Lines in the Sand* (Cambridge: Harvard University Press, 1992), ch. 10.

11. In this last case even though West Germany formally recognized East Germany in 1972, the West German government explicitly maintained that it continued to seek peaceful reunification with East Germany. See for example Wolfram Hanrieder, *Germany, America, Europe: Forty Years of German Foreign Policy* (New Haven: Yale University Press, 1989), chs. 6–7 and William Griffith, *The Ostpolitik of the Federal Republic of Germany* (Cambridge: MIT Press, 1978).

revenue and income that would be generated by the development of the resources. One solution was to divide the territory and thereby share the economic benefits (e.g., Saudi agreements to divide oil-rich neutral zones with Kuwait and Iraq), and another solution was to renounce the claim to territory in exchange for an agreement to enter into joint development projects in the disputed territory (Tunisia and Algeria). These cases reinforce the first point made above that when disputed territory does not become an issue infused with domestic political significance, leaders have far greater flexibility in their diplomatic options. Finally, the relative lack of domestic political attention given to the disputes reflects the fact that the challenger often had more pressing territorial disputes with other states. For example, in Argentina the issues at stake in disputes with both Chile and the British were much more important than those at issue in the dispute with Uruguay. Kuwait was far more concerned about threats to its security from Iraq than from Saudi Arabia, while Iraqi disputes with Iran and Kuwait were more pressing than with Saudi Arabia.

One of the most interesting findings in table 13 is that the presence of minority groups along the border with ethnic ties to the general population of the challenger *did not have a strong effect* on the likelihood of a compromise settlement. It is widely believed that ethnic disputes are explosive and very difficult to resolve through negotiations. The probit results, however, do not strongly support this conclusion. The negative coefficient for the minority variable in table 13 is consistent with H2.2 and is significant (t-ratio $= -3.91$), but in table 14 we find that the presence of a minority group along the border decreased the likelihood of a settlement by only about 4 percent.

An examination of the cases reveals general support for the hypothesis, but nevertheless there are a number of disputes in which the challenger did compromise despite the presence of groups within disputed territory with ethnic ties to the challenger. In total, of the 878 dispute years that a bordering minority was coded as present, about 87 percent were also coded as years of no compromise by the challenger (760). On the other hand, only about 30 percent of all noncompromise years involved disputes with bordering minorities (760/2,541).

In many disputes the challenger's support for the minority group along the border became a foreign policy issue with strong popular and elite backing within the challenger. A number of examples illustrate the point that challenger regimes often received strong domestic support for championing the rights of self-determination for groups that were a minority within the target: Pakistan's support for Muslims in India-controlled Kashmir, Somali claims to the Ogaden region of Ethiopia populated by ethnic Somalis, Turkey's support for Turkish Cypriots, or Afghanistan's dispute with Pakistan over bordering territory populated by Pathan tribes. As a result of the domestic political saliency of the dispute, leaders within the challenger were very unlikely to compromise or withdraw their support for the minority groups along the border. Instead, political leaders within the challenger could generate domestic political support by confronting the target over the treatment and rights of these minority groups, and therefore an agreement to settle the dispute on terms acceptable to the target would not have generated political payoffs for the leadership of the challenger. This combination of nationalistic appeals serving the political interests of elites is precisely why ethnic conflicts can become such intractable international disputes.

However, in a number of cases challengers did, in fact, withdraw their claims to territory populated by minorities. Why is it that leaders within the challenger in these cases did not seem to be tightly constrained by domestic political forces to remain deadlocked in dispute with the target, or did not draw on nationalism to mobilize support against the target? One explanation, which reiterates a point already made, is that in many of these cases the territories in question were not densely populated and were also small in size (Saudi Arabia vs. Qatar; Ethiopia vs. Sudan and Kenya; Tunisia vs. Algeria; Pakistan vs. China; or Iran vs. the Soviet Union). Leaders within the challenger therefore did not attempt to mobilize popular support behind the issue, and political actors outside the government did not put pressure on the political leadership to take a stronger stand in support of the bordering populations.[12] Furthermore, in several cases control of economic resources such as oil or iron ore deposits located within the disputed territory constituted the primary issues at stake (Saudi Arabia vs. Qatar, Morocco vs. Algeria, Tunisia vs. Algeria), and thus the dispute was not framed by the challenger as one over rights of self-determination for ethnic groups.[13]

The two cases involving West Germany's recognition of the postwar borders of Poland and Czechoslovakia are also interesting to consider. In both cases sizable territories were in dispute but the number of Germans still living in the territories was very small in the postwar period. Indeed, most of the Germans who had been living in the territories prior to World War II were forced to relocate after the war. In 1970 West

---

    12. See for example Touval, *The Boundary Politics of Independent Africa*, 246–49, 251–69 and Anwar Syad, *China and Pakistan: Diplomacy of an Entente Cordiale* (Amherst: University of Massachusetts Press, 1974), ch. 4.

    13. See for example Touval, *The Boundary Politics of Independent Africa*, 251–69 and J. B. Kelly, *Arabia, the Gulf and the West* (London: Weidenfeld and Nicolson, 1980), 187–88.

Germany recognized the Oder-Neisse Line as Poland's western frontier, and in 1973 it withdrew all claims to the Sudetenland region of Czechoslovakia. Within West Germany there were considerable domestic political incentives not to formally recognize the postwar borders of either country, but Brandt and other West German leaders forcefully made the argument that the existing policy of nonrecognition was an obstacle to the fundamental goal of German reunification because it isolated the country and weakened its international legitimacy. In essence, then, one of the foundations of West Germany's policy of *ostpolitik* was the recognition that an overly conservative and domestically based policy of appealing to nationalism was, in fact, counterproductive to achieving the actual goal of reunification. Thus, West German leaders recognized the necessity of making some territorial compromises in order to advance the primary goal of German reunification.[14]

The next result in table 13 is that territorial disputes were more likely to be settled by compromise when access to and control over natural resources with economic value were at stake. In table 13 we see that the coefficient for this variable is positive as expected by H4.3, and significant (t-ratio = 3.26). In table 14 we see that challengers are only about 4 percent more likely to compromise when disputed territory contains economically valuable resources. The primary reason for the modest substantive effect of this variable is apparent when we examine the cases in more detail. A pattern emerges that when economic issues are predominantly at stake then compromise settlements are quite likely. In these cases the logic of H4.3 works quite well, since a challenger can agree with the target to an accommodative settlement that still produces domestic political payoffs, that is, the challenger can recognize the target's right to sovereignty over some or all the disputed territory, but nevertheless an agreement can be concluded jointly to develop or divide the resources located within the disputed territory.

The link between the divisibility of economic resources and the resolution of territorial disputes is illustrated by each of the following cases in which various economic agreements either preceded or accompanied territorial compromise by the challenger. For example, the signing of agreements between Argentina and Uruguay on economic cooperation, including plans to develop oil resources in the Rio de la Plata River, was important in finalizing a formal territorial settlement in 1973 over the location of the boundary and the possession of various islands in the river.[15] In a series of settlements with its neighbors, Saudi Arabia

---

14. See Hanrieder, *Germany, America, Europe,* chs. 6–7 and Griffith, *The Ostpolitik of the Federal Republic of Germany.*

15. See Butterworth, *Managing Interstate Conflict,* 430–31.

agreed to the division of bordering territory or offshore islands containing oil deposits with Iran, Iraq, Kuwait, Qatar, and the UAE.[16] Finally, both Morocco and Tunisia signed agreements with Algeria to develp jointly oil or iron ore resources within disputed territory prior to formally renouncing their territorial claims.[17]

Settlements, however, were not as frequent when the disputed territory was valued not only for economic resources but also for its political and strategic importance. In these cases the political issues at stake made it much more difficult for the challenger to compromise or relinquish claims to the disputed territory. The problem for the leadership of the challenger in such cases was that compromise on territorial issues that were intertwined with domestic political significance was more likely to be viewed as a clear foreign policy setback and, thus, provoke strong opposition domestically. For example, the disputes over the Spratly Islands have involved a mix of economic and strategic concerns for the countries of China, Vietnam, Taiwan, and the Philippines. As a result, despite a strong interest by all parties to develop potential oil and natural gas deposits around the islands, no cooperative agreements have been reached and none of the countries have withdrawn their territorial claims.[18] In a number of other cases annexationist goals or public support for decolonization made territorial compromise based on economic side agreements politically unattractive for the challenger. Examples would include North vs. South Yemen; Morocco vs. Mauritania; Mauritania and Morocco vs. Spain; and Venezuela vs. Guyana. The conclusion to be drawn is that when the issues at stake in a dispute include salient domestic political or strategic concerns, leaders within the challenger are not likely to compromise those concerns in order to secure economic gains in a territorial settlement. Clearly, in the absence of such contending considerations leaders within the challenger are often willing to trade territory for economic gains, but economic payoffs are generally not attractive enough to leaders to offset significant domestic political or strategic losses in a territorial settlement.

The International Context of Decisions to Settle Disputes

While the predominant impact of domestic politics is to maintain the status quo of an ongoing territorial dispute, we find that the interna-

---

16. See Kelly, *Arabia, the Gulf and the West* and Amin, *International and Legal Problems of the Gulf,* 98–106, 124–29, 131–38.

17. See Touval, *The Boundary Politics of Independent Africa,* 251–69.

18. See Lo, *China's Policy towards Territorial Disputes* and Marwyn Samuels, *Contest for the South China Sea* (New York: Methuen, 1982).

tional context provides the primary reasons for why challengers seek settlements. This is not to say, however, that international political and strategic considerations do not also at times favor the continuation of disputes. Rather, the point is that when steps are taken toward compromise by the challenger, the impetus is often related to the international political and military context confronted by leaders.

Turning to the results we first see that the military strength of the challenger is not strongly related to a refusal to compromise as predicted by H5.2. The negative coefficient for the military balance variable is consistent with H1.2, but it is of questionable statistical significance (t-ratio $= -1.81$). These relatively weak results are also evident when we examine the results of the marginal impact analysis in table 15, that is, the shift from a very weak to a strong military position for the challenger decreases the probability of compromise ($y = 2$) by only about 3 percent.

These results are based on an interesting pattern in the data. On the one hand, when the challenger had a decisive military advantage, the rate of compromise was quite low. Of the 426 dispute years in which the challenger had at least a three-to-one advantage, the challenger did not compromise in 80 percent of the years (340). However, among the 2,541 dispute years in which the challenger did not compromise, only about 13 percent included challengers who were in a very strong military position. Thus, while military strength may approach being a sufficient condition for not compromising, it is far from being a necessary condition.

Military strength, then, is but one of many determinants of the bargaining resolve of challengers in territorial disputes. A number of cases illustrate the point that when state leaders are in a strong military position they will often adopt a firm negotiating posture and rely on their position of strength to either support a policy of diplomatic pressure on their weaker neighbor, or use their military advantage to take control of disputed territory (Venezuela vs. Guyana; Turkey vs. Greece; Iran vs. UAE; Iraq vs. Kuwait; Libya vs. Chad; India vs. Portugal; China vs. India; and Vietnam vs. Cambodia). In all of these cases (except Venezuela's dispute with Guyana), challengers eventually used military force to take control of disputed territory after diplomacy and negotiations failed to convince the target to make concessions. India overran Goa in 1961 following the refusal of Portugal to decolonize, while China attacked India along the disputed border in 1962 in order to consolidate its control of strategic territory and to counter the "forward policy" of India.[19] Iran occupied disputed islands in the Strait of Hormuz in 1971 as

---

19. See P. D. Gaitonde, *The Liberation of Goa* (London: C. Hurst & Company, 1987); Rubinoff, *India's Use of Force in Goa;* and Allen Whiting, *The Chinese Calculus of Deterrence* (Ann Arbor: University of Michigan Press, 1975), chs. 2–5.

TABLE 15.   The Marginal Impact of Variables Measuring the International Context on the Probability of the Challenger Compromising

Change in Value of Explanatory Variable	Probability of Challenger Compromising (%)		
	$y = 0$	$y = 1$	$y = 2$
Balance of Military Forces			
The ratio of challenger to target capabilities varies from			
1/9 to 1/3	+0.4	+0.2	−0.6
1/3 to 1/1	+0.6	+0.3	−0.9
1/1 to 3/1	+0.7	+0.2	−0.9
3/1 to 9/1	+0.4	+0.1	−0.5
Challenger Dispute Involvement			
In how many other territorial disputes is the challenger involved?			
0 vs. 1	−0.7	−0.2	+0.8
1 vs. 2	−0.6	−0.3	+0.9
2 vs. 5	−1.6	−1.2	+2.8
5 vs. 10	−2.2	−3.2	+5.4
Challenge to Status Quo			
Did the target engage in actions to establish or consolidate control over disputed territory?			
No vs. Yes	+2.9	+0.5	−3.4
Defeat in Armed Conflict			
How many times has the challenger suffered a defeat/ stalemate in the previous armed confrontations with the target?			
0 vs. 1	−5.0	−3.9	+8.9
1 vs. 2	−2.8	−9.0	+11.8
2 vs. 3	−1.4	−12.3	+13.7
3 vs. 4	−0.6	−13.5	+14.1
Common Security Ties			
Are challenger and target military alliance partners?			
No vs. Yes	−6.1	−10.7	+16.8

Note: See the note to table 14 for a description of how the changes in the probability of a settlement were calculated.

the British withdrew their military presence from the Persian Gulf, and Libya took advantage of civil war within Chad in 1972 to occupy the Aozou Strip.[20] Turkey invaded Cyprus in 1974 in support of the Turkish Cypriot community on the island, while Iraq in 1990 invaded Kuwait in

20. See Kelly, *Arabia, the Gulf and the West,* 95–96; Abdulghani, *Iraq and Iran;* and Benyamin Neuberger, *Involvement, Invasion, and Withdrawal: Qadhdhafi's Libya and Chad, 1969–1981* (Tel Aviv: Shiloah Center for Middle Eastern and African Studies, 1982).

part to settle long-standing territorial disputes.[21] Nevertheless, there are a number of cases in which very strong challengers compromised or withdrew claims against their weaker neighbors: China vs. Afghanistan, Burma, and Nepal; and the Soviet Union vs. Iran and Turkey.

Military strength is not a necessary condition for the challenger to remain unyielding in its negotiating position over disputed territory. For example, there are a number of examples in which weak challengers have persisted in their claims without compromising (e.g., Cuba vs. the United States; Bolivia vs. Chile; Madagascar vs. France; Afghanistan vs. Pakistan; and Cambodia vs. Thailand). We know from the results in chapter 5 that the military weakness of the challenger does deter large-scale military conflict, but the lack of a credible military option does not mean that weaker challengers adopt accommodative diplomatic policies over disputed territory. As previously argued in both chapters 4 and 5, leaders from weak states can benefit domestically from continued conflict, and they can also look to international pressure from other states to try to convince the target to make territorial concessions. In sum, military strength is but one of several factors that shape the determination of foreign policy leaders to adopt a hard-line position in territorial disputes. Military power is not unimportant in predicting the outcomes of such disputes, but clearly a convincing explanation of the challenger's behavior requires that a more complex set of factors be taken into account.

The next finding is that challengers were more likely to compromise if they were involved in territorial disputes with other states. The positive coefficient is significant (*t*-ratio = 3.16), which supports H6.2.[22] In table 15 the marginal impact analysis indicates that as the number of territorial disputes increases from zero to ten, the likelihood of the challenger compromising to settle a dispute increases by about 10 percent.

A number of examples illustrate these statistical findings.[23] During

---

21. See for example Tozun Bahcheli, *Greek-Turkish Relations since 1955* (Boulder: Westview, 1990), chs. 3–4 and Lawrence Freedman and Efraim Karsh, *The Gulf Conflict 1990–1991* (Princeton: Princeton University Press, 1993), ch. 3.

22. The alternative measure of the dispute involvement of the challenger (the number of months in each year that the challenger was involved in militarized disputes with states other than the target) produced similar results when it was substituted into the equation. The coefficient was positive and significant ($b = 0.030$ and the *t*-ratio = 5.00) and produced about a 10 percent increase in the likelihood of settlement.

23. While examining the cases in more detail I also considered whether the target's involvement in militarized disputes with other states decreased the likelihood of the challenger compromising. Examples can be cited of cases in which the target's dispute involvement with other states was connected to the decision by the challenger to avoid compromise with the target. Pakistan for example welcomed India's increasingly hostile relations

the period between 1950 and 1990 China was involved in a total of twelve territorial disputes but reached compromise settlements in four cases (Afghanistan, Burma, Nepal, and Pakistan), indicated a willingness to compromise in six others (Japan, Philippines, Malaysia, Bhutan, India, Taiwan), and has maintained relatively inflexible diplomatic positions only in disputes with the Soviet Union and Vietnam. For example, as Chinese relations with India in the late 1950s and early 1960s deteriorated, China settled disputes with several of its Central Asian neighbors—Afghanistan, Burma, Nepal, and Pakistan. Similarly, as pointed out in chapter 5, following the escalation of China's territorial dispute with the Soviet Union to the level of large-scale border clashes in 1969, the Chinese in the early 1970s moved to develop closer

with China in the late 1950s and early 1960s and sought improved relations with China in the hope of putting greater pressure on India. China, in part, took advantage of South Vietnam's weak military position in 1974 to expel South Vietnamese forces from the disputed Paracel Islands, and China reacted to Vietnam's invasion and then occupation of Cambodia beginning in 1977 by increasing diplomatic and military pressure on Vietnam, culminating in the attack against Vietnam in February 1979. The overall conclusion, however, would seem to be that this variable did not play a central role. If we examine a number of cases in which challenger states sought a compromise settlement, we find little evidence that the timing of such decisions were linked to changing assessments of whether the target was preoccupied with conflicts involving other states. For example, as noted above, leaders within China, Pakistan, Morocco, Ethiopia, Kenya, and Iran compromised with some of their neighbors because they valued the support of their neighbors, not because these neighboring countries found themselves in fewer conflicts at the time challengers offered to compromise. Israel was not involved in more conflicts with other states in the late 1970s, but nevertheless Egypt pursued a peace settlement. Similarly, Indonesia ended its policy of confrontation with Malaysia in 1965 and 1966 even though Malaysia at that time was not involved in fewer conflicts with other states than in the period between 1962 and 1964. Morocco is another example: initiatives by King Hassan toward reconciliation with Mauritania and Algeria were not linked to changes in the latter two country's dispute involvement with other states. Finally, the policy by the new government in Argentina in 1984 to seek a settlement with Chile over the Beagle Channel was driven most importantly by the decision by the new president to treat the Falklands dispute with the British as a higher priority. The involvement of Chile in disputes and conflicts with other states seemed to play little, if any, role. Decisions by the challenger to pursue cooperative or conflictual policies in a territorial dispute were driven largely by changes in the foreign policy priorities of the challenger as well as the challenger's assessment of the domestic political feasibility of greater cooperation with the target. In other words, when new pressing foreign policy problems emerge the challenger may in some cases decide that a resolution of a territorial dispute with the target would be desirable. At this point, however, the primary concern of leaders within the challenger state is whether a policy of reconciliation can be packaged in a way that will be supported within his/her own country. In this set of calculations, challenger beliefs about the bargaining resolve of the target are of secondary importance because the challenger has decided that it is in its best interests to seek a settlement and is willing to make unilateral concessions.

ties with Japan as part of a larger strategy to counter Soviet influence and power in the Far East. Another example is Pakistan, which was involved in disputes with China, Afghanistan, and India during the 1950s but agreed to a compromise settlement with China in the early 1960s while refusing to compromise in the other two disputes. In Europe, West Germany was involved in five territorial disputes and compromised in four of the cases. In the Middle East, Saudi Arabia was involved in a total of six territorial disputes but eventually agreed to compromise settlements with most its neighbors in a series of agreements between 1965 and 1981, while Iran under the Shah was involved in four disputes and reached compromise settlements with Saudi Arabia and Bahrain. Finally, in Africa, Morocco had simultaneous disputes with Spain, Algeria, and Mauritania in the 1960s but settled with both Algeria and Mauritania by 1970; Ethiopia had disputes with Kenya, Sudan, and Somalia but reached agreements with both Kenya and Sudan; while Kenya had disputes with Somalia and Ethiopia but settled with Ethiopia.

From these examples two generalizations can be drawn. First, challengers typically compromised in those territorial disputes in which significant military security issues were not at stake. For example, Chinese border agreements with Afghanistan, Burma, Nepal, and Pakistan centered on relatively small sections of territory as did the border agreements between Kenya and Ethiopia, and Saudi Arabia and its neighbors.[24] Second, challengers often sought settlements in order to gain the diplomatic or even military support of the target or other states for disputes that it had with other countries. For example, Pakistan and China compromised with one another in the hope of gaining each other's support against India.[25] Ethiopia and Kenya resolved their border dispute and formed a military alliance in opposition to Somalia,[26] and Morocco settled its disputes with both Algeria and Mauritania with the expectation that those two countries would then extend support to Morocco's claims against Spanish Sahara.[27] Iran pursued accommodative policies with Saudi Ara-

---

24. See appendix A for a summary description of the areas in dispute for each of these cases.

25. The argument that opposition to India has been one of the important foundations of the cooperative relations between Pakistan and China since the early 1960s is developed in works such as Rasul Rais, *China and Pakistan* (Lahore: Progressive Publishers, 1977); Syed, *China and Pakistan;* Yaacov Vertzberger, *The Enduring Entente: Sino-Pakistani Relations, 1960–1980* (New York: Praeger, 1983); and Gurnam Singh, *Sino-Pakistan Relations* (Amritsar: Guru Nanak Dev University Press, 1987).

26. See Touval, *The Boundary Politics of Independent Africa,* 142–43 and 248–49.

27. See ibid., 255–69 and Hodges, *Western Sahara,* ch. 11.

bia to foster Saudi support in opposition to Iraq.[28] Finally, West German leaders by the mid-1960s began to recognize that their goal of German reunification was hindered by its existing policy of refusing to accept the borders of its eastern neighbors (Poland and Czechoslovakia) until a reunified German state was achieved. This policy aroused suspicion within and outside Europe that West Germany still had territorial ambitions. Thus, the failure of their existing policy to generate international support convinced leaders such as Willy Brandt to adopt a bold policy of detente (or *ostpolitik*) with the East and to recognize the territorial status quo in Eastern Europe. Furthermore, Brandt used West German concessions on the recognition of East Germany to pressure the Soviet Union to settle the Berlin dispute. Territorial compromise then was viewed by the West German leadership as promoting their country's longer-term and most important foreign policy goal of eventual reunification with East Germany.[29]

The next set of results indicate that when the challenger and target were military allies, the challenger was more likely to settle the dispute, as proposed by H11.2. The positive coefficient is quite significant (t-ratio = 9.53), and in table 15 this variable produces an approximate 17 percent increase in the likelihood of settlement. The presence of a common territorial dispute adversary between the challenger and target produced similar but weaker results when tested in the equation.[30] Thus, we see the same pattern of findings here as in chapter 5, that is, alliance ties produce stronger effects in dampening conflict between challenger and target than the presence of a common territorial dispute adversary. The more powerful effects of alliance ties in promoting conflict resolution suggest that the formal commitment represented by alliance ties is a stronger indicator of common security interests between states than a less formal security ties. As a result, those stronger shared interests were salient enough to leaders of the challenger that compromise was accepted as the necessary price to pay to maintain that target's support as a reliable ally.[31]

---

28. See Ramazani, *The Persian Gulf,* 48–50, and Ramazani, *Iran's Foreign Policy, 1941–1973,* 409–14.

29. See for example Hanrieder, *Germany, America, Europe: Forty Years of German Foreign Policy,* chs. 6–7 and Griffith, *The Ostpolitik of the Federal Republic of Germany.*

30. When this alternative measure of shared security interests between challenger and target was substituted into the equation, the coefficient was positive ($b = 0.25$), significant (t-ratio = 4.25), and increased the likelihood of compromise by about 7 percent.

31. More generally, these findings also illustrate the point that alliance ties can produce important nonmilitary benefits for a state, that is, a greater ability to exert leverage over the foreign policy of an ally on issues that center on the bilateral relationship between the two countries.

The weaker findings for the common territorial dispute variable reflect the fact that there are a number of cases in which the challenger did not compromise with the target even though they faced a common opponent. For example, the cases in which a common territorial dispute adversary played an important role in promoting a settlement between challenger and target would include China and Pakistan (India); Morocco and Mauritania (Spain); Ethiopia and Kenya (Somalia); and Iran and Saudi Arabia (Iraq). In contrast, there are a series of Middle East cases in which Iran and Saudi Arabia were locked in disputes with the British, but common adversaries such as Iraq did not push Iran or Saudi Arabia to compromise with the British. In Africa, neither Morocco or Mauritania compromised with Spain in an attempt to strengthen their position against one another, and in South Asia, India has not compromised with China to gain an ally in its dispute with Pakistan, nor did China compromise with India in order to gain its support in China's dispute with Pakistan.

As I generally argued in chapter 5, the most important reason why the challenger did not compromise with the target in these disputes was that the challenger did not expect or place a high value on coordinating its policies with the target against a common adversary. For example, in the Middle East the overlapping interests between Iran or Saudi Arabia and the British were outweighed by numerous cases of long-standing territorial disputes. Furthermore, Iran and Saudi Arabia sought to displace the influence and power of the British in the Persian Gulf, and therefore compromise with the British was in opposition to their basic policy goals. As a result, neither Iran nor Saudi Arabia viewed the British as an attractive ally, and the British themselves had few incentives to coordinate policies closely with either country.[32] In the South Asian cases, China placed a higher priority on achieving its territorial goals in its dispute with India than in its dispute with Pakistan. As a result, China had no interest in offering far-reaching concessions to India to gain an ally. India, for its part, was in a relatively strong diplomatic and military position in its dispute with Pakistan, and therefore China was not needed as an ally either.[33]

In sum, the existence of a common territorial dispute adversary did

---

32. See for example Kelly, *Arabia, the Gulf and the West;* Glen Balfour-Paul, *The End of Empire in the Middle East* (Cambridge: Cambridge University Press, 1991); Ramazani, *The Persian Gulf;* and Nadav Safran, *Saudi Arabia: The Ceaseless Quest for Security* (Cambridge: Belknap Press, 1985), chs. 2–4.

33. See Jetly, *India-China Relations;* S. S. Bindra, *India and Her Neighbors* (New Delhi: Deep & Deep Publications, 1984); Syed, *China and Pakistan;* Vertzberger, *The Enduring Entente;* and Singh, *Sino-Pakistan Relations.*

not produce strong and consistent perceptions of shared interests between challenger and target. In many cases in which a common adversary existed, there were also multiple and even severe conflicts between the challenger and target. The weaker findings for this variable reflect the fact that for many challengers the competitive aspect of its relationship with the target exerted more influence over its policies than did the incentives to make substantial concessions based only on limited areas of shared interest.

There are many examples, however, of challengers pursuing accommodative policies with targets who were allies in Western Europe, the Middle East, and Africa. For example, all Western European NATO allies involved in disputes with one another quickly reached settlements. France accepted British control of disputed islands in the English Channel, the Dutch withdrew their claim to Belgian territory, and the Dutch and West Germans were able to reach a compromise settlement over disputed sections of their border. As already argued above, in Africa the common threat of Somali irredentism compelled Ethiopia and Kenya to negotiate a settlement of their border dispute and to become military allies. In the Middle East the common perceived threat of Iraqi hegemony in the Gulf prior to the Iranian revolution contributed to the willingness of Saudi Arabia and Kuwait (both members of the Arab League) to pursue accommodative policies in their territorial disputes with one another.[34]

There are exceptions to this generalization, however. Greece and Turkey have been engaged in a bitter and stalemated dispute over Cyprus despite their common NATO ties, Argentina confronted Chile with the threat of military conflict on several occasions in the Beagle Channel despite their common ties in the Rio Pact, and Iraq applied considerable diplomatic and military pressure against its fellow Arab League ally of Kuwait. As I argued in chapter 4, in each of these cases the challenger did not view the target as a vital ally, and therefore the opportunity cost to the security position of the challenger in losing the military support of the target was quite limited.

The findings in chapters 5 and 6 on alliance ties are also interesting to compare with the findings in chapter 4. In chapter 4 we found that

---

34. There is, however, very limited detailed information on the history of negotiations between Kuwait and Saudi Arabia since the early 1960s. As a result, it is not possible to draw conclusions about this case with confidence. It is certainly the case, however, that both countries viewed Iraq as a primary security threat in the Gulf prior to 1978–79, and Saudi Arabia was a strong supporter of Kuwait's independence and its general policy of resisting pressure from Iraq. See Safran, *Saudi Arabia,* 135–38, 265–79 and Finne, *Shifting Lines in the Sand,* 137–39, 155.

shared alliance ties had only a modest impact in reducing the likelihood of a challenger initiating a dispute. However, shared alliance ties did have much stronger effects in constraining the behavior of a challenger once in a dispute with an ally. Thus, while allies in general may not be strongly deterred from becoming involved in disputes with one another, they do seem quite sensitive to the damage that a severe and protracted conflict over disputed territory could have on their ties of security cooperation with strategically important allies.[35] The critical point to recognize is that military alliances can be formed for a variety of nonmilitary reasons,[36] and when allies do not view their security and defense needs as interdependent, intra-alliance cohesion and cooperation can be difficult to sustain.

The next hypothesis tested was whether challengers would be less likely to seek a settlement if the target had initiated actions designed to establish or consolidate its control over disputed territory (H8.2). In table 13 we see that the coefficient is negative and significant (t-ratio = 7.39), which firmly supports H8.2. In table 15 the marginal impact analysis reveals that this variable is associated with a modest 3 percent decrease in the likelihood of a settlement.

There were over forty cases in which the target undertook some form of action in the disputed territory to change the status quo, and in over thirty cases the challenger either did not compromise at all or for only a small percentage of the years. This pattern of support for the hypothesis is reflected in the fact that in about 86 percent of the years that the target undertook such actions, the challenger did not compromise (508/585 dispute years). Indeed, we know from the findings in chapter 5 that often the response of the target was to increase diplomatic and even military pres-

---

35. Another interesting finding that emerges from the results across chapters 4 through 6 is that while states within an alliance often place a high value on maintaining close ties with their ally, states outside the alliance will often question the reliability of alliance commitments. Previous research on extended deterrence and alliances reveals a similar pattern: formal alliances have little impact in deterring potential attackers, but if deterrence does fail a defender state with alliance ties is very likely to come to the aid of its threatened ally. See Paul Huth, *Extended Deterrence and the Prevention of War* (New Haven: Yale University Press, 1988), ch. 4; Paul Huth and Bruce Russett, "Deterrence Failure and Crisis Escalation," *International Studies Quarterly* 32, no. 1 (1988): 29–45; and Paul Huth, "When Do States Take on Extended Deterrent Commitments?" in Frank wayman and Paul Diehl, eds., *Reconstructing Realpolitik* (Ann Arbor: University of Michigan, 1994), 81–100.

36. See for example James Morrow, "Alliances and Asymmetry," *American Journal of Political Science* 35, no. 4 (1991): 904–33; James Morrow, "Alliances, Credibility, and Peacetime Costs," *Journal of Conflict Resolution* 38, no. 2 (1994): 270–97; and Steven R. David, *Choosing Sides: Alignment and Realignment in the Third World* (Baltimore: Johns Hopkins University Press, 1991).

sure on the challenger. When we examine these cases closely we reach the same conclusion as in chapter 5: both domestic and international factors are necessary to consider in order to understand the behavior of the challenger. We see repeated examples of leaders in the challenger state explaining that increased pressure and opposition to the target was a necessary response to counter the threatening and/or provocative actions of the challenger. At the same time, as argued in chapter 5, the hostile response of the challenger also seems to have been shaped by domestic political concerns, that is, a less than hostile response would have exposed the leadership to elite and public criticism, whereas a hard-line policy toward the target generally bolstered the leadership's own political standing. In this context of heightened confrontation between challenger and target, the likelihood of compromise by the challenger was quite unlikely. Internationally, the challenger was arguing for condemnation of the target and the need for increased pressure, while domestically the leadership was often mobilizing popular opposition to the target's policies. This interplay of leaders within the challenger attempting to shape and influence the views and perceptions of both international and domestic political audiences is clear in a number of cases. For example, Indian political and administrative integration of Kashmir in the 1950s and 1960s consistently provoked a hostile response from Pakistan, and when India in December 1964 took further steps to integrate Kashmir, this reinforced the view of Pakistani leaders that military action had to be taken soon to compel India to make any concessions. Afghanistan responded in the same way to similar measures by Pakistan to tighten its political control of disputed territory along the Durand Line during the 1950s and early 1960s;[37] Israeli steps to establish a more permanent presence in the West Bank and the Golan Heights stimulated a strong and hostile response from the Arab countries;[38] and Turkey's effective partition of Cyprus following the 1974 invasion has been consistently opposed by Greece.[39]

The final result to consider in this section is what impact past military defeats or stalemates had on the willingness of the challenger to seek a settlement. The hypothesis tested posited that prior defeats would compel the leadership of the challenger to seek peace despite the domestic political risks in making concessions (H9.2). The probit results in table 13 provide strong support for the hypothesis. The coefficient for

37. See for example T. V. Paul, *Asymmetric Conflicts: War Initiation by Weaker Powers* (Cambridge: Cambridge University Press, 1994), 121 and Kulwant Kauer, *Pak-Afghanistan Relations* (New Delhi: Deep & Deep Publications, 1985), chs. 3–4.

38. See for example William Harris, *Taking Root: Israeli Settlements in the West Bank, the Golan, and Gaza-Sinai, 1967–1980* (New York: Wiley & Sons, 1980).

39. See Bahcheli, *Greek-Turkish Relations since 1955,* ch. 4.

the military defeat variable is positive and significant with a *t*-ratio of 7.85. Furthermore, this variable has a considerable substantive impact. In table 15 we see that the probability of compromise increases by as much as 49 percent if the challenger had suffered multiple military defeats on the battlefield. The conclusions to be drawn from these probit results, however, need to be stated carefully. If we look at the data more closely we find that when challengers had suffered two or more military defeats, the overall rate of compromise was about 25 percent (36/146 dispute years). This rate of compromise is not high in an absolute sense, but remember that in the entire dataset, the rate of compromise is only about 16 percent. Two or more military defeats, then, roughly increases the likelihood of compromise by 50 percent, and that is why this variable has a positive and significant coefficient in the statistical analysis.

When we look at the individual cases, challengers in the following cases offered concessions or expressed an interest in some form of compromise settlement in the wake of military defeats: both Egypt and Jordan in the early 1950s and then after the 1967 War; Egypt also after the 1973 War; Uganda after its defeat in the war with Tanzania in 1978–79; Indonesia in 1965–66 after its policy of *konfrontasi* had failed toward Malaysia; Cambodia following its occupation by Vietnamese forces in 1977–78; Honduras after its setback in the 1969 football war with El Salvador; and Libya in 1988 after suffering heavy losses to Chad in 1987. A more detailed examination of these cases, however, reveals that the decisions and processes resulting in concessions by the challenger did not always closely fit the causal argument proposed by the modified realist model.

The strongest cases involve Indonesia, Jordan, Egypt, and Libya. The Indonesian case is quite interesting since a new military regime ended the policy of diplomatic and armed opposition to the formation of a Malaysian federation. As already noted, the general pattern has been that military establishments have been strong supporters of claims to disputed territory. However, in this case the military led by General Suharto concluded that the policy of *konfrontasi* initiated by President Sukarno in 1963 was proving counterproductive to the interests of the military in several ways: (1) it was strengthening the position of the communist party within Indonesia, (2) it was isolating Indonesia from critical sources of economic and military aid from Western countries while aligning Indonesia closer to China, and (3) it threatened to embarrass the army due to the superior strength and performance of British forces in armed clashes with Indonesian forces. Thus, contrary to the general pattern of a threatening international environment serving the institutional and political interests of the military, the Indonesian case is an example in which international conflict threatened their interests, and therefore they withdrew their support for the policy of *konfrontasi*.

The new leadership, however, was very sensitive to what they believed would be the damage to their country's international reputation as a result of ending the conflict, and they attempted in negotiations with Malaysia to produce some type of face-saving agreement. Furthermore, Suharto and the military recognized that there would be considerable domestic opposition to a reversal in policy, and therefore they publicly continued to support the policy of *konfrontasi* during the period of transition in political power from Sukarno to Suharto from the fall of 1965 to the spring of 1966. However, once the military had firmly consolidated its position domestically, the decision was made to proceed with an agreement to end the conflict with Malaysia. The costs of accepting a diplomatic and military defeat were regarded as a necessary short-term price to pay in order to prevent the further radicalization of domestic politics, to rejuvenate the economy, and to restore the military's access to arms and aid from the West.[40]

The case of Egypt reveals even more clearly the struggle between the recognition of military weakness and the reluctance to offer concessions to the target for fear of the domestic as well as regional political opposition. For example, President Nasser in the early 1950s pursued behind-the-scenes contacts with Israel on the possibility of some type of peace settlement and then, following the 1967 debacle, he cautiously but publicly moved toward a position of possibly compromising with Israel. Throughout his tenure in power Nasser was constantly struggling to reconcile the competing pressures and priorities of: (1) domestic economic development, (2) leadership of the Arab world and thus opposition to Israel, (3) the recognition that his country was not in a strong military position to confront Israel on the battlefield, and (4) the commitment to recover the Sinai.[41] Sadat also found himself caught be-

---

40. The evolution of Indonesia's policy of *konfrontasi* with Malaysia is presented in Harold James and Dennis Sheil-Small, *The Undeclared War* (London: Leo Cooper, 1971); Michael Leifer, *Indonesia's Foreign Policy* (London: George Allen & Unwin, 1983), ch. 4; J. A. C. Mackie, *Konfrontasi: The Indonesian-Malaysia Dispute, 1963–1966* (New York: Oxford University Press, 1974); Franklin Weinstein, *Indonesia Abandons Confrontation* (Ithaca: Southeast Asia Program, Cornell University, 1969); and Franklin Weinstein, *Indonesian Foreign Policy and the Dilemma of Dependence* (Ithaca: Cornell University Press, 1976), ch. 8.

41. See Mark Tessler, *A History of the Israeli-Palestinian Conflict* (Bloomington: Indiana University Press, 1994), 338–45, 410–11; William Quandt, *Peace Process: American Diplomacy and the Arab-Israeli Conflict since 1967* (Washington, D.C.: Brookings Institution, 1993), ch. 4; Anthony Nutting, *Nasser* (London: Constable and Company, 1972), 389–411, 433–39, 450–55; Robert Stephens, *Nasser: A Political Biography* (New York: Simon & Schuster, 1972), 437–54, 522–28.

tween these crosscutting pressures and also decided that a compromise with Israel was the only real way to meet the priorities of economic development and restoration of Egypt's territorial integrity. Sadat, like Nasser, was acutely aware of the domestic and regional political risks that peace with Israel entailed.[42] The domestic and regional political constraints on King Hussein of Jordan were even greater than in Egypt, and as a result initiatives toward peace with Israel were even more cautiously pursued.[43] Finally, the Libyan leader Qadaffi had shown no inclination to give up control of the Aozou Strip, which his armed forces had occupied since 1972. Only after Chadian forces attacked and inflicted a defeat on Libyan forces in the Aozou in 1987 was Qadaffi willing to begin negotiations over the Aozou and eventually agree to submit the dispute to the ICJ.[44]

In the Ugandan and Cambodian cases military defeats were followed by accommodative policies, but the reasons for the changes in policy clearly do not fit with the arguments of H9.2. The common factor in each of these cases was a change in leadership within the challenger either during or shortly after the armed conflict with the target. In each of these cases the new leadership of the country criticized the former leadership for pursuing ineffective policies that were hurting the country and which were also generating opposition from neighboring states. Thus, when President Amin was toppled in 1979 following the failed invasion of Tanzania, the new leadership of Uganda was quick to distance itself from the discredited policies of the former president and to seek cooperative relations with Tanzania.[45] In the Cambodian case a change in political leadership was directly linked to military defeat, and in this case the new government under the leadership of Heng Samrin was closely aligned to Vietnam—the adversary in armed conflict. Thus,

---

42. See Quandt, *Peace Process*, chs. 7–12; Martin Indyk, *"To the Ends of the Earth" Sadat's Jerusalem Initiative* (Cambridge: Center for Middle Eastern Studies, Harvard University, 1984); Tony Armstrong, *Breaking the Ice* (Washington, D.C.: United States Institute of Peace Press, 1993), 52–67, 84–97, 120-29; and Melvin Frielander, *Sadat and Begin: The Domestic Politics of Peacemaking* (Boulder: Westview Press, 1983).

43. See Quandt, *Peace Process;* Friedlander, *Sadat and Begin*, 150–55, 244–47; and Aaron Kleiman, *Israel, Jordan, Palestine: The Search for a Durable Peace* (Washington, D.C.: Center for Strategic and International Studies, Georgetown University, 1981).

44. See John Allcock et al., *Border and Territorial Disputes*, 229–34.

45. For example in March 1979 the new government of Uganda condemned Amin as follows: "Dictator Amin has not only been a murderer and a terror to Uganda but also to all our immediate neighbors, especially Tanzania and Kenya . . . Ugandans are not enemies of Tanzania and the aggressions, murders and lies of dictator Amin against the people of Tanzania must never be allowed to blur or in any way adversely affect the good relations which have always existed between the two peoples." As quoted in Colin Legum, ed., *Africa Contemporary Record 1978–1979* (New York: African Publishing Co., 1980), B448.

it was to be expected that the new government would adopt a compromising position in subsequent negotiations with Vietnam over outstanding territorial issues.[46]

While the probit results do indicate that military defeat is one factor that will push leaders toward territorial compromise, the effects are by no means always strong enough to overcome domestic political roadblocks. For example, in all of the following disputes the leaders of challenger states generally did not become more accommodative at the bargaining table following military defeats or stalemates on the battlefield: Pakistan vs. India (1947, 1965, 1971); Syria vs. Israel (1948, 1967, 1973, 1982); Argentina vs. the United Kingdom (1982); Greece vs. Turkey (1974); and Somalia vs. Ethiopia (1978). As I argued in chapter 5, the refusal of challengers to accommodate themselves to a more powerful target often reflected a combination of domestic and international political concerns. For example, leaders in these states often had strong political incentives to retain a firm and unyielding diplomatic position following a military setback, in order to maintain public and elite support. In addition, political leaders also avoided compromise in order to protect their personal/country's regional position of influence and stature.

A closer look at several of these cases illustrates both of these dynamics. In the October War of 1973 and the 1982 Lebanon War Syrian military forces suffered heavy losses in battle with Israeli forces. Without doubt, Syrian forces performed far better than in the Six Day War of 1967 but, nevertheless, the military outcome was a stalemate at the very best for Syria. The failure to retake the Golan Heights by threat or force of arms, however, has not led President Asad of Syria to offer substantive concessions at the bargaining table in talks with Israel or the United States for almost two decades. Asad has understood that Syria by itself could not defeat Israel on the battlefield and that the return of the Golan Heights would have to be achieved at the negotiating table. Nevertheless, the bargaining strategy adopted by Asad from the mid-1970s to the late 1980s was to try to pressure Israel into returning the Golan Heights by a combination of a unified Arab diplomatic position at an international conference backed up by a large-scale buildup of Syrian arms, which would pose a credible threat of high costs to Israel in any future war. Asad has been willing to consider a peace agreement with Israel, but in such an agreement Asad has not been willing to make critical concessions over the Golan Heights, that is, all of the occupied territory should be returned to Syria without restrictions on Syria's sovereign rights in the territory. Concern over the domestic political backlash

---

46. See P. C. Pradhan, *Foreign Policy of Kampuchea* (London: Sangam, 1987), ch. 6.

of offering explicit and significant concessions to Israel has constrained the bargaining options of Asad as well as his own desire to see himself and Syria treated as a leader of the Arab world.[47]

In the case of Cyprus, the 1974 Turkish invasion and subsequent occupation of close to 40 percent of the island was a bitter setback for Greece's long-standing goal of enosis with Cyprus. Following the invasion, Turkey consolidated its military and political position in Cyprus and effectively divided the island when an independent Turkish Cypriot state—The Turkish Republic of Northern Cyprus—was proclaimed in 1983. Greece, however, has not been willing to compromise with Turkey in the division of Cyprus. Instead, successive Greek governments have steadfastly supported the Greek Cypriot refusal to recognize the Turkish Republic, have maintained that a single Cypriot state must be reestablished, and have justified a buildup of military forces as a response to the Turkish occupation of Cyprus. Tough rhetoric and diplomatic opposition to Turkish policies in Cyprus command broad political support within Greece, and therefore an anti-Turkish policy has been an attractive political position for Greek leaders to adopt since 1974. At the same time, the Greek policy of firm opposition to the division of Cyprus and the expansion of its military power is designed to redress the national humiliation of the 1974 invasion, to restore the confidence of Greek Cypriots in Greece's role as a protector, and to build international support for their country's position on the Cyprus question.[48]

Finally, in South Asia, military defeats have failed to convince challenger states to make basic concessions with their stronger adversaries. For example, in December 1971 Pakistani forces were defeated on both the western and eastern fronts in armed combat with India. Some analysts have argued that the Simla Agreement signed in July 1972 was a diplomatic setback for Pakistan, since Pakistan pledged to refrain from the threat of force and also made a commitment to settle all disputes peacefully by bilateral negotiations.[49] However, in the two decades following the agreement Pakistan has (*a*) not made any substantive concessions to India on the status of Kashmir or the steps necessary to resolve the dispute, (*b*) firmly opposed Indian attempts to extend its control over the

---

47. See Alasdair Drysdale and Raymond Hinnebusch, *Syria and the Middle East Peace Process* (New York: Council on Foreign Relations Press, 1991), chs. 3–4.

48. See Constantine Danopoulos, *Warriors and Politicians in Modern Greece* (Chapel Hill: Documentary Publications, 1985), ch. 6 and Bahcheli, *Greek-Turkish Relations Since 1955*, ch. 4.

49. See for example Robert Wirsing, *Pakistan's Security under Zia, 1977–1988* (New York: St. Martin's Press, 1991), 171; Ratna Tikoo, *Indo-Pak Relations* (New Delhi: National, 1987), ch. 6 and 237–39; and S. S. Bindra, *Indo-Pak Relations* (New Delhi: Deep & Deep Publications, 1981), ch. 6.

Siachen Glacier region in northern Kashmir, and (c) has aggressively pursued a buildup of conventional forces and initiated a program to develop nuclear weapons to offset India's nuclear capability. The underlying strategic rationale for the Pakistani policy of refusing to concede either diplomatically or militarily to India has been the belief that India's larger goal is to achieve regional dominance, and therefore Pakistan's own regional influence and autonomy are at stake. Public and elite opinion within Pakistan also firmly supports the government's position on Kashmir and a policy of military competition (particularly regarding nuclear weapons). Any sharp reversal in government policy, which would include substantial concessions to India, would therefore be likely to encounter strong opposition across the political spectrum in Pakistan.[50]

India, on the other hand while not a challenger, suffered a stinging defeat in the 1962 war with China, but for three decades there were very few changes in the diplomatic position of India. India has refused to consider concessions over the disputed territory despite some evidence that since the late 1970s China might be willing to consider some type of territorial compromise. As with the other cases examined above, Indian leaders have believed that concessions to China would weaken their country's regional standing and perhaps weaken their position in the dispute with Pakistan. Strategic reasons to remain unyielding, however, are reinforced by the perception that a policy of accommodation with China would risk significant opposition domestically.[51]

Finally, the case of Argentina after its defeat in 1982 deserves a closer examination. At one level, this case illustrates the point that military defeat is not always costly enough to compel political leaders to run the domestic political risks of making concessions to the victor. On another level, however, this case does in fact provide evidence of the powerful effects that military defeats can have on the foreign policy behavior of states. In this case, military defeat played a direct role in convincing the new civilian leadership that took power after the military junta collapsed that the long-standing dispute with Chile had to be resolved. Thus, military defeat prompted concessions toward another historical adversary instead of the state that had inflicted the defeat on Argentina. During the Falklands War large numbers of the best armed and equipped Argentine forces were deployed along the border with Chile for fear that Chile would take advantage of the conflict to attack

---

50. See for example Wirsing, *Pakistan's Security under Zia*, chs. 3–4 for attitudes in the 1970s and 1980s and in the early to mid-1960s see Paul, *Asymmetric Conflicts*, 116.

51. See for example Bhim Sandu, *Unresolved Conflict: China and India* (New Delhi: Radiant Publishers, 1988), 204–17.

Argentina.[52] Settlement of the dispute with Chile was viewed then by the Argentine leadership as bolstering their country's diplomatic as well as military position against Britain in the Falklands dispute.[53]

The Domestic Context of Decisions to Settle Disputes

In this section we shift the analysis to how domestic political conditions affected the willingness of the challenger to act on the issues at stake in the dispute. In the analysis of the results for several hypotheses already tested, I have argued that domestic political forces have often *reduced* the challenger's incentives to settle a dispute. Thus, as with the results in chapters 4 and 5, domestic politics within the challenger generally act as a force favoring continued conflict in territorial disputes.

For example, a history of recent as well as longer-term militarized conflict with the target decreased the willingness of the challenger to seek a settlement as posited by H14.2. In table 13 we see that the variable measuring the total number of militarized disputes between the two countries since 1900 has a negative coefficient which is significant (*t*-ratio = −6.79). The marginal impact analysis in table 16 shows that this variable decreases the likelihood of settlement by as much as 28 percent.

Thus, we see that of the 228 dispute years in which the challenger and target had a history of twenty or more prior militarized disputes, 85 percent of the time (194 years) the challenger did not offer any type of concessions to the target. Similarly strong results are produced if we substitute into the equation the variable measuring whether the challenger had been involved in militarized conflicts with the target in the previous year. The coefficient is negative and significant ($b = -0.65$, *t*-ratio = −10.33) and reduces the likelihood of compromise by over 30 percent.

Thus, parallel to the findings in the previous chapter, rivalry and conflict with the target in both the short and longer term have the domestic political ramifications within the challenger of hardening opposition to the target and reducing the opportunities for diplomatic flexibility in subsequent interactions with the target. In short, a history of armed conflict can be a potent force in creating a domestic political environment in which compromise with an adversary is a controversial and difficult political move for leaders to consider. Thus, very often political leaders are not willing to take risks and undertake diplomatic initiatives that will break a long-standing stalemate in negotiations. Furthermore, leaders

---

52. See Paul, *Asymmetric Conflicts*, 153.
53. See Garrett, "The Beagle Channel Dispute"; Hopkins, *Latin America and Caribbean Contemporary Record 1984–1985*, 229–42; and Lowenthal, *Latin America and Caribbean Contemporary Record 1985–1986*, B3–B21.

themselves are socialized into viewing the target as an adversary and, as a result, they are not predisposed to view concessions as a legitimate option. Finally, as argued in chapter 4 a history of military conflict with the target can be used by the military to justify larger budgets, and thus the military leadership within the challenger state can become strong supporters of continuing confrontation with the target. The combined effect, then, is that the idea of offering concessions and proposing a unilateral initiative to break a stalemate is a policy option quite difficult to get on the policy agenda of political leaders within the challenger. Few voices are advocating such policies within the challenger, and the prevailing climate of opinion (both mass and elite) is opposed to such a change in policy.

A number of cases illustrate the domestic political consequences of extended rivalry and conflict over disputed territory. In South America examples include Argentina vs. Chile, Ecuador vs. Peru, and Bolivia vs. Chile. In Southern Europe there is Greece vs. Turkey, while in the Far East China vs. Japan and the Soviet Union, South Korea vs. Japan, and Japan vs. the Soviet Union are good examples. In all of these disputes political leaders from challenger states frequently referred to the history

TABLE 16.   The Marginal Impact of Variables Measuring the Domestic Context on the Probability of the Challenger Compromising

Change in Value of Explanatory Variable	Probability of Challenger Compromising (%)		
	$y = 0$	$y = 1$	$y = 2$
History of Conflict			
How many militarized disputes were challenger and target involved in since 1900?			
0 vs. 5	+1.8	+1.3	−3.1
5 vs. 10	+2.1	+0.6	−2.7
10 vs. 20	+5.3	−1.0	−4.3
20 vs. 30	+6.9	−3.8	−3.0
30 vs. 40	+8.3	−6.3	−2.0
Democratic Norms			
For how many years has the challenger been democratic in the past twenty-five years?			
0 vs. 5	−1.5	−0.5	+2.0
5 vs. 10	−1.3	−0.9	+2.2
10 vs. 15	−1.1	−1.2	+2.3
15 vs. 20	−1.0	−1.5	+2.5
20 vs. 25	−0.9	−1.8	+2.7

Note: See the note to table 14 for a description of how the changes in the probability of a settlement were calculated.

of conflict and the aggressive policies of the target in the past when addressing their own domestic political audience. The clear message being conveyed by decades of hostile rhetoric and nationalist themes was that their country's position in the territorial dispute was legitimate and that it was incumbent upon the target to make concessions in order to reach a settlement. Furthermore, in all of these cases the military establishments within the challenger were strong supporters of a hard-line policy toward the target.[54]

In two of the cases listed above, however, leaders eventually adopted accommodative policies toward the target: Argentina vs. Chile in 1984 and China vs. Japan in 1978. Nevertheless, a closer examination of these two cases still reveals support for the generalization that political leaders find it quite difficult to take steps toward compromise and are cautious in doing so when the target is a historical adversary.

In November 1984 Argentina finally signed a treaty recognizing Chilean control over disputed islands in the Beagle Channel. Neither a ruling by a court of arbitration in 1977 in favor of Chile nor the subsequent mediation of the Pope was sufficient to convince the military leadership within Argentina to accept a settlement. The new democratic government led by President Raul Alfonsin assumed office in December 1983, and Alfonsin announced his intention to seek a compromise settlement with Chile. By the spring of 1984 a draft treaty had been negotiated with Chile based on the initiatives taken by Alfonsin. From the outset, however, Alfonsin faced strong domestic opposition in certain circles to a policy of compromise with Chile. The leadership of the armed forces denounced the proposed treaty, and some officers even publicly charged the new government with treason. The Peronist Party also opposed the treaty claiming that it was not in the national interest of Argentina. In the face of such opposition, the President called for a national referendum and pledged that ratification of the treaty by the Argentine Congress and Senate would depend on public support. Despite a strong campaign by the Peronist Party to encourage voters to boycott the referendum, 70 percent of the population turned out to vote, and 77 percent voted in favor of the proposed treaty. Backed by public

---

54. See for example Jack Child, *Geopolitics and Conflict in South America* (New York: Praeger, 1985); Douglas Shumavon, "Bolivia: Salida al Mar," in Elizabeth Ferris and Jennie Linclon, eds., *Latin American Foreign Policies* (Boulder: Westview, 1981), 179–90; Danopoulos, *Warriors and Politicians in Modern Greece,* chs. 6–7; A. Doak Barnett, *China and the Major Powers in East Asia* (Washington, D.C: Brookings, 1977), ch. 2; Rajendra Jain, *China and Japan, 1949–1980,* rev. 2d ed. (Oxford: M. Robertson, 1981), ch. 6; Rajendra Jain, *The USSR and Japan, 1945–1980* (Atlantic Highlands, NJ: Humanities Press, 1981), chs. 1,4; and Tsien-hua Tsui, *The Sino-Soviet Border Dispute in the 1970s* (Oakville: Mosaic Press, 1983), chs. 3–4.

support, Alfonsin then pushed strongly for ratification of the treaty and was able to secure ratification by the Congress in November 1984 and in the Senate by one vote in March 1985.[55]

The Argentine case nicely illustrates the point that a policy of territorial compromise with a long-standing adversary is a risky policy to pursue, which will be opposed strongly by domestic political forces (the military and Peronist Party). Furthermore, this case shows how political leaders will push for a settlement against opposition only if they believe they have the domestic political support to form a winning counter coalition. In the Argentine case the results of the referendum legitimized Alfonsin's diplomatic initiative, and he used the results to undercut his domestic opposition. Finally, this case also illustrates that the political backlash against compromise can be managed if the leadership can make a convincing case that concessions will not undermine national security interests and that they are necessary, in fact, to promote such interests. Thus, Alfonsin set the larger context for the domestic debate over the issue of compromise with Chile by arguing that one of the key issues at stake was dealing with the most pressing security problem facing the country—the Falkland Islands. He argued that this dispute could be better managed if Chile was no longer an adversary. Alfonsin, in effect, wanted to convince the public that security concerns required that some concessions be made to Chile. However, the President was also careful to negotiate a treaty that protected the most basic security interests of Argentina in the Beagle Channel while still making concessions to Chile; that is, the final settlement balanced the loss of sovereign rights to islands in the Channel with provisions protecting Argentina's economic and strategic interests in the Atlantic against encroachments by Chile.

In the second case, China tacitly accepted Japanese control over the disputed Senkaku Islands in 1978. When the two countries signed a Treaty of Peace and Friendship in August 1978 Japan announced that China had agreed to de facto Japanese control of the islands. Chinese leaders themselves, however, did not explicitly and openly acknowledge Japanese sovereignty, but at the same time they did not protest or refute the Japanese statement.[56] In this way Japan could claim satisfaction with the outcome without China having to acknowledge formally that it had compromised. This tacit resolution of the dispute may reflect the fact that there was opposition and controversy over the issue of territorial compromise within the Chinese leadership and that an unofficial accep-

---

55. See Garrett, "The Beagle Channel Dispute"; Hopkins, *Latin America and Caribbean Record;* and Lowenthal, *Latin America and Caribbean Record.*

56. See Alan Day, ed., *Border and Territorial Disputes,* 2d ed (London: Longman, 1982), 259.

tance of the Japanese position was one solution acceptable to the military and political leadership.[57]

The second hypothesis tested on the link between domestic politics and compromise over disputed territory was whether a compromise settlement was more likely the more democratic the challenger was (H17.2). In table 13 we see that the coefficient for this variable is positive and significant (t-ratio = 4.88). In table 16 the change from no history of democratic rule to a high level of prior democratic rule for the challenger increases the likelihood of a settlement by approximately 12 percent. Once again, however, these results must be interpreted carefully. When we examine the 216 dispute years coded with high rates of prior democratic rule (twenty years or more), the challenger compromised in about 30 percent of the years (65/216). However, since the overall rate of compromise is only about 16 percent, highly democratic states are almost twice as likely as other challengers to offer concessions to settle a dispute.

If we examine the cases involving democratic challengers we find the strongest support among the disputes in Europe, where democratic challengers accepted compromise settlements in six of nine cases (France vs. Britain; Netherlands vs. Belgium and West Germany; West Germany vs. Czechoslovakia, East Germany, and Poland) and the disputes were relatively short (on average just under eleven years). Furthermore, in two of the three remaining cases (Britain vs. France over islands in the English Channel; and West Germany vs. France over the Saar region), the challenger had in principle agreed to accept a compromise if necessary. The ICJ, however, ruled in favor of the British[58] and the results of a plebiscite in the Saar favored Germany,[59] and therefore no compromise was actually required of either challenger. Even in the case of the long-standing dispute over Northern Ireland, the Irish Republic has made some important concessions. For example, since 1973 the Irish have accepted the principle that unification can only take place with the support of the majority of the population in Northern Ireland. The failure to reach a settlement in this dispute reflects to a considerable extent the political opposition within Northern Ireland to making the concessions that would be a necessary part of any unification agreement.[60]

Outside of Europe the one country's behavior that has not supported the argument that democratic states are more likely to settle

---

57. See Barnett, *China and the Major Powers in East Asia*, 112–22 and Jain, *China and Japan*, ch. 6 for a general discussion of Chinese policy.

58. For a summary of the ICJ ruling see *Yearbook of the United Nations 1953* (New York: United Nations, 1954), 663–68.

59. See Butterworth, *Managing Interstate Conflict*, 144–45.

60. See Allcock et al., *Border and Territorial Disputes*, 120–41.

disputes by offering compromise is India. In decolonization disputes with Portugal and France, India demanded that the colonial powers withdraw from coastal enclaves and islands that they controlled, and India used military force to wrest control of such territories from Portugal when it refused to withdraw. The lack of compromising behavior by India in these cases is not surprising, since they viewed their policies as supporting self-determination for the populations within the colonial territories, and, indeed, by most accounts the local populations favored union with India.[61]

However, the failure of India to compromise with China over their disputed border seems to be clearly at odds with the predictions of H17.2, particularly since China indicated an interest in a compromise settlement in 1960 and again in negotiations and talks since 1980. The "package deal" proposed would require China to recognize the McMahon Line (the Indian position) in the eastern sector of the disputed border while, in return, India would recognize the Chinese position in the western Ladakh sector. In total, China would renounce claims to about 35,000 square miles of territory in exchange for India withdrawing claims to about 13,000 square miles of territory. Indian leaders, however, have not been willing to accept the proposal and some analysts have argued that the hostility of public opinion and the political opposition within India to compromise may have prevented Indian leaders from responding more favorably to Chinese initiatives.[62] The Indian case, then, is an interesting example in which the pull of public opinion and the threat of electoral defeat at the polls have actually pushed democratic leaders to be *more inflexible and confrontational* in their foreign policy. The apparent willingness of leaders within India to consider compromise with China (as predicted by H17.2) has been constrained by other features of the democratic system, that is, a firmer hard-line attitude among the general population and opposition parties. This suggests that for democratic states involved in international disputes which are quite salient to domestic political audiences, democratic leaders may very well find themselves crosspressured by democratic institutions and practices. On the one hand, democratic norms favor compromise and flexibility in diplomacy, but democratic accountability to popular and elite opinion may also convince leaders that compromise is not a politically supportable position in a dispute in which the international adversary is portrayed as an aggressive opponent.

---

61. See Butterworth, *Managing Interstate Conflict,* 112–13, 197–98, Leo Lawrence, *Nehru Seizes Goa* (New York: Pageant Press, 1963), ch. 8, and Rubinoff, *India's Use of Force in Goa,* 94–99.

62. See Sandhu, *Unresolved Conflict,* 208–17; Nancy Jetly, *India China Relations, 1947–1977* (New Delhi: Radiant Publishers, 1979), chs. 4–5; and Neville Maxwell, *India's China War* (New York: Pantheon Books, 1970), 154–70.

When we turn to those disputes in which the challenger is nondemocratic we find that the rate of compromise drops off significantly, as predicted. Of the 2,232 dispute years coded for states with a weak democratic tradition (less than five years), the rate of compromise is only 15 percent (357 years). The probit results reflect the fact that nondemocratic challengers (*a*) are less likely to settle a dispute by compromise compared to democratic states, and (*b*) generally take longer to move toward a compromise settlement compared to democratic states.

Finally, the last finding is for the selection bias variable in table 13. I had expected the coefficient to be negative and significant, based on the argument that challengers who were more likely to initiate a territorial dispute were less likely to compromise since they would typically be characterized by a higher level of resolve to change the territorial status quo. The results in table 13, however, do not support this hypothesis. The coefficient is essentially zero with a very low *t*-ratio (0.57), indicating that prior knowledge about how resolved a state was to initiate a dispute would not help predict whether that state would subsequently compromise to settle the dispute.

I had expected that the selection effects variable would pick up on the fact that many disputes in the post–World War II period had a prior history of protracted conflict and stalemate. As a result, the domestic political incentives for leaders involved in such long-standing disputes would be to avoid controversial policies such as making concessions to the settle the dispute. The lack of a stronger results, I think, can be attributed to two reasons. First, there is the important role that changes in the international political-military position of states played in putting pressure on leaders to make the hard choice of offering concessions to a historical adversary. As already discussed, military defeats and the strategic needs of seeking external support when involved in multiple territorial disputes were important factors associated with compromise by the challenger. The effects of these variables over the course of the period between 1950 and 1990 may have been strong enough to overwhelm the underlying conditions, explaining why states became involved in disputes to begin with. Evidence in support of this argument is found when we take the equation tested in table 13 and run it on progressively smaller time periods approaching 1950. What we find is that the selection effects variable gets stronger and stronger with a negative coefficient. For example, if the analysis is run on the time periods 1950 to 1980, 1950 to 1970, and then 1950 to 1960, the results are as follows: $b = -0.23$, *t*-ratio $= 1.78$, $b = -0.58$, *t*-ratio $= -3.53$, and $b = -1.48$, *t*-ratio $= -4.81$, respectively.

Another piece of evidence supporting this argument is that if we pick out those disputes in which the selection effects variable had a high value but the challenger nevertheless compromised, we find many cases in which military defeats and the involvement of the challenger in multiple disputes with other states played central roles in explaining the decisions of the challenger to compromise.

The second possible explanation for the weak findings for the selection effects variable is that the presence of bordering minorities was a variable that produced very weak results when predicting whether a challenger would be involved in a dispute (see table 3 in chapter 4). However, the results in table 13 indicate that this variable is clearly correlated to the challenger not seeking a compromise settlement. If we look at the cases in more detail we find that there are a number of disputes in which the selection effect variable has a low value but the challenger does not compromise, and a common attribute of many of these cases is that there was an ethnic minority in disputed territory with common ties to the challenger.

Conclusion

Territorial disputes can be resolved in a number of different ways. My focus in this chapter was to try to explain when a challenger state would seek the peaceful settlement of territorial disputes by negotiated compromise or the withdrawal of territorial claims. Hypotheses derived from the modified realist model were empirically tested against the historical record of territorial dispute settlements between 1950 and 1990.

The international political and military environment of states provided the strongest set of incentives for challengers to make concessions and settle a dispute. Specifically, a settlement was more likely when the challenger valued the target as an ally in conflicts with other states, when the challenger was involved in multiple conflicts with other states and the resolution of the dispute would strengthen its position in those other conflicts, and when military defeats convinced leaders that past policies of hostility and the use of armed force were no longer viable approaches to compelling the target to make concessions. On the other hand hypotheses that would explain why the challenger would refrain from seeking a settlement were not as strongly supported. Thus, while it was true that compromise was unlikely when the challenger was in a favorable military position or when strategic issues were at stake, these two variables did not seem markedly to reduce the chances of a settlement compared to other variables tested.

When we shift the analysis to domestic politics within challenger states, the central finding was that leaders were typically constrained by domestic political forces to be very cautious in moving toward a compro-

TABLE 17.   Conventional Realist Model and Ordered Probit Estimates of Probability
of Peaceful Settlement of Territorial Disputes, 1950–90

Explanatory Variables	Coefficient	Standard Errors	Significance Level
Constant	1.403	0.154	<.001
Selection effects	−0.094	0.115	—
Issues at Stake			
Strategic location of territory	−0.387	0.064	<.001
Economic value of territory	0.092	0.044	<.025
International Context			
Balance of military forces	−0.283	0.087	<.001
Challenger disputes	0.030	0.012	<.01
Attempt to change status quo	−0.194	0.066	<.005
Defeat in armed conflict	0.163	0.037	<.001
Common security ties	0.605	0.057	<.001

Note: Number of observations = 3,039; Log-likelihood = −2,194.8; Percentage of cases correctly predicted = 73.7; All significance levels based on one-tailed tests.

mise settlement, since popular and elite opinion, and often the military, was opposed to such a policy. Territorial compromise then was a risky foreign policy for state leaders to adopt from a domestic political perspective. In most situations the leader's position of domestic power and authority was better served by continuing confrontation with the target. The conditions that promoted compromise, however, were when (*a*) the disputed territory was prized largely for its economic value and leaders could then share or divide the economic resources located within the disputed territory in a settlement, and (*b*) when democratic regimes were in power and leaders in challenger states were therefore more likely to accept compromise as an acceptable approach to conflict resolution.

The final point to make is that as with the results in chapters 4 and 5, the inclusion of domestic politics into the analysis adds considerably to the explanatory power of the model tested. If we compare the log-likelihood values of the modified realist model tested in table 13 with a traditional realist model in table 17, we see that, as in the previous chapters, the two values are significantly different ($v = 89.6$, $df = 4$, $p < .001$).[63]

_____

63. See footnote 58 in chapter 4 for a description of how the differences in the two log-likelihood values were calculated.

CHAPTER 7

Conclusion

In this concluding chapter I will step back from the detailed discussion of the statistical findings in the previous chapters and place the results of this book in the larger context of their theoretical as well as policy implications. I begin this chapter with an overall summary of the findings and then draw some connections from those results to the larger body of theoretical work on international conflict and cooperation. In the final section, I focus my attention on policy prescriptions.

Summary of Findings

In chapters 4 to 6 hypotheses derived from a modified realist model were tested in a series of statistical analyses. The hypotheses posited that both domestic political variables as well as international political-military conditions should play important roles in explaining the initiation, escalation, and settlement of territorial disputes. In each of these chapters the statistical tests provided strong support for the modified realist model, and the conclusion that the incorporation of domestic politics into the theoretical model added considerably to our ability to explain patterns of international conflict over disputed territory. One of the central points I want to emphasize is that the domestic and international levels of analysis can be integrated into a single model in a systematic and generalizable fashion. Too often scholars have turned to domestic politics as a vehicle to challenge the predictions of a traditional realist approach without offering an alternative theoretical framework that is logically coherent and which produces testable hypotheses.

My approach to theory building was to turn to the domestic politics literature critiquing realism and to draw generalizable insights from it that could then be used to reformulate and replace some of the questionable assumptions and logic of realism. In my judgment, an important theoretical contribution of the modified realist model is to show that domestic politics can play a central role in foreign policy decisions while we still retain many of the assumptions and insights offered by a traditional realist approach. The incompatibility of according domestic politics a central

181

theoretical role in the study of security policy with the logic of realism is clearly overstated and reflects the unnecessary assumptions and weak logic built into realism. Without question the modified realist model is not as parsimonious as a traditional realist model, but the added theoretical complexity does not preclude generalizable and testable propositions from being formulated. Furthermore, the empirical findings in this book show that the incorporation of additional variables into a model of foreign policy behavior produces a significant increase in explanatory power. A high degree of parsimony in theory building is to be desired if the resulting theories produce very strong results when empirically tested. Traditional realist models, however, have not produced strong results when empirically tested, and it is time that realist scholars accept the challenge of incorporating domestic politics into the study of international conflict in as generalizable and parsimonious a fashion as possible. The partial and incomplete explanations produced by traditional realist models are not satisfactory. If we are to move significantly beyond our current level of knowledge and understanding of international conflict behavior, we need to discard the belief that empirically powerful theories can be developed that do not acknowledge that foreign policy leaders are domestic political leaders who are very sensitive to the potential domestic consequences of foreign policy decisions.

The primary findings for each of the chapters were as follows. In chapter 4 the theoretical question addressed was, When would challenger states confront their neighbors with territorial claims? To answer this question, attention to the international political and security concerns of state leaders provides a starting point. For example, bordering territory that was strategically located was a powerful predictor of whether challengers would be involved in disputes. Nevertheless, less than 20 percent of all disputes involved claims to strategic territory. Challengers were not likely to become embroiled in disputes with their military allies, and challengers were reluctant to dispute territory if it would risk damage to their political reputation for honoring international commitments by having to discard previously signed border agreements. An important finding was that the relative military strength of the challenger was a poor predictor of whether the challenger became involved in a territorial dispute. The weak results reflected the fact that in many disputes the challenger was in a very unfavorable military position.

Domestic politics entered into the decisions of state leaders in a number of ways. For political leaders, the domestic political incentives to dispute territory were multifaceted. In many cases the decision to dispute territory could be linked to the expected political benefits of increased popular support and legitimacy when claims were directed at achieving national unification, the recovery of lost national territory, or gaining access to valuable economic resources. Just as important, however, was the desire of leaders in many cases to avoid the political costs of failing to support a long-standing policy of disputing territory.

The very strong findings for domestic political variables in chapter 4 pointed to an important general conclusion: the reasons why foreign policy leaders adopt or maintain policies that risk conflict with other states is driven in large part by domestic political concerns. The traditional realist expectation that international conflict is fundamentally a result of the clash between states over issues of national security is simply wrong. Military-security issues may be close to being sufficient conditions for conflict and rivalry between states *but by no means are they necessary conditions*. As a result, many of the issues that become the underlying source of political and even military conflict between states have few clear and compelling military-security implications.

In chapter 5 hypotheses from the modified realist model were tested to see how well they could explain levels of political and military conflict over disputed territory. In this chapter the findings for international political-military variables were quite strong. Relative military strength, the strategic value of territory, the presence of common security interests between challenger and target, and the challenger's involvement in disputes with other states all played an important role in predicting levels of escalation. Several variables focusing on domestic politics also produced strong results, and these findings suggested that when domestic political considerations influenced foreign policy, the general effect was to reinforce hostile interstate relations and to encourage leaders to maintain conflictual policies.

Patterns of escalation, then, often reflected the interaction of domestic and international-level variables. Domestic politics would often lead foreign policy leaders to maintain adversarial relations and to consider the option of diplomatic and military escalation, while calculations of relative military strength and assessments of strategic opportunities as well as constraints would either reinforce or moderate those incentives to act forcefully.

The final set of empirical tests in chapter 6 addressed the question of whether a challenger state would seek a peaceful resolution of a territorial dispute by means of compromise or even the withdrawal of territorial claims. The most important findings were that international political and military variables were the principle factors pushing state leaders to move toward a settlement. In contrast, domestic politics within the challenger typically explained why leaders were reluctant to take the initiative and seek a settlement. In short, the concern of leaders that concessions and accommodation with the target would open them to charges of a foreign policy defeat by political opponents was a powerful political reality that obstructed greater international cooperation between challengers and targets.

A challenger was more likely to seek a settlement if: (*a*) it had suffered one or more military defeats at the hands of the target, (*b*) it had common security interests with the target, and (*c*) it was involved in multiple disputes with other states. In contrast, from a domestic politics perspective leaders had few incentives to seek a settlement since territorial concessions that would be offered to the target could be portrayed as a foreign policy defeat for the leadership and risked popular as well as elite opposition. Thus, disputes involving issues of ethnic irredentism, national unification, or the recovery of lost national territory were generally not settled by compromise. The only type of territorial issue amenable to compromise involved access to resources with economic value, since concessions were politically feasible if the division of resources or plans for joint development were substituted for control over disputed territory.

In sum, across these three chapters we found that the explanatory power of domestic- and international-level conditions varied depending on the theoretical questions being addressed. The particular strength of a domestic politics perspective lies in explaining why territorial disputes emerge and why they persist over time. The international strategic environment, on the other hand, is best at explaining varying levels of escalation over disputed territory and why political leaders will sometimes make the difficult choice of offering concessions to settle a dispute.

What do these findings say more broadly about the modified realist model presented in chapter 3? First, I would argue that the traditional realist assumption that the threat or use of military force is the most important means by which states can advance and protect their foreign policy interests is appropriate. There are without doubt other sources of state power and influence, but military strength and the credible threat of its use remain essential for understanding the conflict behavior of states. Second, I would reject another traditional realist assumption that conflict and competition in international politics center around issues of military security. I believe it is correct to argue that when security issues are at stake leaders will place a high priority on protecting such interests. Political and military conflict is by no means, however, largely limited to such issues as the findings in this book demonstrate. Military-security issues are but one of several issues that will receive high priority by foreign policy leaders. Indeed, one of the strengths of the modified realist model is its ability to explain the range of issues over which states become embroiled in conflict with each other.

This comparative advantage of the modified realist model reflects the fact that in the model domestic politics can provide a far richer explanation and understanding of why certain issues are on the policy agenda of foreign policy leaders. Thus, the basic argument of the modified realist model that foreign policy is closely linked to the domestic political needs and concerns of leaders was well supported and should provide a very useful foundation for further theoretical work.

The integration of traditional realist and domestic politics approaches centered on the assumption that a foreign policy setback for a country resulting from a diplomatic/military defeat would impose high political costs on the country's leadership. From this assumption in the modified realist model we were able to build the argument that political leaders have very strong incentives to act strategically and prudently when they are in disputes with other states. In other words, to protect themselves domestically leaders should act like realists in assessing when to escalate disputes and when to avoid conflict. The argument then is that it is good domestic politics for foreign policy leaders to think and act like realists in many ways. Political leaders are rewarded for military and diplomatic successes and punished for the reverse. We see from the results across the chapters that this basic insight of the modified realist model was also strongly supported.

In short, the generally strong results reported in this book indicate that the modified realist model represents a clear advance over traditional realist approaches. With further work and refinement this type of model holds the promise of capturing more fully the reciprocal influences of both domestic politics and the international strategic environment of states on international conflict behavior.

Theoretical Implications

What are the broader theoretical implications of the findings in this book? A number of connections to existing work on the causes of international conflict and cooperation can be identified.

The Domestic Sources of Security Policy. One of the central themes that emerges from the empirical results is that foreign policy decision makers are political leaders who view security policy as both a potential threat to their position of domestic political power as well as an opportunity to strengthen their domestic political position. From this perspective there are domestic political gains to be secured from a well-designed security policy but, at the same time, there are also substantial political risks in a foreign policy setback for the leadership of a country. Given the domestic political stakes involved in many security policy decisions, domestic politics is intertwined with foreign policy in two related ways: (a) domestic political factors can shape how leaders define what issues and problems are given priority in foreign policy, and (b) the foreign policy response of leaders to international events and the actions of other states is shaped by expectations regarding the domestic political support or opposition that a policy response is expected to produce. If we can understand how alternative foreign policy choices are likely to impact on the domestic political interests of leaders, we then have a strong basis for understanding whether conflict or cooperation with other states should be expected.

The conception then of international politics as a two-level game of bargaining between and within states[1] is a more fruitful starting point for theorizing than the standard realist assumption that decisions on security policy are unlikely to be shaped by the domestic political concerns of leaders. In taking this position I do not mean to imply that almost all security decisions are driven by domestic political forces. Indeed, there are surely cases in which the security policy choices of state leaders do not have implications for their domestic political position. Rather, the principal point is that theoretical analysis should begin with the assumption that foreign policy leaders will pay very close attention to the domestic political implications of security policy if they believe there is a connection between the two. I am also not arguing that domestic politics leaves no room for flexibility or maneuvering by state leaders in foreign policy. In many respects the results in this book suggest that the primary effect of domestic politics is to promote a status quo bias in foreign policy. Sharp departures and initiatives in foreign policy risk challenging the political interests of groups who have attached themselves to existing policies. These constraints on changing policies, however, are not insurmountable. The critical requirement is that leaders be able to make a credible case that the payoffs to be secured by a change in foreign policy will compensate for any potential losses or risks. For example, a major theme of chapter 6 was that offering territorial concessions to a target was often a risky domestic political move for leaders of the challenger state. However, such concessions were made in a number of cases and what we found was that political leaders often argued to their domestic political audience that a favorable trade-off had been achieved, that is,

1. See Robert Putnam, "Diplomacy and Domestic Politics: The Logic of Two-Level Games," *International Organization* 42, no. 3 (1988): 427–60.

claims to territory were exchanged either for concrete plans to share economic resources or the political support of the target in another more pressing dispute. In sum, the results of this book strongly confirm one of the central critiques of the traditional realist model: an important weakness of this theoretical approach is its failure to accord domestic politics a central role in explaining the security policy choices of state leaders.

The findings in chapter 5 and 6 on the impact of democratic institutions and norms on conflict behavior have potentially important implications for what is commonly referred to as the democratic peace literature. The findings in this book challenge the conventional wisdom that democratic states are only more pacific in their political and military relations with other democracies.[2] Thus, according to this approach we would expect democratic states to avoid the use of force and to seek compromise settlements only in territorial disputes *with other* democratic states. The findings in this book, however, show that increasing levels of democracy reduce escalation and promote peaceful conflict resolution consistently, regardless of who the adversary was in a territorial dispute. The theoretical literature on democracy and international conflict behavior, therefore, needs to move away from the prevailing dyadic approach and take a much more careful and rigorous approach to developing the individual state-level connections between democratic institutions and foreign policy behavior. Much of the existing theoretical literature has been driven by the two-sided empirical observation that democratic states do not go to war against one another but they do often use force against nondemocratic states. Unfortunately, the second part of this empirical observation is taken as conventional wisdom when, in fact, it is not well established.[3] The findings in this book provide further evidence that this conventional wisdom needs to be reexamined much more closely.

Deterrence Theory. The results of chapters 5 and 6 have important implications for the study of conventional deterrence and international conflict. First, the strong results for both domestic- and international-level variables in chapter 5 demonstrate that the most powerful explanations of international conflict require careful attention to both the domestic and international context of crises and disputes. Even though I argued above that it is essential to build theories of foreign policy that take into account the domestic political incentives of leaders, I also firmly believe

---

2. There is an extensive theoretical and empirical literature on this subject which I cited and discussed in chapter 3.

3. See for example James Lee Ray, *Democracy and International Politics* (Columbia: University of South Carolina Press, 1995), ch. 1.

that domestic-based explanations of war and deterrence outcomes are quite incomplete by themselves. At the same time, theoretical explanations focusing only on variables such as relative military power and the resolve to use force are incomplete as well. As a result, the most important task for future work is to place deterrence theory in a broader rational choice model of the foreign policy behavior of states, recognizing that security policy and domestic politics are interrelated.

One issue that needs to be worked out more systematically is how domestic political incentives to use force interact with strategic assessments of the likely risks and costs of armed conflict. The argument that domestic political weakness causes decision makers to engage in a systematic and biased appraisal of the strategic environment which, in turn, results in the failure of deterrence[4] is not consistently supported by historical evidence.[5] Nevertheless, at times it does seem that the political incentives to escalate are more salient to decision makers than military deterrents, but in other cases deterrent measures do temper escalatory pressures. Clearly, domestic political instability and weakness are not sufficient conditions to cause escalation, but at times their effects do seem powerful. Careful theoretical work is required to clarify the contingent nature of this relationship.

The results of this book also address the larger question, What actions and policies of an adversary can be deterred by a state possessing military strength, that is, What is the utility of military power as an instrument of foreign policy? The answer, I think, is that military power has a somewhat narrow but still very important role to play in foreign policy. Military strength is critical in deterring large-scale attacks against national territory and that of allies. However, below that level of threat military strength is much less useful in preventing probes and attacks driven by limited aims and even less so when the threats are small-scale border raids and armed insurgencies. Furthermore, military strength does not deter weak countries from making territorial claims or compel weak countries to make territorial concessions. Military strength and a credible deterrent posture are vital then in preventing war and the frequent use of force at high levels of escalation by a determined adversary.

Successful deterrence, however, may not contribute very much to conflict resolution. Indeed, continued deterrence success, coupled with

---

4. See for example Richard Ned Lebow, *Between Peace and War* (Baltimore: Johns Hopkins University Press, 1981), ch. 4 and Robert Jervis, Richard Ned Lebow, and Janice Gross Stein, *Psychology and Deterrence* (Baltimore: Johns Hopkins University Press, 1985), chs. 3, 5.

5. See for example Ellie Lieberman, "The Rational Deterrence Theory Debate," *Security Studies* 3, no. 3 (1994): 384–427.

a diplomatic stalemate or the absence of active political steps toward conflict resolution, is likely to lead to renewed armed conflict. The exercise of military power by imposing military defeats on states, however, does compel weaker states to move cautiously toward peace. Thus, in a dialectical fashion deterrence failures and the harsh realities of battlefield outcomes can turn out to be more conducive to conflict resolution than a protracted military standoff in which mutual deterrence is quite robust between adversaries.[6]

Policy Implications

In this final section I focus my attention on policy prescriptions directed at third parties (the United Nations, regional organizations, as well as individual countries) that might become involved in territorial disputes between states. They are offered as general guidelines that can be applied to current territorial disputes or to situations where the potential for a dispute seems high.

Preventive Diplomacy and Intervention. Given that once territorial disputes emerge, domestic political incentives encourage leaders to remain deadlocked in conflict, timely diplomatic intervention is necessary to try and avoid protracted disputes. Furthermore, we know from chapter 6 that territorial settlements are difficult to conclude once a dispute has become a salient domestic political issue within the challenger state. This suggests that discrete mediation efforts should be actively pursued by third parties as early as possible and, particularly, before the issue of a territorial claim becomes politicized within the domestic system of the challenger. In cases in which the claims of the challenger lack legal or historical support, third parties should make clear the likely opposition of the international community and the possibility of sanctions. However, at this early stage of the dispute any threats of possible sanctions by third parties should be communicated in private to avoid public pressure on the leaders of the challenger.

It must be recognized, however, that many territorial issues are difficult to resolve, and thus many latent disputes will become active and open conflicts. Once a dispute does emerge, third parties should give high priority to preventing armed conflicts in disputed border regions, since they will only further harden domestic opposition within the challenger to making concessions to the target. In situations in which armed

---

6. See ibid., 414–16 and Jonathan Shimshoni, *Israel and Conventional Deterrence* (Ithaca: Cornell University Press, 1988), chs. 3–5 for a similar conclusion based on the experience of the adversarial relationship between Egypt and Israel from 1948 to 1979.

conflict is a real threat, the United Nations or regional organizations should consider the preventive deployment of some type of peacekeeping forces within the disputed territory, if possible, or along the border if only one party agrees to such a deployment.[7] The preventive deployment of forces would contribute to preventing armed conflicts from developing and thus minimize the loss of life. The prevention of casualties, in turn, would undercut the emergence of domestic political forces within the challenger, which would obstruct a peaceful resolution of the dispute. A peacekeeping presence might also play an important role in deterring or limiting the extent to which the challenger supports some type of insurgency or armed rebellion within the disputed territory. However, in situations in which the threat of armed conflict or rebellion seems quite low, the preventive deployment of a peacekeeping force would be counterproductive in that it would heighten attention and publicity around the dispute and put political pressure on leaders within the challenger to respond in a defiant manner.

Minimize Domestic Political Costs of a Settlement for a Challenger. Third parties must approach the search for the terms of settlement with a keen awareness that political leaders will be very reluctant to make territorial concessions because of their political costs. The substance of the territorial issues at stake also make a difference, but the key stumbling block may very well be the domestic political struggle within the challenger to accept a settlement. Third parties then should avoid open and explicit pressure on challengers as long as possible. This does not mean that international opposition should not be communicated, but very open support for the target will weaken the legitimacy of the third party's role as a mediator. Certainly, in disputes in which the challenger aggressively resorts to the use of force, public condemnation by third parties is appropriate. In many disputes, however, the legitimacy of opposing claims are not so clear-cut, and therefore third parties should try to steer a middle course. International pressure will harden domestic political opposition to an agreement and will further expose political leaders within the challenger to charges of sacrificing national interests.

Third parties must recognize that to induce the challenger to make concessions, the terms of a settlement need to be formulated so that leaders can counter charges of appeasement and capitulation. Thus, if claims to territory have to be withdrawn, some form of concessions by the target on policies within the disputed territory (e.g., treatment of ethnic minorities) may be critical to packaging a politically viable agree-

---

7. See for example Boutros Boutros-Ghali, *An Agenda for Peace 1995*, 2d ed. (New York: United Nations, 1995), 46–51.

ment. Third parties then need to think very hard about what groups will be vocal and influential in their opposition to a settlement within the challenger and whether side payments or agreements could be reached that would split or weaken the opposition.

Limits to Military Intervention. It will be difficult for third parties to make credible threats to intervene with military force (as opposed to a peacekeeping presence) in support of a target state. The territorial goals of a challenger are very often limited and specific in geographic scope, and thus military forces on the ground are much more important than potential forces in being. It should be expected that challengers will not be easily deterred by threats of outside military intervention. Furthermore, for intervention to be effective in the context of an ongoing armed conflict, enough forces would have to be introduced to inflict a military defeat on the target. Challengers will learn from military defeat that use of force carries with it high costs and thus move (slowly) toward compromise. The conflict in Bosnia was an example of a case in which limited threats of outside military intervention and the deployment of lightly armed peacekeeping forces largely failed to convince the Serbian challenger to stop its military attacks or to accept a settlement based on territorial concessions.

Formalize Settlements. It is very important that explicit and formal documents be signed which clearly specify the terms of a territorial settlement. Governments generally do not repudiate well-defined agreements, and therefore the durability of a territorial settlement is greatly strengthened by such agreements. As an extension, third parties could play a very valuable role in the implementation of a settlement by providing technical and financial assistance to the challenger and target so that they could quickly and fully demarcate the boundaries established by any border agreement.

The Consequences of Changing Support for Norms of Self-Determination. Territorial disputes will be more common and more violent if international norms shift from favoring state sovereignty to rights of self-determination for substate groups. Ethnic irredentism will increase, and such issues are more likely to escalate to high levels of conflict. There are trade-offs to be considered no matter which international norms are given greater support. If priority is accorded to the principles of protecting the territorial integrity of states and noninterference in domestic affairs, then minorities are vulnerable to state repression and violence.[8] In contrast, if greater recognition is given to rights of self-determination for substate

---

8. See for example Ted Robert Gurr, *Minorities at Risk* (Washington, D.C: United States Institute of Peace Press, 1993).

groups, then we can expect greater interstate violence. A possible solution is to preserve the norm of maintaining the borders of sovereign states but move toward accepting the international norm of monitoring the treatment of minorities within states and to hold governments responsible for policies of political, economic, and cultural discrimination.[9]

Encourage Economic Cooperation as Solutions to Disputes When Feasible. When access to economic resources is a primary issue at stake in a territorial dispute, the prospects for a peaceful settlement are increased. Third parties should strongly encourage both parties to develop plans for the joint development of economic resources as a solution to disputes over territory. Bilateral as well as multilateral assistance should be used to help finance and plan such projects. It is vital to recognize, however, that economic solutions are only likely to work if both parties have already resolved their political conflicts over disputed territory. Thus, third parties should attach priority to resolving and managing political conflict, if it exists, before turning to economic agreements. Once political differences have been hammered out then economic cooperation can be quite useful in cementing improved political relations and bolstering the durability of a territorial settlement.

---

9. For a broad-ranging discussion of alternative international policies to deal with problems of ethnic conflict within states see Morton Halperin and David Scheffer, *Self-Determination in the New World Order* (Washington, D.C.: Carnegie Endowment for International Peace, 1992), chs. 5–6 and Gidion Gotlieb, *Nation against State* (New York: Council on Foreign Relations Press, 1993).

Appendixes

Summary Description of Territorial Dispute Cases, 1950–90

Listed below are summary descriptions for the 129 cases of territorial disputes that were initiated by challenger states between 1950 and 1990. These 129 territorial disputes constitute: (*a*) the complete dataset utilized for the empirical tests conducted in chapters 5 and 6, and (*b*) one-half of the dataset (the other half consisting of the nondispute cases listed in appendix B) relied upon for the empirical analysis in chapter 4. In the empirical tests the territorial disputes were analyzed from 1950 to 1990, and therefore the profiles in this appendix summarize diplomatic and military developments during this period. I do, however, include an update for those disputes that were not settled prior to the end of 1990 by summarizing recent developments through the end of 1994. The cases are grouped together by geographic region, and at the end of this appendix in section 3 is a bibliography of the sources utilized to build the summary descriptions for each case.

The summary profile of each case includes the following information.

1. The starting and end dates of the territorial dispute between 1950 and 1990.
2. A description of the territory in dispute and which states had territorial claims.
3. The dates of militarized disputes over disputed territory.
4. The outcome of the dispute through the end of 1990 (as well as an update on those disputes that had not been settled prior to the end of 1990).

My goal was to identify the complete population of territorial disputes in the international system during the period between 1950 and 1990. Unfortunately, there is no single source that lists all current and past territorial disputes between states during the postwar period. As a result, I had to consult a broad range of sources in an attempt to compile a complete list. If my list of disputes is compared to the cases included in the two other studies of territorial disputes that are the most comprehensive in their coverage, we find a high degree of convergence.[1] If we examine those cases in *Border and Territorial Disputes,*

---

1. John Allock, Guy Arnold, Alan Day, D. S. Lewis, Lorimer Poultney, Roland Rance, and D. J. Sagar, *Border and Territorial Disputes,* 3d ed. (London: Longman, 1992)

which match my definition of a territorial dispute, there is agreement on approximately 93 percent of the borders that are in dispute (fifty-four out of fifty-eight cases). The list of cases in *Border and Territorial Disputes* is shorter than my list since that study included only ongoing disputes as well as borders that had a high potential of becoming disputed. Similarly, the level of agreement with the cases listed in *Peace and Disputed Sovereignty* was very high (92 percent, or seventy-eight out of eighty-five borders). Once again, the smaller number of cases that can be compared reflects the primary focus of *Peace and Disputed Sovereignty* on current disputes, with a partial listing of prior disputes that had been previously settled.

Nevertheless, there will undoubtedly be some debate and questions raised about the inclusion and exclusion of specific cases. I have included, therefore, in section 2 of this appendix a discussion of a number of potential cases of territorial conflicts which I considered—including the cases of disagreement when my list is compared to *Border and Territorial Disputes* and *Peace and Disputed Sovereignty*—but decided not to include in my population of dispute cases.

In identifying the population of dispute cases, I required confirmation of a dispute from at least two different sources, and in most cases it was possible to find documentation from more than two sources. Not surprisingly, only limited documentation was available for short-lived disputes involving limited diplomatic conflict and no militarized confrontations. In identifying and coding each case, determination of precisely when the dispute began was in some cases problematic. It was not difficult to identify when negotiations over disputed territory were initiated, or when public statements were issued by state leaders that a dispute existed. The more demanding question to answer was whether prior to such events an official, but not public, claim had been issued by one or both governments.

A similar problem was encountered in determining the end dates of some disputes. In certain cases the challenger state did not sign any agreement, issue any public statement, or publish any diplomatic document in which it renounced its territorial claim. The lack of continued public diplomatic initiatives and conflict over a sustained period of time could be interpreted as evidence that the dispute had, in fact, ended. However, in such cases I did not code the dispute as resolved until evidence was found that the challenger government had, in fact, withdrawn its claim to the disputed territory. As a result, a dispute can lapse into a period of inactivity on the part of the challenger state without it being coded as resolved.

The final issue to discuss about each territorial dispute is that the militarized disputes listed for each case include only those disputes in which: (1) the actions of the challenger state were clearly connected to the territorial issue in contention and not some other issue, and (2) the actions of the challenger state were taken with the direction and authority of the central government. When there

---

and Friedrich Kratochwil, Paul Rohrlich, and Harpreet Mahajan, *Peace and Disputed Sovereignty* (Lanham, MD: University Press of America, 1985).

was evidence that the local forces initiated military actions along disputed territory without the prior consent of the government, I would exclude such cases.

Summary of Territorial Dispute Cases

Central and South America

Countries: Argentina vs. Chile
Years: 1950–90
Challenger: Argentina 1950–90
Disputed Territory: Three areas have been in dispute between the two countries. The claims of Argentina have a long history that can be traced back to each country's independence from Spain in the early nineteenth century. At the time of independence the borders between the two former Spanish provinces in certain regions were only vaguely, or even inaccurately, defined by treaties and agreements. As a result, the two newly independent countries presented differing interpretations of where their common border was located. Agreements signed in 1881 and 1902 failed to resolve disputes in three regions. The first area of contention centered on a small strip of territory approximately forty-five miles in length along the north-south Andean border referred to as the Palena region. The second area centered on the Laguno del Desierto region along the southern portion of the Andean frontier. The third and most contentious area of dispute involved a group of small islands—primarily Picton, Nueva, and Lennox—at the southern tip of the continent in the Beagle Channel.
Militarized Disputes Initiated by Challenger: (1) July–September 1952, (2) August 1955, (3) November 1958, (4) August–September 1959, (5) July 1964, (6) November–December 1965, (7) November 1967–May 1968, (8) August 1977–February 1978, (9) August 1978–January 1979, (10) October 1980–February 1981
Outcome of Dispute: The disputes over the Palena and the Laguna del Desierto regions were not a source of open and acute conflict after the mid-1960s, when British arbitration helped resolve many of the disputes; a comprehensive settlement, however, was not reached over all of the disputed territory in each region. It was not until August 1991 that an agreement was signed between the two countries settling almost all points of contention, except for small sections of the Laguna de Desierto. It was agreed, however, that the remaining dispute in this region would be submitted to a panel of judges from the OAS for a final decision. Both countries submitted their claims to the panel in August 1993, but no ruling had been issued by the end of 1994. The dispute over islands in the Beagle Channel, however, was resolved in November 1984 in a Treaty of Peace and Friendship signed by the two countries. A panel of former ICJ judges had issued a ruling in 1977 favoring Chile, but Argentina refused to accept the panel's decision. Papal mediation eventually helped bring about an agreement. In the 1984 treaty Argentina recognized Chilean sovereignty over the disputed islands, but Chile did accept tight restrictions on its maritime rights to the Atlantic in close proximity to the islands.

Countries: Argentina vs. United Kingdom/Falkland Islands
Years: 1950–90
Challenger: Argentina 1950–90
Disputed Territory: Argentina has disputed the British claim to sovereignty over the Falkland Islands (or Malvinas) and their dependencies (located in the South Atlantic some 300 miles off the Argentine coastline) since 1833. In the post–World War II period Argentina began actively pressing its claim in 1965. The Argentine claim is based on geographic proximity and occupation of the islands prior to 1833. Britain, in turn, claims sovereignty as a result of its occupation of the islands since 1833 and because the expressed preference of the local population is to remain British.
Militarized Disputes Initiated by Challenger: (1) February 1976, (2) December 1976, (3) March–April 1982
Outcome of Dispute: The conflicting claims to sovereignty over the islands persist. Multiple rounds of negotiations were held between the mid-1960s and the early 1980s but no settlement was reached. In 1982 Argentina and Britain went to war when Argentina attempted to seize the islands, but Argentine military forces were compelled to withdraw after a successful British counterattack. Since 1982 there has been no change in the diplomatic position of either side on the basic issue of sovereignty in several rounds of talks and negotiations. Trade relations, however, were resumed between the two countries in the course of 1985–1986, and since 1990 full diplomatic relations have been restored and the two countries have cooperated on joint fishing rights around the disputed islands.

Countries: Argentina vs. Uruguay
Years: 1950–73
Challengers: Both Argentina and Uruguay 1950–73
Disputed Territory: The Uruguay River and the Rio de la Plata have been considered to form in principle the boundary between Argentina and Uruguay since the preliminary Peace Convention of August 1828 was signed by the two countries. A treaty to delimit the boundary was signed in September 1916 but neither country ratified the agreement. The dispute centered on exactly where the boundary between the two countries should be located along the Rio de la Plata River, including sovereignty over several islands and rights to oil deposits under the river. Uruguay's position was that the boundary should be located at the geographic center of the river, while Argentina insisted that the boundary should follow the deep channel.
Militarized Disputes Initiated by Challenger: Argentina, (1) January 1969, (2) January 1973
Outcome of Dispute: A partial agreement was reached in April 1961 when a treaty was signed allocating islands between the two countries in the Uruguay River. Following agreements on joint development of oil resources, a general settlement was concluded in November of 1973. The treaty contained the following provisions: (*a*) the center of the Rio de la Plata river was accepted as the boundary, (*b*) international use of the river channels was established, and (*c*) possession of various small islands was determined.

Countries: Bolivia vs. Chile
Years: 1950–90
Challenger: Bolivia 1950–90
Disputed Territory: Bolivia has sought a territorial outlet to the Pacific Ocean ever since the loss of coastal territory to Chile in the Pacific War of 1879–1884. Bolivia has called for a port in the region along the border between Chile and Peru known as the Tacna and Arica provinces. While Chile has refused to cede the territory requested by Bolivia, it has granted Bolivia duty-free use of the ports of Africa and Antofagasta and of the railroads connecting them.
Militarized Disputes Initiated by Challenger: ———
Outcome of Dispute: The two countries, along with Peru, have exchanged proposals for a resolution of the issue since the mid-1970s. At one point Chile proposed to grant to Bolivia a corridor to the sea but only in exchange for Bolivian territorial and financial compensation. In 1987 Bolivia proposed that Chile cede 1,000 square miles of territory, which Chile rejected. By the end of 1992 Bolivia was moving in the direction of seeking a rapprochement with Chile, and there was discussion within Bolivia about possibly dropping its demand for a sea outlet. However, by the summer of 1993 Bolivia was reaffirming its demand for a sea outlet and criticizing Chile for refusing to adopt a more flexible policy.

Countries: Cuba vs. United States
Years: 1959–90
Challenger: Cuba 1959–90
Disputed Territory: Since Fidel Castro came to power Cuba has considered the U.S. military base at Guantanamo to be illegally occupied and has demanded that the United States withdraw from the base. The United States has countered that it has full jurisdiction and control over the base and its surrounding territory (117 square miles), based on treaties signed with Cuba in 1903 and 1934, and that it has no intention of withdrawing. The Cuban claim to Guantanamo was reaffirmed in 1976 when, by referendum, a provision was included in the Cuban constitution declaring that all international treaties signed under conditions of inequality and pressure were null and void.
Militarized Disputes Initiated by Challenger: (1) April 1960–April 1961
Outcome of Dispute: The dispute remains deadlocked in stalemate. The United States continues to use the base at Guantanamo and has given no indication that it intends to change its policy despite continuing Cuban calls for complete withdrawal.

Countries: Ecuador vs. Peru
Years: 1950–90
Challenger: Ecuador 1950–90
Disputed Territory: Since its independence in the nineteenth century, Ecuador has laid claim to a large section of the Amazon Basin of northern Peru, known as the Orient, in an attempt to gain direct access to the Amazon River and therefore the Atlantic Ocean. The territory has been in dispute since 1802 when the trans-Andean Maranon river basin was transferred from the Spanish authorities

in Quito to those in Lima. When Spain was evicted in the 1820s, both Peru and Ecuador laid claim to the territory. The territory in dispute covers some 125,000 square miles and includes the Amazon and Maranon rivers and Peru's primary oil-producing region. Following its defeat in armed conflict with Peru in 1941, Ecuador signed the Rio Protocol in 1942, which awarded most of the disputed territory to Peru and denied Ecuador direct access to the Amazon River. By 1950 Ecuador was openly calling for the revision of the Rio Protocol based upon (a) the discovery of the Rio Cenepa River, which was not a part of the Protocol and, if controlled by Ecuador, would provide it with access to the Amazon River, and (b) the charge that the Protocol was invalid because it had been signed under duress. In 1960 Ecuador unilaterally declared the Rio Protocol null and void and called on Peru to reopen border negotiations. Peru, however, has maintained that the Rio Protocol remains in force and that therefore there is no dispute over the delimitation of the border between the two countries.

Militarized Disputes Initiated by Challenger: (1) February–July 1953, (2) May–October 1954, (3) August–September 1955, (4) June 1977–January 1978, (5) January–March 1981

Outcome of Dispute: The dispute persists because Peru has not been willing to negotiate with Ecuador on a revision of the Rio Protocol. Militarized confrontations along the border occurred in 1991, but some movement toward a possible settlement did take place during late 1991 until early 1993. Peru offered joint economic development projects and navigation rights to Ecuador on the Amazon, and the two countries were working on an agreement for mediation by the Vatican and the possibility of permitting an outside expert to help resolve the dispute. The apparent movement toward a more accommodative position by Peru, however, ended when the Peruvian president announced in September 1993 and again in March 1994 that the Rio Protocol remained fully in force and should not be revised.

Countries: Guatemala vs. United Kingdom/Belize
Years: 1950–90
Challenger: Guatemala 1950–90
Disputed Territory: Guatemala has claimed sovereignty over the neighboring territory of Belize (formerly British Honduras) since its independence from Spain in the mid-nineteenth century. Guatemala claimed Belize on the grounds that it had inherited the territory (8,866 square miles) from Spain. In 1859 Guatemala signed a treaty with Britain recognizing British sovereignty over Belize and delimiting the border. Adherence to the treaty was contingent upon the building of a road across the jungle from Guatemala to the Caribbean coast (article 7). Guatemala has argued that Britain nullified the Boundary Treaty of 1859 by failing to meet the requirements of article 7. In turn, Britain denies that it bears sole responsibility for the failure to implement article 7. Furthermore, Britain has maintained that the colony had the right to self-determination and that the population favored independence as opposed to annexation by Guatemala.

Militarized Disputes Initiated by Challenger: (1) January–April 1972, (2) October–December 1975, (3) April–July 1977

Outcome of Dispute: Despite periodic rounds of talks between the two countries in the 1960s and 1970s, a negotiated settlement could not be reached providing for the independence of Belize on terms acceptable to Guatemala. Accordingly, Britain went ahead with plans for independence, which was achieved by Belize in 1981. By 1983 Guatemala had greatly reduced the size of its territorial claims against Belize, and by 1989 relations between the two countries had improved. In mid-1990 it was agreed that a joint commission would be formed to draft a treaty in which Guatemala would recognize Belize independence, and the two countries would also establish a joint economic development zone along their border. By November 1992 the president of Guatemala, with the support of a Constitutional Court, had decided to recognize Belize officially and to withdraw any territorial claims.

Countries: Honduras vs. El Salvador
Years: 1950–90
Challenger: Honduras 1950–90
Disputed Territory: Delimitation of the common frontier between the two countries had been a source of conflict since the 1880s. About one-third of the approximately 200-mile border had been in dispute, with Honduras refusing to recognize specific provisions of a border convention originally signed in 1884 but never ratified. In addition to the border, the two countries disputed several small islands in the Gulf of Fonseca.
Militarized Disputes Initiated by Challenger: (1) July–August 1976
Outcome of Dispute: In October 1980 the Lima Peace Treaty was signed which: (*a*) delimited about two-thirds of the disputed border, (*b*) included provisions for establishing border commissions to delimit the remaining disputed areas, as well as (*c*) an agreement that if the border commissions and governments could not reach an agreement within five years, any remaining disputes would be submitted to the ICJ. In 1986 the two countries submitted their disputes over remaining areas to the ICJ. A ruling was issued by the ICJ in September 1992 in which two-thirds of the disputed territory was awarded to Honduras.

Countries: Honduras vs. United States
Years: 1950–72
Challenger: Honduras 1950–72
Disputed Territory: Honduras claimed sovereignty over the Swan Islands, which the United States had secured control over after signing a lease agreement in 1863.
Militarized Disputes Initiated by Challenger: ———
Outcome of Dispute: In 1972 the United States terminated its lease and returned the island to Honduras.

Countries: Mexico vs. United States
Years: 1950–63
Challenger: Mexico 1950–63
Disputed Territory: The dispute can be traced back to the 1890s when Mexico

presented a claim to several small tracts of territories along the Rio Grande totaling some 3,000 acres. The dispute arose because changes in the course of Rio Grande raised questions about the location of the border. The largest area of dispute (the Chamizal Tract) was brought before an abitration panel, which ruled in 1911 in favor of Mexico. The United States, however, refused to accept the ruling.

Militarized Disputes Initiated by Challenger: ———

Outcome of Dispute: In August 1963 a final settlement was reached in which both countries made concessions, though the United States ceded more territory in the prinicpal area of dispute—Chamizal.

Countries: Netherlands/Suriname vs. France/French Guiana
Years: 1950–90
Challengers: Netherlands 1950–74 and Suriname 1975–90
Disputed Territory: The Dutch prior to 1975 and Suriname since then have claimed a triangular area of land (approximately 3,000 square miles) near the Maroni river along the southern border of French Guiana.
Militarized Disputes Initiated by Challenger: ———
Outcome of Dispute: A treaty was drawn up in 1977 stipulating that Suriname would recognize French sovereignty over the disputed territory in exchange for French economic aid to develop resources jointly in the area. Suriname, however, has not signed or ratified the treaty, and therefore the dispute continues to exist though Suriname has not actively pursued the dispute since the early 1980s.

Countries: Netherlands/Suriname vs. United Kingdom/Guyana
Years: 1950–90
Challengers: Netherlands 1950–74 and Suriname 1975–90
Disputed Territory: The Dutch prior to 1975 and Suriname since then have claimed a triangular area of land (approximately 6,000 square miles) with little economic value near the New River along the southern border of Guyana.
Militarized Disputes Initiated by Challenger: Suriname, (1) April 1976, (2) January 1978
Outcome of Dispute: Several rounds of negotiations were held in the 1970s and 1980s to resolve the dispute, but no agreement has been reached and a border commission established in 1989 has made no further progress toward a settlement.

Countries: Nicaragua vs. Colombia
Years: 1980–90
Challenger: Nicaragua 1980–90
Disputed Territory: In February 1980 the Nicaraguan government declared null and void a 1928 treaty establishing Colombian sovereignty over the Caribbean archipelago of San Andreas and Providencia. Nicaragua claimed that the 1928 treaty was invalid because it been imposed on Nicaragua under United States pressure. In response, Colombia reaffirmed its claim to sovereignty over the archipelago and stated its willingness to take the dispute before the ICJ.
Militarized Disputes Initiated by Challenger: ———

Outcome of Dispute: The two governments have held talks on the issue in the 1980s, but neither side has compromised or changed its position.

Countries: Nicaragua vs. Honduras
Years: 1950–60
Challenger: Nicaragua 1950–60
Disputed Territory: In 1906 Nicaragua refused to accept an arbitration ruling awarding some 5,000 square miles of disputed border territory to Honduras. The dispute remained relatively dormant until 1957 when Honduras sought to take control over the disputed territory in order to develop recently discovered oil deposits.
Militarized Disputes Initiated by Challenger: (1) April–June 1957
Outcome of Dispute: The dispute was submitted to the ICJ, which ruled in November 1960 that the arbitration award of 1906 should be enforced. Within the following year Nicaragua withdrew from the territory, and new boundary lines were fixed in accord with the 1906 award.

Countries: Nicaragua vs. United States
Years: 1950–71
Challenger: Nicaragua 1950–71
Disputed Territory: Nicaragua claimed sovereignty over Corn Island, which had been leased by agreement to the United States in 1916.
Militarized Disputes Initiated by Challenger: ———
Outcome of Dispute: In 1971 the United States returned the island to Nicaragua when it terminated its lease agreement.

Countries: Panama vs. United States
Years: 1950–77
Challenger: Panama 1950–77
Disputed Territory: The Panamanian government desired complete sovereignty over the Panama Canal Zone. The United States exercised sovereignty over the Canal Zone based on a treaty signed in 1903, which granted the United States sovereign rights for 99 years.
Militarized Disputes Initiated by Challenger: ———
Outcome of Dispute: After multiple rounds of negotiations and tentative agreements being signed since the 1950s, a general settlement was reached in 1977. In the treaty the two governments agreed that Panama would assume full sovereignty and operational control of the Canal Zone by the year 2000.

Countries: Uruguay vs. Brazil
Years: 1950–90
Challenger: Uruguay 1950–90
Disputed Territory: Two short sections of the border are contested by Uruguay. The first is the Arroyo de la Invernda area of the Rio Quarai, and the second centers on islands situated at the confluence of the Rio Quarai and the Uruguay. A treaty signed in October 1851 delimited the border between the two countries,

but the boundary disputes are based on opposing interpretations of the treaty by each country. According to the treaty the boundary follows the Cuchilla Negra to the headwaters of the arroyo to the Rio Quarai. Brazil and Uruguay, however, identify different streams as the Arroyo de la Invernada, and thus the dispute centers on the area between the different streams as well as the sovereignty of Brasilera Island at the confluence of the Uruguay and the Rio Quarai. Uruguay claims that the boundary follows the more easterly rivers, while Brazil claims the more westerly rivers. Established boundary pillars favor the Brazilian position. The 1851 treaty states that islands in the Rio Quarai at its embouchure into the Uruguay belong to Brazil, but Uruguay claims that Brasilera Island is in the Uruguay river and does not belong to Brazil.

Militarized Disputes Initiated by Challenger: ———

Outcome of Dispute: The dispute has not been a source of acute conflict between the two countries, and periodic talks have been held but no settlement has been reached.

Countries: Venezuela vs. United Kingdom/Guyana
Years: 1951–90
Challenger: Venezuela 1951–90
Disputed Territory: Venezuela claims a large section of Guyanese territory (50,000 square miles) west of the Essequibo river, which includes areas rich in oil deposits. In 1899 the territory in dispute was awarded by a court of arbitration to Guyana (then British Guiana). In 1951 Venezuela publicly questioned the validity of the award and reopened the border issue, and in 1962 Venezuela officially announced that it no longer would accept the 1899 ruling.

Militarized Disputes Initiated by Challenger: (1) October 1966, (2) January 1969, (3) February 1970, (4) April 1976, (5) July 1981–September 1982

Outcome of Dispute: The June 1970 Protocol of Port of Spain signed by Britain, Guyana, and Venezuela placed a twelve-year moratorium on the territorial dispute. Venezuela announced in December 1981, however, that it would not extend the moratorium and that it still claimed the Essequibo territory. United Nations mediated talks were held in the mid-1980s without a breakthrough, but by the end of the 1980s relations between the two countries had improved as economic ties were developed. Nevertheless, Venezuela maintains its claim to the Essequibo territory.

Europe

Countries: East Germany/Soviet Union vs. West Germany/United States/United Kingdom/France
Years: 1950–71
Challenger: Soviet Union/East Germany 1950–71
Disputed Territory: East Germany, with the support of the Soviet Union, sought to establish control over West Berlin and terminate the occupation rights of the United States, Britain, and France concluded at the end of World War II and to compel West Germany to abandon its claims to Berlin. The Soviets and East

Germans viewed the Western presence in Berlin as a threat to the stability and legitimacy of the East German regime and therefore turned to a combination of threats and negotiations with their NATO adversaries in an attempt to end the Western presence in and claims to Berlin.

Militarized Disputes Initiated by Challenger: Soviet Union, (1) November 1958–June 1959, (2) July–October 1961

Outcome of Dispute: The erection of the Berlin Wall in 1961 effectively sealed off East Berlin from West Berlin and removed the perceived threat of the Western powers to East Germany. In September 1971 a four-power agreement was signed settling the confrontation over Berlin. The Soviet Union declared its desire to eliminate tension in the area and agreed to respect the rights of the Western Powers in West Berlin, improve transit traffic between West Berlin and West Germany, and allow travel from West to East Berlin.

Countries: France vs. United Kingdom
Years: 1950–53
Challengers: France and Great Britain 1950–53
Disputed Territory: France and Great Britain both claimed sovereignty over the small islands of Minquiers and Ecrehos located off the French coast in the English Channel.
Militarized Disputes Initiated by Challenger: ———
Outcome of Dispute: The dispute was submitted to the ICJ in 1951, and a ruling was announced in 1953 wherein British sovereignty over the islands was recognized. France accepted the ICJ ruling.

Countries: Greece vs. Albania
Years: 1950–71
Challenger: Greece 1950–71
Disputed Territory: Greek governments had expressed reservations about its borders with Albania since the latter had become an independent state in 1913. Greece considered the southern section of Albania, which is populated by ethnic Greeks, to be a part of the Greek region of Epirus. Following the end of World War II Greek governments reaffirmed their desire to annex this Albanian territory.
Militarized Disputes Initiated by Challenger: ———
Outcome of Dispute: Albania steadfastly insisted that the territory was part of its national territory as established by international agreement in 1913 and would not negotiate over the issue. In May 1971 diplomatic relations were established between the two countries, and a peace treaty was signed in which Greece tacitly recognized the existing borders of Albania.

Countries: Greece vs. Turkey vs. United Kingdom/Cyprus
Years: 1951–90
Challengers: Greece 1951–90 and Turkey 1955–90
Disputed Territory: Throughout the post–World War II period Greece and Turkey have competed for control and influence over the island of Cyprus. Until the

late nineteenth century Cyprus was a part of the Ottoman Empire, but in 1878 the island was occupied by Great Britain and then annexed in 1914 by the British. Approximately 80 percent of the population is composed of Greek Cypriots and the remainder are Turkish Cypriots. From the early 1950s onward Greece has favored union with Cyprus through a policy of enosis, but since 1974 Greek policy has focused on opposing the partition of Cyprus following the Turkish invasion. Turkey has opposed the Greek policy of enosis and instead has favored the partition of Cyprus in order to protect the position of Turkish Cypriots. Up until 1960, when Cyprus attained independence, Great Britain was the target of opposing Turkish and Greek claims to the island, and since then the two countries have directly competed for influence over Cyprus.
Militarized Disputes Initiated by Challenger: Greece (1) November 1963–August 1964, (2) November–December 1967, and Turkey (1) July 1974–February 1975
Outcome of Dispute: In an uneasy compromise Greece and Turkey agreed that an independent Cypriot state would be established in 1960. Rivalry and conflict, however, continued between the two states for influence on the island, and following the Turkish military intervention in July 1974 Cyprus has been effectively divided into Greek and Turkish Cypriot controlled areas. In February 1975 a Turkish Cypriot Federated State was proclaimed, and in November 1983 a Turkish Republic of Northern Cyprus was formed. Greece has not recognized Turkish control over portions of Cyprus since 1974 and has called for the reestablishment of a single Cypriot state. Several rounds of talks have been held under United Nations direction (e.g., 1977–80, 1983–85, 1988–92) between Greek and Turkish Cypriots without any resolution of the dispute.

Countries: Ireland vs. United Kingdom
Years: 1950–90
Challenger: Ireland 1950–90
Disputed Territory: Since the partition of Ireland in 1922, the independent Catholic Irish Republic has sought reunification with Protestant Northern Ireland. Great Britain has maintained that reunification can be achieved only if the majority of the people of Northern Ireland expressly support such a policy.
Militarized Disputes Initiated by Challenger: ———
Outcome of Dispute: The dispute has not been settled though limited progress has been achieved since the early 1970s. In 1973 the Irish Republic declared that it accepted the principle that reunification would require that the majority of the population of Northern Ireland supported such a policy, while the British endorsed the principle that power-sharing arrangements should be established. In the Anglo-Irish Agreement of 1985 Dublin was allowed an official consultative role in the affairs of Northern Ireland, and in 1992 British and Irish officials held direct talks for the first time in several decades.

Countries: Netherlands vs. Belgium
Years: 1950–59
Challenger: Netherlands 1950–59
Disputed Territories: Dutch governments claimed sovereignty over two small

areas along the Belgium border that had been awarded to Belgium in a boundary convention concluded in 1943.
Militarized Disputes Initiated by Challenger: ———
Outcome of Dispute: The dispute was submitted to the ICJ in 1957, and a ruling was announced in 1959 confirming that the two areas were part of Belgian territory. The Dutch accepted the ICJ ruling.

Countries: Netherlands vs. West Germany
Years: 1950–60
Challenger: Netherlands 1950–60
Disputed Territory: Following the conclusion of World War II the Netherlands advanced territorial claims against Germany totaling some 700 square miles. By 1949 those claims had been reduced to only twenty-six square miles by a provisional recommendation of a Western demarcation commission. Most of the territories in question were areas that were lightly populated and of little economic value.
Militarized Disputes Initiated by Challenger: ———
Outcome of Dispute: In April 1960 a treaty was signed between the two governments the dispute which settled through mutual compromise.

Countries: Spain vs. United Kingdom
Years: 1950–90
Challenger: Spain 1950–90
Disputed Territory: Spanish governments have claimed sovereignty over the British naval base of Gibraltar (two and one-quarter square miles), situated at the very tip of southern Spain. Gibraltar was occupied by the Spanish from 1462–1704 and by the British ever since. Spain argues that the 1713 Treaty of Utrecht transferred ownership, but not sovereignty, of Gibraltar to Britain. The British reject the Spanish claim and state that any change in the status of Gibraltar must be supported by the local population.
Militarized Disputes Initiated by Challenger: (1) June–November 1969
Outcome of Dispute: Since the mid-1960s multiple rounds of talks have been held between the two countries (most recently between 1985 and 1987 and then again from 1989 to 1992), but they have failed to achieve a breakthrough on the central question of sovereignty with both sides maintaining their opposing positions. Nevertheless, the border, which had been closed since 1969, was reopened in 1985, and some cooperative agreements on customs and drug trafficking have been signed by the two governments.

Countries: West Germany vs. Czechoslovakia
Years: 1955–73
Challenger: West Germany 1955–73
Disputed Territory: The Munich Agreement of September 1938 ceded to Germany the Sudetenland areas of Czechoslovakia. Following World War II, West German governments did not officially renounce that agreement even though the territory had been restored to Czechoslovakia after the war. The position of

West German governments was that a final settlement of Germany's eastern borders could not be concluded until German reunification had been achieved.
Militarized Disputes Initiated by Challenger: ———
Outcome of Dispute: In a treaty signed by West Germany and Czechoslovakia in December 1973, West Germany formally declared that the Munich Agreement was null and void and that it had no territorial claims against Czechoslovakia.

Countries: West Germany vs. East Germany
Years: 1955–72
Challenger: West Germany 1955–72
Disputed Territory: Following its defeat in World War II Germany was divided into two states with West Germany closely aligned to the United States and NATO, while East Germany was aligned with the Soviet Union and the Warsaw Pact. Successive West German governments, however, refused to recognize the sovereignty of the East German state.
Militarized Disputes Initiated by Challenger: ———
Outcome of Dispute: In a treaty signed in December 1972 West Germany recognized the territorial integrity and sovereignty of the East German state. At the same time, West Germany reaffirmed its goal of seeking the peaceful reunification of Germany through free self-determination. The collapse of the communist regime in East Germany in late 1989 reopened the issue of German reunification. West German plans for reunification were approved by the United States, the Soviet Union, Great Britain, and France in September 1990 and in the following month Germany was formally reunified.

Countries: West Germany vs. France
Years: 1955–57
Challenger: West Germany 1955–57
Disputed Territory: Following the end of World War II the coal and steel producing region of the Saar was placed under the control of France. West Germany, however, sought the return of the Saar as part of its national territory.
Militarized Disputes Initiated by Challenger: ———
Outcome of Dispute: An agreement was reached in January 1957 for the incorporation of the Saar into West Germany.

Countries: West Germany vs. Poland
Years: 1955–70
Challenger: West Germany 1955–70
Disputed Territory: At the conclusion of World War II Poland's western frontier was extended at Germany's expense to the Oder-Neisse Line. East Germany officially recognized the new border with Poland but West German governments, however, did not, and thus maintained a claim to the territories gained by Poland. The position of West German governments was that a final settlement of Germany's eastern borders could not be reached until German reunification had been achieved.
Militarized Disputes Initiated by Challenger: ———

Outcome of Dispute: In a treaty signed by the two governments in November 1970, West Germany formally accepted the Oder-Neisse Line as the western border of Poland and stated that it had no territorial claims against Poland. In the Moscow Agreement of September 1990 a reunified Germany pledged to respect the Oder-Neisse Line and in November of that year the newly reunified German government signed a treaty with Poland reaffirming the Oder-Neisse Line.

Countries: Yugoslavia vs. Italy
Years: 1950–75
Challenger: Yugoslavia 1950–75
Disputed Territory: At the end of World War II Yugoslavia laid claim to the territory of Trieste, which was occupied by the Western powers following Italy's defeat. Trieste had been awarded to Italy following the conclusion of World War I, and the Rapallo Treaty of 1920 confirmed Italy's control of Trieste by Yugoslavia.
Militarized Disputes Initiated by Challenger: (1) October–December 1953
Outcome of Dispute: In 1954 the Western powers agreed to transfer control of Trieste to Italy. Yugoslavia did not directly challenge this decision, but it did not formally accept Italian control until the Treaty of Osimo was signed in November 1975. In the treaty Yugoslavia officially accepted the status quo in Trieste as permanent and fully recognized its frontier with Italy.

Middle East

Countries: Egypt vs. Israel
Years: 1950–89
Challenger: Egypt 1950–89
Disputed Territory: In the interwar period Egypt opposed the creation of a Jewish state in Palestine. When the United Nations General Assembly passed a resolution in November 1947 to partition Palestine and create a new Jewish state, Egypt announced its intention to prevent by force of arms the establishment of an independent Israeli state. Egypt's official position was that the territories comprising the state of Israel should form the basis of an independent Palestinian state, but Egypt also had ambitions to annex some of the territory that would have formed an independent Palestinian state. In addition, following its defeat in the 1967 Six Day War, Egypt sought to end the Israeli occupation of the Sinai (approximately 22,500 square miles) and the Taba Strip.
Militarized Disputes Initiated by Challenger: (1) January–March 1960, (2) May–June 1967, (3) September–October 1967, (4) September–October 1968, (5) March 1969–August 1970, (6) April–June 1973, (7) October 1973
Outcome of Dispute: The signing of the 1979 Egyptian-Israeli Peace Treaty contained four basic provisions relating to territorial issues: (*a*) the formal acceptance by Egypt of the existence of Israel, (*b*) an agreement by Israel to return the Sinai to Egypt over a three-year period, (*c*) an agreement by both countries that United Nations forces would occupy the Taba Strip pending a final negotiated settlement, and (*d*) an agreement to hold talks on autonomy for Palestinians in

the West Bank and Gaza Strip. The Israeli withdrawal from the Sinai was completed by April 1982 while binding arbitration was accepted in 1986 to settle the dispute over the Taba Strip. A ruling favoring Egypt was issued in September 1988 (by March 1989 Taba was formally incorporated as a part of Egypt). Finally, Israeli-Egyptian autonomy talks quickly deadlocked by the end of 1980, and Israeli-Egyptian negotiations were subsequently replaced by direct contacts and negotiation between Israeli and Palestinian representatives. In August 1993 Israel and the Palestinian Liberation Organization signed an agreement to establish self-rule for Palestinians in the Gaza Strip and Jerhico.

Countries: Egypt vs. United Kingdom
Years: 1950–54
Challenger: Egypt 1950–54
Disputed Territory: Following the end of World War II Egypt sought an agreement with the British to terminate British occupation and control of territory surrounding the Suez Canal. British rights in the canal zone had been recently reaffirmed in a treaty signed with Egypt in 1936. The British, however, considered the canal to be vital to the defense of Europe and therefore were reluctant to withdraw completely from the canal zone.
Militarized Disputes Initiated by Challenger: (1) February 1953–July 1954
Outcome of Dispute: The dispute was settled with the signing of an evacuation agreement in October 1954 providing for the withdrawal of 80,000 British forces over a twenty-month period. The agreement also stipulated that during this transition the two countries would share responsibilities for the operation of technical installations regarding the Canal and its defense.

Countries: Iran vs. United Kingdom/Bahrain
Years: 1950–70 and 1979–90
Challenger: Iran 1950–70 and 1979–90
Disputed Territory: Iran had a long-standing claim (dating back to the mid-nineteenth century) to sovereignty over the island of Bahrain, located off the coast of Saudi Arabia. Iran began to press its claim more forcefully in 1968 following the announcement by the British of their intention to withdraw from the Persian Gulf.
Militarized Disputes Initiated by Challenger: ———
Outcome of Dispute: Britain brought the dispute before the United Nations, and a fact-finding mission in 1970 reported that the population of Bahrain preferred independence to absorption by Iran. The Shah of Iran then backed away from pressing his country's claims, and in December 1970 the Iranian government endorsed a United Nations Security Council Resolution affirming the independence of the state of Bahrain. In September 1979, however, the new regime in Iran renewed its claim to sovereignty over Bahrain and during the 1980s supported efforts to destabilize the Bahrain regime. By the end of the 1980s, however, Iran sought to improve relations with Bahrain, and in December 1989 a document was signed in which Iran agreed not to interfere in the internal affairs

of Bahrain and not to use military force against the country. By December of 1990 the two countries had resumed full diplomatic relations.

Countries: Iran vs. United Kingdom/United Arab Emirates
Years: 1950–90
Challenger: Iran 1950–90
Disputed Territory: Iran and the United Arab Emirates have competing claims to sovereignty over the islands of Abu Musa, Greater Tunb, and Lesser Tunb. These islands are located at the entrance to the Persian Gulf, opposite the Strait of Hormuz and were controlled by the British until the UAR's independence in 1971. Iran had contested British control over the islands since the late nineteenth century.
Militarized Disputes Initiated by Challenger: Iran, (1) November 1970, (2) November 1971
Outcome of Dispute: In November 1971 Iranian forces occupied the islands, which was immediately condemned by the UAE Council of Ministers as an act of aggression violating the sovereignty of the UAE, and Iran was called upon to withdraw from the islands. Iran, however, continues to occupy the islands, and the UAE still claims sovereignty over the islands.

Countries: Iran vs. Iraq
Years: 1950–90
Challengers: Iran 1950–75 and Iraq 1979–90
Disputed Territory: The dispute centers on the boundary between the two countries along the Shatt-al-Arab Waterway. The Shatt-al-Arab extends for 160 miles and flows into the Persian Gulf. For both countries major oil export centers are located along the waterway. Iraq claims jurisdiction over the entire waterway, whereas Iran has consistently argued that the boundary should be based on the Thalweg line principle (the median line in the deepest channel of the waterway). Agreements signed in 1913 and 1937 delimited the boundary and established a regime of administration largely in accord with the Iraqi position, which Iran sought to change in the postwar period.
Militarized Disputes Initiated by Challenger: Iran (1) November 1959–January 1960, (2) February–April 1961, (3) December 1965–April 1966, (4) April–July 1969, (5) January 1972–March 1973, (6) March–May 1974, (7) August 1974–March 1975, and Iraq (1) October 1979–March 1980, (2) September 1980–July 1988
Outcome of Dispute: In June 1975 the two governments signed the Algiers Accord and related protocols, which, at the time, seemed to have settled the territorial dispute in favor of Iran. It became apparent, however, that Iraq did not consider the Accord a definitive settlement. In September 1980 Iraq officially abrogated the Accord and claimed sovereignty over all of the Shatt-al-Arab Waterway and invaded Iran. When a cease-fire was signed in 1988 ending the Iran-Iraq War, Iraqi forces occupied the Shatt-al-Arab Waterway. Subsequent peace talks between the two countries, however, failed to resolve the

dispute over the waterway. It was not until August 1990, shortly after the Iraqi invasion of Kuwait, that Saddam Hussein agreed to settle the dispute by accepting the terms established by the 1975 Algiers Accord.

Countries: Jordan vs. Saudi Arabia
Years: 1950–65
Challengers: Both Jordan and Saudi Arabia 1950–65
Disputed Territory: Both countries had competing claims to where their common border should be located. Great Britain in the 1920s and 1930s had attempted to delimit the borders of Trans-Jordan, but an agreement could not be reached with Saudi Arabia. The territories in dispute were largely uninhabited deserts of little economic value.
Militarized Disputes Initiated by Challenger: ———
Outcome of Dispute: Talks were held periodically from 1961 to 1963 without a resolution of the dispute. In August 1965 a compromise agreement was signed settling the dispute. Jordan received 3,600 square miles of territory and its coastline was extended by twelve miles, while Saudi Arabia received 4,200 square miles of land.

Countries: Iran vs. Saudi Arabia
Years: 1950–68
Challengers: Both Iran and Saudi Arabia 1950–68
Disputed Territory: The two countries had competing claims to sovereignty over the islands of Farsi and Al-Arabiyah.
Militarized Disputes Initiated by Challenger: ———
Outcome of Dispute: In 1968 a boundary agreement was ratified by both governments whereby Iran was given Farsi and Saudi Arabia Al-Arabiyah.

Countries: Iraq vs. United Kingdom/Kuwait
Years: 1950–90
Challenger: Iraq 1950–90
Disputed Territory: In 1951 the Iraqi government resumed active diplomatic efforts to gain control of Bubiyan and Warba Islands, which were under U.K./Kuwaiti sovereignty following stalemated talks in the 1930s. In 1961 the Iraqi government laid claim to all of Kuwait at the time of its independence from Great Britain. In 1963, following a change in regime, the claim was withdrawn by the Iraqi government and Kuwait was recognized as a sovereign state. Iraq, however, did not renounce its claims to the islands of Warba and Bubiyan, which are located strategically close to Iraq's military base at Umm Qasr.
Militarized Disputes Initiated by Challenger: (1) June 1961–February 1962, (2) April 1967, (3) December 1972–June 1973, (4) March–June 1975, (5) July 1990–March 1991
Outcome of Dispute: Periodic negotiations were held over the disputed islands in the 1970s and early 1980s but no agreement was reached. In August 1990 Iraqi military forces invaded and occupied Kuwait and shortly thereafter Kuwait was

annexed by Iraq. Kuwaiti sovereignty was restored following Iraq's defeat in the Gulf War by U.S. and allied forces in March 1991.

Countries: Jordan vs. Israel
Years: 1950–90
Challenger: Jordan 1950–90
Disputed Territory: Jordan refused to recognize the existence of an independent Israeli state since the Jewish state declared its independence in 1948. Furthermore, Jordan's official position was that the territories comprising the state of Israel should form the basis of an independent Palestinian state, but Jordan also had ambitions to annex some of the territory that would have formed an independent Palestinian state. Finally, following its defeat in the 1967 Six Day War, Jordan called for an end to the Israeli occupation of the West Bank (which it had annexed in 1950) and East Jerusalem.
Militarized Disputes Initiated by Challenger: (1) May–June 1967
Note: Large numbers of guerrilla raids along the Jordanian-Israeli border were carried out between 1950 and 1970. These raids, however, were not considered to be militarized disputes initiated by the Jordanian government because they did not involve regular Jordanian armed forces and were often opposed by the Jordanian government. Furthermore, numerous border incidents involving Jordanian and Israeli armed forces occurred, but I did not code them as militarized dispute cases because they seemed either to be localized clashes initiated without the direction of the Jordanian government, or they were responses to Israeli reprisal attacks against guerrilla forces and not attempts by Jordan to overturn the territorial status quo.
Outcome of Dispute: Jordan's dispute with Israel over the occupation of the West Bank ended in July 1988 when the Jordanian government renounced all ties and claims to the West Bank. Jordan, however, has not withdrawn its claim to East Jerusalem though Jordan did sign a peace treaty and establish full diplomatic relations with Israel in the fall of 1994.

Countries: North Yemen vs. United Kingdom/South Yemen
Years: 1950–90
Challenger: North Yemen 1950–90
Disputed Territory: The initial dispute centered on North Yemen's claim to nine regions along its border with the port of Aden. Negotiations with the British had been held in the interwar period, but the two countries could not reach an agreement. Aden had been annexed by the British in 1839 and had become an important base for supporting British naval operations in the Persian Gulf. By 1958, however, North Yemen's claims had expanded to include the entire territory of what was to become South Yemen.
Militarized Disputes Initiated by Challenger: (1) June 1956–January 1958, (2) February–October 1972, (3) June 1978–March 1979
Outcome of Dispute: South Yemen became an independent state in 1967, but North Yemen did not renounce its desire to incorporate South Yemen into a

greater Yemen Republic. An agreement was reached, however, by the end of 1981 on a plan for eventual unification of the two states. In 1990 a transitional interim government was formed between the states, and the two countries united to form the Republic of Yemen. A new government, however, was never consolidated, and by May of 1994 civil war erupted with large-scale armed clashes in both the northern and southern regions of the country. Northern armed forces, however, defeated Southern forces by early July and since that time President Ali Abdulla Saleh has been attempting to rebuild the legitimacy of the government.

Countries: Oman vs. United Arab Emirates
Years: 1977–81
Challenger: Oman 1977–81
Disputed Territory: Oman laid claim to substantial parts of Ras al-Khaimah (one of the member states of the UAE), particularly sections of its northern coast.
Militarized Disputes Initiated by Challenger: ———
Outcome of Dispute: The UAE government announced in April 1981 that an agreement had been worked out which would enable the two countries to resolve all outstanding territorial issues.

Countries: Qatar vs. United Kingdom/Bahrain
Years: 1967–90
Challenger: Qatar 1967–90
Disputed Territory: Qatar disputes Bahrain's claim of sovereignty over the Hawar and adjacent islands, which are situated just off the east coast of Qatar. Deposits of oil are believed to exist on the islands.
Militarized Disputes Initiated by Challenger: (1) April 1986
Outcome of Dispute: Despite ongoing talks and mediation efforts by Saudi Arabia since the 1970s there has been no resolution of the dispute. A militarized confrontation over the islands in April of 1986 was followed by a further round of talks and mediation efforts, which culminated in an agreement by the two countries to submit the dispute to international arbitration if a bilateral agreement could not be reached. In July 1991 the dispute was brought before the ICJ for possible consideration, but in mid-1992 Qatar withdraw its support for ICJ deliberations over the dispute.

Countries: Saudi Arabia vs. Iraq
Years: 1950–81
Challengers: Both Saudi Arabia and Iraq 1950–81
Disputed Territory: In the Uqair Convention of 1922 the border between the two countries was defined and a neutral zone was established. The treaty, however, did not precisely delimit the border at all points or the neutral zone. As result, opposing interpretations and claims based on the 1922 treaty were advanced by both governments.
Militarized Disputes Initiated by Challenger: ———
Outcome of Dispute: In July 1975 a preliminary agreement was reached to divide

equally the neutral zone. In December 1981 it was announced that a final settlement had been reached on all border questions as well as the neutral zone.

Countries: Saudi Arabia vs. Kuwait
Years: 1961–90
Challengers: Saudi Arabia 1961–90 and Kuwait 1961–65
Disputed Territory: There have been two areas of contention. The first centered on the division of oil-rich territory in the neutral zone (2,500 square miles) between the two countries. The second was based on Saudi Arabia's claim of sovereignty over the Kuwaiti islands of Qaru and Umm el-Maradim.
Militarized Disputes Initiated by Challenger: ———
Outcome of Dispute: There has been no resolution of the dispute over the islands. Kuwait maintains its claim to exclusive sovereignty over the islands, which Saudi Arabia continues to contest though the dispute has not been a source of open conflict. It is reported that Kuwait has offered to share half of the oil revenues from these islands if Saudi Arabia would recognize Kuwaiti sovereignty over the islands. The division of the neutral zone was settled by an agreement in July 1965 that divided the zone into two equal parts.

Countries: Saudi Arabia vs. United Kingdom/Qatar
Years: 1950–65
Challenger: Saudi Arabia 1950–65
Disputed Territory: Saudi Arabia had claims to approximately twenty-three miles of coastline along Qatar dating back to the mid-1930s.
Militarized Disputes Initiated by Challenger: ———
Outcome: Reportedly in December 1965 a compromise agreement was reached between Suadi Arabia and Qatar that settled the dispute.

Countries: Saudi Arabia vs. United Kingdom/United Arab Emirates
Years: 1950–74
Challenger: Saudi Arabia 1950–74
Disputed Territory: Saudi Arabia had claims to oil-rich sections along the border with Abu Dhabi (one of the states of the UAE) dating back to the early 1930s.
Militarized Disputes Initiated by Challenger: (1) August–October 1952
Outcome of Dispute: An agreement was signed in August 1974 that settled the dispute. The agreement has not been published, but it is believed that Saudi Arabia gained a triangular strip of land on Abu Dhabi's eastern border and a land corridor to the Gulf Coast, while Saudi Arabia ceded several villages in the Buraimi Oasis to Abu Dhabi.

Countries: Syria vs. Israel
Years: 1950–90
Challenger: Syria 1950–90
Disputed Territory: Syria has refused to recognize the existence of an independent Israeli state. Syria strongly opposed the United Nations General Assembly resolution of November 1947 to partition Palestine and create a new Jewish

state. Syria's official position was that the territories comprising the state of Israel should form the basis of an independent Palestinian state, but Syria also had an interest in annexing some of the territory that would have formed an independent Palestinian state. In addition, following its defeat in the 1967 Six Day War, Syria has sought to end the Israeli occupation of the Golan Heights. *Militarized Disputes Initiated by Challenger:* (1) March–May 1951, (2) March–June 1954, (3) October–December 1955, (4) March–July 1957, (5) November–December 1958, (6) January–February 1960, (7) June–December 1962, (8) July–December 1964, (9) June–August 1965, (10) March–July 1966, (11) January–June 1967, (12) June 1969–November 1970, (13) September 1972–February 1973, (14) October 1973–May 1974

Outcome of Dispute: There has been no resolution of the multiple issues in dispute. Syria continues to withhold recognition of Israel as an independent state, Israel remains in control of the Golan Heights, and Syria continues to support the formation of an independent Palestinian state. However, in the spring of 1994 stalemated talks on the Golan Heights and a peace treaty with Israel were given new life when Israel put forward new proposals to return the territory to Syria over a phased period of withdrawal.

Africa

Countries: Benin vs. Niger
Years: 1960–65
Challenger: Both Benin and Niger 1960–65
Disputed Territory: The dispute between the two countries to sovereign rights over Lete island in the Niger River can be traced back to the period of French colonial rule.
Militarized Disputes Initiated by Challenger: Benin, (1) December 1963
Outcome of Dispute: The two governments announced in June 1965 that the dispute was effectively settled. The exact basis of the settlement is not clear, however, entailing either a partition of the island or a condominium.

Countries: Comoros vs. France/Mayotte
Years: 1975–90
Challenger: Comoros 1975–90
Disputed Territory: In 1975 Comoros attained independence, but a majority of the population of one of the Comoro islands, Mayotte (about 220 square miles), expressed a desire to remain a French dependency rather than be part of an independent Comoros. Comoros, however, maintains that Mayotte is part of its national territory, while the French government insists that people of Mayotte have the right to self-determination.
Militarized Disputes Initiated by Challenger: ———
Outcome of Dispute: Despite opposition from the United Nations Security Council and General Assembly, France has not altered its policy of support for Mayotte's continued status as a French colony.

Countries: Egypt vs. United Kingdom/Sudan
Years: 1950–90
Challenger: Egypt 1950–90
Disputed Territory: In the immediate post–World War II period Egypt called for the British to accept Egyptian sovereignty over the Sudan. That claim was effectively withdrawn with the signing of the Anglo-Egyptian Agreement in 1953, and Sudan attained its independence in 1956. In 1958, however, Egypt claimed sovereignty over all territories north of the twenty-second parallel, including the Wadi Halfa salient, along its border with Sudan. Sudan has consistently rejected the Egyptian claim.
Militarized Disputes Initiated by Challenger: (1) February 1958
Outcome of Dispute: There has been no resolution of the dispute, but Egypt had not pressed the issue since the early 1960s until late 1992 when Sudan charged that Egyptian military forces had been deployed in the disputed territory. During the first half of 1993 both countries increased their military presence in and around the disputed territory, but by the end of the year the confrontation had dissipated.

Countries: Ethiopia vs. France/Djibouti
Years: 1950–77
Challenger: Ethiopia 1950–77
Disputed Territory: Ethiopia had pressed claims to sovereign rights over the French colony of Djibouti following World War II. Ethiopia's claim was designed in part to counter the Somalia claim to the colony as well as to protect an important railway link that extended from within Ethiopia, across the border, and then all the way to the port of Djibouti.
Militarized Disputes Initiated by Challenger: ———
Outcome of Dispute: In 1966 the French gave assurances to Ethiopia concerning the railway link, and thus Ethiopia in 1967 supported the results of a referendum held in Djibouti in which the majority of the population voted in favor of continued rule by France. Ethiopia, however, did not formally withdraw its claim until Djibouti achieved independence in 1977. Ethiopia at that time officially recognized the sovereignty of the new country and pledged to respect its territorial integrity.

Countries: Ethiopia vs. United Kingdom/Sudan
Years: 1950–72
Challenger: Ethiopia 1950–72
Disputed Territory: Ethiopia contested sections of its northern and southern border with Sudan. Earlier border agreements concluded between Ethiopia, Britain, and Italy at the turn of the century did not clearly establish the location of the border with Sudan, and as a result Ethiopia disputed the border as early as 1909.
Militarized Disputes Initiated by Challenger: (1) July 1967
Outcome of Dispute: All outstanding territorial issues were settled by an ex-

change of notes between the two governments in 1972 in which Ethiopia accepted the existing borders of Sudan.

Countries: Ethiopia vs. United Kingdom/Kenya
Years: 1950–70
Challenger: Ethiopia 1950–70
Disputed Territory: Both countries claimed sovereignty over a small section of territory along the border where the Gadaduma and Gadama wells are located.
Militarized Disputes Initiated by Challenger: ———
Outcome of Dispute: In several rounds of talks in the 1950s the British were firm in maintaining that the disputed territory remain a part of Kenya. Shortly before attaining independence in 1963, however, the Kenyan government reached a partial agreement to concede the Gadaduma wells to Ethiopia and in turn Ethiopia conceded the Gadama wells to Kenya. Further negotiations were held after independence, and by 1970 a comprehensive agreement was reached between Kenya and Ethiopia.

Countries: Ghana vs. Ivory Coast
Years: 1959–66
Challenger: Ghana 1959–66
Disputed Territory: Under the regime of President Nkrumah, Ghana sought to annex the Sanwi district in the southeastern section of the Ivory Coast.
Militarized Disputes Initiated by Challenger: ———
Outcome of Dispute: Following the overthrow of President Nkrumah in 1966, the new leadership of Ghana withdrew its claim to the Sanwi district.

Countries: Lesotho vs. South Africa
Years: 1966–90
Challenger: Lesotho 1966–90
Disputed Territory: Lesotho claims sovereignty over large sections of territory within the Orange Free State and Natal and the eastern Cape Province of South Africa.
Militarized Disputes Initiated by Challenger: ———
Outcome of Dispute: There has been no change in the positions of each state in the dispute despite an improvement in relations in the late 1980s.

Countries: Liberia vs. France/Guinea
Years: 1950–58
Challenger: Liberia 1950–58
Disputed Territory: Liberia had a long-standing dispute over its border with French West Africa, claiming that the French had unjustly annexed Liberian territory.
Militarized Disputes Initiated by Challenger: ———
Outcome of Dispute: Shortly after Guinea's independence in October 1958 the President of Liberia announced that all of his country's claims to the bordering territory of Guinea had been withdrawn.

Countries: Liberia vs. France/Ivory Coast
Years: 1950–60
Challenger: Liberia 1950–60
Disputed Territory: Liberia had a long-standing dispute over its border with French West Africa, claiming that the French had unjustly annexed Liberian territory.
Militarized Disputes Initiated by Challenger: ———
Outcome of Dispute: Shortly after the Ivory Coast's independence in August of 1960 the President of Liberia announced that all of his country's claims to the bordering territory of the Ivory Coast had been withdrawn.

Countries: Libya vs. Chad
Years: 1954–90
Challenger: Libya 1954–90
Disputed Territory: Libyan claims to the Aozou Strip, which extends along the entire border with Chad (approximately 684 square miles), date back to the early 1950s. The territory runs through barren and sparsely populated sections of the Sahara Desert, but it is believed to be rich in deposits of minerals, including uranium and iron ore. Following Colonel Qaddafi's assumption of power in Libya in 1969, the claim to the Aozou Strip was actively pursued. The foundation for the Libyan claim is specific provisions in a Franco-Italian protocol signed in January 1935 that ceded the territory to the Italian colony of Libya. Chad, however, rejects the validity of the 1935 agreement since France never ratified it.
Militarized Disputes Initiated by Challenger: (1) April–November 1972
Outcome of Dispute: In April 1972 Libyan forces occupied the Aozou Strip and later that year compelled the Chadian government to recognize the Libyan annexation of the territory. Since then, Chadian governments and the OAU have called upon Libya to withdraw from the Aozou strip, but Libya continued its occupation of the territory. It was not until 1987 that the Libyan presence in the Aozou was militarily challenged by Chad. In heavy fighting during August–September 1987 Libyan forces suffer substantial losses in the Aozou. Subsequently, five rounds of talks were held between Libya and Chad over the status of the Aozou Strip but no agreement could be reached. As a result, in 1990 both countries agreed to submit the dispute to the ICJ, and a ruling was issued in February 1994 supporting Chadian claims to the disputed territory.

Countries: Madagascar vs. France
Years: 1960–90
Challenger: Madagascar 1960–90
Disputed Territory: Since independence Madagascar has claimed sovereignty over the French islands of Glorioso, Juan de Nova, Bassas da India, and Europa.
Militarized Disputes Initiated by Challenger: ———
Outcome of Dispute: In the 1970s Madagascar attempted to mobilize international support for its claims by pressing the issue at the United Nations. The General Assembly took up the question of the dispute at Madagascar's request, and in December 1979 a resolution was passed fully supporting Madagascar's

claim. The French government, however, rejected the U.N. resolution in 1980 but after a decade of friendly relations indicated in June 1990 its willingness to accept United Nations resolutions, and, in return, Madagascar agreed to compensate French companies nationalized in 1972.

Countries: Mali vs. Mauritania
Years: 1960–63
Challenger: Mail 1960–63
Disputed Territory: Mali claimed sovereignty over the Eastern Hodh and territories along the western sector of the Mauritanian border (some 3,000 square miles), which had been ceded to Mauritania by France in 1944. The territory in dispute was largely desert and was sparsely populated.
Militarized Disputes Initiated by Challenger: ———
Outcome of Dispute: A border agreement was reached in February 1963 in which Mauritania returned to Mali most of the territories ceded by France in 1944. In addition, it was agreed that nationals from each country would be guaranteed nomadic rights and the use of wells in the disputed areas.

Countries: Mali vs. Burkino Faso
Years: 1960–87
Challenger: Mali 1960–87
Disputed Territory: Since the independence of the two countries in 1960, Mali had claimed sovereignty over Burkino Faso territory (approximately 500 square miles) along the Beli River in the Dori district.
Militarized Disputes Initiated by Challenger: (1) November 1974–June 1975, (2) December 1985
Outcome of Dispute: Despite periodic negotiations throughout the 1960s and 1970s, no resolution of the issue was achieved. In 1983 the dispute was taken up by the ICJ, but a militarized confrontation occurred in December 1985 with casualties on both sides. The ICJ issued a ruling in December 1986 evenly dividing the disputed territory between the two countries, and the ruling was accepted by both countries in 1987.

Countries: Mauritania vs. Spain/Western Sahara
Years: 1960–75
Challenger: Mauritania 1960–75
Disputed Territory: Following its independence in 1960 Mauritania laid claim to Rio de Oro, and by 1965 it claimed sovereignty over all of the Western Sahara (125,000 square miles with large deposits of phosphate reserves).
Militarized Disputes Initiated by Challenger: ———
Outcome of Dispute: The Tripartite Agreement signed in November 1975 among Spain, Mauritania, and Morocco divided up the Western Sahara between the latter two countries, with Mauritania receiving about one-third of the Spanish colony. In August 1979 Mauritania relinquished all claims to the Western Sahara in a peace agreement signed with the Polisario Front.

Countries: Mauritius vs. France/Tromelin Island
Years: 1976–90
Challenger: Mauritius 1976–90
Disputed Territory: In April 1976 Mauritius claimed sovereignty over the French-controlled island of Tromelin, which is less than one square mile and has little economic value.
Militarized Disputes Initiated by Challenger: ———
Outcome of Dispute: The French rejected the Mauritius claim in December 1976, and there has been no change in the position of the opposing governments since then. Nevertheless, cooperative economic and political relations between the two countries have been maintained.

Countries: Mauritius vs. United Kingdom/Diego Garcia and islands
Years: 1980–90
Challenger: Mauritius 1980–90
Disputed Territory: Under an agreement reached in 1965 Mauritius recognized British sovereignty over Diego Garcia as part of the British Indian Ocean Territory. By 1980, however, Mauritius called for the return of Diego Garcia on the grounds that Britain had violated an agreement not to allow military bases on the island. Britain maintains that no such agreement on military bases (involving the United States) was ever reached and views the agreements of 1965 as valid and in force.
Militarized Disputes Initiated by Challenger: ———
Outcome of Dispute: There has been no resolution of the disputing claims. The Mauritius claim of sovereignty over the entire Chagos Archipelago was formally endorsed by the OAU at a summit in June 1980, and in the following month the OAU called for the demilitarization of Diego Garcia and its unconditional return to Mauritius. Period talks in the 1980s failed to resolve the dispute, and in 1992–93 a newly elected Mauritius government renewed its claim to the islands and threatened to take the issue to the United Nations and the ICJ.

Countries: Morocco vs. France/Algeria
Years: 1956–70
Challenger: Morocco 1956–70
Disputed Territory: Morocco laid claim to western sections of southern Algeria, particularly in the Tindouf area where large deposits of iron ore are located, based on the historical argument that the territories had been part of Morocco in precolonial times.
Militarized Disputes Initiated by Challenger: (1) July–October 1962, (2) September–November 1963
Outcome of Dispute: In May 1970 the two countries announced that the border had been settled with Morocco withdrawing its claims. A border treaty signed in 1972 between the two countries formally ratified the agreement of 1970. Plans had been drawn up for the joint economic development of resources along the border, but they have not materialized as a result of Algeria's support for the Polisario in the conflict with Morocco over the Western Sahara.

Countries: Morocco vs. France/Mauritania
Years: 1957–70
Challenger: Morocco 1957–70
Disputed Territory: Morocco claimed sovereignty over all of Mauritania, arguing that in the precolonial period Mauritania had been a province of Morocco. As a result, Morocco withheld recognition of Mauritania's independence in 1960.
Militarized Disputes Initiated by Challenger: ———
Outcome of Dispute: In 1969 Morocco formally recognized Mauritania, and in June 1970 a treaty was signed in which Morocco agreed to respect the territorial integrity of Mauritania.

Countries: Morocco vs. Spain/Spanish Sahara and enclaves/islands
Years: 1956–90
Challenger: Morocco 1956–90
Disputed Territory: Since its independence in 1956 Morocco has laid claims to Spain's North African territories and in the early 1960s began to press the issue aggressively before the United Nations. The claims can be divided into two distinct sets of territorial issues: the first centers on Moroccan claims to sovereignty over all of the Spanish (Western) Sahara; the second, over several small Spanish enclaves and islands along the Moroccan coast.
Militarized Disputes Initiated by Challenger: (1) June–November 1975
Outcome of Dispute: In the Tripartite Agreement of November 1975 Spain ceded to Morocco approximately two-thirds of the Western Sahara and the remaining one-third to Mauritania. Since 1975 the Polisario Front with the active support of Algeria has fought for the independence of the Western Sahara against Morocco (and Mauritania until 1979). In 1969 Spain returned the enclave of Ifni in the Treaty of Fez to Morocco, but Spain has refused to return four remaining enclaves—Ceuta, Melilla, Penones of Alhucemas, and Velz de la Gomera—and the Chafarinas Islands to Morocco. In 1990 U.N. mediation was initiated to resolve the dispute but no settlement was reached. Some progress was achieved, however, in July 1991 when the two countries signed a treaty of friendship and cooperation in which both parties pledged to resolve the dispute peacefully.

Countries: Seychelles vs. France/Tromelin Islands
Years: 1976–90
Challenger: Seychelles 1976–90
Disputed Territory: Since its independence Seychelles has claimed sovereignty over the French island of Tromelin.
Militarized Disputes Initiated by Challenger: ———
Outcome of Dispute: France has refused to recognize Seychelles claims to sovereignty and has established military bases on Tromelin Island.

Countries: Italy/Somalia vs. Ethiopia
Years: 1950–90
Challengers: Italy 1950–59 and Somalia 1960–90

Disputed Territory: Somalia seeks self-determination for, if not the annexation, of all Somali–inhabited areas of the Ogaden region in Ethiopia. Prior to Somalia's independence in 1960, Italian governments maintained that the Italian Somaliland border with Ethiopia was in dispute, but negotiations with Ethiopia failed to settle the conflict and by the late 1950s Somalian leaders were actively pressing their claims to the Ogaden.

Militarized Disputes Initiated by Challenger: Somalia (1) December 1960–September 1961, (2) November 1963–April 1964, (3) March–June 1966, (4) May 1974, (5) March 1977–March 1978, (6) August–November 1980

Outcome of Dispute: There has been no resolution of the conflict over the Ogaden region. The OAU has consistently supported the Ethiopian position, but several attempts at mediation have proven unsuccessful. Intensified fighting in the Ogaden between rebels and Ethiopian forces occurred in 1982–83, and Italian mediation efforts in the mid- and late 1980s failed to break the stalemate. However, tension was reduced with a joint agreement signed in 1988 in which both sides were to demilitarize the disputed region and to stop supporting insurgency movements against one another. The dispute has not been a source of open conflict since civil war broke out in Somalia in 1990–91.

Countries: Somalia vs. France/Djibouti
Years: 1960–77
Challenger: Somalia 1960–77
Disputed Territory: Somalia sought self-determination for, if not the annexation of, Djibouti.
Militarized Disputes Initiated by Challenger: ———
Outcome of Dispute: In declarations in December 1976 and January 1977 the Somali government stated its intention to recognize the independence and sovereignty of Djibouti and to respect its territorial integrity after its attainment of independence. Djibouti became independent in June 1977, and Somalia carried through with its stated policy.

Countries: Somalia vs. United Kingdom/Kenya
Years: 1960–1981
Challenger: Somalia 1960–1981
Disputed Territory: Somalia sought self-determination for, if not the annexation of, the Somali-inhabited areas of the northeastern province of Kenya (approximately 50,000 square miles of territory).
Militarized Disputes Initiated by Challenger: (1) December 1963–March 1964, (2) March–August 1967
Outcome of Dispute: In the Arusha Agreement of October 1967, mediated by the OAU, the two countries agreed to reestablish cooperative and normal diplomatic relations. As a result, Somalia has not actively pressed the territorial issue with Kenya since 1967. The OAU has supported Kenya's position in the dispute, and successive Kenyan governments have called on Somalia to renounce publicly its territorial claims. In September 1981 Somalia President Barre, however, did announce that his country had no territorial ambitions against Kenya and

that ethnic Somalis in Kenya should be considered Kenyans. Since 1981 Somali governments have not issued irrendentist claims, and in 1984 the two countries signed an agreement on border security.

Countries: Togo vs. Ghana
Years: 1958–90
Challenger: Togo 1958–90 and Ghana 1958–66
Disputed Territory: Togo has laid claim to Ghanaian territory along their southern border populated by the Ewe tribe, which comprises one of the predominant ethnic groups within Togo. Ghana, in turn, had called for the unification of Togo with Ghana.
Militarized Disputes Initiated by Challenger: ———
Outcome of Dispute: Ghana's call for unification with Togo was withdrawn in 1966 after a coup in Ghana removed President Nkrumah from power. Ghana, however, has steadfastly refused to surrender any of the territory claimed by Togo, but Togo has not aggressively pressed its claims since the late 1970s. Relations during the 1980s, however, were strained as a result of a series of minor border incidents and political instability in both countries. Nevertheless, the territorial dispute did not reemerge as a source of open conflict. Bilateral relations have improved since late 1991.

Countries: Tunisia vs. France/Bizerte Naval Base
Years: 1956–62
Challenger: Tunisia 1956–62
Disputed Territory: In the late 1950s Tunisia pressed France to withdraw from its naval base at Bizerte, which the French were reluctant to agree to.
Militarized Disputes Initiated by Challenger: (1) July–September 1961
Outcome of Dispute: A comprehensive agreement was reached between the two governments by August 1962, and French forces completed their withdrawal by mid-October 1963.

Countries: Tunisia vs. France/Algeria
Years: 1956–70
Challenger: Tunisia 1956–70
Disputed Territory: Tunisia claimed sovereignty over a section of the oil-rich Sahara within Algeria.
Militarized Disputes Initiated by Challenger: ———
Outcome of Dispute: Through agreements signed and ratified in 1968 and 1970 Tunisia accepted the existing borders of Algeria and therefore withdrew its claim of sovereignty over the disputed Saharan territory.

Countries: Uganda vs. Tanzania
Years: 1972–79
Challenger: Uganda 1972–79

Disputed Territory: In September 1972 President Amin of Uganda laid claim to the Kagera Salient along the border of Tanzania. Anglo-German agreements signed in 1890 and 1914 had originally allocated the salient to German East Africa (Tanzania).

Militarized Disputes Initiated by Challenger: (1) July 1974–September 1975, (2) February–May 1977, (3) October 1978–June 1979,

Outcome of Dispute: Since the removal of Amin from power following the war between Uganda and Tanzania in 1978–79, Ugandan governments have renounced the earlier claim to the Kagera Salient.

Countries: Zaire vs. Congo
Years: 1970–90
Challenger: Zaire 1970–90
Disputed Territory: The boundary along the Congo River is in dispute and, as a result, so is sovereignty over numerous islands.
Militarized Disputes Initiated by Challenger: ———
Outcome of Dispute: The boundary along the Congo River has not yet been officially established as following the median line or the Thalweg principle. Periodic talks have been held without a settlement, but the dispute has not been a source of acute conflict.

Countries: Zaire vs. Zambia
Years: 1980–90
Challenger: Zaire 1980–90
Disputed Territory: The dispute centers on a small area in and around Lake Mweru, which is located along Zambia's northern border with Zaire. The area in dispute is referred to as the Kaputa district. In 1981 Zambia asserted that Zaire was pressing claims against it. In 1982 the two governments, in a joint statement, declared that there was no dispute between them.
Militarized Disputes Initiated by Challenger: (1) February–September 1982, (2) September 1983
Outcome of Dispute: It was announced in 1987, following several rounds of talks, that the two countries had reached an agreement on a general formula for eventually settling the dispute. Further progress was reported in 1989–90 but all points of dispute had not been resolved at that time.

Countries: Zambia vs. Malawi
Years: 1981–86
Challenger: Zambia 1981–86
Disputed Territory: The dispute centers on a small section of Zambia's eastern province border with Malawi.
Militarized Disputes Initiated by Challenger: ———
Outcome of Dispute: In 1984 a joint border commission was formed to address the dispute and held regular meetings during 1985 and the early part of 1986. Zambia withdrew its claims based on the recommendations of a border commission report issued in 1986.

Central Asia

Countries: Afghanistan vs. Pakistan
Years: 1950–90
Challenger: Afghanistan 1950–90
Disputed Territory: Afghan governments have refused to accept boundary lines of its eastern border with Pakistan (the so-called Durand Line established in 1893 and further developed by agreements in 1905, 1921, and 1930) wherein Pathan tribes are populated. Afghanistan has called for: (*a*) the incorporation of all Pathan tribes within Afghanistan, including sections of Pakistani territory, or (*b*) an autonomous or independent state of Pakhtoonistan. The Pakistani government has steadfastly maintained that the Durand Line is not open to question.
Militarized Disputes Initiated by Challenger: (1) September–October 1950, (2) March–September 1955, (3) September–December 1960, (4) May 1961–January 1962
Outcome of Dispute: Afghan governments had actively pursued the dispute until the mid- to late 1970s without any change in Pakistan's policy of refusing to discuss the issue. However, as a result of the Soviet invasion of Afghanistan in 1979 and the subsequent civil war in Afghanistan, the territorial dispute with Pakistan has not been a source of conflict.

Countries: China vs. Afghanistan
Years: 1950–63
Challenger: China 1950–63
Disputed Territory: The eastern border of Afghanistan with China (forty-seven miles in length) had never been carefully delimited by the British in the nineteenth century. In the early twentieth century Chinese governments advanced claims to much of the mountainous Pamir region along the ill-defined border, and those claims were maintained by the new communist government after it came to power in 1949.
Militarized Disputes Initiated by Challenger: ———
Outcome of Dispute: An agreement was concluded in November 1963 that fully delimited the border between the two countries.

Countries: China vs. Bhutan
Years: 1979–90
Challenger: China 1979–90
Disputed Territory: The border between the two countries extends for about 300 miles, and China lays claim to small sections of territory at several points.
Militarized Disputes Initiated by Challenger: ———
Outcome of Dispute: Multiple rounds of talks have been held since 1984 with both parties expressing an interest in a friendly settlement. Nevertheless, no final resolution of the dispute has been achieved.

Countries: China vs. Burma
Years: 1950–60

Challenger: China 1950–60
Disputed Territory: The Chinese government had advanced claims to a small section of territory in northern Burma along the common border of the Chinese province of Yunnan, which was largely uninhabited. The Chinese claim was based on political ties dating back to the Ming dynasty in the sixteenth century.
Militarized Disputes Initiated by Challenger: (1) May–September 1959
Outcome of Dispute: Sino-Burmese talks on the border began in 1954, and a general settlement was reached by October 1960. The 1960 Treaty gave 132 square miles of Burmese land to China while Burma gained control of eighty-five square miles of Chinese territory.

Countries: China vs. India
Years: 1950–90
Challenger: China 1950–90
Disputed Territory: The two governments contest much of their common 2,000-mile-long border. The focus of the border dispute centers primarily on two separate areas: (*a*) in the eastern section where Tibet borders on Arunachal Pradesh (formerly the North-East Frontier Agency), and (*b*) in the western section where Kashmir borders on Tibet and Xinjiang (the Ladakh Frontier). China has not accepted either the McMahon Line in the eastern sector (which India does), or Indian claims (based on a treaty signed in 1842) to the Aksai Chin region in the western sector. The dispute over the Aksai Chin is particularly important to China because the only passable route to Tibet from Sinkiang, China's westernmost province, is through the Aksai Chin. The two countries also dispute the border at Bara Hoti, Wu Ju, and the central border at Sikkum.
Militarized Disputes Initiated by Challenger: (1) September 1956, (2) June–November 1958, (3) September–December 1958, (4) July 1959–February 1960, (5) April–November 1962
Outcome of Dispute: There has been no resolution of the conflicting claims in either the eastern or western sectors. The prevailing status quo has been defined by the territory held by China following its defeat of India in the 1962 border war. China has been satisfied with the status quo since 1962 because it had achieved its primary goal of establishing effective control over the strategic Aksai Chin region. As a result, since 1962 China has favored a settlement on the basis of territory actually controlled by each country. India has refused to accept this premise as the basis for a settlement. Several rounds of talks were held in the 1980s and early 1990s, but little progress was achieved on resolving the central issues. Nevertheless, both sides agreed to reduce the number of military forces deployed along the disputed border in 1990, and trade along the border was reopened in 1991 for the first time since the 1962 war. Further progress was achieved when the Indian-prime minister recognized the actual line of control along the disputed border in an agreement signed in September 1993. Following this agreement talks have been held on further troop reductions and confidence-building measures along the border.

Countries: China vs. Nepal
Years: 1950–61
Challengers: Both China and Nepal 1950–61
Disputed Territory: The dispute centered on the lack of a clearly defined border. As a result, both governments advanced opposing interpretations of where the 670-mile border between Tibet and Nepal was located. Several treaties were negotiated between Nepal and Tibet in the eighteenth and nineteenth centuries. However, the boundary lines established in the treaties were often unclear or contradictory. As a result, both countries advanced claims to the territory of the other along the border in twenty different sectors, including Rasua, Kimathauka, Nara Pass, Tingribode, Mt. Everest, and the Nelu River.
Militarized Disputes Initiated by Challenger: China, (1) April 1959–August 1960
Outcome of Dispute: Border talks were initiated in late 1959, and by October 1961 a border pact was signed settling all outstanding issues. Most of the disputes were settled in favor of Nepal.

Countries: China vs. Pakistan
Years: 1950–63
Challengers: China and Pakistan 1950–63
Disputed Territory: The territory centered on the 325-mile border between Pakistani-controlled Kashmir and the Chinese region of Xinjiang. Approximately 3,400 square miles were in dispute with both parties claiming the territory of the other.
Militarized Disputes Initiated by Challenger: ———
Outcome of Dispute: In late 1959 Pakistan announced its willingness to consult on the boundary question, and over the next four years talks were held. An agreement was signed between the two governments in March 1963 dividing up the disputed territory. A protocol to the agreement was added in March 1965.

Countries: China vs. Soviet Union
Years: 1950–90
Challenger: China 1950–90
Disputed Territory: During the 1950s China did not press its territorial claims against the Soviet Union. By the early 1960s, however, the dispute over territory was public and was a primary source of conflict between the two countries. China has disputes with the Soviet Union in the Far Eastern sector along the border between Manchuria and Eastern Siberia, and in the Central Asian sector between Xinjiang and the Soviet Republics of Khazakhstan, Kirghizia, and Tajikistan. The Chinese government considers the treaties defining the border in these regions (signed in the mid- and late nineteenth century) as "unequal" and therefore subject to renegotiation. Chinese claims to Soviet territory amounted to over 500,000 square miles.
Militarized Disputes Initiated by Challenger: (1) November 1964, (2) October 1966–January 1967, (3) March–October 1969
Note: Large numbers of border violations and incidents were reported by both governments during the 1960–63 period. Unfortunately, reliable and detailed

data on border clashes during this period are not available, and therefore I was not able to identify with confidence militarized disputes during this three-year period. Several border incidents also occurred during the 1970s and 1980s, but the available evidence indicates that these were minor clashes initiated by local forces without larger diplomatic or military goals relating to the territorial dispute.
Outcome of Dispute: Periodic rounds of talks were held from 1964 to 1982 between the two governments without any substantial progress. In 1986 the Soviet leader Gorbachev indicated that his country was willing to make some concessions and further talks were held. In 1991 the Soviets made several concessions to China in the Far Eastern sector, including the transfer of Damansky Island and the Amur, Argun, and Ussuri rivers. With the collapse of the Soviet Union, Chinese territorial claims are directed not only against Russia but also Kazakhstan, Kirghizia, and Tajikstan. Thus, any further progress toward a settlement will require agreements with all four states.

Countries: India vs. France/Pondicherry, Karaikal, Mahe, and Yanam
Years: 1950–54
Challenger: India 1950–54
Disputed Territory: When India gained its independence it laid claim to several French enclaves—Pondechery, Mache, Kerikal, Yaman—within its national territory.
Militarized Disputes Initiated by Challenger: ———
Outcome of Dispute: In 1954 France agreed to transfer sovereignty over the territories to the Indian government. It was not until 1962, however, that the agreement was formally signed and ratified by France.

Countries: India vs. Portugal/Goa, Damao, Diu
Years: 1950–74
Challenger: India 1950–74
Disputed Territory: Following its independence, India advanced claims to several Portuguese port enclaves situated along the Adriatic Sea—Goa, Damao, and Diu.
Militarized Disputes Initiated by Challenger: (1) August 1954–June 1955, (2) November–December 1961
Outcome of Dispute: In December 1961 Indian forces successfully invaded the Portuguese territories, and shortly thereafter the territories were incorporated into India. It was not until 1974, with the change of regime in Portugal, that Indian sovereignty over the territories was recognized by the Portuguese government.

Countries: India vs. Bangladesh
Years: 1973–90
Challengers: Both India and Bangladesh 1973–90
Disputed Territory: Since independence the two countries have contested sovereignty over a small section of their border (Tripura), and since the late 1970s the two countries have disputed an island (called New Moore by India and South Talpatty by Bangladesh) in the Bay of Bengal.

Militarized Disputes Initiated by Challenger: ——
Outcome of Dispute: Partial agreements were reached in the late 1950s to exchange some territory along the disputed border, but a final settlement has not
been reached. Nevertheless, the remaining sections of territory have not been a
source of open conflict since the early 1970s. The dispute over the island has also
not engendered intense conflict, and both governments have expressed the desire to settle the dispute peacefully. Several rounds of talks were held over the
disputed island in the 1980s but no final agreement has been reached.

Countries: Pakistan vs. India
Years: 1950–90
Challenger: Pakistan 1950–90
Disputed Territory: Two primary areas along the Indo-Pakistani border have
been contested by Pakistan: Kashmir and the Rann of Kutch. In October 1947
the accession of approximately two-thirds of Kashmir to India was announced,
and since that time Pakistan has contested the accession, demanding instead that
a plebiscite be held in Kashmir to determine its status. Pakistan believes that the
people of Kashmir would vote for union with Pakistan if given the opportunity.
Pakistan therefore contests Indian claims to sovereignty over Kashmir and seeks
to incorporate all of Kashmir (85,000 square miles) within its own national
territory. India, in turn, has been willing to accept the division of Kashmir and
has pressed Pakistan to treat the border in Kashmir as the interstate border
between the two countries. Pakistan also contested a smaller section of desolate
Indian territory in the Rann of Kutch totaling some 3,500 square miles. In 1947
the Kutch State had acceded to India, and Pakistan claimed that the northern
part of the Rann of Kutch was part of the Sord State of Pakistan.
Militarized Disputes Initiated by Challenger: (1) July–August 1951, (2) February–
March 1956, (3) September–November 1962, (4) July 1963, (5) March–September 1964, (6) January–July 1965, (7) April–December 1965, (8) April–August
1966, (9) July–November 1981, (10) June 1984, (11) June–September 1985, (12)
October 1986–February 1987
Outcome of Dispute: The dispute over Kashmir continues without resolution.
Several rounds of talks were held in the 1980s and early 1990s with neither
country willing to change their positions. Several militarized disputes during the
1980s centered on the Siachin glacier region in Kashmir. The dispute in the Rann
of Kutch, however, was settled in February 1968 by a ruling of the Indo-Pakistan
Western Boundary Case Tribunal, awarding almost all of the disputed territory
(about 90 percent) to India.

Countries: Soviet Union vs. Iran
Years: 1950–54
Challengers: Both Soviet Union and Iran 1950–54
Disputed Territory: The two governments contested a number of points along
their 1,000-mile border both east and west of the Caspian Sea.
Militarized Disputes Initiated by Challenger: ——
Outcome of Dispute: A convention was signed in December 1954 delimiting the

entire border and settled all points of dispute through compromise. Demarcation of the border was completed by the end of 1957.

Countries: Soviet Union vs. Turkey
Years: 1950–53
Challenger: Soviet Union 1950–53
Disputed Territory: In 1945–46 the Soviet Government called on Turkey to cede the districts of Kars and Ardahan (10,000 square miles) along the Caucasian frontier. These territories were annexed by Russia in 1878 by the Treaty of Berlin but were returned to Turkey in the Soviet-Turkish Treaty of Moscow 1921.
Militarized Disputes Initiated by Challenger: ———
Outcome of Dispute: In a note delivered to the Turkish government in May 1953 the Soviet government renounced all territorial claims against Turkey.

East and Southeast Asia

Countries: China vs. Japan
Years: 1951–90
Challenger: China 1951–90
Disputed Territory: The Chinese government has contested the Japanese claim to sovereignty over the Senkaku Islands, located some 100 miles northeast of Taiwan. In 1968 U.N.-sponsored surveys of the seabed and continental shelves in the East and South China Seas indicated that large oil deposits were likely in areas contiguous to the islands. Japan occupied the islands during the 1894–95 war with China and maintains that China accepted the annexation of the islands in the 1895 Peace Treaty. China, however, contends that the islands have historically always been a part of China, that the 1895 Peace Treaty did not cede sovereignty of the islands to Japan, and that Japan as a result of its defeat in World War II renounced all claims to overseas territories.
Militarized Disputes Initiated by Challenger: ———
Outcome of Dispute: During the period from 1951 until 1972 the United States exercised administrative rights, though not sovereignty, over the islands based on the terms of the 1951 San Francisco Peace Treaty. It was not until the late 1960s that both countries (as well as Taiwan—see below) actively pressed their claims over the islands. In 1972 Japan reassumed full sovereignty over the islands after the signing of the Okinawa Reversion Treaty with the United States, which China and Taiwan both protested. In August 1978 a Treaty of Peace and Friendship was signed between the Japan and China, and Japan announced at that time that China had recognized de facto Japanese control over the islands. Chinese officials have stated that their country would avoid conflict over the issue, but they have not formally renounced their claim to the islands.

Countries: China vs. Taiwan
Years: 1950–90
Challengers: Both China and Taiwan 1950–90

Disputed Territory: There are two distinct disputes between the two countries. First, China does not recognize the independence of Taiwan and claims sovereignty over the island. Following their defeat in the Chinese Civil War, nationalist forces fled to the island of Taiwan and smaller offshore islands in 1949 and established their own regime, claiming that they were the sole legitimate government of China. The communist Chinese government, however, considers itself the sole legal government of China and maintains that the island of Taiwan and other smaller offshore islands have always historically been under the sovereignty of the mainland Chinese government. Second, Chinese nationalist forces since 1947 have occupied Itu Abu, the largest of the Spratly Islands, and it is still currently administered from Taipei. Furthermore, Taiwan has claimed sovereignty over the entire Spratly Island chain, as has China since 1949. The Spratlys had been annexed by Japan in 1939, but in the San Francisco Treaty of 1951 Japan renounced its claims to the Spratly Islands.
Militarized Disputes Initiated by Challenger: China, (1) January–August 1950, (2) August 1954–May 1955, (3) August–October 1958
Outcome of Dispute: There has been no resolution of either dispute. China now seeks the peaceful return of Taiwan but refuses to renounce the right to use military force to reconquer the island. Taiwan, in turn, has not expressed an interest in proposals for peaceful reunification. Nevertheless, by the late 1980s and early 1990s bilateral relations had improved between the two countries, as some restrictions on travel were lifted and economic ties were expanded. The dispute over the Spratly Islands remains unresolved, though the two countries have not actively confronted one another over the islands. A 1990 Chinese proposal for joint economic development of the islands, issued to all countries with claims to the islands (Malaysia, Philippines, Taiwan, Vietnam), has not elicited a cooperative response.

Countries: China vs. South Vietnam/Vietnam
Years: 1951–90
Challengers: Both China and South Vietnam/Vietnam 1951–90
Disputed Territory: The two countries have disputes along their common land border as well as over the sovereignty of islands in the South China Sea, due to differing interpretations of the 1887 Sino-French boundary convention. The border dispute centers on numerous small sections of territory (in total less than twenty-five square miles), which both sides claim as theirs. In the South China Sea the countries have competing claims to sovereignty over the Paracel and Spratly Islands. In 1932–33 the Paracel and Spratly Islands were annexed by France, but in 1939 both groups of islands were occupied by Japanese forces. Japan, however, formally renounced its claims to both islands in 1951. From 1951–75 the South Vietnamese government disputed Chinese claims along the border and over the islands, and since 1976 the communist Vietnamese government has adopted a similar position. Before 1974 the eastern Paracels were occupied by China and the western Paracels by South Vietnam. In 1974 the Chinese evicted South Vietnamese forces from the islands. Vietnam occupies several of the Spratly Islands that China claims sovereignty over.

Militarized Disputes Initiated by Challenger: China (1) January–February 1974, (2) April 1978–March 1979, (3) April–May 1983, (4) April–July 1984, (5) November 1984–May 1985, (6) October 1986–March 1987, (7) January–May 1988, and South Vietnam (1) June–October 1956
Outcome of Dispute: Neither conflict over disputed border regions or islands has been resolved between China and Vietnam. Talks held in the mid-1970s on the disputes over the border and islands failed to reach an agreement, and since the border war in 1978–79 little further progress has been made in resolving the territorial disputes. Border clashes have sporadically occurred throughout the 1980s, with heavy fighting in 1987, while in 1988 Vietnamese and Chinese forces clashed in the Spratlys and each country has since increased its military presence among the islands. In 1990 China presented a proposal for the joint economic development of the Spratly islands to all of the other countries that have claims to the islands—Malaysia, Philippines, Taiwan, Vietnam—on the condition that all countries remove their military forces from the islands. No significant cooperative measures, however, have been taken in this direction by the various countries.

Countries: Indonesia vs. Netherlands/New Guinea
Years: 1950–62
Challenger: Indonesia 1950–62
Disputed Territory: Following its independence in 1949, Indonesia called for the complete incorporation of New Guinea (or West Irian as named by Indonesia) within its national territory. The Dutch maintained that the population had the right to self-determination and therefore would not permit Indonesia to incorporate West Irian.
Militarized Disputes Initiated by Challenger: (1) May 1953, (2) October 1954, (3) February–November 1957, (4) November 1961–August 1962
Outcome of Dispute: By 1961 the dispute had escalated to armed conflict short of war. In August 1962 a settlement was reached between the two governments in which it was agreed that Indonesia would assume administrative control over the territory in 1963, and self-determination for the local population would be exercised by the end of 1969.

Countries: Indonesia vs. United Kingdom/Malaysia
Years: 1961–66
Challenger: Malaysia 1961–66
Disputed Territory: When Great Britain and Malaya began discussing plans in 1961 for a Malaysian federation, the Indonesian government expressed its opposition. The federation was to consist of Malaya, Sabah, Sarawak, and Singapore. The Indonesian government insisted that the peoples of Sarawak and Sabah had the right to self-determination, and it did not accept a U.N. report in September 1963 that concluded that a majority of the population in the territories favored participation in the federation.
Militarized Disputes Initiated by Challenger: (1) February 1963–November 1965
Outcome of Dispute: Beginning in late 1963, Indonesia pursued a policy of direct

confrontation, involving the provision of arms and aid to rebels as well as the involvement of regular Indonesian armed forces in attacks against Malaysia. By late 1965 Indonesian armed attacks against Malaysia had greatly diminished, and a peace agreement was signed with Malaysia in August 1966 in which Indonesia effectively withdrew its demand of self-determination for Sarawak and Sabah.

Countries: Japan vs. Soviet Union
Years: 1951–90
Challenger: Japan 1951–90
Disputed Territory: Japan has contested Soviet (now Russian) occupation of a number of islands off the northeast coast of Japan. The islands are the Habomai group along with Shikotan, Kunashiri, and Etorofu, which were occupied by Soviet forces at the very end of World War II. In the 1951 Peace Treaty (which the Soviet Union did not sign), Japan accepted the loss of Sakhalin and the Kurile Islands, but with the provision that the latter did not include Kunashiri, Etorofu, Shikotan, or the Habomais. Japan claims sovereignty over all of these islands, but the Soviet Union maintained that their sovereignty over the islands was established by agreements reached with allied powers just prior to the end of World War II. In total, approximately 3,000 square miles of territory are in dispute.
Militarized Disputes Initiated by Challenger: ———
Outcome of Dispute: There has been no resolution of the competing claims, and Russia continues to control the disputed islands. Under Soviet leader Gorbachev, talks were resumed in 1986 and several rounds were subsequently held. Russian troops began to withdraw from the islands in 1991, and agreements were reached on fishing and travel rights in 1991–92. During 1992–93 the possibility of Russia exchanging the islands for large-scale economic aid from Japan was discussed between the two countries, but no such agreement has been reached.

Countries: Malaysia vs. China
Years: 1979–90
Challenger: Malaysia 1979–90
Disputed Territory: Malaysia has claimed sovereignty over several of the Spratly Islands, located on its continental shelf.
Militarized Disputes Initiated by Challenger: ———
Outcome of Dispute: There has been no resolution of the dispute. As previously noted, China proposed in 1990 the joint economic development of the Spratlys, but Malaysia and other countries have not cooperated with China in such a plan. In 1991 Malaysia announced plans for the development of tourist resorts in the Spratlys, which was denounced by China and other governments.

Countries: North Korea vs. South Korea
Years: 1950–90
Challenger: North Korea 1950–90
Disputed Territory: North Korea has sought to create a single unified Korea (by the use of force if necessary) and for decades has refused to recognize the

independence of South Korea. In June 1950 North Korea invaded South Korea in an attempt at unification, which failed as a result of U.S. and U.N. armed intervention in support of South Korea. The present border is a provisional line established by the 1953 armistice agreement, which brought an end to the Korean War.

Militarized Disputes Initiated by Challenger: (1) June 1950–July 1953

Note: Numerous border incidents and armed exchanges have occurred along the border and at sea since the end of the Korean War, but they were not included as cases of militarized disputes due to a lack of reliable evidence indicating that these confrontations were attempts by the North Korean government to overturn the territorial status quo. The limited evidence available indicates that these clashes were intended only to harass U.S. and South Korean forces and/or were initiated by local forces without central government direction.

Outcome of Dispute: The two countries have held numerous rounds of talks on reunification since the early 1970s without a general settlement. An important step toward a settlement, however, was taken when the two countries signed an "Agreement on Reconciliation, Non-Aggression, and Exchanges and Cooperation" in December 1991. In the accord North Korea formally recognized South Korea, pledged not to attack South Korea and to resolve all disputes peacefully, and agreed to promote economic, scientific and cultural ties with South Korea. Since 1992 further progress in implementing the 1991 accord has been blocked by the controversy over the potential development of nuclear weapons in North Korea and the failure of North Korea to permit full-scope inspections of nuclear facilities by the International Atomic Energy Agency.

Countries: North Vietnam vs. South Vietnam
Years: 1956–75
Challenger: North Vietnam 1956–75
Disputed Territory: The Geneva agreements of 1954 provisionally split Vietnam into a northern and southern zone until reunification could be achieved through national elections to be held in 1956. The national elections, however, were not held, and South Vietnam disassociated itself from the 1954 agreements for reunification. North Vietnam, however, continued to seek the reunification of Vietnam and therefore did not accept the independence of South Vietnam.
Militarized Disputes Initiated by Challenger: (1) December 1964–April 1975
Outcome of Dispute: During the period from 1956 until late 1960 North Vietnam sought peaceful reunification with South Vietnam. By the fall of 1960, however, North Vietnam decided to support the Viet Cong armed struggle. By late 1964 regular armed forces of the North Vietnamese army were infiltrating into South Vietnam and were preparing to engage in direct combat with South Vietnamese and U.S. forces. The Vietnam War ended with the capture of Saigon in 1975, and in 1976 a unified Vietnam under communist rule was proclaimed.

Countries: Philippines vs. China
Years: 1956–90
Challenger: Philippines 1956–90

Disputed Territory: The Philippine government has claimed several of the Spratly Islands, all of which China has claimed sovereignty over since 1949. In 1956 the Philippine government indirectly laid claim to the islands, and in 1971 openly, and more formally, reiterated its claim. In 1978 a presidential decree annexed several islands to the Philippine province of Palawan.

Militarized Disputes Initiated by Challenger: (1) May 1982

Outcome of Dispute: An agreement was reached between the two governments in March 1979 to resolve the dispute "in a spirit of conciliation and friendship," but no formal settlement has been concluded. As previously noted, Chinese proposals for the joint economic development of the Spratly Islands has not received support from the other countries with claims to them. The Philippines has established a military presence on several of the islands and has actively sought to develop oil deposits around the islands.

Countries: Philippines vs. United Kingdom/Malaysia

Years: 1961–90

Challenger: Philippines 1961–90

Disputed Territory: In 1961 Great Britain and Malaya began discussing plans for the formation of a Malaysian federation that would include the territory of Sabah (North Borneo). The Philippine government, however, claimed sovereignty over the territory itself on historical grounds.

Militarized Disputes Initiated by Challenger: (1) April–December 1968

Outcome of Dispute: In 1977 the Philippine government announced its intent to withdraw its claim to sovereignty over Sabah, and subsequent Philippine governments have not renounced that policy and have not questioned Malaysian sovereignty. Several rounds of talks in the mid- and late 1980s were held between the two countries, and in August 1988 the Philippine Foreign Secretary stated that his country was willing in principle to drop the claim. Nevertheless, no formal settlement has been reached in which the Philippine government has conclusively renounced its territorial claims.

Countries: Portugal vs. Indonesia

Years: 1975–90

Challenger: Portugal 1975–90

Disputed Territory: Following the outbreak of civil war in East Timor in August 1975, Indonesian armed forces intervened in December, and by August 1976 East Timor was proclaimed Indonesia's twenty-seventh province. Portugal condemned the Indonesian action, refused to accept Indonesian annexation of East Timor, and still considers East Timor to be under its sovereignty.

Militarized Disputes Initiated by Challenger: ———

Outcome of Dispute: The United Nations condemned the Indonesian invasion and called for East Timor to be given the right of self-determination. Indonesian leaders, however, continue to insist that East Timor is a province of their country and deny charges of widespread human rights abuses against the local population and Fretilin resistance movement. Portugal, in turn, has refused in several rounds of talks in the 1980s and 1990s to recognize Indonesian sovereignty and supports U.N. resolutions for self-determination in East Timor.

Countries: South Korea vs. Japan
Years: 1951–90
Challenger: South Korea 1951–90
Disputed Territory: South Korea has contested Japanese sovereignty over the small group of islands known as Takeshima (or Tak-do as named by the South Koreans). The islands are located in the southern portion of the Sea of Japan, approximately equidistant between the two countries. Japan had formally annexed the islands in 1905, but following World War II South Korea challenged the legitimacy of the Japanese annexation, claiming that it was an act of imperialism and therefore illegal and that Japan relinquished all rights to the islands after its defeat in World War II.
Militarized Disputes Initiated by Challenger: (1) February 1953–February 1954, (2) July 1954
Outcome of Dispute: Negotiations were held over the islands in the 1950s and 1960s with South Korea pressing for full sovereignty over the islands while declining Japanese proposals for international arbitration. An agreement, however, was reached in the mid-1960s to neutralize the islands, and since the late 1970s South Korea has exercised de facto sovereignty over the islands. Nevertheless, Japan has not formally conceded sovereignty of the islands to South Korea, and therefore the dispute has not been officially settled.

Countries: South Vietnam/Vietnam vs. Cambodia
Years: 1956–83
Challengers: South Vietnam 1956–75, Vietnam 1976–83, and Cambodia 1956–83
Disputed Territory: The length of the common border between Vietnam and Cambodia is approximately 760 miles long and is based on treaties negotiated between France and Cambodia in the nineteenth century and from decrees issued by the Governor General of Indochina during the period of French colonial rule. South Vietnam and Cambodia, however, were unable to reach an agreement on the delimitation of their border following their independence. As a result, several sections of the border were in dispute, as was sovereignty over several islands in the Gulf of Thailand, with both sides claiming territory of the other. Disputes over the border existed in the following areas: (1) in the Prek Binh Gi area in junction with Bassac, (2) between Bassac and Mekong proper, (3) northeast of Loc Ninh between Dak Jerman and Dak Huyt, (4) between Srepok and the Se San, and (5) near the Laos tripoint. In most of these areas Cambodia claimed Vietnamese territory populated by sizable Cambodian minorities. In the Gulf of Thailand, Vietnam and Cambodia disputed sovereignty over the offshore islands of Quan Phu Quoc and the smaller Wei Islands.
Militarized Disputes Initiated by Challenger: South Vietnam (1) May–June 1958, (2) June 1959, (3) November 1962, Vietnam (1) July 1977–December 1982, and Cambodia (1) May 1975, (2) March 1977–January 1979

Outcome of Dispute: Following their invasion of Cambodia in December 1977, Vietnamese forces assumed control over disputed territory. An agreement was reached in February 1979 to begin negotiations on resolving the border dispute. By July 1982 an agreement had been reached on defining territorial waters and maritime zones, and in July of the following year a treaty was signed resolving all outstanding issues along their land border. The provisions of the treaty settled the dispute on terms favorable to Vietnam. The validity of the treaty is questioned by many countries since Cambodia was occupied by Vietnam forces at the time of the settlement and the Cambodian government itself was heavily dependent upon Vietnam for support.

Countries: Taiwan vs. Japan
Years: 1951–90
Challenger: Taiwan 1951–90
Disputed Territory: Just as the Chinese government has contested the Japanese claim to sovereignty over the Senkaku Islands, so has the Taiwanese government. Taiwan lays claim to the islands on historical grounds as well as geographic proximity and maintains that Japan renounced all rights to the islands as a result of its defeat in World War II and peace treaties signed in 1951 and 1952.
Militarized Disputes Initiated by Challenger: ———
Outcome of Dispute: Taiwan did not actively press its claims until the early 1970s. Seismic surveys in 1968 indicated the likely presence of oil deposits in close proximity to the islands, and in early 1972 Taiwan announced that the islands were to be incorporated as a part of their national territory. Later in that year, however, Japan reasserted its full sovereign control over the islands in the Reversion Treaty signed with the United States, whereby U.S. administrative control was terminated. The Japanese government therefore has refused to accept the Taiwanese claim and has exercised control over the islands since 1972.

Countries: Thailand vs. France/Cambodia
Years: 1950–82
Challengers: Thailand 1950–82 and Cambodia 1954–70
Disputed Territory: In 1946 the provinces of Siem Reap and Battambang were returned to Cambodia. In 1941, under Japanese occupation, the provinces had been granted to Thailand. The Thai government, however, disputed the return of the provinces to Cambodia, maintaining claims to sovereignty over them. Most importantly, the two countries laid claim to the ancient Khmer Temple of Preah Vihear and its surrounding territory, which was of little economic value and not heavily populated. Both countries claimed that the Franco-Siamese Treaty of 1907 established that the Temple was within their own national territory.
Militarized Disputes Initiated by Challenger: Thailand (1) November 1953, (2) July–November 1963, (3) April 1966, (4) June–July 1967, (5) June–August 1968, (6) March–June 1970, and Cambodia (1) June–December 1961, (2) June–November 1962
Outcome of Dispute: The ICJ ruled in 1962 that the Temple was within Cambodian territory. Thailand, however, was reluctant to accept the ICJ ruling and

wavered on its commitment to respect the decision throughout the 1960s. In 1970 the Thai government declared its willingness to respect the existing borders of Cambodia but did not explicitly accept the earlier ICJ ruling. By 1982, however, it seems that Thailand had formally withdrawn its claims to the disputed territory.

Countries: Thailand vs. Laos
Years: 1984–90
Challengers: Thailand 1984–90
Disputed Territory: Two areas along the border are in dispute. The first centers on approximately twenty square kilometers of territory along the northern border west of the Mekong. The second area covers eighty square kilometers of bordering territory between the Laos province of Sayaboury and the Thai province of Phitsanuloke, referred to as Ban Rom Klao.
Militarized Disputes Initiated by Challenger: (1) May–October 1984, (2) December 1987–February 1988
Outcome of Dispute: Multiple rounds of talks were held between 1984–88 with some limited progress reported. A border commission was established during 1988, and surveys and inspections of the border areas were carried out during 1989–90, but no settlement has been reported.

Countries: Vanuata vs. France
Years: 1982–90
Challengers: Vanuata 1982–90
Disputed Territory: Vanuata lays claim to the South Pacific Islands of Matthew and Hunter, which France maintains are part of New Caledonia.
Militarized Disputes Initiated by Challenger: ———
Outcome of Dispute: There has been no settlement of the dispute, but the deadlock over the disputed islands has not been a source of conflict since 1988.

Excluded Cases

Listed below are a number of potential cases of territorial disputes that I considered but finally decided not to include, generally because either: (1) there was not sufficient evidence that the potential challenger had, in fact, presented any official territorial claims against its neighbor, or (2) a territorial claim issued by a challenger in the pre–World War II period was not reiterated and pressed against its neighbor in the period between 1950 and 1990. As noted in the introduction to this appendix, there are a limited number of cases in which my codings disagree with those listed in *Border and Territorial Disputes* or *Peace and Disputed Sovereignty,* and those cases are considered here.

In the Caribbean and Central America two cases were considered. First, Haiti has a long-standing claim to sovereignty over U.S.-held Navassa Island (included in *Border and Territorial Disputes* and *Peace and Disputed Sovereignty*). I was unable, however, to find documentation of Haitian governments in the postwar period diplomatically confronting the U.S. over this issue. Second, for many years Mexico reserved the right to claim the territory of Belize if adequate steps toward self-determination for Belize were not achieved. Mexico expressed full support for the independence of Belize in 1981 and therefore withdrew any potential claims to its territory.

In South America four cases were considered. First, Brazil and Paraguay have not delimited a short section of their border in the Guaira Falls area of the Rio Parena. While there is no formal agreement on the location of the border in this area, I was unable to find evidence that Paraguay had challenged de facto Brazilian control of the disputed territory. In fact, it seems that the two countries have suspended the question of sovereignty while cooperating in joint projects to develop the economic resources of the river. Second, Argentina and Paraguay have had difficulties delimiting a small section of their northeastern border along the Polcomayo River because the course of the river has periodically changed over time thus shifting the boundary between the two countries (included in both *Border and Territorial Disputes* and *Peace and Disputed Sovereignty*). In my judgment this is not a dispute in principle over where the border should be fixed, but a problem of the border changing for naturally occurring reasons. Third, in *Peace and Disputed Sovereignty* Bolivia and Brazil are listed as having a dispute over several islands. I consulted several other sources, including *Border and Territorial Disputes* and *The World Factbook* and could not find confirming evidence that a dispute existed, and therefore I excluded the case. Fourth, while Colombia has been in a dispute with Venezuela over rights in the Gulf of Venezuela, it has not contested Venezuela's sovereignty over the Los Monjes Islands. The dispute instead has centered on the delimitation of marine and submarine areas in the Gulf, which are in close proximity to the Los Monjes Islands.

In Europe there were two cases considered. First, there was the potential case of Albanian interest in the Kosovo province of the former Yugoslavia (included in *Peace and Disputed Sovereignty*). The Kosovo province of Yugoslavia is predominantly populated by Albanians (about 90 percent of the population speaks Albanian). In 1941 the Kosovo province was annexed by Italian-controlled Albania. After World War II Kosovo was restored to Yugoslavia in a 1947 peace treaty with Italy. While Albanian governments have provided support for groups within Kosovo seeking secession from Yugoslavia and union with Albania, I was not able to find evidence that Albanian governments had ever actually presented a claim to the territory. Second, there is the case of possible Swedish claims to the Finnish-controlled Aaland Islands (included in *Peace and Disputed Sovereignty*). In 1921 the League of Nations awarded the islands to Finland, and since that time the local population on the islands have expressed their desire to return to Swedish rule. However, I did not find evidence that the Swedish government had officially called for the return of the islands.

Several cases were considered in the Persian Gulf region. First, Saudi Arabian borders with Oman and Yemen have not yet been delimited and, in principle, Saudi Arabia has claims to the territory of both its neighbors based on demands originally made in 1935. However, I was unable to find evidence of an actual ongoing dispute or confrontation over the borders in the postwar period, except for a small border clash in late 1969 near the Saudi border oasis of Al-

Wadiah between Saudi and South Yemen troops. Second, the rulers of Bahrain have a long-standing claim to Zubarah along the northwestern coast of Qatar. However, the claim is to political jurisdiction over and the allegiance of the tribes within Zubarah, and not an actual claim to sovereignty over the territory itself. Third, several sources have noted that the former South Yemen had a claim to Omani territory in the Dhofar region along the border (included in *Peace and Disputed Sovereignty*), but I could not find clear evidence that this claim had been actively pursued by South Yemen. The two countries had strained relations stemming from South Yemen's support for a rebel group operating against the Omani government in the Dhofar region. However, it did not seem to be the case that South Yemen's support for the rebel group was linked to territorial claims.

In Central Asia there is a potential dispute between Syria and Turkey. In 1939 France ceded to Turkey the Syrian territory of Alexandretta (the Turkish refer to it as Hatay), despite the strenuous objections of the Syrian regime. In March 1946 an agreement was reached in which Turkey would not press Syria to recognize Turkish sovereignty over the territory, and Syria, in return, would not officially demand its return. Thus, while Syria has not renounced its claim to Alexandretta it has not officially issued a demand against Turkey that the territory be returned.

In Africa there were five cases that I considered. First, there were reports that upon attaining independence Congo claimed sovereignty over territory in the Upper Ogooue region of Gabon. However, I was unable to find clear evidence that this claim was officially presented to Gabon in 1960 or that the claim has been reiterated since that time. Second, there is some evidence that in 1967 the Tanzanian government claimed that its border with Malawi should lie not along the eastern shore of Lake Nyasa but instead along the median line of the lake (included in *Border and Territorial Disputes* and *Peace and Disputed Sovereignty*). It is not clear, however, whether this was an official claim at the time, and I was not able to find evidence that the claim had extended beyond 1967. Third, a border clash in 1981 was followed by reports of a border dispute between Nigeria and Cameroon (included in *Border and Territorial Disputes*). The available evidence, however, would seem to indicate that the dispute did not involve competing claims to territory but instead centered on the alledged "harassment" of Nigerians located along the border, and questions of defining where the maritime boundary was located.

In the Far East several cases require some discussion. First, there exists a potential dispute between China and North Korea. Both governments claim territory along a twenty-mile section of their 880-mile long common border. The area is known as Pai-T'ou Shan and is relatively uninhabited. I could not find any evidence that two governments, however, had actually confronted one another over the territory. The next two cases were difficult to code, but I finally decided to exclude them because the focus of conflict in each case seemed to be over when sovereign rights would be restored to China and not whether they would be. I did not include the future status of Hong Kong as a dispute case because the conflict between China and Britain in the postwar period has centered on the colony's political and economic structure once the British ninety-nine-year lease expires in 1997 and China resumes sovereign rights over the territory. I did not consider China and Portugal to be in a territorial dispute over the future of Macao since postwar negotiations similarly centered on the colony's political and economic future once China resumes complete sovereignty over the territory. Finally, a note of clarification is required concerning the dispute over the Spratly Islands. This is a very complex dispute with multiple states issuing claims to specific islands. In trying to sort out the competing claims and to break them down into individual cases, I decided to treat China as the primary target of competing claims because China has the longest standing claim including all of the islands in dispute.

In the Oceania region there was a long-standing British claim to U.S.-held islands near Gilbert Island. The United States relinquished control of the islands to Kirbati when that country became independent in 1979, but I could not find evidence that the British had actively pressed the United States on this issue prior to their transfer in 1979.

Finally, while a number of countries have claims to portions of Antarctica I did not include this as a set of disputes because no single country is recognized as having sovereign rights over Antarctica. As a result, there is no clearly identifiable country that is the target of claims from several competing challenger states.

Bibliography

The first set of sources provide either global coverage or provide information on disputes across multiple regions. I utilized these sources to construct a tentative list of the population of territorial disputes in the international system between 1950 and 1990. I then turned to region- or country-specific sources (listed in the second section of the bibliography) to confirm these cases and to see if additional cases could be identified as well.

Global Sources

Allcock, John, Guy Arnold, Alan Day, D. S. Lewis, Lorimer Poultney, Roland Rance, and D. J. Sagar. *Border and Territorial Disputes* rev. 3d ed. London: Longman, 1992.

Anderson, Ewan. *An Atlas of World Political Flashpoints* London: Pinter Publishers, 1993.

Brecher, Michael, Jonathan Wilkenfeld, and Sheila Moser. *Crises in the Twentieth Century*, vol. 1. New York: Pergamon Press, 1988.

Brogan, Patrick. *The Fighting Never Stopped*. New York: Vintage Books, 1990.

Butterworth, Robert. *Managing Interstate Conflict, 1945–74: Data with Synopses*. Pittsburgh: University Center for International Studies, University of Pittsburgh, 1976.

Central Intelligence Agency. *The World Factbook 1993*. Washington, DC: Government Printing Office, 1993.

Correlates of War Project. "Militarized Interstate Dispute Dataset, 1816–1990" University of Michigan, 1993.

Day, Alan ed. *Border and Territorial Disputes.* 2d ed. London: Longman, 1987.

Downing, David. *An Atlas of Territorial and Border Disputes.* London: New English Library Limited, 1980.

Grundy-Warr, Carl ed. *International Boundaries and Boundary Conflict Resolution.* Durham: International Boundaries Research Unit, University of Durham, 1990.

International Boundary Study. Washington, DC: The Geographer, Bureau of Intelligence and Research, Department of State.

———. No. 3 (revised) Chad-Libya Boundary, December 15, 1978.

———. No. 8 British Honduras-Guatemala Boundary, July 21, 1961.

———. No. 9 Morocco-Spanish Sahara Boundary, September 14, 1961.

———. No. 18 Sudan-United Arab Republic (Egypt), July 27, 1962.

———. No. 21 British Guiana-Venezuela Boundary, March 14, 1963.

———. No. 23 Mali-Mauritania Boundary, December 16, 1963.

———. No. 25 (revised) Iran-USSR Boundary, February 28, 1978.

———. No. 27 Iraq-Turkey Boundary, January 30, 1964.

———. No. 29 Turkey-USSR Boundary, February 24, 1964.

———. No. 31 Germany-Netherlands Boundary, April 6, 1964.

———. No. 36 Honduras-Nicaragua Boundary, October 12, 1964.

———. No. 40 Cambodia-Thailand Boundary, November 16, 1964.

———. No. 42 Burma-China Boundary, November 30, 1964.

———. No. 45 Indonesia-Malaysia Boundary, March 15, 1965.

———. No. 50 China-Nepal Boundary, May 30, 1965.

———. No. 55 Tanzania-Uganda Boundary, September 1, 1965.

———. No. 60 Jordan-Saudi Arabia Boundary, December 30, 1965.

———. No. 64 (revised) China-USSR Boundary, February 13, 1978.

———. No. 67 Bolivia-Chile Boundary, March 15, 1966.

———. No. 68 (revised) Argentina-Uruguay Boundary, October 1, 1975.

———. No. 80 Burma-India Boundary, May 15, 1968.

———. No. 85 China-Pakistan Boundary, November 15, 1968.

———. No. 86 India-Pakistan Boundary (Rann of Kutch), December 2, 1968.

———. No. 87 (revised) Djibouti-Somalia Boundary, May 18, 1979.

———. No. 89 Afghanistan-China Boundary, May 1, 1969.

———. No. 101 Argentina-Chile Boundary (Palena Sector), May 25, 1970.

———. No. 103 Kuwait-Saudi Arabia Boundary, September 15, 1970.

———. No. 113 Albania-Greece Boundary, August 18, 1971.

———. No. 116 Albania-Yugoslavia Boundary, October 8, 1971.

———. No. 127 Congo-Zaire Boundary, September 8, 1972.

———. No. 134 Kenya-Somalia Boundary, May 14, 1973.

———. No. 143 Lesotho-South Africa Boundary, January 25, 1974.

———. No. 149 Mauritania-Spanish Sahara Boundary, January 8, 1975.

———. No. 152 Ethiopia-Kenya Boundary, October 15, 1975.

———. No. 153 Ethiopia-Somalia Boundary, November 5, 1975.

———. No. 155 Cambodia-Vietnam Boundary, March 5, 1976.

————. No. 164 Iran-Iraq Boundary, July 13, 1978.

————. No. 170 Brazil-Uruguay Boundary, November 23, 1979.

————. No. 172 Ecuador-Peru Boundary, May 19, 1980.

James, Alan. *Peacekeeping in International Politics*. London: International Institute for Strategic Studies, 1990.

Kacowicz, Arie. *Peaceful Territorial Change*. Columbia: University of South Carolina Press, 1994.

Keesing's Contemporary Archives 1950–1986. London: Keesing's Publications, 1950–86.

Keesing's Record of World Events 1987–1990. London: Longman, 1987–90.

Kratochwil, Friedrich, Paul Rohrlich, and Harpreet Mahajan, *Peace and Disputed Sovereignty: Reflections on Conflict over Territory*. Lanham, MD: University Press of America, 1985.

Munro, David, and Alan Day. *A World Record of Major Conflict Areas*. London: Edward Arnold, 1990.

Prescott, J. R. V. *Political Frontiers and Boundaries*. Boston: Allen & Unwin, 1987.

Sharma, Surya. *International Boundary Disputes and International Law*. Bombay: N. M. Tripathi Private Limited, 1976.

Tillema, Herbert. *International Armed Conflict since 1945*. Boulder: Westview Press, 1991.

Yearbook of the United Nations 1950–1990. New York: United Nations, 1951–91.

Regional and Country-Specific Sources

Central and South America

Beck, Peter. "Cooperative Confrontation in the Falkland Island Dispute." *Journal of Inter-American Studies and World Affairs* 24, no. 1 (1982): 37–57.

Bender, Lynn. *Cuba vs. United States*. San Juan: Inter American University Press, 1981.

Bianchi, William. *Belize: The Controversy between Guatemala and Great Britain over the Territory of British Honduras in Central America*. New York: Las Americas Publishing Co., 1959.

Braveboy-Wagner, Jacqueline. *The Venezuela-Guyana Border Dispute*. Boulder: Westview Press, 1984.

Bustamante, Fernando. "Ecuador: Putting an End to Ghosts of the Past?" *Journal of Inter-American Studies and World Affairs* 34, no. 4 (1992–93): 195–224.

Calvert, Peter. *Boundary Disputes in Latin America*. London: Institute for the Study of Conflict, 1983.

Charlton, Michael. *The Little Platoon: Diplomacy and the Falklands Dispute*. New York: Blackwell, 1989.

Child, Jack. *Geopolitics and Conflict in South America*. New York: Praeger, 1985.

DeSoto, Anthony. *Bolivia's Right to an Access to the Sea*. Pasadena: Jensen Publishing Co., 1962.

Documents on the Territorial Integrity of Guyana: Guyana and Venezuela. Georgetown, Guyana: Ministry of Foreign Affairs, 1981.

Farnsworth, David, and James McKenney. *U.S.-Panama Relations 1903–1978*. Boulder: Westview, 1983.

Jessup, Philip. "El Chamizal." *American Journal of International Law* 67 (1973): 423–45.

Ireland, Gordon. *Boundaries, Possessions, and Conflicts in South America*. Cambridge: Harvard University Press, 1938.

Kinney, Douglas. *National Interest/National Honor: The Diplomacy of the Falklands Crisis*. New York: Praeger, 1989.

Krieg, William. *Ecuadorean-Peruvian Rivalry in the Upper Amazon*, 2d ed. Bethesda, MD: William Krieg, 1986.

LaFeber, Walter. *The Panama Canal*. New York: Oxford University Press, 1978.

Lamborn, Alan, and Stephen Mumme. *Statecraft, Domestic Politics, and Foreign Policy Making: The El Chamizal Dispute*. Boulder: Westview Press, 1988.

Lanus, Juan. *De Chapultepec al Beagle: Politica Exterior Argentina, 1945–1980*. Buenos Aires: Emece Editores, 1984.

Liss, Sheldon. *A Century of Disagreement*. Washington, DC: The University Press, 1965.

Manfedo Jr., Fernando. "The Future of the Panama Canal." *Journal of Inter-American Studies and World Affairs* 35, no. 3 (1993): 103–28.

Moraga, Oscar. *El Precio de la Paz Chileno-Argentina, 1810–1969*, vol. 3. Santiago: Editorial Nascimento, 1969.

Osborne, Alfred. "On the Economic Cost to Panama of Negotiating a Peaceful Solution to the Panama Canal Question." *Journal of Inter-American Studies and World Affairs* 19, no. 4 (1977): 509–21.

Zammit, J. Ann. *The Belize Issue*. London: Latin American Bureau, 1978.

Zook, David. *Zarumilla y Maranon: The Ecuador-Peru Dispute*. New York: Bookman Associates Inc., 1964.

Europe

Bahcheli, Tozun. *Greek-Turkish Relations since 1955*. Boulder: Westview Press, 1990.

Davison, W. Phillips. *The Berlin Blockade*. Princeton: Princeton University Press, 1958.

Ehrlich, Thomas. *Cyprus 1958–1967: International Crises and the Role of Law*. New York: Oxford University Press, 1974.

Ertekien, N. M. *The Cyprus Dispute*. London: K. Rusten and Brother, 1981.

Freymond, Jacques. *The Saar Conflict*. London: Stevens, 1960.

George, Alexander, and Richard Smoke. *Deterrence in American Foreign Policy*. New York: Columbia University Press, 1974.

Griffith, William. *The Ostpolitik of the Federal Republic of Germany*. Cambridge: MIT Press, 1978.

Hanrieder, Wolfram. *Germany, America, Europe: Forty Years of German Foreign Policy.* New Haven: Yale University Press, 1989.

Hitchens, Christopher. *Cyprus.* London: Quartet Books, 1984.

Levie, Howard. *The Status of Gibraltar.* Boulder: Westview Press, 1983.

Necatigil, Zaim. *The Cyprus Question and the Turkish Position in International Law.* New York: Oxford University Press, 1989.

McAdams, James. *Germany Divided.* Princeton: Princeton University Press, 1993.

McGhee, George. *At the Creation of a New Germany.* New Haven: Yale University Press, 1989.

Polyviou, Polyvios. *Cyprus: Conflict and Negotiation 1960–80.* London: Gerald Duckworth & Co. Ltd., 1980.

Slusser, Robert. *The Berlin Crisis of 1961.* Baltimore: Johns Hopkins University Press, 1973.

Middle East

Adamiyat, Faridun. *Bahrain: A Legal and Diplomatic Study of the British-Iranian Controversy.* New York: F. A. Praeger, 1955.

Abdulghani, J. M. *Iran and Iraq: The Years of Crisis.* Baltimore: Johns Hopkins University Press, 1984.

Albaharna, Husain. *The Arabian Gulf States.* rev. 2d. ed. Beirut: Libraire Du Liban, 1975.

Amin, S. H. *International and Legal Problems of the Gulf.* London: Middle East and North African Studies Press Limited, 1981.

Balfour-Paul, Glenn. *The End of Empire in the Middle East.* Cambridge: Cambridge University Press, 1991.

Bar-Siman-Tov, Yaacov. *Linkage Politics in the Middle East.* Boulder: Westview, 1983.

Drysdale, Alasdair, and Raymond Hinnebusch. *Syria and the Middle East Peace Process.* New York: Council on Foreign Relations Press, 1991.

Fahmy, I. *Negotiating for Peace in the Middle East.* London: Croom Helm, 1983.

Finne, David. *Shifting Lines in the Sand.* Cambridge: Harvard University Press, 1992.

Gause, F. Gregory. *Saudi-Yemeni Relations.* New York: Columbia University Press, 1990.

Hassouna, Hussein. *The League of Arab States and Regional Disputes.* New York: Oceana Publications, Inc., 1975.

Ismael, Tareq. *Iran and Iraq: Roots of Conflict.* Syracuse: Syracuse University Press, 1982.

Kaikobad, Kaiyan. *The Shatt-al-Arab Boundary Question: A Legal Reappraisal.* New York: Oxford University Press, 1988.

Kelly, J. B. *Arabia, the Gulf and the West.* London: Weidenfeld and Nicholson, 1980.

Khouri, Fred. *The Arab-Israeli Dilemma.* 3d ed. Syracuse: Syracuse University Press, 1985.

Korany, Bahgat, and Ali Hillal Dessouki eds., *The Foreign Policies of Arab States*. Boulder: Westview, 1984.

Laquer, Walter, and Barry Rubin eds., *The Arab-Israeli Reader: A Documentary History of the Middle East Conflict*, rev. ed. New York: Penguin Books, 1984.

Middle East Contemporary Survey 1976–1990. New York: Holmes & Meir, 1977–85, Boulder: Westview Press, 1986–92.

Little, Tom. *South Arabia: Arena of Conflict*. New York: Praeger, 1968.

Ma'oz, Moshe, and Avner Yaniv eds., *Syria under Assad*. New York: St. Martin's Press, 1986.

Marlowe, John. *Anglo-Egyptian Relations, 1800–1956*, 2d ed. London: Frank Cass, 1965.

Peterson, John. *Conflict in the Yemens and Superpower Involvement*. Washington, DC: Center for Contemporary Arab Studies, Georgetown University, 1981.

Phillips, Wendell. *Oman: A History*. New York: Reynal and Company, 1967.

Pipes, Daniel. *Greater Syria*. New York: Oxford University Press, 1990.

Quandt, William. *Peace Process: American Diplomacy and the Arab-Israeli Conflict since 1967*. Washington, DC: Brookings Institution, 1993.

Rabinovich, Itamar. *The War for Lebanon 1970–1985*, rev. ed. Ithaca: Cornell University Press, 1985.

Rabinovich, Itamar. *Syria Under the Ba'ath, 1963–66*. New Brunswick, NJ: Transaction, 1972.

Ramazani, Rouhallah. *Iran's Foreign Policy, 1941–1973*. Charlottesville: University Press of Virginia, 1975.

Schofield, Richard. *Kuwait and Iraq: Historical Claims and Territorial Disputes*. London: Royal Institute of International Affairs, 1991.

Schofield, Richard. *Evolution of the Shatt-al-Arab Boundary Dispute*. Wisbech, Cambridgeshire, England: Middle East & North African Studies Press, 1986.

Schonfield, Hugh. *The Suez Canal in Peace and War*. Coral Cables: University of Miami Press, 1969.

Seale, Patrick. *Asad of Syria*. London: Tauris, 1988.

Stephens, Robert. *Nasser: A Political Biography*. New York: Simon & Schuster, 1972.

Taryam, Abdullah. *The Establishment of the United Arab Emirates*. New York: Croom Helm, 1987.

Tessler, Mark. *A History of the Israeli-Palestinian Conflict*. Bloomington: Indiana University Press, 1994.

Zahlan, Rosmarie. *The Making of the Modern Gulf States*. Boston: Unwin Hyman, 1989.

Africa

Avirgan, Tony, and Martha Honey. *War in Uganda*. Westport, CT: Lawrence Hill, 1982.

Brownlie, Ian. *African Boundaries: A Legal and Diplomatic Encyclopedia.* London: C. Hurst & Company, 1979.

Africa Contemporary Record 1968–1989. London: Africa Research Limited, 1969, New York: Holmes & Meier, 1970–1992.

Farer, Tom. *War Clouds on the Horn of Africa,* 2d rev. ed. New York: Carnegie Endowment for International Peace, 1979.

FitzGibbon, Louis. *The Betrayal of the Somalis.* London: R. Collings, 1982.

Gorman, Robert. *Political Conflict on the Horn of Africa.* New York: Praeger, 1981.

Hodges, Tony. *Western Sahara.* Westport, CT: Lawrence Hill and Company, 1983.

Hoskyns, Catherine, ed., *The Ethiopian-Somalia-Kenya Dispute.* London: Oxford University Press, 1969.

Lemarchand, Rene, ed., *The Green and the Black.* Bloomington: Indiana University Press, 1988.

McEwen, A. C. *The International Boundaries of East Africa.* New York: Oxford University Press, 1971.

Neuberger, Benyamin. *Involvement, Invasion, and Withdrawal: Qadhafi's Libya and Chad, 1969–1981.* Tel Aviv: Shiloah Center for Middle Eastern and African Studies, 1982.

Rezette, Robert. *The Western Sahara and the Frontiers of Morocco.* Paris: Nouvelles Editions Latines, 1975.

Thomas, Graham. *Sudan, 1950–1985.* London: Darf Publishers Ltd., 1990.

Sabry, Hussein. *Sovereignty for Sudan.* London: Ithaca Press, 1982.

Thompson, Virginia, and Richard Adloff. *Conflict in Chad.* Berkeley: Institute of International Studies, 1981.

Thompson, W. Scott. *Ghana's Foreign Policy, 1957–1966.* Princeton: Princeton University Press, 1969.

Touval, Saadia. *The Boundary Politics of Independent Africa.* Cambridge: Harvard University Press, 1972.

Touval, Saadia. *Somali Nationalism.* Cambridge: Harvard University Press, 1963.

Trout, Frank. *Morocco's Saharan Frontiers.* Geneva: Droz, 1969.

Wright, John. *Libya, Chad and the Central Sahara.* New York: Barnes and Nobles Imports, 1989.

Central and South Asia

Ali, Mehrunnisa, ed., *Pak-Afghan Discord.* Karachi: Pakistan Study Centre, University of Karachi, 1990.

Asian Recorder 1955–1990. New Delhi: K. K. Thomas, 1956–1991.

Bindra, S. S. *India and Her Neighbors.* New Delhi: Deep & Deep Publications, 1984.

Bindra, S. S. *Indo-Pak Relations.* New Delhi: Deep & Deep Publications, 1981.

Chakravarti, P. C. *India's China Policy.* Bloomington: Indiana University Press, 1962.

Chawala, Sudershan. *The Foreign Relations of India*. Encino: Dickenson Publishing Co., 1976.

Gaitonde, P. D. *The Liberation of Goa*. London: C. Hurst & Company, 1987.

Gupta, Sisir. *Kashmir: A Study in India-Pakistan Relations*. Bombay: Asia Publishing House, 1966.

Gurtov, Melvin, and Byoon-Moo Hwang. *China under Threat*. Baltimore: Johns Hopkins University Press, 1980.

Heimsath, Charles. *A Diplomatic History of Modern India*. Bombay: Allied Publishers 1971.

Hinton, Harold. *China's Relations with Burma and Vietnam*. New York: Institute of Pacific Relations, 1958.

Hoffmann, Steven. *India and the China Crisis*. Berkeley: University of California Press, 1990.

Jetly, Nancy. *India-China Relations 1947–1977*. New Delhi: Radiant Publishers, 1979.

Kaplan, Stephen. *Diplomacy of Power*. Washington, DC: Brookings, 1981.

Kaur, Kulwant. *Pak-Afghanistan Relations*. New Delhi: Deep & Deep Publications, 1985.

Krishna, Rao. *The Sino-Indian Boundary Question and International Law*. New Delhi: Indian Society of International Law, 1963.

Kuniholm, Bruce. *The Origins of the Cold War in the Near East*. Princeton: Princeton University Press, 1980.

Lawrence, Leo. *Nehru Seizes Goa*. New York: Pageant Press, 1963.

Maxwell, Neville. *India's China War*. New York: Pantheon Books, 1970.

Murty, T. S. *India-China Boundary: India's Options*. New Delhi: ABC Publishing House, 1987.

Prakhar, Gulab Mishra. *Indo-Pakistan Relations*. New Delhi: Ashish Publishing House, 1987.

Rais, Rasul. *China and Pakistan*. Lahore: Progressive Publishers, 1977.

Rowland, John. *A History of Sino-Indian Relations*. Princeton: D. Van Nostrand Co., 1967.

Rubinoff, Arthur. *India's Use of Force in Goa*. Bombay: Popular Prakashan, 1971.

Rubinstein, Alvin. *Soviet Policy towards Turkey, Iran, and Afghanistan*. New York: Praeger, 1982.

Sagar, Vidya. *India in World Affairs*. New Delhi: Swastik Prakashan, 1973.

Sandhu, Bhim. *Unresolved Conflict: China and India*. New Delhi: Radiant Publishers, 1988.

Shahi, Agha. *Pakistan's Security and Foreign Policy*. Zaildar Park: Progressive Publishers, 1988.

Syed, Anwar. *China and Pakistan*. Amherst: University of Massachusetts Press, 1974.

Tahir, Bashir Ahmed, and Shabbir Ahmed Khalid. *Chronology of Pakistan's Relations with Afghanistan 1947–1988*. Islamabad: National Institute of Pakistan Studies, 1989.

Tharoor, Shashi. *Reasons of State*. New Delhi: Vikas Publishing House, 1982.

Tikoo, Ratna. *Indo-Pak Relations*. New Delhi: National, 1987.
Whiting, Allen. *The Chinese Calculus of Deterrence*. Ann Arbor: University of Michigan Press, 1975.
Wirsing, Robert. *Pakistan's Security under Zia, 1977–1988*. New York: St. Martin's Press, 1991.
Woodman, Dorothy. *The Making of Burma*. London: Cresset, 1962.

Far East and Southeast Asia

Agung, Ide Anak Agung Gde. *Twenty Years Indonesian Foreign Policy, 1945–1965*. Mouton: The Hague, 1975.
Barnett, A. Doak. *China and the Major Powers in East Asia*. Washington, DC: Brookings, 1977.
Chang, Pao-min. *The Sino-Vietnamese Territorial Dispute*. New York: Praeger Special Studies, 1986.
Chen, King. *China's War with Vietnam, 1979*. Stanford: Hoover Institution Press, 1987.
Chin, Kin Wah. *The Defense of Malaysia and Singapore*. Cambridge: Cambridge University Press, 1983.
Chiu, Hungdah ed., *China and the Question of Taiwan*. New York: Praeger, 1973.
Duiker, William. *China and Vietnam*. Berkeley: Institute of East Asian Studies, 1986.
Gelman, Harry. *Russo-Japanese Relations and the Future of the U.S.-Japanese Alliance*. Santa Monica, CA: RAND, 1993.
Gilks, Anne. *The Breakdown of the Sino-Vietnamese Alliance, 1970–1979*. Berkeley: Institute of East Asian Studies, 1992.
Ginsburg, George, and Carl Pinckle, *The Sino-Soviet Territorial Dispute, 1949–64*. New York: Praeger, 1978.
Hellmann, Donald. *Japanese Foreign Policy and Domestic Politics*. Berkeley: University of California Press, 1969.
James, Harold, and Dennis Sheil-Small. *The Undeclared War: The Story of the Indonesian Confrontation 1962–1966*. London: Leo Cooper, 1971.
Jain, Rajendra. *China and Japan, 1949–1980*, rev. 2d ed. Oxford: M. Robertson, 1981.
Jain, Rajendra. *The USSR and Japan, 1945–1980*. Atlantic Highlands, NJ: Humanities Press, 1981.
Jones, Peter. *China and the Soviet Union, 1949–1984*. New York: Facts on File Publications, 1985.
Kalicki, John. *The Pattern of Sino-American Crises*. Cambridge: Cambridge University Press, 1975.
Lawson, Eugene. *The Sino-Vietnamese Conflict*. New York: Praeger, 1984.
Leifer, Michael. *Indonesia's Foreign Policy*. London: Allen & Unwin, 1983.
Long, Simon. *Taiwan: China's Last Frontier*. New York: St. Martin's, 1991.
Lo, Chi-kin. *China's Policy towards Territorial Disputes: The Case of the South China Sea Islands*. London: Routledge, 1989.

Mackerras, Colin. *Modern China: A Chronology from 1842 to the Present.* London: Thames and Hudson, 1982.

Mackie, J. A. C. *Konfrontasi: The Indonesia-Malaysia Dispute, 1963–1966.* New York: Oxford University Press, 1974.

Palmier, Leslie. *Indonesia and the Dutch.* London: Oxford University Press, 1962.

Park, Choon-ho. "Oil under Troubled Waters." *Harvard International Law Review* 14, no. 2 (1973): 212–60.

Phuangkasem, Corrine. *Thailand's Foreign Relations, 1964–1980.* Singapore: Institute of Southeast Asian Studies, 1984.

Pluvier, Jan. *Confrontations: A Study in Indonesian Politics.* London: Oxford University Press, 1965.

Pradhan, P. C. *Foreign Policy of Kampuchea.* London: Sangam Books Limited, 1987.

Rees, David. *Soviet Border Problems: China and Japan.* London: Institute for the Study of Conflict, 1982.

Reinhardt, Jon. *Foreign Policy and National Integration.* New Haven: Yale University Southeast Asia Studies, 1971.

Robertson, Myles. *Soviet Policy towards Japan.* Cambridge: Cambridge University Press, 1988.

Ross, Robert. *The Indochina Tangle: China's Vietnam Policy, 1975–1979.* New York: Columbia University Press, 1988.

Samuels, Marwyn. *Contest for the South China Sea.* New York: Methuen, 1982.

Smith, Roger. *Cambodia's Foreign Policy.* Ithaca: Cornell University Press, 1965.

Stolper, Thomas. *China, Taiwan, and the Offshore Islands.* Armonk, NY: M. E. Sharpe, 1985.

Thies, Wallace. *When Governments Collide: Coercion and Diplomacy in the Vietnam Conflict, 1964–1968.* Berkeley: University of California Press, 1980.

Tsui, Tsien-Hua. *The Sino-Soviet Border Dispute in the 1970's.* Oakville, Ontario, Canada: Mosaic Press, 1983.

Upton, Peter. "International Law and the Sino-Japanese Controversy over the Territorial Sovereignty of the Senkaku Islands." *Boston University Law Review* 52, no. 4 (1972): 763–90.

Weinstein, Franklin. *Indonesian Foreign Policy and the Dilemma of Dependence.* Ithaca: Cornell University Press, 1976.

Whiting, Allen. *China Crosses the Yalu.* New York: Macmillian, 1960.

Wun, Kin Wah. *A Documentary Analysis of Sino-Soviet Relations: The Border Negotiations.* Singapore: Institute of Humanities and Social Sciences, Nanyang University, 1976.

APPENDIX B

Random Sample of Bordering States Not Involved in Territorial Disputes, 1950–90

In this appendix I summarize the procedures I utilized to generate the 129 nondispute cases that comprise one-half of the dataset analyzed in chapter 4. The first step was to identify the universe of interstate borders that existed during the period between 1950 and 1990 in which neighboring states did not have at any time a territorial dispute with one another. The following criteria were employed to determine the universe of such interstate borders.

1. All contiguous land borders between independent states and colonies/ overseas territories between 1950 and 1990 were identified with the reference of various atlases. For each border the time period during which independent states and/or colonies existed was recorded.[1]
2. All cross-water borders of up to 200 miles were also identified for the period between 1950 and 1990. All islands within 200 miles of one another and subject to some form of colonial rule or administration by two different states were included as well.[2]
3. I excluded all land or cross-water borders that were the source of an interstate dispute at any point between 1950 and 1990, as identified in appendix A.

In total, 240 borders were identified between 1950 and 1990. The next step was to then generate two potential cases for each border by designating each neighboring state as a potential challenger. The only exception to this general rule was in the case of cross-water borders where the overseas islands of one country were proximate to the homeland of another state (a total of thirty-three cases). In such cases, I excluded the state with control over the islands as a potential challenger. From this population of 447 cases of potential challengers

---

1. The dates of independence for all states were taken from Melvin Small and J. David Singer, *Resort to Arms* (Beverly Hills: Sage Publications, 1982), 47–51, and for the identity of colonial powers and their overseas territories, David Henige, *Colonial Governors from the Fifteenth Century to the Present* (Madison: University of Wisconsin Press, 1970) and *The World Factbook 1993* (Washington, D.C.: U.S. Government Printing Office, 1993) were relied upon.

2. The Correlates of War Project dataset "States, Nations, and Entities, 1816–1986" and *The World Factbook 1993* were relied upon to identify all cross-water borders.

(207 × 2 + 33) and 18,327 challengers years of nondisputed borders (414 × 41 + 33 × 41), 129 nonterritorial dispute cases were randomly selected to equal the exact number of territorial dispute cases between states from 1950 to 1990. Thus, these 129 nondispute cases equaled approximately 29 percent of the total population of challenger years of nondisputed borders (129 × 41 = 5,289 and 5,289/18,327 = 28.9 percent). As a result, there are 258 cases in the dataset (which is analyzed in chapter 4) with 5,289 annual observations for the 129 nondispute cases and 3,039 observations for the 129 dispute cases. The bordering dyads and countries designated as potential challengers for the 129 nonterritorial dispute cases are listed below in table A.1.

TABLE A.1.   List of Randomly Selected Borders and Potential Challengers for Nondispute Cases, 1950–90

North America
US-Canada: PC = Canada
Central America and the Caribbean
  Mexico-UK/Belize: PC = UK/Belize
  Mexico-Guatemala: PC = both
  Guatemala-Honduras: PC = both
  Nicaragua-Costa Rica: PC = both
  Costa Rica-Colombia (Isla de San Andres): PC = Costa Rica
  Costa Rica-Panama: PC = both
  Haiti-Dominican Republic: PC = both
  Cuba-UK/Cayman Islands: PC = Cuba
  UK/Jamaica-UK/Cayman Islands: PC = UK/Jamaica
  Haiti-US/Nevassa Island: PC = Haiti
  UK/Bahamas-UK/Turks and Caicos Islands: PC = UK/Bahamas
  UK/Trinidad and Tobago-UK/Grenada: PC = UK/Trinidad and Tobago
South America
  Colombia-Venezuela: PC = both
  Colombia-Peru: PC = Peru
  Colombia-Ecuador: PC = Ecuador
  Colombia-Brazil: PC = both
  Guyana-Brazil: PC = Brazil
  Brazil-Netherlands/Suriname: PC = Brazil
  Brazil-Paraguay: PC = Brazil
  Venezuela-Brazil: PC = Brazil
  Venezuela-Netherlands/Aruba: PC = Venezuela
  Peru-Chile: PC = Peru
  Bolivia-Paraguay: PC = both
  Bolivia-Argentina: PC = both
  Paraguay-Argentina: PC = Argentina
Western Europe
  Belgium-West Germany: PC = West Germany
  Belgium-France: PC = both
  France-Luxembourg: PC = both
  France-Italy: PC = both
  Switzerland-France: PC = both

TABLE A.1—*Continued*
West Germany-Austria: PC = West Germany
Sweden-Finland/Aaland Island: PC = Sweden
Sweden-Norway: PC = Sweden
USSR-Finland: PC = both
Portugal-Spain: PC = Portugal
UK/Malta-Italy/Sicily: PC = Italy
Eastern Europe
USSR-Poland: PC = Poland
USSR-Czechoslovakia: PC = both
Poland-Czechoslovakia: PC = both
Poland-East Germany: PC = Poland
Czechoslovakia-East Germany: PC = Czechoslovakia
Hungary-Czechoslovakia: PC = both
Austria-Czechoslovakia: PC = both
Romania-Hungary: PC = Romania
Romania-Yugoslavia: PC = both
Bulgaria-Romania: PC = both
Bulgaria-Yugoslavia: PC = Yugoslavia
Bulgaria-Turkey: PC = Bulgaria
Africa
France/Algeria-Spain/Western Sahara: PC = both
France/Mauritania-France/Algeria: PC = both
France/Algeria-Italy/Libya: PC = both
Italy/Libya-Egypt: PC = both
Italy/Libya-UK/Sudan: PC = Italy/Libya
France/Chad-UK/Sudan: PC = UK/Sudan
UK/Sudan-UK/Kenya: PC = both
France/Senegal-France/Guinea: PC = France/Guinea
France/Senegal-Portugal/Guinea-Bissau: PC = Portugal/Guinea-Bissau
Liberia-UK/Sierra Leone: PC = both
France/Benin-UK/Nigeria: PC = UK/Nigeria
France/Benin-France/Burkina: PC = France/Burkina
France/Niger-UK/Nigeria: PC = France/Niger
UK/Nigeria-France/Chad: PC = both
France/Niger-France/Burkina: PC = France/Burkina
France/Ivory Coast-France/Burkina: PC = France/Ivory Coast
France/Burkina-UK/Ghana: PC = France/Burkina
France/Cameroon-Spain/Equatorial Guinea: PC = France/Cameroon France/Gabon-
France/Congo: PC = France/Congo
France/Gabon-Spain/Equatorial Guinea: PC = France/Gabon
UK/Sudan-France/Central African Republic: PC = UK/Sudan
Belgium/Zaire-UK/Tanzania: PC = UK/Tanzania
Belgium/Zaire-Portugal/Angola: PC = both
Middle East
Lebanon-UK/Cyprus: PC = Lebanon
Lebanon-Syria: PC = Syria
Syria-Jordan: PC = Syria

TABLE A.1—*Continued*

Syria-Iraq: PC = Iraq
Iraq-Jordan: PC = Iraq
Turkey-Syria: PC = Turkey
Iran-Turkey: PC = both
Iraq-Turkey: PC = Iraq
Saudi Arabia-North Yemen: PC = North Yemen

Central and South Asia

Iran-Afghanistan: PC = both
Iran-Pakistan: PC = both
India-Burma: PC = India
USSR-Afghanistan: PC = USSR
USSR-Mongolia: PC = USSR
USSR-North Korea: PC = USSR

Southeast Asia and Oceania

Thailand-UK/Malaysia: PC = both
Burma-Thailand: PC = both
UK/Malaysia-UK/Singapore: PC = both
Indonesia-India/Nicobar Island: PC = both
Indonesia-Australia/Christmas Island: PC = Indonesia
Indonesia-Australia/Papua New Guinea: PC = Indonesia
UK/Christmas Island-US/Jarvis Island: PC = UK

Note: PC = potential challenger.

APPENDIX C

Measurement of Exogenous Variables

In this appendix I describe the operational measures for each of the hypotheses derived from the modified realist model in chapter 3 that are empirically tested in chapters 4 through 6. Annual data was collected for the challenger and target in each of the 129 nondispute cases for the entire period between 1950 and 1990, while annual data for the 129 dispute cases was collected for all of the years that a dispute existed between a challenger and target during the period between 1950 and 1990. In the nondispute dataset the identity of the challenger and target remained constant over the period between 1950 and 1990 in most cases (see app. B). However, in cases in which the challenger or target was not an independent state for the entire period, the colonial power was designated as the challenger or target during the period of colonial rule and data was collected on the colonial power for the appropriate years.

Variables Measuring Issues at Stake

Strategic Location of Bordering Territory (H1.1–1.2). This variable was coded a 1 if bordering territory was strategically located and 0 otherwise. To code for the strategic value of bordering territory one or more of the following conditions must be met: (*a*) it is located in close proximity to major shipping lanes or choke points of narrow straits; (*b*) it is located in close proximity to military bases of the challenger; (*c*) it would provide an outlet to the sea for an otherwise land-locked country; (*d*) it was being used as a military base site for the target; (*e*) it could be used to establish a second military front against the target; and (*f*) control of disputed territory blocked the principal route through which a challenger could attack a target. Proximity to major shipping lanes, choke points, access to the sea, and second military fronts were based on Chaliand and Rageau,[1] while country-specific sources listed in the bibliography to appendix A were relied upon to determine the location of military bases and whether disputed territory was the location from which a challenger would seek to attack a target.

Minority Groups along Border with Ties to Challenger (H2.1–2.2). This variable attempts to measure the presence of bordering populations that are a

---

1. Gerard Chaliand and Jean-Pierre Rageau, *Strategic Atlas,* 3d ed. (New York: Harper Perennial, 1992) and Gerard Chaliand and Jean-Pierre Rageau, *Strategic Atlas,* rev. 2d ed. (New York: Harper & Row, 1985).

minority within the target state but share ties of a common language and ethnicity with the largest comparable ethnic group within the challenger. For the nondispute dyads the language and ethnic background of populations living within fifty miles of the challenger border were determined, while in the territorial dispute cases the characteristics of the population living only within disputed territory were examined. The variable was coded a 1 if groups along the border or within disputed territory, which were a minority within the target, spoke the same language and shared the same ethnic background as the largest ethnic group within the challenger and 0 otherwise.[2]

Political Unification Based on Similarity of Challenger and Target Populations (H3.1–3.2). This variable was coded a 1 if the predominant language and ethnic group of the populations of the challenger and target were the same, and 0 otherwise.[3]

Economic Value of Bordering Territory (H4.1–4.3). This variable was coded a 1 if bordering territory was of economic value to the challenger and 0 otherwise. Bordering territory on land was coded as economically valuable due to its resource endowment, while bordering islands were economically valuable if they were located in close proximity to rich fishing grounds or seabed minerals and deposits. This variable was coded a 1 for each year that natural resources which could generate export earnings were believed or known to be located within fifty miles of land borders or two hundred miles for islands and coastal territory for the nondispute cases, and within disputed territory for the dispute cases. If such resources were not located along the border, a value of 0 was coded. The list of natural resources included oil, manganese, iron ore, lead, titanium, bauxite, sulfur, copper, nickel, chromium, cobalt, tin, tungsten, zinc, phosphate, gold, silver, uranium, and diamonds. In addition, the presence of water supplies in arid bordering territory was also coded as economically valuable. Multiple atlases, which spanned the period between 1950 and 1990, as well as many of the sources listed in the bibliography to appendix A were consulted to determine the location of these natural resources and principal fishing grounds.

Variables Measuring International Context

The Balance of Conventional Military Capabilities (H5.1–5.2). To measure the relative military capabilities of challenger and target, annual data was collected on national military expenditures and the number of men under arms from 1950 to 1990. The Correlates of War Project dataset on "The National Capabilities of

---

2. The primary sources consulted in the coding of this variable were R. E. Asher ed., *The Encyclopedia of Language and Linguistics,* 10 vols. (New York: Pergamon Press, 1994); *Demographic Yearbook, 1950–1990* (New York: United Nations, 1951–1992); *The World Factbook 1993* (Washington, D.C.: Central Intelligence Agency, 1993); A. I. Asiwaju, ed., *Partitioned Africans: Ethnic Relations across Africa's International Boundaries 1884–1984* (London: C. Hurst, 1985); Ted Robert Gurr, *Minorities at Risk* (Washington, D.C.: United States Institute of Peace Press, 1993).

3. For the sources relied upon to code this variable see footnote two.

States, 1816–1990" was the source utilized to gather data on expenditures and military personnel. The data on expenditures was converted into constant 1990 dollars and was then supplemented (when data was available for both countries in a dyad for the same year) with the constant 1990 dollar equivalent of annual military arms imports over the period between 1950 and 1990.[4] The arms import data was collected because countries do not reliably report on expenditures for such arms and/or what arms were acquired from abroad. Arms imports, however, are a critical component of the overall military strength of many countries, particularly in most developing countries, which lack the capacity to produce their own arms. As a result, it is important when trying to measure the military capabilities of states to factor in their arms imports when possible. The challenger's capabilities were then calculated as the percentage of the combined capabilities of challenger and target for each of three separate indicators of military capabilities—the number of men under arms, total military expenditures, and total expenditures per soldier. When necessary the capabilities of challenger and target were discounted to reflect the impact of distance on the power projection capabilities of each state.[5] The overall balance of forces was then calculated by taking the average percentage across the three indicators. The balance of forces variable could range in value from 0 to 1. A value approaching 0 would indicate that the challenger had very limited capabilities, whereas a value close to 1 would indicate that the challenger was much stronger militarily than the target.

Prior Gain of Territory by the Challenger (control variable). This variable was coded a value of 1 for each year in either of the following situations: (1) if the challenger had previously achieved a net gain of territory from the target prior to 1950, or (2) if the challenger gained territory from the target after 1950 and subsequently extended its claims to new territory or maintained claims to other territories of the target. If neither condition applied then a value of 0 was coded. For example, in the United States-Mexico dyad the United States would be coded a value of 1 throughout the period between 1950 and 1990 because it had made large territorial gains at the expense of Mexico during the nineteenth century. Morocco was coded as gaining territory from Spain for the period of 1969 to 1990 since it gained control of (*a*) the enclave of Ifni in 1969 and then (*b*) much of the Western Sahara in 1976 but continued to press claims against remaining Spanish enclaves and offshore islands.[6]

---

4. For the period between 1950 and 1980 arms import data was taken from Michael Brzoska and Thomas Ohlson, *Arms Transfers to the Third World, 1971–85* (New York: Oxford University Press, 1987) and for the years between 1981 and 1990 data was collected from *World Military Expenditures and Arms Transfers 1991–1992* (Washington, D.C.: U.S. Arms Control and Disarmament Agency, 1994).

5. I utilized the index developed by Bruce Bueno de Mesquita, *The War Trap* (New Haven: Yale University Press, 1981), 105.

6. I relied upon Gary Goertz and Paul Diehl, *Territorial Changes and International Conflict* (New York: Routledge, 1992), 147–64 and the Correlates of War dataset on "States, Nations, and Entities, 1816–1986" for data on exchanges of territory between challenger and target.

Dispute Involvement of Challenger with Other States (H6.1–6.2). Two different measures were constructed for this variable. The first measure was coded as the number of months within each year that the challenger was engaged in militarized disputes with states other than the target. The Correlates of War Project dataset on "Militarized Interstate Disputes, 1816–1992" was the primary source utilized to code this variable.

The second measure was the territorial dispute involvement of the challenger with other states. This variable was coded as the number of territorial disputes in each year that the challenger was engaged in with states other than the target. Appendix A was utilized to code this variable.

Stalemate in Negotiations (H7). To test this hypothesis data was collected on the outcome of negotiations or talks between the challenger and the target at the end of each year. The outcome of the negotiations was coded from the perspective of the challenger state, and the sources listed in the bibliography at the end of appendix A were utilized to code diplomatic developments on an annual basis. If the outcome of negotiations and diplomatic efforts by the challenger during a given year was the failure to convince the target to make even limited concessions on the territorial issue, then a value of 1 was coded and 0 otherwise. This variable attempts to measure when diplomatic efforts by the challenger had failed to persuade the target to make concessions over disputed territory.

To code this variable the following procedures were followed. The first requirement was that a round of talks or negotiations had been completed or the challenger had proposed that talks be held. The second requirement was that diplomatic efforts by the challenger failed to bring about a favorable change in the territorial status quo. Continued stalemate and the failure of diplomatic efforts was defined by one or more of the following: (*a*) the absence of any territorial concessions by the target, or any indication by the target that it was willing to consider compromise over disputed territory, (*b*) the inability of some type of border commission to resolve either specific or larger territorial questions on terms favorable to the challenger, and (*c*) a ruling by the ICJ or some other arbitrator or mediating body that favored the position of the target.

Target Attempt to Change Status Quo (H8.1–8.2). A value of 1 was coded for each year that a target undertook actions that were viewed by a challenger as significant steps to alter the prevailing political, economic, or military status quo within the area of disputed territory, and 0 otherwise. The actions of the target could be directed at (*a*) establishing economic, political, or military control over disputed territory, (*b*) consolidating such control, or (*c*) enabling local authorities in the disputed territory to establish greater control in preparation for eventual independence from the target.

More specifically, the following actions by the target were given a value of 1: (*a*) the exploration for as well as mining and production of natural resources within disputed territory, (*b*) the establishment of permanent military bases and fortifications in disputed territory, (*c*) legislative and constitutional measures that formally moved toward the incorporation of disputed territory within the political structure of the target, or (*d*) legislative and constitutional measures that formally moved toward an independent political entity within the disputed territory. The sources listed in the bibliography to appendix A were utilized to code this variable.

Defeat or Stalemate for the Challenger in Armed Conflict (H9.1–9.2). The number of past military defeats for the challenger was recorded for each year following the defeat or stalemate of the challenger's armed forces in a war with the target, or in a militarized dispute short of war in which at least several hundred troops were engaged. The number of past defeats was recorded for each subsequent year until the challenger in another war or militarized dispute was able to achieve a victory or favorable outcome, and then a value of 0 was coded from that point forward. The codings for war outcomes were taken from Small and Singer,[7] and for militarized disputes short of war, I coded the outcomes on the basis of whether the challenger was able to seize or hold disputed territory while suffering fewer casualties than the target. A wide range of individual sources (listed in the bibliography to appendix A) were consulted in the coding of outcomes for such cases. As an example, Egypt was coded as having suffered one defeat in battle with Israel for the years 1950 to 1956 (the outcome of the 1948 war of Israeli independence), two defeats for the years 1957 to 1967 (following the outcome of the 1956 Suez War), three defeats for the years 1968 to 1970 (after the Six Day War in 1967), four defeats for the years 1971 to 1973 (the failure of the War of Attrition), and five defeats for the years 1974 to 1989. (The final setback was the stalemate in the 1973 October War.)

Deterrent Alliance Ties of Target (H10). This variable was coded a 1 for each year in which (*a*) the target had either a defense pact or entente alliance with another state and (*b*) the challenger was not a member of that defense pact or entente. If neither condition applied then a value of 0 was coded.

An alliance was classified as a defense pact if one or both parties had agreed to assist the other in the event of an armed attack. If the alliance partners had only agreed to consult in the event of armed conflict, I coded this as an entente. Agreements that only stated the general intent of the parties to cooperate on military and security issues were not coded as ententes. The defense pact and entente ties of the challenger were then examined to determine whether the agreed-upon commitments were limited to a particular geographic region or threat from a specific country. As a result, some challenger defense pacts or ententes were not coded as deterrent alliances because the terms of the alliance excluded assistance against the target involved in the territorial dispute with the challenger. For example, NATO defense commitments to Britain were not coded as extending to conflicts that the British might have become embroiled in as a result of territorial disputes with countries in Central or South America.[8]

---

7. Melvin Small and J. David Singer, *Resort to Arms* (Beverly Hills: Sage Publications, 1982), ch. 11.

8. The sources consulted for the coding of alliance ties were Nonah Alexander and Allan Nanes, eds. *The United States and Iran* (Fredrick, MD: University Publications of America, Inc., 1980); Charles Chikeka, *Britain, France, and the New African States* (Lewiston, NY: Edwin Mullen Press, 1990); John Chipman, *French Power in Africa* (Oxford: Basil Blackwell Ltd, 1989); Henry Degenhardt, *Treaties and Alliances of the World,* 4th ed.

Common Security Ties between Challenger and Target (H11.1–11.2). Two different measures of this variable were constructed. The first measure coded whether the challenger and target were members of the same alliance. This variable was coded a 1 for each year in which the target and challenger were members of the same defense pact, entente, or nonaggression/neutrality pact and 0 otherwise. A neutrality or nonaggression pact was coded as present if states had agreed that they would not attack each other or would not join adversarial alliances. The second measure was based on whether the challenger and target were involved in a territorial dispute with the same state. A value of 1 was coded for each year in which the challenger and target shared such a common adversary and 0 otherwise. The identification of territorial disputes, the states involved, and the duration of the disputes were taken from appendix A.

Prior Settlement by Challenger (H12). A value of 1 was coded for the period between 1950 and 1990 for a case if the challenger prior to 1950 had agreed to a compromise settlement of a territorial dispute with the target, or had agreed to a general border agreement in which the delimitation of the border was clearly established. If neither condition applied then a value of 0 was coded. The primary sources consulted were those listed in the bibliography in appendix A, particularly the *International Boundary Study* series published by the United States Department of State.

Variables Measuring the Domestic Context

Unsettled Prior Territorial Dispute (H13). This variable was coded a 1 for the period between 1950 and 1990 if the challenger had been involved in a territorial dispute with the target that had not been resolved on terms accepted by the challenger prior to the beginning of World War II, and 0 otherwise. The sources listed in the bibliography to appendix A were relied upon to code this variable, particularly the *International Boundary Study* series published by the United States Department of State.

Prior History of Militarized Disputes (H14.1–14.2). Two related measures were constructed to test this variable. For the first measure the total number of militarized disputes between challenger and target dating back to 1900 was recorded on an annual basis from 1950 to 1990. Thus, for each year the variable included the number of such disputes from 1900 to the end of the most recent previous year. The Correlates of War dataset "Militarized Interstate Disputes,

---

(New York: Scribner's, 1986); J. C. Hurewitz, *Diplomacy in the Near and Middle East: A Documentary Record: 1914–1956,* vol. 2 (Princeton: D. Van Nostrand Company, Inc., 1956); George Lenczowski, *The Middle East in World Affairs,* 4th ed. (Ithaca: Cornell University Press, 1980); Ido Oren, "The War Proneness of Alliances," *Journal of Conflict Resolution* 34, no. 2 (1990): 208–33; Pedro Ramet, *The Soviet-Syrian Relationship since 1955* (Boulder: Westview Press, 1990); Grant Rhode and Reid Whitlock *Treaties of the People's Republic of China, 1949–1978* (Boulder: Westview Press, 1980); Melvin Small and J. David Singer, "Formal Alliances, 1816–1965: An Extension of the Basic Data," in J. David Singer and Paul F. Diehl, eds., *Measuring the Correlates of War* (Ann Arbor: University of Michigan Press, 1990), 159–90.

1816–1992" was the primary source utilized to code this variable. The second measure utilized the same data on the total number of prior militarized confrontations between challenger and target, but the variable was coded annually as the number of such disputes that took place between the two states within the past year. The first measure taps the longer-term historical pattern of conflict behavior as well as more recent confrontations, while the second measure focuses only on the short-term pattern of militarized conflicts between challenger and target.

Prior Loss of Territory for the Challenger (H15). This variable was coded a value of 1 for each year if the challenger had previously suffered a net loss of territory to the target through an agreement and/or defeat in armed conflict, and 0 otherwise. For example, Syria was coded a value of 1 for this variable from 1968 to 1990 following its defeat in the Six Day War of 1967 and Israel's occupation of the Golan Heights.[9]

Decolonization Norm (H16). If the territory of a target was a colony or overseas dependency and the challenger did not possess any colonial territory of its own, then a value of 1 was coded for this variable and 0 otherwise.[10]

Democratic Norms of Challenger (H17.1–17.2). This variable was constructed from the *POLITY II* dataset.[11] For each year the challenger's autocracy score was subtracted from its democracy score generating a net democracy score.[12] This net score (which could range in value from −10 to 10) was then converted into a dummy variable with values of 5 or greater equaling 1, indicating that the challenger was relatively democratic, and 0 otherwise.[13] The next step then was to determine within the past twenty-five years how often the challenger had been democratic. The measure then attempts to weigh the cur-

---

9. Data was collected from Goertz and Diehl, *Territorial Changes and International Conflict,* 147–64, the Correlates of War dataset on "States, Nations, and Entities, 1816–1986," and the country-specific sources listed in the bibliography in appendix A.

10. I utilized *The World Factbook 1993* and David Henige, *Colonial Governors from the Fifteenth Century to the Present* (Madison: University of Wisconsin Press, 1970) to code this variable.

11. The *POLITY II* dataset is on deposit at the Inter-University Consortium for Political and Social Research, University of Michigan. I had to supplement the *POLITY II* dataset with codings for the years 1987 to 1990 since *POLITY II* did not extend beyond 1986. I relied upon *Freedom in the World, 1987–1990* (New York: Freedom House, 1988–1991), *The Europa World Yearbook 1990,* vols. 1–2 (London: Europa Publications Limited, 1990), and George Delury ed., *World Encyclopedia of Political Systems and Parties,* vols. 1–2, 2d ed. (New York: Facts on File Publications, 1987) to code cases from 1987 to 1990.

12. The features of a political system which were utilized by *POLITY II* to code for the level of autocracy and democracy were: (1) competitiveness of participation, (2) regulation of participation, (3) competitiveness of executive recruitment, (4) openness of executive recruitment, and (5) constraints on chief executive.

13. Missing data from *POLITY II* constituted less than 3 percent of the observations for this variable for the years 1950 to 1986. I relied upon *Freedom in the World 1978–1986* (New York: Freedom House, 1979–1987); *The Europa World Yearbook 1990;* and George Delury, ed., *World Encyclopedia of Political Systems and Parties* to code missing data for the years 1950 to 1986.

rent democratic status of the challenger by the relatively recent past history of democratic rule in the country. Since this variable attempts to measure the impact of democratic norms, it is vital to develop an indicator measuring how long democratic institutions and practices have been a feature of the political system. A twenty-five-year lag was chosen because it roughly measures the generational experiences of leaders that would be currently in power. For example, to code Turkey for 1962 it was necessary to determine how many years Turkey had been democratic during the period from 1937 to 1961. During that period Turkey was democratic a total of eight years, and therefore a value of 8 was recorded for the democratic norms variable in 1962.

APPENDIX D

Questions of Research Design and Statistical Analysis

In this appendix I explain the logic behind a number of decisions that I made in (a) constructing the datasets that were analyzed in chapters 4 through 6 and (b) in choosing the statistical estimators that were relied upon to conduct the empirical tests presented in each of those chapters.

Construction of the Datasets

The population of 129 territorial dispute cases described in appendix A and the random sample of 129 nondisputed borders listed in appendix B comprise the two datasets that are analyzed. For the dataset of nondisputed borders, information on the variables to be tested (see appendix C) was collected on an annual basis for all of the years from 1950 to 1990, while data was collected only for those years that a dispute existed in the dataset of dispute cases. The reason why each case in the two datasets was organized as a time series of data was driven by the logic of the theoretical questions tested in each of the chapters. For example, in chapter 4 the basic theoretical question addressed was when a challenger state would dispute the territory of a bordering country. To answer this question, it is vital to have complete information on all of the years in which a dispute existed, not only the year when the dispute first originated. The same general logic applies to the research design for testing the theoretical questions addressed in chapters 5 and 6. In chapter 5 the theoretical question is, When can we expect challengers to escalate disputes to high levels of diplomatic and military conflict? To answer that question we should systematically compare all years in which levels of conflict were high to those years where they were not. Finally, in chapter 6 the empirical tests seek to answer the question, When will a challenger state seek the peaceful settlement of disputes through compromise and accommodation? Once again, a convincing answer to that question cannot be formed until all years of compromise have been compared to all years of no compromise.

The next question that I had to address was whether the annual level data collected for each case should be aggregated—for example, five- or ten-year intervals—before the empirical tests were conducted. My position was that unless there were compelling theoretical reasons to aggregate the data, it should be left in its annual level form. My assumption was that decisions by the leaders of a challenger state on the initiation, escalation, and settlement of territorial disputes were theoretically possible in any given year, and that there was not a convincing argument to be made that such decisions were only made periodically, that is, every three, five, or ten years. Furthermore, aggregation of the data would have resulted in the loss of a good deal of information about intracase variance in the values of the endogenous and exogenous variables, which, in turn, would have introduced distortions and errors into the statistical analysis.[1] Given that I did not see any strong theoretical argument for aggregating the data to any specific time interval and the clear risks in doing so for the empirical analyses, I decided to keep all of the data as annual level observations for all of the variables.

The empirical tests reported in chapters 4 through 6 are therefore carried out on pooled cross-sectional time series datasets. In chapter 4 the dataset consisted of 258 cases equally divided between territorial disputes and non-disputed borders, totaling 8,328 observations (5,289 in the nondispute set of cases and 3,039 in the dispute cases). The datasets for chapters 5 and 6 consisted of the 129 cases of territorial disputes over the period between 1950 and 1990 with a total of 3,039 observations.

Statistical Tests of the Data

To test these pooled cross-sectional time series datasets, I had to consider the relative strengths and weaknesses of alternative statistical approaches. Unfortunately, no single estimator could simultaneously meet all of the demands imposed by the basic structure of the datasets. As a result, I selected the estimator that I believed could correct for the most important potential problems which might undermine the validity of the statistical results, while recognizing that some other problems still existed but could not be corrected for.

The basic tradeoff in choosing between alternative estimators was minimizing error in the estimation of the coefficients versus estimating as accurately as possible the standard errors of the coefficients. Given this choice, I decided that it was most important to produce the most accurate estimates of the coefficients—the correct sign and magnitude of beta—while accepting some loss of confidence in my ability to engage in hypothesis testing due to incorrect estimates of the standard errors. In the statistical analyses for chapters 4 through 6, I relied upon logit and probit estimators to test the specified equations. Logit and probit estimators were appropriate because the endogenous variables in those chapters were either dichotomous or trichotomous. Both estimators produce very similar results, and therefore decisions on which estimator to use were based largely on practical grounds.[2] The logit (probit) model

---

1. See for example John Freeman, "Systemic Sampling, Temporal Aggregation, and the Study of Political Relationships," *Political Analysis* 1 (1989): 61–98.

2. I selected the logit model for the results reported in table 3 because it is not difficult to correct for over- or undersampling in a logit model whereas it is quite difficult with a probit model. The dataset used to produce the results reported in table 3 was constructed by undersampling the number of nondisputed borders in the international

produced consistent estimates of the coefficients despite positive autocorrelation in the data.[3] The drawback with the logit (probit) estimator was that it could not take into account autocorrelation when estimating the standard errors of the coefficients.

The logit (probit) model therefore treated each of the observations in the datasets as independent from one another. We know, however, from research on the use of ordinary least squares regression with time series data that estimates of standard errors are incorrect if there is positive autocorrelation in the data. At the same time, it is quite difficult to predict whether the standard errors will be over- or underestimated.[4] While there is only limited research on the use of logit (probit) models with time series data, it would seem reasonable to expect that the estimates of standard errors in a logit (probit) analysis will also be incorrect if there is positive autocorrelation. I adopted the conservative position and assumed that the standard errors were underestimated for all of the equations tested, and therefore I had to be cautious in drawing conclusions about the significance levels of the estimated coefficients. As a rough rule of thumb that I applied to all of the results reported, my confidence in the statistical significance of coefficients with t-ratios above 3.00 was very high to high, high to moderate for coefficients with t-ratios between 2.00 and 3.00, and moderate to low for coefficients with t-ratios below 2.00 but above 1.30.

As an alternative to logit (probit) analysis, I could have utilized a generalized least squares (GLS) estimator which would have estimated more accurately the standard errors by taking into account positive autocorrelation in the data.[5] However, a substantial amount of error would have been introduced in the estimates of the coefficients with a GLS estimator. Systematic error would have been introduced because the endogenous variables for all of the equations tested are categorical while a GLS estimator assumes a continuous interval level measure. The magnitude of the error introduced by the use of a GLS estimator increases as the proportion of cases in the dataset lie close to either tail of the probability distribution in a logit (probit) model. In all of the equations tested, however, there were a substantial number of cases that were located near either the lower ($p < .30$) or upper ($p > .70$) tail of the distribution. As a result, the

system between 1950 and 1990, and this must be taken into account in the estimation of the equation tested. In a logit model the bias introduced by undersampling can be corrected by adding to the constant the natural log of the proportion of the sample underselected. For the results reported in table 2 the proportion of sample selected was .289.

3. See C. Gourieroux, "Estimation and Test in Probit Models with Serial Correlation," in J. P. Florens, M. Mouchart, J. P. Raoult, and L. Samir, eds., *Alternative Approaches to Time Series Analysis* (Bruxelles: Publications des Facultes universitaires Saint-Louis, 1984), 169–209.

4. See for example Andrew Harvey, *The Econometric Analysis of Time Series,* 2d ed. (Cambridge: MIT Press, 1990), 197–98 and George Judge, W. E. Griffiths, R. Carter Hill, Helmut Lutkepohl, and Tsoung-Chao Lee, *The Theory and Practice of Econometrics,* 2d ed. (New York: John Wiley & Sons, 1985), 281–82.

5. See for example Jan Kmenta, *Elements of Econometrics,* 2d ed. (New York: Macmillan Publishing Company, 1986), 616–35.

use of a GLS estimator would have introduced a significant amount of error into the estimation of the coefficients.

Another estimator that was considered was survival analysis. Survival analysis basically attempts to predict how much time will pass before a specified event will take place given some initially designated starting point in time.[6] In the context of my research on territorial disputes, this statistical approach would be designed to answer questions such as: When will a challenger first initiate a dispute? How long will it be before a challenger resorts to a high level of diplomatic or military pressure in a dispute? How long will a dispute persist before the challenger proposes a settlement? Each of these questions are important to address, but they fail to capture the full range of challenger behavior that I am interested in explaining. For example, I am interested in understanding not only when a challenger will initiate a dispute but if the dispute will be short or protracted. I want to know not only how quickly a dispute will escalate to high levels of conflict but if such levels of conflict will persist over time. Survival analysis, however, is not designed to answer these types of questions, and therefore I did not rely upon this estimator in my statistical tests.

The final issue that I had to consider in the statistical analyses was the potential effects of selection bias. In chapters 5 and 6 I tested various hypotheses on the behavior of challenger states involved in a territorial dispute. For each of these chapters the datasets included only those borders that were disputed at some point between 1950 and 1990. The fact that some borders, however, were never disputed and therefore did not make it into the population of cases to be analyzed had to be taken into account when estimating the effects of the variables in the equations tested. The reason is that a number of variables which were related to levels of escalation over disputed territory or the willingness to settle a dispute were also related to decisions by a challenger state to become involved in a dispute to begin with. Therefore, when I was estimating the effects of all the variables in the equations tested in chapters 5 and 6, I had to account for the impact that these particular variables had in the emergence of territorial disputes. If I did not take into account these potential selection effects, the probit analyses might have produced inaccurate estimates of the coefficients, including both the sign and magnitude of beta.[7]

To test these equations I therefore had to estimate first what variables determined whether a border was disputed or not. The equation tested in chapter 4 served as the selection equation for the empirical analyses in chapters 5 and 6. The one essential requirement was that at least one exogenous variable from the equation in chapter 4, which is significant when empirically tested, should *not be* included in the other equations because it is not expected to be a significant explanatory variable.[8]

---

6. See for example Paul Allison, *Event History Analysis* (Beverly Hills: Sage Publications, 1984).

7. For example, see Christopher Achen, *The Statistical Analysis of Quasi-Experiments* (Berkeley: University of California Press, 1986), ch. 4.

8. See ibid., ch. 5.

Logit analysis was utilized to estimate the selection equation, and the results are reported in table 3 in chapter 4. From the results in table 3 we can see that there are five variables in this equation which are significant but are not included in the outcome equations tested in chapters 5 and 6 (see tables 8 and 13).

The next step then was to take the estimated probabilities for each of the disputed border cases generated by the equation reported in table 3 and include them as a control variable in the outcome equations for chapters 5 and 6. By including the estimated probabilities in the equations, the error terms are no longer correlated with the exogenous variables, and therefore consistent estimates of the coefficients can be produced. I then estimated the outcome equations with probit models.[9]

---

9. Currently available software does not include selection bias models programmed to utilize logit analysis to estimate the selection and outcomes equations. As a result, I utilized a logit-probit setup that introduces some error when calculating lambda—see ibid., 99. The amount of error, however, is quite small since logit and probit models produce very similar predicted values, which are utilized to calculate lambda.

Index